Vital Historical Records of Jackson County, Missouri 1826-1876

Including a Full Name and Subject Index

Originally Collected, Compiled, and Published
by the Kansas City Chapter
Daughters of the American Revolution
Kansas City, Missouri
1933-1934

85th Anniversary Edition

Volume 2: Family Burying Grounds and Early Cemeteries

The Orderly Pack Rat
Greenwood, Missouri
2019

© 2019 David W. Jackson

All rights reserved. Without permission in writing from the publisher, no part of this work may be reproduced or transmitted in any form or by any means, electronic or mechanical, including photocopying, recording, or by any information storage and retrieval system.

David W. Jackson, 1969-
Vital Historical Records of Jackson County, Missouri, 1826-1876. Volume 2. Family Burying Grounds and Early Cemeteries.
  210 p. cm.

1. Epitaphs—Missouri—Jackson County. 4. Jackson County (Mo.)—Genealogy. I. Jackson, David W., 1969-. II. Title.

ISBN: 978-1-7343686-1-1 (The Orderly Pack Rat)

85th Anniversary Edition, 2019. 3 Volumes.

Volume 1: Early Churches.	Pages i-xii + 13-224
Volume 2: Family Burying Grounds and Early Cemeteries.	**Pages 225-430**
Volume 3: Miscellany and Index.	Pages 431-694

Originally Collected, Compiled, and Published by the Kansas City Chapter, Daughters of the American Revolution, Kansas City, Missouri, 1933-1934. Expanded and improved from a 2009 publication compiled by David W. Jackson and Suzanne V. Vinduska. With thanks to the Kansas City Chapter, Daughters of the American Revolution.

Front cover image: "About twenty members of the Elizabeth Benton Chapter, Daughters of the American Revolution, yesterday held memorial services at the grave of Nathaniel Lewis, Revolutionary War soldier, who is buried in a family plot on the Lewis farm north of Independence. A marker bearing a brass plate designed by the DAR was placed on the grave. Mrs. Carl L. Immele, 2120 E. 68th St, who is a descendant of Lewis, read the services at the graveside. Descendants of Nathaniel Lewis, who own the farm, attended" [*Kansas City (Mo.) Times, 21 May 1938*]. The cemetery became known as the Lewis-Gregg Cemetery. The Civil War Roundtable of Western Missouri asked David W. Jackson and Kathleen Tuohey to plot the cemetery's burials. Many unmarked graves were located through dowsing/divining. It was also discovered that Nathaniel Lewis' marker is set beside his actual resting place; that is, there is no burial in the location where the 1938 stone was set. **Back cover images**: 1928 monument dedication for William Moore, Revolutionary War and War of 1812 soldier, courtesy the Independence Pioneers Chapter, Daughters of the American Revolution.

Published in the United States of America by:
The Orderly Pack Rat
Greenwood, Missouri 64034
david.jackson@orderlypackrat.com
orderlypackrat.com

CONTENTS

JACKSON COUNTY, MISSOURI VIII
PREFACATORY NOTE IX

VOLUME 1
PART ONE: EARLY CHURCHES

BAPTIST 13
CATHOLIC 89
CHRISTIAN OR DISCIPLES OF CHRIST 119
CONGREGATIONAL 143
EPISCOPALIAN 151
EVANGELICAL 155
JEWISH 171
LATTER DAY SAINTS 173
LUTHERAN 175
METHODIST 191
PRESBYTERIAN 199
PRESBYTERIAN (CUMBERLAND) 211
UNITARIAN 223

VOLUME 2
PART TWO: FAMILY BURYING GROUNDS AND EARLY CEMETERIES
Tombstone inscriptions arranged by townships in which these grounds are located.

FORT OSAGE TOWNSHIP 227
BLUE TOWNSHIP 245
KAW TOWNSHIP 263
SNI-A-BAR TOWNSHIP 329
WASHINGTON TOWNSHIP 353
VAN BUREN TOWNSHIP 373
PRAIRIE TOWNSHIP 389
WESTPORT TOWNSHIP 411
BROOKING TOWNSHIP 419

VOLUME 3
PART THREE: MISCELLANY AND INDEX

MISCELLANY 431

KANSAS CITY CHAPTER, DAR, REGENTS, 1906-2019 453

HISTORY OF THE KANSAS CITY CHAPTER, DAR 454

FULL NAME & SUBJECT INDEX 459

PART TWO

CEMETERIES

The cemeteries herein given are listed alphabetically in the Township in which the cemetery is located.

No claim is made that the list and records of the cemeteries are complete, but the Committee did its best in securing all data as was available. In the larger cemetery lists, no death date after 1875 was copied unless the birth date was before 1850, except in a few instances, where the stones showed signs of soon becoming illegible.

No attempt was made to copy records in the larger cemeteries of the county organized after 1875. Complete records of burials in these newer cemeteries are found in the offices of the cemeteries.

By request of the Independence Pioneers Chapter, Daughters of the American Revolution, the records of Woodlawn Cemetery, Independence, Missouri, one of the older cemeteries in the county, are not entered here, as the members of the Independence Pioneers Chapter expect to copy and publish these records.

*Time is hastening on, and we
What our fathers are shall be,—
Shadow-shapes of memory!
Joined to that vast multitude
Where the great are but the good,
And the mind of strength shall prove
Weaker than the heart of love.*
—Whittier

FORT OSAGE TOWNSHIP
Organized May 22, 1827

BONE HILL CEMETERY
Section 29, Township 50 N., Range 29 W

Bickel, Mary E., mother, born 1842, died 1915
Bickel, M. J., born 1837, died 1907
Bergschneider, Henry F., born May 17, 1838, died April 14, 1921
Bergschneider, Wilhelmina, wife of Henry F. Bergschneider, born September 12, 1837, died March 24, 1920
Bierbaum, Wilhelmina Gebohrne, born January 17, 1840, died April 3, 1912
Dieckmann, Floring, born February 10, 1838, died November 3, 1904
Holte, ——, born September 10, 1810, died January 22, 1901
Horstmann, Henriette, born December 28, 1839, died December 9, 1910
Schaberg, John W., born August 17, 1834, died November 17, 1910
Schaberg, Mary L., wife of John W. Schaberg, born November 24, 1839, died May 29, 1908
Schuster, Elizabeth, born February 13, 1840, died November 12, 1916
Schuster, Fredrick W., born October 3, 1832, died September 1, 1909
Stock, Charles W., born October 12, 1869, died January 9, 1899
Stock, Fritz, born February 25, 1822, died January 23, 1911
Stock, Louisa, wife of Fritz Stock, born January 17, 1830, died July 1, 1903
Schuster, John J., born 1837, died 1914
Stoenner, E. R. A., born February 20, 1812, died ——
Stoenner, F. W., born 1848, died 1919
Stoenner, Louise S., wife of F. W. Stoenner, born November 6, 1854, died November 10, 1930
Stoenner, George H., born December 16, 1853, died November 24, 1919
Stoenner, Louise S., wife of George H. Stoenner, born January 15, 1854, died July 30, 1926
Twente, Katharine, wife of Heinrich Twente, born January 28, 1827, died April 29, 1904

Copied July 24, 1933, by Miss Julia Kinney and Miss Ethel Merwin

BUCKNER CEMETERY
Section 22, S. E., Township 49, Range 30

Allen, Flavius, born December 16, 1842, died April 16, 1916
Allen, Rachel, wife of Flavius Allen, born June 4, 1842, died September 7, 1919
Beckett, Andrew J., born May 9, 1833, died February 21, 1909

Beckum, Thomas E., born March 14, 1833, died August 1, 1910
Botts, R. A., father, born October 30, 1846, died October 26, 1930
Botts, Parthinia A., wife of R. A. Botts, born January 10, 1854, died September 12, 1901
Bowling, John W., father, born 1838, died 1924
Bowling, Elizabeth, wife of John W. Bowling, born 1842, died 1924
Brown, Ida F., born February 12, 1842, died April 14, 1909
Bucker, Janett B., born March 21, 1838, died December 2, 1922
Campbell, Joseph E., born 1848, died 1918
Campbell, Margaret E., wife of Joseph E. Campbell, born 1849, died 1920
Cannon-Lewis-Kitch
    Cannon, Miranda R., mother, born 1843, died 1911
    Lewis, Claud H., Jr., died October 19, 1921
    Kitch, Eva V., born 1900, died 1931
Carmean, John W., born 1849, died 1930
Carmean, Emily J., wife of John W. Carmean, born 1855, died 1925
Chiles, Joel F., born July 18, 1848, died February 1, 1915, son of J. F. and Azubah S. Chiles
Chiles, Lucy Vernon, daughter of Vernon and Elizabeth Chiles Mason, born June 27, 1914, died July 8, 1916
Chiles, J. Franklin, born September 14, 1891, died October 31, 1931, son of Joel F. and Lucy T. Chiles
Chiles, Samuel H., father, born 1844, died 1929
Chiles, Hughes W., son of Samuel H. Chiles, born 1875, died 1915
Cole, C. E., Uncle, born 1825, died 1899. Erected by Kinsey sisters
Corn, William E., born March 7, 1843, died July 3, 1931
Corn, Matilda C., wife of William E. Corn, born March 7, 1847, died February 7, 1915
Costillo, Patrick, born 1847, died 1928
Costillo, Emma Alice, wife of Patrick Costillo, born 1856, died 1906
Costello, Michael, born 1850, died 1931
Douglass, Edmond T., born July 6, 1827, died April 20, 1910
Douglass, Phoebe, mother, wife of Edmond T. Douglass, born October 2, 1836, died January 4, 1917
Edwards, Jona, born January 18, 1838, died February 14, 1906
Edwards, Fannie, wife of Jona Edwards, born September 10, 1853, died May 23, 1904
Gogswell, W. M., born February 22, 1822, died June 5, 1901
Gogswell, Anna E., wife of W. M. Gogswell, born December 5, 1837, died May 6, 1885
Gordry, born December 23, 1849, died April 20, 1925
Hall, Thomas G., born October 6, 1821, died November 23, 1892
Hall, Nancy, wife of Thomas G. Hall, born October 26, 1826, died January 8, 1903
Hanway, Francis M., born 1833, died 1873
Hanway, Rebecca, wife of Francis M. Hanway, born 1836, died 1910
Hanway, Geneta, born 1864, died 1871
Hanway, William W., born October 14, 1857, died May 10, 1929, Woodman of the World Emblem
Hanway, Victoria J., born August 8, 1873, died August 1, 1932
Harra, George H., born February 5, 1817, died September 16, 1894
Harra, Suesa, born August 30, 1820, died April 21, 1905
Harra, William H., born August 22, 1836, died May 3, 1928
Harra, Aura Ellen, born August 1, 1852, died April 16, 1929
Harra, Christian F., father, born 1847, died 1926
Hewitt, Elvira J., wife of H. L. Hewitt, died March 13, 1886; age, 46 years, 10 months, 23 days
Houghton, Ervin Orlando, born December 14, 1841, died April 6, 1925
Howell, Samuel, born 1844, died 1903
Howell, Perlina J., wife of Samuel Howell, born 1845, died 1927

CEMETERIES—FORT OSAGE TOWNSHIP

Hudson, Samuel W., father, born March 2, 1842, died April 20, 1903
Hudson, Emma D., born October 9, 1850, died January 22, 1910
Hudspeth, William, born July 2, 1843, died May 23, 1915
Hudspeth, Martha J., wife of William Hudspeth, born August 31, 1850
Hudspeth, Thomas B., born 1849, died 1926
Hudspeth, Mattie, wife of Thomas B. Hudspeth, born 1859, died 1930
Knapheide, F. W., born April 12, 1849, died April 23, 1919
Knapheide, Matilde M., wife of F. W. Knapheide, born January 14, 1854, died February 27, 1909
Mathews, James P., born March 28, 1821, died November 24, 1898
Mackey, Joseph, born June 13, 1840, died September 17, 1920
Mackey, Margaret, wife of Joseph Mackey, born January 11, 1845, died April 12, 1916
Martin, Jacob, died July 22, 1900; age, 76 years, 5 months, 5 days
Martin, Charity, wife of Jacob, died November 12, 1886; age, 66 years, 4 months, 6 days
Mershon, Eli, father, born 1839, died 1926
O'Donnell, Dominic, died January 6, 1902; age, 73 years
Owens, James H., born September 3, 1840, died March 19, 1919
Owens, Katherine, wife of James H. Owens, born April 12, 1844, died March 10, 1917
Owen, Nephi, born 1838, died 1906
Owen, Elizabeth, wife of Nephi Owen, born 1843, died ——
Plum, Levi, born June 22, 1836, died October 25, 1907
Plum, Laura, wife of Levi
Propst, William, born June 24, 1810, died June 11, 1899
Propst, Elizabeth, wife of William, born January 2, 1824, died February 1, 1904
Pryor, John Shelby, born 1832, died 1918
Pryor, Miriam D., wife of John Shelby Pryor, born 1859, died 1917
See, Salathiel H., born 1847, died 1915
Sheriff, Isaac, father, born 1847, died 1930
Sheriff, Helen, wife of Isaac Sheriff, born 1856, died 19—
Sheriff, Julia Stock, daughter of Helen and Isaac Sheriff, born 1902, died 1929
Stapp, Emily S., born 1878, died 1931
Swearingen, Sarah Wood, born May 25, 1843, died April 23, 1912
Thatcher, John, born March 16, 1815, died April 13, 1899
Thomas, Delila, wife of P. B. Thomas, died December 6, 1883; age, 62 years, 10 months, 5 days
Truitt, Mary F., wife of O. Truitt, died July 21, 1886; age, 47 years, 3 months, 24 days
Ucker, John, father, born 1835, died 1920
Ucker, Mathilda, mother, born 1844, died 1920
Ucker, Nancy, mother, born 1840, died 1878
Vest, Noah, born 1838, died 1912
Vest, Alice, born 1878, died 1900
Vest, Ariel C., born 1849, died 1919
Watson, George W., born 1845, died 1922
Watson, Nancy A., wife of George W. Watson, born 1848, died 1907
West, Francis M., died August 7, 1890; age, 48 years, 24 days
West, Emily Alice, died February 19, 1928; age, 73 years
Wood, Christian, wife of Samuel Wood, died February 7, 1899; age, 67 years, 5 months, 7 days
Wyatt, Joseph M., father, born 1844, died 1929

Compiled and copied May 14, 1933, by Miss Julia Kinney and Miss Ethel Merwin

CHILES BURYING GROUND
Section 14, Township 50, Range 31 W
Data contributed by Mrs. Anna A. Perrin, daughter of Joel F. Chiles

John Henry Chiles and his wife, Sarah, were buried on their farm. Mr. Chiles died before his wife did and Mrs. Perrin remembers that Mrs. Chiles died about 1848. There are no markers at their graves. They came from Clark County, Kentucky, to Jackson County, Missouri. They were the parents of the following:

    John, born November 25, 1790
    Richard, born November 20, 1792
    Susan, born August 14, 1793
    Henry, born February 1, 1796
    Christopher, born December 18, 1800
    James, born August 16, 1803
    Joel Franklin, born January 20, 1806
    William, born February 20, 1808
    Joseph Ballinger, born July 16, 1810
    Alexander M. E., born November 14, 1814

All of their children settled in Jackson County, Missouri.

                      Compiled by Miss Jessie M. Crosby

CHILES CEMETERY
Section 12, Township 50, Range 31 W

Chiles, Franklin, died June 15, 1851; age, 27 years, member of Presbyterian Church
Chiles, Sally, wife of R. B. Chiles, died November 11, 1858; age, 62 years
Hamilton, James L., born October 9, 1817, died October 16, 1846
Hamilton, James William, infant son of James L. and Jane Hamilton, born January 8, 1847, died February 9, 1847
Mockbee, Richard C., infant son of Thomas and Eliza A. Mockbee, died September, 1837
Potts, Jessie, died July 3, 1849; age, 42 years, 4 months, 5 days.

CHILES CEMETERY
Section 13, Township 50, Range 31 W

Chiles, Joel F., died February 18, 1855; age, 49 years, 29 days
Chiles, Azubah, wife of Joel F. Chiles, died August 5, 1873; age, 64 years, 4 months, 22 days
Chiles, Caldwell, son of J. F. and Azubah Chiles, born June 28, 1840, died May 18, 1900
Chiles, Sarah Margaret, daughter of J. F. and Azubah Chiles, born June 14, 1846, died May 6, 1899
Chiles, Mary Jane, daughter of J. F. and Azubah Chiles, born March 5, 1844, died February 6, 1928
Chiles, Elijah G., son of J. F. and Azubah Chiles, born June 19, 1850, died February 29, 1852
Chiles, Richard B., son of J. F. and Azubah Chiles, born November 30, 1833, died October 30, 1850
Chiles, William G., son of J. F. and Azubah Chiles, born June 22, 1836, died December 10, 1915
Chiles, Phineas, son of W. G. and M. E. Chiles, born July 5, 1877, died August 10, 1879
Chiles, Mary Emily Murfee, wife of William G. Chiles, born April 23, 1849, died May 27, 1907
Chiles, infant son of W. G. and M. E. Chiles, born August 21, 1871
Chiles, Mattie Adams, late consort of P. S. Chiles, departed March 6, 1869
Chiles, Charlie A., son of P. S. and M. A. Chiles, died July 5, 1869; age, 3 months, 27 days
Chiles, Anne Azubah, daughter of Joel F. and Lucy T. Chiles, born December 3, 1885, died July 11, 1887

P. S. Chiles and Joel F. Chiles were sons of Joel F. and Azubah Chiles.

        Copied April 15, 1933, by Miss Mary Sue Chiles and Miss Jessie M. Crosby

CLEMENTS CEMETERY
Section 25, Township 50, Range 30
Located on the Berry Farm

Clements, Zachariah B., born 1858, died 1919
Clements, Henry B., died May 22, 1900; age, 77 years, 5 months
Clements, Frances J., wife of Henry B. Clements, born July 5, 1821, died October 4, 1896
Clements, Jesse W., son of Henry B. and Frances J. Clements, born June 1, 1851, died January 12, 1887
Clements, Robert S., son of Henry B. and Frances J. Clements, born August 18, 1849, died August 1, 1861
Clements, Minnie E., wife of Luther H. Clements, born September 10, 1867, died July 28, 1872
Neathery, Martha P., daughter of Milton and Mary M. Neathery, died January 25, 1883; age, 6 years, 10 months, 12 days
Five unmarked graves

    Copied July 22, 1933, by Miss Julia Kinney and Miss Ethel Merwin

CORN CEMETERY
Section 23, Township 50, Range 31 W

Corn, Samuel, died March 25, 1854, in 64th year of his age
Corn, Mary, wife of Samuel Corn, died January 11, 1862; age, 66 years
Corn, Samuel, son of S. and M. Corn, born June 14, 1828, died August 14, 1852
Corn, Joshua, died April 23, 1881; age, 59 years, 6 months, 28 days
Corn, Adaline, died March 8, 1855; age, 26 years

    Copied July 5, 1933, by Miss Jessie M. Crosby and Mrs. Ernest L. Harris

CUSENBARY CEMETERY
Section 7, Township 50, Range 30 W

Cusenbary, Sarah E., wife of Daniel Cusenbary, died July 26, 1847; age, 26 years, 11 months, 21 days
Cusenbary, Dannie F., son of Daniel and Celia F. Cusenbary, born September 10, 1853, died October 8, 1853
Cusenbary, Fannie A., daughter of Daniel and Celia F. Cusenbary, born March 25, 1855, died April 8, 1855
Cusenbary, Emma C., daughter of Daniel C. Cusenbary, born March 6, 1858, died April 25, 1858
Cusenbary, Sarah R., daughter of Daniel and Celia F. Cusenbary, born December 18, 1856, died December 26, 1856
——, born September 10, 18—, died April 4, 1854

    Copied April 15, 1933, by Miss Mary Sue Chiles and Miss Jessie M. Crosby

DIXON CEMETERY
Section 6, Township 50, Range 30 W

Dixon, William M., born July 23, 1842, died January 15, 1892
Dixon, Elizabeth A., born July 18, 1849, died February 18, 1911
Dixon, Jesse W., son of W. M. and L. A. Dixon, died August 10, 1882; age, 4 months
Dixon, Ebenezer, died March 22, 1884; age, 84 years, 5 months, 7 days

Dixon, Harriet, born March 16, 1807, died February 5, 1894
Donehew, Sarah, wife of Henry Donehew, born November 1, 1804, died December 22, 1851

Copied April 15, 1933, by Miss Mary Sue Chiles and Miss Jessie M. Crosby

DOUGLAS CEMETERY
Section 7, Township 50, Range 30 W

Cameron, Polly A., daughter of J. and F. S. Cameron, died October 1, 1853; age, 20 years, 2 months, 25 days

Conner, James, died October 2, 1817, in 33rd year of his age

Conner, Ann Mirum, daughter of J. and J. J. Conner, died August 20, 1848; age, 6 years, 2 months

Douglass, Thomas, born February, 1785, died January 10, 1817

Douglass, Mirum, wife of Thomas H. Douglass, born January 8, 1800, died May 27, 1849

Douglass, William, born May, 1825, died May 18, 1884
    Mildred J., wife of William Douglass, born December 5, 1832, died September 22, 1909
    Thaddeus T., their son, born July 7, 1859, died January 24, 1911

Douglass, Gamelus, died June 5, 1876; age, 33 years, 2 months, 25 days

Douglass, Emily Jane, daughter of E. T. and T. E. Douglass, born March 22, 1857, died January 14, 1861

Eckles, Joyce J., born March 28, 1817, died October 23, 1872

Eckles, Robert C., born November 9, 1801, died April 5, 1875

Eckles, Susan, daughter of R. C. and A. Eckles, born August 23, 1874, died January 25, 1878

Henderson, Mary E., wife of John Henderson, born February 10, 1863, died December 14, 1888

Sanders, Nancy, wife of J. H. Sanders, born 1811, died 1890; age, 79 years

Copied April 15, 1933, by Miss Mary Sue Chiles and Miss Jessie M. Crosby

FRANKLIN CEMETERY
Section 14, Township 50, Range 31 W

Cowley, Nancy, wife of William Cowley, died November 20, 1858; age, 53 years, 1 month, 15 days

Franklin, John, Sr., died August 7, 1845, in the 82nd year of his age

Franklin, Mary Ann, wife of John Franklin, Sr., died March 12, 1846, in the 83rd year of her age

Franklin, Lewis, died November 2, 1860; age, 67 years, 8 months

Franklin, Sarah, wife of Lewis Franklin, died February 21, 1862; age, 68 years, 1 month, 27 days

Franklin, Benjamin, born October 22, 1818, died August 9, 1848, in the 30th year of his age

Franklin, Albert M., born October 11, 1823, died April 29, 1848, in the 25th year of his age

Franklin, Marietta, wife of J. L. H. Franklin, died August 18, 1873; age, 27 years, 14 days

Franklin, James, son of J. L. H. and M. Franklin, died July 19, 1872; age, 1 year, 13 days

Franklin, William D.

Montgomery, Elizabeth, wife of David H. Montgomery, died November 19, 1858; age, 28 years, 9 months, 18 days

Montgomery, Isabel, wife of R. V. Montgomery

Copied March 11, 1933, by Miss Mary Sue Chiles and Miss Jessie M. Crosby

GREEN CHAPEL CEMETERY
Section 31, Township 50, Range 29 W

Adams, Sarah J. Herd, wife of Wm. G. Adams, died October 2, 1882; age, 33 years, 11 months, 7 days

Ames, Stephen D. A., died October 5, 1871; age, 20 years, 4 months, 12 days

Axline, Joseph, born May 21, 1824, died October 15, 1871

Axline, Amanda J., wife of Joseph Axline, born January 19, 1830, died April 27, 1888

Axline, Alpheus Samuel, son of J. E. and A. J. Axline, died August 14, 1865; age, 11 years, 5 months, 18 days

Axline, Carrie Blanche, daughter of Joseph and Amanda J. Axline, born August 19, 1871, died November 4, 1871

Axline, David G., son of J. E. and A. J. Axline, died August 15, 1870; age, 8 months, 2 days

Axline, Maggie May, daughter of Joseph and A. J. Axline, died April 11, 1868

Axline, Martha H., daughter of C. and P. Axline, born August 20, 1871, died September 29, 1871

Barnes, Temperance, wife of M. Barnes, died April 10, 1849; age, 47 or 67 years, 1 month, 11 days

Barnes, Malvina, daughter of M. and T. Barnes, died August 23, 1849; age, 17 years, 8 months, 7 days

Beavers, James, died November 9, 1865; age, 66 years, 7 months

Beavers, John W., died April 9, 1869; age, 59 years, 1 month

Beavers, Susan J., daughter of Moses and Margaret Beavers, died March 6, 1869; age, 5 months

Biffe, infant daughter of Peter B. and Sally Biffe, died May 8, 1863; age, 2 days

Blocher, Frankie, son of Joshua and Eliza J. Blocher, born November 26, 1868

Blocher, Henry T., son of J. and Jane Blocher, born November 8, 1870, died August 7, 1871

Bishop, Mary, died February 21, 188—; age, 74 years

Brockman, C. G., born December 28, 1820, died January 24, 1874

Brockman, N. J., wife of C. G. Brockman, born August 2, 1823, died August 2, 1873

Brockman, Lee Elmer, son of W. J. and E. J. Brockman, died January 7, 1869: age, 4 days

Brockman, Mary E., daughter of C. G. and N. J. Brockman, died September 7, 1851; age, 11 months, 28 days

Brockman, Nancy J., daughter of C. G. and N. J. Brockman, died June 1, 1852; age, 11 months, 23 days

Brockman, Joseph A., son of C. G. and N. J. Brockman, died October 22, 1847; age, 2 years, 2 months, 14 days

Brockman, Fanny A., daughter of C. G. and N. J. Brockman, died March 13, 1844; age, 15 days

Brockman, Cecilia F., born October 23, 1847, died April 7, 1859

Burnley, Norburn N., died May 6, 1896; age, 74 years, 7 months, 17 days

Burnley, Nicholas D., son of N. N. and M. Burnley, died November 21, 1871; age, 22 years, 8 months, 8 days

Burnley, Alvira E., daughter of N. N. and M. Burnley, died August 19, 1871; age, 17 years, 2 months, 20 days

Campbell, James, died March 24, 1858; age, 61 years, 5 months, 17 days

Campbell, John B., born January 20, 1822, died March 4, 1885 (Mason)
  Rachel Ann Grubb, wife of John B. Campbell, born October 6, 1822, died September 10, 1910

Campbell, Ruth Hanah, daughter of John B. Campbell, Jr., died June 30, 1866; age, 10 months, 5 days

Campbell, James R., son of J. B. and R. A. Campbell, died June 7, 1856; age, 2 months, 7 days

Campbell, Charity R., daughter of J. B. and Rachel A. Campbell, died August 24, 1859; age, 6 years, 5 months, 11 days

Chamblin, John, born 1849, died 1926
  Girtie, wife of John Chamblin, born 1843, died 1924
Chilton, B. R., born 1808, died 1891
  Urial, nephew of B. R. Chilton, born 1820, died 1887
Chilton, Nannie H., wife of R. H. Chilton, died December 5, 1899; age, 69 years
Cogswell, Col. William, born December 25, 1793, died December 23, 1866 (Mason)
Cogswell, Fanny Ann, wife of William Cogswell, died August 15, 1858, "in the 65th year of her age and the 43rd year of her marriage"
Cogswell, James M., born July 1, 1821, died April 11, 1855
Cogswell, Joseph W., born December 6, 1816, died October 20, 1843
Conard, Ira Clayton, son of Abner and Ann Conard, born September 4, 1868, died September 26, 1868
Conrad, Claria G., daughter of H. and S. A. Conrad, born August 27, 1863, died July 18, 1869
Conrad, Jennie M., daughter of H. and S. A. Conrad, born December 21, 1869, died August 9, 1870
Cox, Mary J., wife of William Cox, born August 1, 1825, died March 12, 1901
  William, born February 22, 1822, died November 15, 1882
Dickenson, Samuel, died August —, 1834; age, 37 years
Dickenson, Hugh, born June 15, 1802, died April 24, 1871
Dickenson, Milly Templeton, wife of Hugh Dickenson, died December 28, 1882; age, 86 years, 1 month, 11 days
Dickerson, Rebecca, wife of Griffith Dickerson, died August 22, 1860, in the 75th year of her age
Dunn, Charlotte F., wife of A. F. Dunn, died August 2, 1872; age, 42 years, 1 month, 11 days
Dunn, Jane A., daughter of A. F. and C. F. Dunn, died November 20, 1858; age, 1 month
Evans, Alice B., daughter of J. and A. E. Evans, died September 24, 1855; age, 9 months, 12 days
Evans, Mary B., daughter of J. and A. E. Evans, died September 17, 1861
Filler, Alphaous Eugine
Gardner, J. Elmer, son of E. H. and M. G. Gardner, died May 3, 1879; age, 8 months, 20 days
Gardner, Margarett C., wife of Rev. E. H. Gardner, born January 30, 1837, died September 22, 1907
Gray, Ed, died June 7, 1868; age, 21 years
Grubb, Rachel, died February 3, 1874; age, 72 years, 4 months, 20 days
Harra, Stroad Albert, son of C. A. and H. T. Harra, died December 28, 1870; age, 5 years, 2 months, 26 days
Heard, Jessee, died October 24, 1872; age, 55 years, 7 months, 19 days
Heard, John J., died January 29, 1869; age, 17 years, 1 month, 5 days
Hightower, John, born March 1, 1816, died May 6, 1897
Hightower, William H., son of John and S. A. Hightower, died October 11, 1886; age, 42 years, 6 months, 13 days
Ish, daughter of J. and M. M. Ish, died May 24, 1859; age, 2 years, 11 months, 28 days
Jeans, Columbus F., born July 25, 1835, died September 11, 1863
Jeans, James L., born August 6, 1832, died January 1863
Jeans, Nancy, wife of Elijah Jeans, born October 21, 1807, died September 24, 1867
Jeans, Richard U., born April 4, 1826, died January, 1863
Jeans, Bealie G., died April 15, 1862; age, 3 months, 13 days
  Maggie, died January 6, 1870; age, 6 months, 26 days
  Children of B. E. and M. E. Jeans
Johnson, John W., died July 17, 1851, in the 26th year of his age
King, Viola B., daughter of M. P. and M. L. King, died October 1, 1871; age, 2 years
Klutz, William, born November 7, 1841, died November 23, ——
  Mary A., wife of Wm. Klutz, born October 24, 1847, died April 14, 1903
Keshlear, Cob
Keshlear, Mariar L., daughter of J. and S. B. Keshlear

Lane, Jennie B., daughter of V. and S. E. Lane, died September 3, 1874; age, 2 months, 11 days
Lentz, Mary C., wife of N. Lentz, born December 25, 1848, died March 20, 1868
Lentz, son of J. and M. M. Lentz, died October 26, 1872; age, 4 months
Littell, Archibald, born February 7, 1824, died July 15, 1903
 Catherine, wife of A. Littell, born May 3, 1822, died January 31, 1908
Littell, Tennie M., mother, born May 1, 1858, died October 9, 1931
Little, John, son of A. and C. Little, died August 28, 1868; age, 21 days
Luther, Solomon, born 1855, died 1866
 John David, born 1861, died 1928
 Charles H., born 1847, died 1869
Morison, John, born July 1, 1811, died May 22, 1860
Mulford, James W., born August 11, 1845, died September 23, 1899
Murphy, John C., born July 13, 1838, died January 1, 1910
Murphy, Agnes B., wife of J. C. Murphy, born March 8, 1853, died December 6, 1896
McMurtry, Miss Belle, born February 19, 1838, died May 7, 1925
McMurtry, J. W., born February 16, 1834, died November 17, 1910
 Mary, wife of John McMurtry, died August 12, 1878; age, 74 years, 2 months, 23 days
Neer, L. C., born January 29, 1841, died October 9, 1912
Neer, Narcissa, wife of L. C. Neer, born March 12, 1834, died September 16, 1902
Newton, Josiah C., born January 30, 1816, died July 3, 1869
 Serena G., wife of J. C. Newton, born May 30, 1828, died April 1, 1903
Noggle, George, died December 30, 1863; age, 50 years, 9 months, 29 days
Pallett, Jane, wife of Abraham Pallett, born March 31, 1773, died October 10, 1852
Pallett, William, born October 26, 1799, died October 28, 1837
Pallett, James Y., born March 31, 1803, died August 6, 1840
Pallette, Thomas A., born October 18, 1805, died May 12, 1882
 Sarah, wife of Thomas A. Pallette, born October 22, 1804, died March 15, 1892
Pallette, A. C., died November 12, 1875; age, 65 years, 1 month, 23 days
 Martha B., wife of A. C. Pallette, died January 13, 1892; age, 79 years, 1 day
Pallette, Robert S., son of A. C. and M. B. Pallette, born February 13, 1843, died December 13, 1860
Pallette, James M., son of T. A. and S. Pallette, born March 22, 1832, died August 24, 1843
Pallette, Louisa R. M., daughter of T. A. and S. Pallette, born December 15, 1833, died September 26, 1837
Pallette, Thomas B., son of T. A. and S. Pallette, born July 20, 1838, died May 5, 1842
Pallette, Saraha H., daughter of T. A. and S. Pallette, born November 16, 1840, died December 7, 1840
Pinkard, Lucinda Jane, daughter of Robert and Jane Pinkard, died September 18, 1858; age, 20 years, 10 months, 2 days
Pinkard, Martha Ann, daughter of Robert and Jane Pinkard, died September 16, 1858; age, 16 years, 8 months, 4 days
Renick, William, died December 30, 1879; age, 78 years, 10 months, 14 days
 Sallie, wife of Wm. Renick, died November 1, 1859; age, 55 years
Renick, John T., born April 1, 1834, died May 23, 1907 (Mason)
Renick, Lucy, infant daughter of W. S. and A. Renick, died December 18, 1858
Robertson, Nancy E., wife of James Robertson, born August 9, 1846, died November 26, 1882
Robinson, Dr. Eldridge, died August 31, 1845; age, 37 years
Robinson, Sarah E., daughter of Dr. E. and Celia F. Robinson, born December 14, 1840, died August 18, 1845
Robinson, W. Benny, born January 18, 1843, died "A Martyr to Freedom" February 28, 1863
Russel, Louisa J., daughter of J. C. and S. M. Russel, died May 24, 1854; age, 5 years, 8 months, 6 days
Russel, William A. T., son of J. C. and S. M. Russel, died January 12, 1859; age, 8 months, 23 days

Sanders, Thomas S. H., died April 17, 1855; age, 21 years, 1 month, 20 days
Sanders, W. M. A., died November 11, 1859; age, 32 years, 2 months, 2 days
Scothorn, Ellnora M., daughter of F. A. and J. K. Scothorn, died 1869; age, 6 months, 20 days
Smith, Sterling, born September 15, 1837, died January 22, 1897
Steele, Samuel J., born December 14, 1815, died January 30, 1898
    Mary C., wife of S. J. Steele, born September 27, 1832, died January 17, 1899
Steele, Alexander, born May 30, 1804, died June 18, 1863; age, 59 years
Steele, Sarah, wife of Alexander Steele, born November 6, 1806, died May 9, 1890; age, 84 years
Steele, Millard Filmore, son of G. D. and Mary Steele, born April 20, 1857, died January 15, 1858
Strickland, Mary C., wife of W. B. Strickland, daughter of J. and S. A. Hightower, born in Kentucky, December 24, 1841, died February 12, 1861
Strickland, Renick, son of Geo. W. and Saiab Strickland, died February 1, 1859; age, 3 months, 5 days
Thomas, George, died August 11, 1873; age, 24 years, 2 months, 4 days
Walraven, Catharine A. M. (Sweet Mother), wife of T. B. Walraven, born July 22, 1835, died December 26, 1860
Wilke, Anna E., wife of E. Wilke, born April 27, 1827, died December 29, 1880; age, 52 years, 8 months, 2 days
Wilkinson, John Walker, died April 18, 1858
Wilkerson, children of J. T. and Fannie Wilkerson, died August 30, 1874
Williams, Oliver C., son of R. V. and E. J. Williams, died December 21, 1875; age, 2 years, 5 months, 23 days
Wilson, Thomas H., died September 29, 1868; age, 63 years
Wilson, Lucinda D., wife of T. H. Wilson, died September 7, 1875; age, 38 years, 2 months, 12 days
Wilson, William C., son of T. H. and L. B. Wilson, died February 26, 1865; age, 27 years, 7 months, 24 days
Wilson, Albert H., son of H. P. and E. J. Wilson, died December 7, 1869; age, 41 years, 11 days
Wilson, Mary Jane, daughter of T. H. and L. B. Wilson, died July 31, 1858; age, 6 years, 6 months, 27 days
Worley, Albert H., died 1881, born 1840
Worley, Laura E., daughter of A. H. and M. E. Worley, died June 12, 1873; age, 4 months, 14 days
Worley, Sarah M., daughter of J. and M. Worley, born March 14, 1848, died May 15, 1857

    Copied March 18, 1933, by Mrs. May T. Crosby and Miss Jessie M. Crosby

HUDSPETH CEMETERY
Section 13, Township 50, Range 31 W

Beall, Rufus, and his wife, Paralee, 1825-1913
Broughton, Eliza J., daughter of P. M. Broughton, died November 10, 1866; age, 5 years, 7 months, 7 days
Hudspeth, William, born in North Carolina May 1, 1778, died August 16, 1867 (father)
Hudspeth, William H., born January 15, 1842, died May 24, 1907
Hudspeth, Joel, died January 8, 189—; age, 71 years, 8 months, 23 days
Hudspeth, Silas B., son of W. and Tabitha Hudspeth, died October 12, 1885; age, 71 years, 9 months, 6 days
Hudspeth, Robert N., son of W. and Tabitha Hudspeth, died March 23, 1885; age, 63 years, 28 days

Hudspeth, George W., born February 27, 1820, died April 19, 1903
  Elizabeth C., born May 6, 1830, died February 4, 1899
Hudspeth, William J., son of G. W. and E. Hudspeth, died February 14, 1863; age, 10 months, 22 days
Hudspeth, Adhor B., daughter of G. W. and E. Hudspeth, died November 9, 1858; age, 9 months, 7 days
Hudspeth, Joel Rufus, son of Joseph W. and Amanda Hudspeth, born November 21, 1839, died February 27, 1895
Hudspeth, George E., born September 7, 1851, died October 25, 1910
  ——, his wife, born July 7, 1847, died 1923
Jacobs, Amanda E., wife of M. C. Jacobs, born April 19, 1836, died March 13, 1862
    "Death lies on her, like an untimely
    Frost upon the sweetest Flower of the Field."
Melliston, John, born 1843, died 1873
  Susan, his wife, died March 13, 1916
Morrow, Jesse, died July 16, 1886; age, 75 years, 4 months, 6 days
  Silvia, wife of Jesse Morrow, died June 10, 1872; age, 64 years, 10 months, 3 days
Morrow, Benjamin H., born December 16, 1840, died January 27, 1916
  Amanda E., his wife, born September 29, 1848, died May 15, 1922
Morrow, George, born 1845, died 1864
Morrow, James O. S., son of J. and S. Morrow, died July 2, 1886; age, 53 years, 10 months, 1 day
Morrow, William T., son of J. and S. Morrow, died March 2, 1862; age, 23 years, 6 months, 9 days
Morrow, Mary L., daughter of J. and S. Morrow, died January 3, 1867; age, 31 years, 5 months, 16 days
Morrow, Missouri, daughter of J. S. Morrow, died May 25, 1868; age, 25 years, 3 months, 24 days
Morrow, Tabitha H., daughter of J. and S. Morrow, died May 2, 1874; age, 43 years, 1 month, 28 days
Morrow, Nathan H., son of J. and S. Morrow, died September 11, 1883; age, 48 years, 11 months, 28 days
Shepherd, Henrietta S., wife of F. F. Shepherd, born April 23, 1834, died September 24, 1855

Copied June 21, 1933, by Miss Jessie M. Crosby and Mrs. May T. Crosby

HALL CEMETERY
Section 23, Township 50, Range 31 W

Dixon, David, died February 18, 1863; age, 22 years, 1 month, 10 days
Dixon, Maudie M., daughter of G. and M. E. Dixon, died March 12, 1878; age, 2 years, 10 months, 21 days
Hall, John J., died June 26, 1884; age, 23 years, 7 months, 24 days
  Mollie E., died December 5, 1882; age, 16 years, 4 months, 8 days
Hall, May, died October 25, 1882; age, 13 years, 11 months, 3 days
  Mattie A., wife of J. A. Warren and daughter of L. and E. Hall, died October 20, 1882; age, 25 years, 6 months, 23 days
  Lucinda I., died August 31, 1879; age, 27 years, 4 months, 3 days
  Charles W., died August 7, 1868; age, 4 years, 2 months, 10 days
Lewis, Susan, wife of Joshua Lewis, born May 6, 1831, died September 30, 1852

Copied June 8, 1933, by Mrs. John H. Twyman and Miss Jessie M. Crosby

LATIMER CEMETERY
On the C. Piepmeyer Farm, SW of Bone Hill

Latimer, John, born 1821, died November 12, 1863; age, 42 years
Latimer, Christy, born May 23, 1795, died September 5, 1867; age, 72 years
Latimer, Mary A., wife of Christy Latimer, born November 16, 1811, died August 20, 1876; age, 65 years
Latimer, Silas S., son of Christy and Mary A. Latimer, born December 18, 1854, died September 11, 1859
Latimer, William H., son of Christy and Mary A. Latimer, born April 23, 1851, died October, 1852
Latimer, Robert C., son of Christy and Mary A. Latimer, born May 6, 1836, died January 12, 1853; age, 16 years
Latimer, Washington, died March 25, 1868; age, 37 years, 1 month, 13 days
Ward, Virginia S., wife of George J. Ward, born September 18, 1845, died April 27, 1874

Copied September 3, 1933, by Miss Julia Kinney and Miss Ethel Merwin

NECESSARY CEMETERY
Section 27, Township 50 N, Range 30 W

Located on the H. S. Burgess Farm

This is a very old cemetery with about fifteen graves, but no stones. Several people were buried here before it was used as a family burial ground by the Necessary family. The only information obtained so far is that Mrs. Dude Ames, about 40 years old, was buried here about 28 years ago.

Compiled by Miss Julia Kinney and Miss Ethel Merwin September 22, 1933

RICE BURYING GROUND
Section 12, Township 50, Range 31 W

Murfee, Emily, wife of J. Murfee, born January 12, 1827, died June 20, 1849
Peace, Caroline, wife of Isaac Peace, died January 27, 1869; age, 48 years, 3 months, 13 days
Peace, Isaac, died October 22, 1878; age, 54 years, 10 months, 22 days
Peace, Joseph M., son of Isaac and Caroline Peace, born May 27, 1850, died April 2, 1858
Rice, Michael, born in St. Mary, Devonshire, England, December 28, 1791, died February 11, 1854
Rice, Nancy, wife of Michael Rice, born in K. T., November 30, 1800, died October 9, 1837
Rice, James, son of Michael and Nancy Rice, born October 9, 1837, died February 1, 1838
Rice, John M., son of Michael and Ann C. Rice, born December 2, 1848, died November 2, 1850

Copied March 11, 1933, by Miss Mary Sue Chiles and Miss Jessie M. Crosby

DRAKE CEMETERY
Section 12, Towship 50, Range 31 W

Adams, Lynchburg, died December 6, 1873; age, 69 years, 14 days
Adams, Elizabeth D., wife of Lynch B. Adams, daughter of a Rev. soldier, died January 24, 1859; age, 50 years, 1 month, 17 days
Drake, Isaac, (no dates) stone reads Isaac Drake N. J. Mil. Rev. War
Drake, Fannie, wife of Isaac Drake, died September 5, 1849; age, 74 years, 5 months, 26 days
Drake, A. J., born 1812, died 1887
  Elizabeth, his wife, born 1823, died 1864

Copied March 11, 1933 by Miss Mary Sue Chiles and Miss Jessie M. Crosby

SIBLEY CEMETERY
Section 2, Township 50 N, Range 30 W

This is probably the oldest cemetery in Jackson County, Missouri. It is located near the site of Fort Osage. In August, 1930, the Sibley Cemetery Association was organized and granted a state charter. The object of the association is to beautify and maintain the cemetery.

Alderman, Mary J., wife of C. B. Alderman, died May 25, 1859; age, 30 years, 1 month, 16 days

Baker, John, died December 18, 1893; age, 64 years, 11 months, 23 days
Caroline J., wife of J. Baker, died November 3, 1898; age, 69 years, 6 months, 23 days

Bault, Annie May, daughter of J. G. and J. Bault, died December 21, 1871; age, 11 months, 21 days

Brown, Eliza V., wife of J. W. Brown, died January 29, 1875; age, 24 years, 10 months, 11 days

Bryant, James M., died May 13, 1868; age, 43 years, 11 months, 28 days

Bryant, Jane, wife of James Bryant, born November 28, 1817, died November 5, 1869

Cameron, Jonathan, died February 16, 1868 (broken stone)

Campbell, Alexander, born September 3, 1811, died November 15, 1879

Charlton, Dorinda, wife of R. G. Charlton, born October 28, 1835, died June 14, 1871

Charlton, W. E., son of R. G. and D. Charlton, born January 23, 1865, died June 4, 1873

Childs, Joel F., son of W. G. and Susan H. Childs, born December 27, 1840, died October 1, 1864

Childs, Thomas, son of Wm. G. and Susan H. Childs, died July 27, 1856; age, 22 years, 5 months, 2 days (Odd Fellow)

Childs, Norah C., daughter of S. I. and M. E. Childs, died April 2, 1856; age, 6 months, 12 days

Colcord, Lafayette W., born October 16, 1829, died February 5, 1903
Rebecca, born May 7, 1801, died January 21, 1870

Collins, Martha, died August 26, 1871; age, 84 years, 10 days

Coonce, James, born January 28, 1825, died August 6, 1858

Dixon, infant daughter of J. M. and H. L. Dixon, died October 28, 1869

Garrison, Armilda M., born December 20, 1820, died March 26, 1885; age, 64 years, 3 months, 6 days

Gibbs, W. W., died March 7, 1871; age, 39 years, 7 months, 6 days

Hambright, John W., died January 1, 1875; age, 68 years, 11 months, 5 days

Hambright, Missouri L., wife of John W. Hambright, died October 15, 1878; age, 67 years, 6 months, 7 days

Hambright, John W., died October 26, 1874; age, 72 years

Hambright, James W., born Jan. 29, 1838, died July 1, 1920

Haines, Michael D., born February 24, 1818, died March 28, 1848

Haines, Michael H., died August 22, 1874 (stone broken)

Haines, John White, son of M. H. and M. A. Haines, died July 26, 1871; age, 6 years, 9 months, 26 days

Haines, Susanna R., wife of Simpson Haines, died February 13, 1881; age, 65 years, 3 months, 21 days

Hamilton, Christopher C., born November 23, 1823, died March 6, 1875

Hamilton, James B., born August 6, 1824, died August 25, 1898
Mrs. James B., born November 4, 1845, died November 7, 1925

Hamilton, John B., died October 26, 1874; age, 72 years, 8 months, 29 days

Hamilton, Samuel W., born September 17, 1852, died November 2, 1856

Hamilton, Willie G. D., son of W. H. and G. A. Hamilton, died February 9, 1869; age, 3 months, 4 days

Hanna, James T., son of J. A. and E. G. Hanna, died October 17, 1856; age, 4 years, 10 months, 19 days
Hanna, Martha E., daughter of J. A. and M. E. Hanna, died October 29, 1856; age, 1 year, 11 days
Harrelson, Jeremiah, died October 4, 1839; age, 61 years, 9 months
Harrelson, Martha, wife of Jeremiah Harrelson, died September 27, 1839; age, 57 years, 11 months, 27 days
Harrelson, Jeremiah T., died October 7, 1839; age, 19 years, 5 months, 12 days
Harrelson, James C., died April 6, 1852; age, 40 years, 7 months, 26 days
Harrelson, Joseph A., died January 23, 1852; age, 43 years, 8 months, 19 days
Harrelson, Barbara W., wife of Joseph A. Harrelson, died September 17, 1842; age, 32 years, 6 months, 2 days
Hollis, Anna, daughter of J. A. and A. E. Hollis, born at Utica, Miss., August 5, 185-, died August 17, 1856
Holmes, John R., died June 5, 1872; age, 29 years, 8 months, 22 days
Holmes, Martie E., son of J. R. and M. L. Holmes, died January 22, 1873; age, 5 years, 2 months, 14 days
Hudson, Mary G., wife of S. W. Hudson, died July 15, 1873; age, 21 years, 2 months, 17 days
Hudson, Minnie A., daughter of S. W. and M. G. Hudson, died November 20, 1873; age, 8 months
Hughes, Mary H., wife of Henry H. Hughes, born November 1, 1850, died December 26, 1871
Hull, Milton, died November 30, 1889; age, 55 years, 11 months, 8 days
Hullis, James H., died July 8, 1881; age, 55 years, 5 months
Huston, A. H., died October 7, 1879; age, 31 years, 5 months, 26 days
Jackson, Leonard N., died April 24, 1904; age, 59 years, 4 months, 5 days
Jackson, Sarah, born 1848, died 1921
Jackson, W. S., died January 26, 1877; age, 44 years, 2 months, 6 days
Jackson, Willie, son of W. S. and M. A. Jackson, born February 26, 1870, died September 23, 1875
Jackson, Rosey, daughter of W. S. and M. A. Jackson, born September 2, 1873, died September 7, 1873
Johnson, Samuel R., died March 18, 1891; age, 57 years, 11 months, 20 days
Johnson, Catharine, died December 11, 1897; age, 60 years, 8 months, 8 days
Johnson, Nancy J., born 1843, died 1924
Johnson, infant daughter of B. J. and S. E. Johnson, died March 14, 1861
Johnson, John Franklin, son of Benjamin and S. E. Johnson, died October 27, 1856; age, 1 year, 7 months, 2 days
Johnson, William Thomas, son of Benjamin and S. E. Johnson, died October 7, 1850
Kimsey, James W., died January 20, 1893; age, 54 years, 3 months, 16 days
Kimsey, Missouri Ann, born November 29, 1837, died October 18, 1921
Kimsey, Samuel, died November 13, 1875; age 39 years, 7 months, 17 days
Kimsey, Emily H., wife of Samuel Kimsey, born —, —14 (broken stone)
Lambert, William H., died July 7, 1898; age, 59 years, 8 months, 9 days
Lee, E. R., born 1841, died 1927 (Mason)
Lee, James S., son of E. R. and E. A. Lee, born January 13, 1867, died September 21, 1867
Leonard, Elizabeth, died May 14, 1849; age, 11 years, 5 months, 25 days
Leonard, Isabel B., wife of Zenas Leonard, died August 11, 1851; age, 37 years, 1 month, 12 days
Lillard, John H., no dates. The Masonic Emblem and Odd Fellow Emblem on the stone
Locke, George K., son of J. F. and M. J. Locke, born March 10, 1848, died April 14, 1854
Locke, Dr. Pelides, born March 17, 1824, died May 2, 1849
Locke, infant daughter of Dr. P. and M. A. Locke, died July 1849
Locke, Samuel H., son of J. F. and M. J. Locke, born June 16, 1853, died Sept. 16, 1853
Long, Josephus, born 1830, died 1916
    Anna E., wife of Josephus Long, born 1834, died 1903
Loud, Eliza A., wife of Granville Loud, died June 2, 1880

CEMETERIES—FORT OSAGE TOWNSHIP

McCarty, Mary Nancy D., wife of J. C. McCarty, died March 29, 1879; age, 85 years
McClellan, Abraham, died September 18, 1851; age, 77 years, 11 months, 9 days
McClellan, Jane, wife of Abraham McClellan (no dates, next to John M. Walker)
McClellan, Barbara W., daughter of A. and J. McClellan, died October 23, 1823; age, 3 years, 1 month
McClellan, Susan W., daughter of A. and J. McClellan, died June 18, 1851; age, 28 years, 11 months, 25 days
McCown, Martha A., died August 16, 1849; age, 33 years, 8 months, 12 days
    Barbarae, died August 23, 1847; age, 8 months, 19 days
McCune, Ella May, daughter of N. and M. McCune, died December 13, 1874; age, 4 years, 9 months, 13 days
McMillen, Abagail G., daughter of J. S. and A. McMillen, died September 21, 1856; age, 2 years, 9 months, 21 days
McMillin, James S., died August 10, 1891; age, 76 years, 5 months, 22 days (Mason)
McMillin, Abigail, wife of J. S. McMillin, died June 13, 1896; age, 74 years, 10 months, 25 days
McQueary, children of T. and B. McQueary
Myler, Susan, wife of H. F. Myler, died June 2, 1853; age, 33 years
Neill, W. T., born May 9, 183-, died October 28, 1911
    Louisa, wife of W. T. Neill, born October 24, 1833, died March 7, 1907
Pollard, William C., died December 17, 1872; age, 46 years, 11 months, 16 days
Pollard, Hettie, wife of W. G. Pollard, died June 28, 1884; age, 57 years, 3 months, 2 days
Pryor, Jane G. (or C.), wife of L. W. Pryor, died December 20, 1869; age, 59 years, 8 months, 3 days
Pryor, Isaac D., son of J. S. and M. E. Pryor, died October 5, 1869; age, 6 months, 15 days
Pryor, Laura Ann, daughter of J. S. and M. E. Pryor, died July 10, 1859; age, 1 year, 2 days
Radcliff, Martha, wife of William Radcliff, died September 7, 1881; age, 40 years
Ragland, James W., died January 30, 1870 (incomplete)
Ragland, Jane, wife of James W. Ragland, died September 1, 1870; age, 22 years, 11 months
Ray, William, died May 22, 1872; age, 56 years
Raber, Artemesia, daughter of H. and A. M. Raber, died September 19, 1871; age, 1 month
Rolen, John, died May 2, 1874; age, 58 years, 3 months, 23 days
Rolen, children of J. M. and M. L. Rolen, 1851
Simpson, Squire, died September 18, 1861, in the 22nd year of his age
Sharp, Emma, daughter of T. and N. J. Sharp, died August 1, 1867; age, 3 years
Sharp, infant son of T. and N. J. Sharp, died November 21, 1870; age, 8 months
Smith, Lafayette French, son of N. M. and M. Smith, born October 5, 1853, died January 26, 1854
Smith, Viola, daughter of N. M. and M. Smith, born October 27, 1850, died August 2, 1854
Steele, A. G., Sr., died December 31, 1894; age, 84 years
Steele, Emily, wife of A. G. Steele, born January 11, 1819, died April 9, 1888
Steele, Albert G., son of A. G. and Emily Steele, died January 14, 1881; age, 35 years, 3 months, 3 days
Steele, George A., son of A. G. and Emily Steele, died October 9, 1863 at Fort Delaware and was buried in the prisoners' burying ground in New Jersey; age, 22 years, 10 months, 8 days
Steele, James T., son of A. G. and Emily Steele, died March 5, 1863; age, 22 years, 10 months, 8 days
Steele, Joseph E., son of A. G. and Emily Steele, died July 7, 1864, and buried at Hamburg, Alabama; age, 25 years, 6 months, 23 days
Sommerville, Alex A., died March 19, 1899; age, 79 years, 1 month
Taulbee, Rebecca (mother), born 1838, died 1916
Thomas, Zackariah E., died January 16, 1854; age, 48 years, 9 months, 20 days. Erected by his son, A. J. Thomas
Thompson, John, died February 6, 1898; age, 62 years, 2 months, 25 days

Thompson, Mary A., wife of John Thompson, died April 19, 1883; age, 44 years, 23 days
Triplet, Eli, died February 9, 1879; age, 61 years, 6 months, 22 days
    Margaret E., wife of Eli Triplet, died March 6, 1887; age, 56 years, 4 months, 8 days
Triplet, Elijah W., son of Eli and M. E. Triplet, born November 2, 1860, died August 25, 1862
Triplet, Eleanor, daughter of Eli and M. E. Triplet, born December 11, 1862, died January 15, 1868
Triplet, Marshal D., son of Eli and M. E. Triplet, born November 28, 1864, died August 22, 1866
Triplet, Sue, daughter of Eli and M. E. Triplet, born December 25, 1868, died September 4, 1869
Triplet, infant son of E. and M. E. Triplet, died July 18, 1870
Tunstall, Marye, Consort of J. V. Tunstall, died August 18, 1866; age, 43 years, 3 months, 15 days
Ueker, Nancy, wife of John D. Ueker, died August 24, 1879; age, 39 years, 7 months, 15 days
Vesey, Louisa A., wife of Zadek Vesey, born March 19, 1819, died October 30, 1855
Vest, Norah E., daughter of N. and A. G. Vest, died February, 1875; age, 11 years, 4 months, 22 days
Walker, John M., died May 8, 1844
Willis, Little Jodie, son of Jos. and S. J. Willis, died 1871
Willis, Joseph W., son of Joseph and Sarah J. Willis, born May 26, 1858, died (broken)
Willis, Maggie L., daughter of Joseph and Sarah Willis, born June 27, 1864, died August 17, 1865
Young, Dr. S. J., died April 28, 192—; age, 83 years

    Copied March 11, 1933, by Mrs. Max A. Christopher, Miss Mary Sue Chiles and Miss Jessie M. Crosby

SIX MILE BAPTIST CHURCH CEMETERY
Section 7, Township 50, Range 30 W

Bittle, David (father), born 1838, died 1923
    Mollie (mother), born 1858, died 1923
Bittle, William, born May 3, 1826, died July 28, 1908
Charlton, Rufus G., born in Montgomery Co., Va., November 15, 1833, died October 27, 1901
Charlton, Francis M. (father), born 1844, died 1929
Charlton, Martha, wife of W. R. Charlton, born October 14, 1845, died September 4, 1913
Clark, D. G., born February 27, 1831, died 1914
    Amanda, wife of D. G. Clark, born February 15, 1843, died 1902
Corn, Caroline, wife of Joshua Corn, born January 21, 1842, died September 28, 1908
Douglas, James H., born June 5, 1828, died March 11, 1911
    Henrietta, wife of J. H. Douglas, born January 24, 1835, died September 18, 1879
Dixon, Polk, born January 3, 1846, died September 11, 1910
Dixon, Virginia, born February 3, 1848, died December 7, 1928
Dyer, M. Josie, wife of D. P. Dyer, born 1837, died 1914
Fristoe, Mary L., wife of Richard Fristoe, died September 23, 1870; age, 77 years
Harland, Z. T., born March 31, 1849, died February 25, 1904
Hock, Joseph, born November 4, 1822, died April 8, 1899
Hock, Elizabeth, wife of Joseph H. Hock, born July 27, 1831, died February 28, 1894
Hock, Joseph H., born March 11, 1849, died December 4, 1914
Hock, Martha, wife of Joseph H. Hock, born July 31, 1849, died November 9, 1916
Hunter, Edna, born 1819, died 1893
Johnston, William L., born May 29, 1816, died July 24, 1875
    Eliza A., wife of Wm. L. Johnston, born December 29, 1825, died July 4, 1897
Jones, Rev. Albert T.
    Sarah, wife of Rev. Albert T. Jones

CEMETERIES—FORT OSAGE TOWNSHIP

Jones, James H., born August 1, 1845, died November 29, 1911
Kimbrel, Lewis, died April 24, 1903; age, 96 years, 6 months
Kimbrel, Jane, wife of Lewis Kimbrel, died May 17, 1902; age, 81 years
Kimbrel, William, born December 15, 1841, died July 29, 1912
Kittle, Amassa, born 1823, died 1893
   Martha E., wife of Amassa Kittle, born 1830, died 1908
Kuster, George H. (father), born 1848, died 1922
Kuster, Mary L. (mother), born 1851, died 1926
Mann, Ambrose (father), born 1836, died 1928
Mann, Ezra, born January 8, 1832, died March 12, 1904
Mann, Lucy A., wife of Ezra, August 9, 1838
Minter, John D., born December 10, 1814, died August 22, 1871
Minter, Ann R., born September 8, 1818, died March 13, 1903
Peace, William R., born 1844, died 1888
Pem, Joseph, born January 21, 1842, died December 26, 1931
Pem, Charlotte, wife of Joseph Pem, born February 1, 1844, died October 12, 1910
Potter, Bettie, wife of R. M. Potter, died July 5, 1894; age, 54 years
Rolen, James M., born 1848, died 1910
Rolen, Hannah, wife of John Rolen, died January 21, 1891; age, 64 years, 11 months, 12 days
Stone, W. J., born November 16, 1844, died December 26, 1915
Twyman, L. W., M. D., born February 28, 1825, died August 4, 1902
   Fannie, wife of Dr. L. W. Twyman, born April 22, 1829, died April 1, 1909
  Dr. L. W. Twyman and Miss F. C. Fristoe were married March 22, 1848, by J. J. Robinson
Twyman, Julia, daughter of L. W. and F. C. Twyman, born February 6, 1849, died April 11, 1864
Tyer, Lewis, died January 3, 1877; age, 62 years, 9 months, 23 days
Tyer, Mary, wife of Lewis Tyer, born January 10, 1816, died June 8, 1872

        Copied June 23, 1933, by Mrs. May T. Crosby and Miss Jessie M. Crosby

UNNAMED CEMETERY
Section 12, Township 50, Range 31 W

This cemetery is on land which was owned by the Childs family. It is one of the oldest burying places in the county. It is referred to as "The Cemetery in the Woods." The graves are marked with native stones. It is impossible to record the names of those buried there but it is known that some of the Potts family are here and a Mrs. Colston who died about 1888.

        Contributed by Miss Jessie M. Crosby

WEIR CEMETERY
Section 19, Township 50 N, Range 30 W

Moore, George S., born December 13, 1818, died April 4, 1851
Moore, there were several of the Moore family buried in this cemetery
Morgan, Martin M., born May 27, 1803, died July 6, 1849
Morgan, Nancy D., wife of Benjamin F. Morgan, born September 21, 1834, died December 21, 1854
Morgan, there were other Morgans buried in this cemetery
Weir, Andrew H., died January 9, 1881; age, 62 years, 3 months, 29 days
A stone, "died June 17, 1855" (the stone is broken)

This is one of the most neglected cemeteries in the county. It is known that some of the Hudspeth family were buried there. There is a suggestion of what was, long ago, a rock vault. Many of the tombstones have been missing for years and the cemetery is becoming a place of tradition only.

        Copied June 21, 1933, by Miss Jessie M. Crosby

BLUE TOWNSHIP

Organized May 22, 1827

ADAMS CEMETERY
Section 16, Township 50, Range 31 W

Adams, Catherine, wife of William Adams, died March 27, 1876; age, 28 years, 3 months, 20 days

Adams, Elizabeth, second wife of Stephen Adams, born March 18, 1811, died September 24, 1884; age, 73 years, 6 months, 6 days

Adams, Mary, wife of Stephen Adams, born March 12, 1810, died October 28, 1857; age, 47 years, 7 months

Adams, Mary Jane, daughter of Stephen and Polly Adams, died March 25, 1847; age, 9 years, 4 months, 4 days

Adams, Rachel, daughter of Stephen and Polly Adams, died October 25, 1849; age, 18 years, 7 months, 1 day

Adams, Stephen A., son of William and Catharine Adams, born July 7, 1867, died November 15, 1869

Wood, Ann, wife of Edward Wood, born November 6, 1827, died July 15, 1857; age, 30 years, 7 months, 9 days

Copied June 8, 1933, by Mrs. John H. Twyman and Miss Jessie M. Crosby

ANDERSON CEMETERY
Section 19, Township 50, Range 31 W

Anderson, George W., born September 3, 1810, died January 18, 1859

Anderson, Sallie A., wife of G. W. Anderson, born September 10, 1809, died May 24, 1881

Anderson, George W., born September 4, 1846, died June 26, 1880

Anderson, Minerva S., daughter of G. W. and Juliet Anderson, died July 4, 1879; age, 3 years

Anderson, Little Mary, daughter of James R. and Annie Anderson, died April 11, 1881; age, 15 years, 3 months, 27 days

Daniel, Rachel J., died July 6, 1881; age, 33 years, 2 months, 29 days

Howell, Grace, daughter of J. A. and Annie Howell, died May 3, 1882; age, 1 year, 8 months 15 days

Copied by Mrs. Ernest L. Harris and Miss Crosby

BATES GRAVE
Section 32, Township 50, Range 32 W

Bates, Mary E. Alton, wife of S. P. Bates, born August 8, 1842, died September 3, 1876; age, 34 years, 27 days

Mr. S. P. Bates was the teacher at the Reed school

Copied July 20, 1933, by Mrs. Ernest L. Harris and Miss Jessie M. Crosby

BELCHER CEMETERY
Section 20, Township 50, Range 31 W

Adams, Bowen C., son of L. and Emeline Adams, born November 8, 1853, died June 27, 1855
Belcher, John, born December 25, 1776, died September 26, 1843
Powell, Lilly B., wife of Alvis Powell, who departed this life January 10, 1848; age, 21 years, 6 months, 11 days

> "Remember friends
> as you pass by
> As you are now
> so once was I.
> As I am now
> so you must be
> Prepare for death
> and follow me."

A broken stone, Sarah E., daughter of   J. and Rachel
There are several unmarked graves

Copied July 5, 1933, by Miss Jessie M. Crosby and Mrs. Ernest L. Harris

BURNS CEMETERY
Section 32, Township 50, Range 32 W
Contributed by Jesse Reed, grandson of Mathias Reed

Mrs. Benson, from Indiana
Burns, Felix
Sage, Angeline
Sage, Walker
Simmons, Jack
Todd, George

Copied by Mrs. Ernest L. Harris and Miss Jessie M. Crosby

CAMP CEMETERY
Section 26, Township 49 N, Range 31 W

Balwyman,   , born May 4, 1835, died September 7, 1918
Bryant, Mary Ann, born 1841, died 1917
Burch, William, died April 15, 1911; age, 69 years
Burch, C. R., born 1870, died 1920
Burch, Catherine, wife of John Burch, born March 12, 1852, died August 2, 1909
Clarkson, Thomas G., died May 7, 1858; age, 40 years
Kinchle, Drucilla, born December 17, 1847, died March 28, 1925
Nave, Henry, no dates
Nave, Abraham, born September 30, 1805, died August 10, 1885
Nave, Eliza C., first wife of Abraham Nave, died May 24, 1877; age, 67 years
Nave, Mary, wife of Henry Nave, died 1896; age, 57 years, 3 months, 22 days
Nave, Nora, wife of Ulysses Nave, died October 29, 1893; age, 26 years, 7 months, 10 days
Sharp, James, born September 29, 1837, died August 18, 1893
Stover, Abigail, died March 5, 1928; age, 89 years, 11 months, 25 days
Stover, Charles, died October 1, 1876; age, 45 years, 1 month, 25 days
Wilson, Emily, wife of A. R. Wilson, born December 10, 1826, died December 14, 1883
Wilson, Samuel, son of A. R. and E. Wilson, born January 12, 1873, died February 23, 1896
Wilson, G. E., no dates
Wilson, Mary B., wife of G. E. Wilson, died October 28, 1888; age, 28 years

Copied June, 1933, by Miss Julia Kinney and Miss Ethel Merwin

CEMETERIES—BLUE TOWNSHIP

CHRISMAN CEMETERY
Section 33, Township 50, Range 31 W

Data Contributed by A. M. Chrisman

Chrisman, Sanders
Chrisman, Elizabeth, wife of Sanders Chrisman
Chrisman, two children of Mr. and Mrs. Sanders Chrisman
Goforth, Eliza Ann, wife of E. G. Goforth, died January 18, 1876; age, 38 years, 2 months, 30 days

There are fifteen graves marked with native stones but without inscriptions on them.
Copied July 12, 1933, by Mrs. Ernest L. Harris and Miss Jessie M. Crosby

CHRISTOPHER MANN CEMETERY
Section 23, Township 50, Range 32 W

The land for this cemetery was given by a Mr. Waldo. There are as many as 150 buried here but only three markers are left. Their inscriptions follow:

Mallison, Mary A., wife of J. H. Mallison, died January 10, 1884; age, 18 years, 11 months, 20 days
Monroe, Mary E., wife of W. N. O. Monroe, died June 22, 1868; age, 33 years, 4 months, 28 days
Monroe, Julia A., daughter of W. N. O. and M. E. Monroe, died October 2, 1869; age, 3 months, 18 days

The above inscriptions were copied July 20, 1933, by Miss Jessie Crosby, Mrs. Hale Houts and Mrs. Ernest L. Harris.

The following data given by Mrs. Scott Davis and Mrs. Pertilla (nee Mallison).

Mallison, Lillie Elizabeth, died 1877; age, 16 years
Mallison, Edward, died 1869; age, 2 and one-half years old
Mallison, George, died 1884; age, 21 years
Moore, William, and three of his children
Mrs. Meador and children
Monroe, Daniel, died about 1874
Monroe, Frances Agnes, died about 1864

COURTNEY CEMETERY
Section 13, Township 50, Range 32 W

Birge, Mary Noble, born January 25, 1867, died March 2, 1897
Bokamper, Gottleib, born May 18, 1833, died December 18, 1908
Burton, Levi R., born 1847, died 1880
Davis, John, born May 19, 1834, died February 28, 1867; erected 1883 by his son, Walter S. Davis
Davis, Agnes, wife of John Davis, born August 10, 1834, died December 17, 1869
Engle, Lorinda M., died May 29, 1903; age, 47 years, 5 months, 5 days
Fann, J. W., Co. I, 6th Kansas Cav.
Fann, Maria, wife of J. Fann, died July 28, 1880; age, 34 years, 11 months, 27 days
Fann, G. S., Co. M, 15th Kansas Cav.
Fann, W. E., Co. M, 15th Kansas Cav.
Fann, David B., Co. B, 2nd Mo. S. M. Cav.
Hobbs, W. M., Co. B, 2nd Mo. S. M. Cav.

Julian, William E., born September 27, 1840, died September 14, 1915
Julian, Mary Moore, born May 3, 1852, died December 25, 1918
Julian, John S., born May 4, 1835, died October 23, 1903
Julian, R. C., died February, 1860; age, 21 years, 5 months, 20 days
Julian, Jane, wife of John Julian, died July 24, 1885; age, 75 years, 9 months, 16 days
Julian, Prior L., born May 5, 1831, died April 28, 1900
Julian, Benjamin, born May 8, 1846, died April 20, 1900
Julian, Myli Williams, born February 15, 1847, died November 3, 1925
Kelley, Joseph C., died February 19, 1868; age, 38 years, 9 months, 4 days
Kelley, Samuel Mann, born August 4, 1837, died May 30, 1862
Lyday, D. H., Co. B, 6th Mo. Cav.
Mayo, P. L.
Mann, Benjamin F., born June 4, 1833, died October 17, 1913
Marlow, Robert, born February 5, 1820, died February 22, 1896
Marlow, Martha E., wife of R. Marlow, born August 30, 1826, died January 19, 1886
Murphy, John C., born February 2, 1846, died June 24, 1854
Neal, Clabern C., born February 2, 1879; age, 30 years
Noble, Albert W., born July 27, 1829, died August 24, 1872
Noble, Albert, born October 5, 1851, died February 17, 1889
Noble, Mary C., beloved wife of A. W. Noble, born November 13, 1826, died February 14, 1894
Pail, Lula Bell M.
Pierce, John A., died March 15, 1868; age, 37 years, 7 months, 25 days
Purcell, Catherine, wife of James Purcell, born December 19, 1840, died October 7, 1882
Smith, Enoch, born 1814, died 1910
Smith, Sarah E., wife of E. Smith, died July 14, 1850; age, 44 years
Smith, Harriett T., born 1834, died 1922
Stewart, Elizabeth, wife of Zeghariah Stewart, born January 25, 1815, died February 4, 1900
Turner, Sarah, born November 17, 1818
Williams, G. M., Co. B, 2nd Mo. Cav., died September 7, 1869; age, 30 years, 4 months, 6 days
Williams, S. S., died March 11, 1874; age, 59 years, 4 months, 24 days
Williams, Meyliann, wife of S. S. Williams, died October 4, 1880; age, 61 years, 11 months, 23 days
Williams, Millie, died May 19, 1855; age, 24 years
Williams, Susan, born November 25, 1830, died September 15, 1851

Copied July 20, 1933, by Mrs. Ernest L. Harris and Miss Jessie M. Crosby

DALTON CEMETERY, sometimes known as LUTTRELL CEMETERY
Section 19, Township 49, Range 31 W

Carr, James, died May 15, 1901; age, 89 years, 9 months, 5 days
    Anna, wife of James Carr, died April 20, 1895; age, 78 years, 5 months, 6 days
Cruwell, William, born December 31, 1838, died August 10, 1928
Cruwell, William, Co. E, 4 U. S. R. O. Mo. Inf.
Dalton, Lewis, died June 22, 1879; age, 80 years, 10 months, 4 days
    Matilda, died February 19, 1879; age, 76 years, 7 months, 4 days
Harris, Eliza, born December 25, 1820, died March 1, 1875

Harris, William, born October 31, 1847, died April 2, 1875
Huls, Elizabeth, born November 7, 1789, died August 5, 1859
Luttrell, Sarah, wife of W. Luttrell, died October 13, 1860; age, 71 years, 11 months, 6 days
Luttrell, Greenville S., died December 22, 1866; age, 41 years, 8 months, 24 days
Luttrell, William M., born January 31, 1833, died June 29, 1851
Luttrell, Willis, died January 27, 1833; age, 19 years, 9 months
Luttrell, Samuel, died February 26, 1893; age, 74 years, 4 months, 12 days
    Armilda J., died February 12, 1914; age, 82 years, 7 months, 25 days
Luttrell, L. P. S., husband of S. E. Luttrell, born December 12, 1827, died October 22, 1887
Luttrell, Charlie, son of S. H. and A. J. Luttrell, died July 3, 1865; age, 1 year, 3 months, 5 days
Meyer, Christena, born April 22, 1833, died September 4,
Sneed, George B., son of J. M. and E. E. Sneed, died March 14, 1875; age, 6 months, 7 days

    Copied June 17, 1933, by Miss Jessie M. Crosby and Mrs. May T. Crosby

HARRIS-JOHNSON CEMETERY
Section 24, Township 49, Range 32
On old Luttrell Farm

(39th St. and Lee's Summit Rd., No. 10 E. One-fourth mile west of 10 E and about 100 ft. over fence on 39th Street.)

We are deeply grateful to the following for their assistance in securing information about this cemetery.

    Mrs. E. L. Harris, Kansas City, Mo.
    Mrs. W. H. Carr, Rural Route, Independence, Mo.
    Mrs. Carlton, Rural Route, Lee's Summit

Johnson, Larkin, born 1794, died 1877
Johnson, Sarah Harris, wife of Larkin Johnson, born 1798, died 1865
Harris, Reuben, died May 16, 1842, aged 82 years
Harris, Samuel, son of Reuben Harris, born 1807, died 1854, uncle of Mrs. Carr
Harris, Secky, son of Reuben Harris, uncle of Mrs. Carr
Harris, Secretary, son of Samuel and Jane Hall Harris; age, 9 years
Luttrell, Sarah Smith, wife of John Luttrell, died just after the Civil War

    Copied October 1, 1933, by Miss Jessie Crosby and Mrs. Hale Houts

HEDGES FAMILY BURYING GROUNDS
Section 18, Township 50, Range 31 W
Section 12, Township 47, Range 33 W

Data contributed by Mrs. Henry Kemper, daughter of
George S. and Martha Gaitskill Hedges

George S. Hedges and Martha Gaitskill were married April, 1837, and moved from Bourbon County, Kentucky, to Jackson County, Missouri.

The Records in the office of Recorder of Deeds, Independence, Missouri, Court House, show in Book G, pages 163 and 328, that on August 26, 1840, George S. Hedges bought from Lilburn W. Boggs and Thomas Jeffries, the East one-half of the Southeast Quarter of Section 18, Township 50, Range 31 W. The Price paid for the 80 acres was $1800.00, according to the records.

Martha Gaitskill, Consort of George S. Hedges, born June 22, 1819, died May 22, 1850, in her 31st year, and was buried in the Burying Ground on the Hedges Farm.

Mr. Hedges married again, and a baby by his second wife was also buried here.

During the Civil War, Mr. Hedges moved his family to Johnson County, Missouri, and lived about two miles from the town of Columbus, Missouri.

The records in the Independence, Missouri, Recorder of Deeds office, show that on April 10, 1866, Mr. George S. Hedges bought from Samuel Gregg, 130 acres in Section 12, Township 47, Range 33 W, for a consideration of $5000.00.

George S. Hedges, born February 11, 1811, died February 7, 1879; age, 67 years, 11 months, 16 days

Mr. Hedges died on the farm and was buried there.

Ambrose George Hedges, son of George S. Hedges, born May 5, 1850, died November 8, 1872, was buried in this ground.

Data compiled by Miss Jessie M. Crosby

HILL CEMETERY
Section 9, Township 49, Range 32 W

Now Hill Park near Independence, Missouri

Hill, Adam, born August 29, 1799, died February 24, 1886

Hill, Ann Woods Moberley, wife of Adam Hill, born August, 1808, died June 12, 1851

Hill, William Moberley, born July 6, 1836, died November 27, 1912

Hill, Curtis, born December 29, 1845, died June 17, 1867

Hill, Ann Elizabeth Gossett, wife of William Hill, born November 10, 1850, died November 4, 1880

A sister-in-law and a nephew of Adam Hill, while visiting the Hill family, died there about the close of the Civil War, and were buried in the family cemetery.

Land, Peter, a confederate soldier killed during the battle at Independence, Missouri, June, 1861

Four small babies and seven children, all descendants of the Hill family, are buried there.

The last three records contributed by Mrs. Frank Abston

Copied June 11, 1933, by Miss Jessie M. Crosby and Mrs. May T. Crosby

HOWARD CEMETERY
Section 17, Township 48, Range 31 W

Farm still owned by Howard family

Howard, William B., born March 10, 1821, died July 13, 1896

Howard, Maria D., wife of William B. Howard, born November 22, 1825, died February 16, 1865

Howard, William B., son of William B. and M. D., born May 10, 1846, died May 23, 1857

Emmerson, Mary M., daughter of S. and M. R. White, died September 12, 1882; age, 67 years, 10 months, 5 days

White, Ann R., daughter of S. and M. R. White, died May 31, 1838; age, 19 years, 4 months, 9 days

CEMETERIES—BLUE TOWNSHIP

White, Samuel, son of S. and M. R. White, died June 21, 1839; age, 10 years, 5 months, 18 days
White, Samuel, died October 23, 1844; age, 60 years, 5 months, 12 days
White, Martha R., wife of S. White, died April 19, 1881; age, 91 years, 7 days
Richardson, William D., died December 12, 1869; age, 53 years, 2 months, 2 days
Richardson, Leathy J., wife of William D. Richardson, died July 9, 1873; age, 24 years, 2 months, 1 day
Richardson, Willie J., son of William and L. J. Richardson, died August 29, 1873; age, 1 month, 20 days

Copied August 14, 1933, by Mrs. Hale Houts

IRWIN CEMETERY
Section 30, Township 50, Range 31 W

The Irwins owned 420 acres of land, on which this cemetery is located

Infant son born and died August 10, 1848
Infant daughter born and died April 7, 1849
Joseph S., born April 7, 1847, died October 11, 1848
In Memory of five children of J. C. and Mary H. Irwin
Mary S. Irwin, born November 10, 1852, died July 3, 1853

Copied August 17, 1933, by Mrs. Ernest L. Harris and Miss Jessie M. Crosby

JOHNSON CEMETERY
Section 31, Township 48, Range 32

On farm now owned by Mr. Albert Johnson, formerly owned by Mr. Green Johnson

Judy Shepherd, born November 15, 1802, died May 4, 1870
J. B. Johnson, born April 23, 1824, died May 24, 1874

Copied September 21, 1933, by Mrs. Hale Houts

JONES CEMETERY
Section 9, Township 50, Range 31 W

Beets, Mamie J., born March 22, 1871, died February 12, 1882
Bell, Frank M., born March 13, 1859, died June 2, 1922
Bell, Minnie M., wife of F. M. Bell, died December 6, 1881; age, 20 years, 11 months, 29 days
Bell, Samuel, born August 5, 1797, died June 27, 1854
Bittle, Immanuel, born April 28, 1814, died March 28, 1896
Burhle, William H., son of J. and M. A. Burhle, died January 13, 1864; age, 4 months, 29 days
Cannaday, William H., born November 18, 1818, died February 29, 1888
Cannaday, W. R., born 1840
  Mary, wife of W. R. Cannaday, born 1853, died 1906
Cannaday, Alice, daughter of H. H. and S. C. Cannaday, died August 20, 1872; age, 6 years, 5 months, 17 days
Cannaday, Sarah, wife of H. H. Cannaday, died April 29, 1872; age, 62 years, 3 months, 12 days
Clack, Mary J., wife of B. S. M. Clack, died June 18, 1855, in her 29th year
  W. T. and J. S., son of the above, 3 years, 5 months

Clack, Sarah Mc., wife of B. S. M. Clack, died January 27, 1859; age, 29 years, 26 days
Clack, Catharine P. J., daughter of B. S. M. and S. Mc. Clack, died September 13, 1858; age, 1 year, 2 months, 23 days
Clack, Casander, born April 4, 1792, died April 1, 1867
Davis, Ethelbert, born 1829, died 1877
Fuhr, Fannie E., daughter of L. and J. S. Fuhr, died May 10, 1875; age, 7 years, 6 months, 29 days
Fuhr, Robert, son of L. and J. S. Fuhr, born May 28, 1869, died September 12, 1870
Fuhr, Florence, daughter of L. and J. S. Fuhr, born September 9, 1855, died November 28, 1861
Fuhr, Budy, son of L. and J. S. Fuhr, born May 13, 1864, died July 9, 1865
Fuhr, John W., son of L. and J. S. Fuhr, born February 20, 1866, died October 7, 1867
Glenn, Mr. and Mrs. Hugh Glenn
Herring, Rosella, daughter of G. and S. Herring, died August 2, 1873; age, 11 months, 10 days
Herrins, George, died April 6, 1873; age, 37 years, 1 month
Huntsucker, T. H., born 1843, died 1907
Inman, S. R., died February 28, 1880; age, 44 years, 5 months, 24 days
Inman, Henry C., son of S. R. and M. W. Inman, died January 13, 1875; age, 14 years, 2 months, 5 days
Jepson, Ephram M., died April 27, 1861; age, 37 years, 11 months, 14 days
Jepson, James W., died December 21, 1877; age, about 20 years
Linsdale, Susan, born 1831, died 1867
Stewart, Charles, born 1806, died 1874
Stewart, Susan, daughter of Charles Christopher Stewart
Strange, Helen, wife of John Strange, died January 9, 1877
Thompson, Sarah Francis, born April 15, 1845, died December 21, 1887
Wright, Henry, died October 10, 188—; age, 50 years, 9 months, 18 days
Wright, Sarah G., born September 4, 1836, died August 2, 1918
Wright, Armitage, born 1855, died 1875
Young, Harriet, died December 19, 1871; age, about 36 years

Copied June 8, 1933, by Mrs. John H. Twyman and Miss Jessie M. Crosby

LEWIS CEMETERY
Section 17, Township 50, Range 31 W

Burgess, Eliza A., born June 13, 1872, died June 5, 1873
Burgess, Dicy, born October 17, 1878, died July 12, 1879
Burgess, Susan, born March 27, 1835, died February 18, 1884
Davis, Mr. and Mrs. William Davis
Gregg, H., died June 23, 1857; age, 82 years, 5 months, 6 days
Gregg, Harmon, died June 7, 1868; age, 52 years, 5 months, 7 days
Gregg, Harmon, died August 19, 1841; age, 71 years, 5 months, 28 days
Gregg, Susan, wife of Harmon Gregg, died June 23, 1857; age, 82 years, 11 months, 6 days
Lentz, J. W., son of N. and E. Lentz, born January 8, 1880, died July 28, 1880
Lentz, Eliza J., wife of N. Lentz, born October 8, 1849, died June 27, 1880
Lentz, O. F., son of N. and Lou Lentz, by 2nd wife, born July 9, 1882, died August 24, 1883
Lewis, Dicy A., died May 22, 1897; age, 41 years, 5 months, 9 days
Lewis, John E., died January 10, 1884; age, 43 years, 9 months, 8 days
Lewis, Nathaniel, died 1851
Lewis, Susan, wife of John E. Lewis
Lewis, Polly, died May 28, 1897; age, 84 years, 4 months, 9 days
Lewis, James Walker, died July 14, 1889; age, 90 years, 7 months, 28 days

CEMETERIES—BLUE TOWNSHIP

Lewis, James H., died October 2, 1842; age, 2 years, 19 days
Lewis, Emaline, died May 24, 1846; age, 9 years, 6 months
Mason, James, born June 22, 1789, died January 11, 1858
Mason, wife of James Mason
Copied by Mrs. Ernest L. Harris and Miss Jessie Crosby

LONG CEMETERY
Section 26, Township 50, Range 32 W

Enclosed by an iron fence with a locked gate—all dates were not visible

Long, Robert Nicholas
Long, Aletha A., wife of Robert Nicholas Long
Long, Robert Nicholas
Long, Frances Agnes, born July 28, 1836, died May 5, 1916
Lucas, Coretta
Ward, James
Contributed by Mrs. Hale Houts and Miss Jessie M. Crosby

McGUIRE BURYING GROUND
Section 29, Township 50, Range 31 W

Clark, Cordelia, wife of J. A. Clark, born August 2, 1822, died August 24, 1882
McGuire, Jepthah, born May 30, 1819, died May 10, 1849
McGuire, infant daughter of W. and J. McGuire, born February 5, 1882, died February 6, 1882
Copied June 8, 1933, by Mrs. John H. Twyman and Miss Jessie M. Crosby

MOORE CEMETERY
On farm formerly known as the Grinter Farm. Now owned by Hans Dierks
Section 12, Township 49, Range 32

Moore, William, born 1757, died 1843; Revolutionary Soldier, enlisted February 14, 1776 in Col. Morgan's Virginia Regiment; handsome D. A. R. marker at grave
Moore, William, Corporal, War of 1812; 1812 marker on monument
Copied September 21, 1933, by Mrs. Hale Houts

OVERTON CEMETERY
Section 5, Township 49, Range 32 W
Van Horn Road and Evanston

Contributed by Mrs. Lizzie Moore of Liberty, Mo.

Jesse Overton came from New Orleans, La., to Jackson County, Missouri, before the Civil War. His wife was Debrah Cameron, daughter of Dave and Rachel Rose Cameron. They were from near Dallas, Texas. Both Mr. and Mrs. Jesse Overton were buried in this cemetery. She died during the second year of the Civil War, after the battle of Wilson Creek. There were also eight of the Overton children and thirty of the Overton slaves buried there.
Mary Jane Wales, wife of William P. Overton, oldest son of J. and D. Overton, died 1852; age, 23 years; she was from Boston, Mass., and was the daughter of Loring and Marie (Du Pont) Wales
John Maxwell and daughter, Emma, later removed to Independence cemetery
John Maxwell's wife was Matilda Overton
Mrs. Tom Duncan

Mrs. John Wallace
William Smitzen
Mr. and Mrs. Dorton
Dave Farlow, removed to Independence cemetery
Three children of James Franklin Overton, youngest son of Jesse and Debrah Overton

As Jesse Overton and Aaron Overton were related by marriage, some people might think that they came from the same Overton family, but Mrs. Moore emphasized the fact that there was no blood relationship.

Copied by Miss Jessie M. Crosby

PITCHER CEMETERY
Section 17, Township 49, Range 32 W
Thirty-third and Blue Ridge Boulevard

Baker, Sarah Hall, daughter of Jesse and Lydia Hall, died 1875
Bishop, John N., born July 9, 1853, died February 27, 1894
Bishop, David, died May 3, 1876; age, 75 years, 11 months, 19 days
Dunham, Harley, born October 7, 1855, died May 3, 1856
Glascock, E. L., died November 30, 1867; age, 70 years
Glascock, Henrietta, died November 5, 1865; age, 84 years
Hall, Lydia, born December 24, 1813, died September 2, 1887
Hamilton, Gertrude M., daughter of Thos. and Annie Hamilton, died July 4, 1899; age, 1 year, 9 months, 28 days
Henkle, George W., born November 22, 1810, died April 19, 1857
Henkle, George, son of G. W. and A. E. Henkle, born March 29, 1849, died August 18, 1855
Mason, Grover Brock, son of W. R. and J. B. Mason, died October 29, 1895; age, 1 year, 1 month, 19 days
McCormick, D. J., born September 23, 1824, died September 25, 1900; "She Believed and Sleeps in Jesus"
Noland, Ledstone, Smith's N. G. Mil. Revolutionary War
Noland, Mary, wife of William Noland, Sr., born June 19, 1801, died December 18, 1871
Noland, Nancy H., wife of J. D. Noland, born February 18, 1848, died January 30, 1868
Stewart, Susan, died January 14, 1879; age, 75 years, 3 months, 5 days
Tyler, Charles H., born March 13, 1845, died May 30, 1896

The above inscriptions were copied from the tombstones. The following record of interments was furnished by Mr. John H. Twyman of Kansas City, Mo. These were all members of his mother's family and were buried in this cemetery:
Brock, Perry, and his wife
Brock, John
Hale, Elsie, died 1859
Hale, Farlow J., born November 12, 1840
Hale, John
Hale, Lusia J., born December 5, 1836
Hale, James L., son of Bennet Hale, born October 29, 1832
Hale, Nancy, born October 28, 1832
Mason, Ember, and his wife

Mrs. M. A. Pitcher contributed the following names of the family buried in this cemetery:
Pitcher, Col. Thomas Pitcher, served in Price's army in the Civil War
    Col. Thomas Pitcher's wife
    A daughter of Bolley Pitcher
    Lafayette Pitcher
    Bettie Frye Pitcher
    Nancy Noland Pitcher died about 1866

CEMETERIES—BLUE TOWNSHIP

Bess Pitcher, daughter of Baldwin Pitcher

During the Civil War there was a skirmish near the Pitcher School house. It is claimed that these killed were buried in the Pitcher cemetery.

Hinkle, George Washington, and wife
Armstrong, William
Armstrong, Sallie Harrington, wife of William Armstrong

The last two names were contributed by a Granddaughter.
Compiled and copied March 3, 1933, by Mrs. Max A. Christopher and Miss Jessie M. Crosby

POTEET CEMETERY
Section 4, Township 49, Range 31 W

Poteet, Jane, wife of E. P. Poteet, born February 8, 1806, died January 30, 1855
Poteet, Katharine, wife of William Poteet, born June 3, 1763, died April 4, 1844
Poteet, Lucy L., daughter of E. and E. J. Poteet, died February 27, 1864; age, 1 year, 27 days
Poteet, William C., died February 14, 1875; age, 49 years, 11 months, 15 days
Poteet, William, Jr., born October 4, 1767, died September 3, 1844
Poteet, (?), died February 10, 1872; age, 74 years, 10 months, 9 days

Copied July 12, 1933, by Mrs. Ernest L. Harris and Miss Jessie M. Crosby

SALEM BAPTIST CHURCH CEMETERY
Section 21, Township 50, Range 31 W

Adams, Nelson, born May 15, 1829, died October 30, 1898
Adams, Mary J., wife of Nelson Adams, born January 30, 1839, died February 4, 1916
Adams, R. W., born 1840, died 1921
Adams, Stephen, born November 17, 1803, died November 13, 1887
Adams, Rosetta, born 1848, died 1929
Adams, William, born November 2, 1835, died July 18, 1892
Aid, James D., born March 22, 1842, died December 30, 1909
    Tishia Ann, wife of James D. Aid, born May 2, 1847, died April 14, 1932
Alford, Gabriel, died September 6, 1884; age, 52 years, 10 months, 24 days
Bedford, Anna, born May 29, 1845, died January 5, 1928
Bedford, Caroline H., born January 17, 1818, died May 2, 1907
Bedford, Green, born June 2, 1816, died May 22, 1910
Bedford, Margus A., born September 2, 1838, died August 8, 1920
Beets, James, died May 21, 1894; age, 77 years, 2 months, 10 days
Beets, Elizabeth I., born January 9, 1823, died April 3, 1902
Beets, Joseph B., born 1843, died 1932
    Laanar E., wife of Joseph E. Beets, born 1837, died 1912
Breedlove, Eliza (mother), born 1842, died 1925
Carpenter, J. W., born March 4, 1841, died December 18, 1916
    John J., died January 23, 1893; age, 71 years, 7 months, 13 days
    Lucinda J., wife of John J. Carpenter, died September 26, 1892; age, 74 years, 4 months
Cooper, Samuel H., born December 7, 1849, died December 16, 1897
Davis, Ethelbert, born 1829, died 1877
    Mary A., wife of Ethelbert Davis, born 1822, died 1902
Donohew, Algan G. (father), born 1840, died 1918
Donohew, Martilla V., wife of A. G. Donohew, born January 28, 1844, died May 31, 1880
Edwards, Sallie A. (mother), born 1843, died 1922
    John F. (father), born 1841, died 1924
Fowler, James, died December 25, 1881; age, 78 years, 11 months, 7 days

Fuhr, Lorenz, born February 7, 1832, died May 23, 1908 (Mason)
　J. Susan, wife of L. Fuhr, born August 28, 1835, died January 16, 1901
Giffin, T., born March 23, 1828, died December 10, 1887
　Nancy, wife of T. Giffin, born October 24, 1833, died July 18, 1906
Gilvin, Bettie R., born 1840, died 1917
Goodwin, Sallie F., mother of W. A. Dodson, born 1844, died 1912
Hammontree, Martha, wife of Wm. Hammontree, died December 25, 1884; age, 51 years
Harding, Sarah E., born 1837, died 1919
Hatten, Noah C., born October 22, 1808, died September 8, 1899
　Elizabeth, wife of Noah C. Hatten, died December 5, 1873; age, 52 years
Hensley, A., died December 26, 1896; age, 75 years, 7 months
　Elizabeth, wife of A. Hensley, died November 5, 1892; age, 70 years, 3 months, 20 days
Hifner, George H., born February 11, 1833, died August 1, 1920
　Eliza J., wife of George Hifner, born June 20, 1828, died April 18, 1906
Hogue, Ozias, born 1843, died 1906
Iams, M. H., born March 11, 1820, died November 21, 1896
Iams, Ella L., born July 9, 1840, died February 1, 1903
Irwin, Daniel H., born October 20, 1845, died September 15, 1898
Jackson, William R., born 1842, died 1908
　Martha A., wife of Wm. R. Jackson, born 1846, died 1927
Johnston, Rev. M. T., born 1849, died 1927
　Sarah C., wife of Rev. M. T. Johnston, born 1856, died 1917
Jones, W. K., born February 2, 1832, died January 18, 1904
Jones, Marinda R., born April 28, 1838, died May 23, 1905
Lenox, Charles, died December 5, 1898; age, 67 years
Lweray, William, born October 1, 1824, died September 17, 1898
　Nancy A., wife of Wm. Lweray, born June 22, 1833, died July 27, 1878
Lentz, Jacob, died November 21, 1880; age, 54 years, 5 months, 5 days
　Mary M., wife of Jacob Lentz, born December 4, 1850, died October 27, 1921
Malbaff, Lewis, born January 9, 1812, died November 2, 1906
　Cynthia A., wife of Lewis Malbaff, born November 15, 1825, died December 5, 1909
McBroome, James S., born 1849, died 1911
McCandless, H. M., born 1819, died 1902
　Mary J., wife of H. M. McCandless, born 1837, died 1901
McFarland, William C., born January 28, 1830, died March 8, 1887
　Nancy A., wife of Wm. C. McFarland, born July 13, 1843, died November 1, 1900
Morrow, Jacob C., born March 28, 1830, died December 11, 1902
　Nancy I., born August 12, 1843, died February 4, 1881
Mounts, W. S., 1842
　Emma J., wife of W. S. Mounts, born 1847, died 1913
Myers, John, died February 17, 1896; age, 63 years, 7 months, 27 days
　Rachel A., wife of John Myers, born February 27, 1850, died March 26, 1905
Parker, Preston P., born September 4, 1840, died April 20, 1932
　Elizabeth F., wife of Preston P. Parker, born September 30, 1850, died March 4, 1921
Pettyjohn, Amanda Lee, born 1844, died 1924
Prince, John (father), born October 15, 1827, died August 27, 1895
Reed, Jasper, born February 4, 1828, died December 8, 1908
Ricketts, Jerry, born December 7, 1845, died April 5, 1898
Roberts, Nora, daughter of F. W. and E. J. Roberts, born 1836, died 1895
Rogers, George W., born 1839, died 1907
Rogers, Joseph, born October 8, 1842, died September 22, 1922
Rogers, Martha F., born November 24, 1849, died November 11, 1925
Rogers, Winslow, born January 12, 1816, died October 14, 1906
Rogers, Nancy A., wife of Winslow Rogers, died June 1, 1896; age, 76 years
Searcy, Ambrose W., born February 27, 1816, died March 25, 1892

Shrank, Sara A., wife of Fred Shrank, born February 28, 1844, died September 17, 1902
Stewart, Charley, born March 17, 1840, died May 6, 1897
    Mary (mother), born 1806, died 1888; "Real Daughter of D. A. R."—marker
Stewart, John, born November 30, 1831, died May 17, 1905
Stewart, Wesley, died April 27, 1890; age, 53 years, 5 months, 4 days
Stewart, Emeline, wife of Wesley Stewart, died February 13, 1884; age, 43 years, 3 months, 20 days
Thompson, Mary C., born 1822, died 1914
Webb, Preston, born July 6, 1836, died January 31, 1899
Webb, William, died February 25, 1886; age, 62 years, 10 months, 10 days
Whitney, Elijah, born August 8, 1812, died September 3, 1897
    Julana F., wife of E. K. Whitney, born May 11, 1811, died January 1, 1884
Wiest, Anna Marie, born 1845, died 1921
Wood, Francis, born January 21, 1837, died May 28, 1914
Wood, Elizabeth, wife of Francis Wood, born September 25, 1843, died July 3, 1914

    Copied June 21, 1933, by Mrs. May T. Crosby and Miss Jessie M. Crosby

SMITH CEMETERY
Section 15, Township 48, Range 32

Only one marker now standing, which is as follows:
Sally, a wife of James Landers, died June 14, 1851; age, 30 years, 24 days and 8 months

Information concerning those buried upon this site received by Mrs. Hale Houts from Mrs. L. E. Harris and from Mrs. M. A. Tucker, of Warsaw, Missouri.

Oby Davis, Dee Davis, twins
Davis, Jane Billings, died 1870
Davis, child of Jane Billings Davis
Billings, mother of Jane Billings Davis
Father Star, Mother Star, died before 1849; sons went West in Oregon Gold Rush
Annie Star Crabtree, daughter of Father and Mother Crabtree
Mahala Harris Shusher, died before 1860
William Shusher, husband of Mahala
Laura Fristoe Harris, wife of Reuben M. Harris
Margaret (Peggy) Harris Taylor, died 1869; age, 61 years
Sarah Margaret Harris, died August 24, 1848
Mary Ellen Harris Tucker, died October 13, 1869
Nancy Harris McCorkle Lilley, died November 10, 1872
1. Jabes McCorkle, died June 2, 1863
2. James Lilley, died March 9, 1875
Virginia Harris, died March 11, 1879 (last one to be buried)
Richard Sly, died October 28, 1853
3. Capt. Ferdinand Scott, died 1863
4. Boone Muir, died 1863

---

5. Susan Crawford Vandevere, died August, 1863
6. Armenia Crawford Selvey, died August, 1863
7. Charity McCorkle Kerr, died August, 1863
    1, 2, 3, 4 were confederate soldiers
    5, 6, 7, women died in the prison at 14th and Grand Ave.
    Father Star a Revolutionary soldier
                            (Josephine Anderson Claybor)
   Kate Harris, struck by lightning about 1880
   Mary Ellen Crabtree, a daughter of Monroe Crabtree
   One large circular grave containing the remains of from 12 to 15 soldiers of the Civil War

STAPLES CEMETERY
Section 30, Township 50, Range 31 W

Chiles, Isabella, wife of Thomas Chiles, died September 19, 1852; age, 62 years

Eddie, William, son of J. G. and E. G. Eddie, died October 23, 1822; age, 1 year, 10 months, 11 days

Mason, James G., born July 6, 1811, died February 15, 1891 (Mason)

Mason, Mary W., wife of J. G. Mason, born August 5, 1826, died February 10, 1909

Mason, James M., son of J. G. and Mary W. Mason, born November, 1848, died June 9, 1850

Mason, Virginia, daughter of J. G. and Mary W. Mason, born January 12, 1868, died April 25, 1868

Mason, James E., son of J. G. and Mary W. Mason, born March 12, 1869, died March 26, 1869

Mason, Emma, daughter of J. C. and M. W. Mason, born April 10, 1865, died January 24, 1897

Overfelt, Elizabeth P., consort of J. A. Overfelt

Parker, Elcy T., wife of Charles Parker and daughter of J. G. and Mary W. Mason, died February 1, 1871

Parker, Clay, son of C. and E. T. Parker, died December 16, 1870; age, 2 months, 17 days

Staples, A. F., born July 16, 1790, died July 31, 1868; age, 78 years, 15 days

Staples, Elcy, wife of A. F. Staples, born December 6, 1793, died September 3, 1865; age, 72 years, 8 months, 27 days

Staples, John M., died March 14, 1862; age, 39 years, 7 months, 3 days

Staples, Felix G., born January 26, 1829, died September 17, 1865

Staples, Thomas J., born June 28, 1835, died May 26, 1863; age, 27 years, 10 months, 28 days

Copied June 8, 1933, by Mrs. John H. Twyman and Miss Jessie M. Crosby

STEAGALL CEMETERY
Section 22, Township 49, Range 32 W

Stigall, John Marshall, son of R. W. and M. R. Stigall, died July 21, 1854; age, 18 years

Steagall, Memory of Martha A. A., born March 30, 1832, died June 24, 1851

Steagall, Sarah S., born May 17, 1835, died August 11, 1851

Copied August 9, 1933, by Mrs. Ernest L. Harris and Miss Jessie M. Crosby

WEBB CEMETERY
Section 28, Township 50, Range 31 W

Bafee, Joseph, son of T. J. and N. G. Bafee, died March 31, 1886, age, 3 months

Bafee, Thomas W., son of T. J. and N. G. Bafee, died July 5, 1879; age, 1 year, 6 months

Botts, Catherine, died May 26, 1853; age, 10 years, 5 months, 12 days

Botts, Joseph, died August 17, 1862; age, 22 years, 10 days

Botts, Marana, wife of Thomas Botts, born June 3, 1820, died June 21, 1897; age, 77 years, 18 days

Botts, Margaret, died July 20, 1859; age, 75 years, 9 months, 1 day

Botts, Susan M., died February 9, 1860; age, 9 days

Botts, Thomas H., died March 7, 1886; age, 74 years, 17 days

Bridges, Thomas, died March 3, 1862

Bridges, Martha, died January 9, 1856

Horne, T. A., born March 19, 1832, died January 13, 1906

Horne, N. J., wife of T. J. Horne, born July 31, 1832, died December 27, 1901

Mayes, David A., died October 12, 1851; age, 26 years, 2 months, 14 days

CEMETERIES—BLUE TOWNSHIP

Mays, Permelia, wife of W. Mays, died July 17, 1868
McGuire, Katherine, born August 28, 1816, died March 5, 1868
Sale, Mary C., wife of James T. Sale, died December 2, 1884; age, 47 years, 6 months (monument in southeast corner, inscription almost obliterated)
Sale, infant children of J. T. and M. C. Sale
Webb, Asa, born March 3, 1806, died September 3, 1888
Webb, Mary, wife of Asa Webb, died January 16, 1889; age, 82 years, 4 months, 18 days
Webb, Elizabeth, born March 3, 1833, died November 26, 1906
Webb, Joseph, died May 25, 1869; age, 21 years, 7 months, 23 days

Copied March 18, 1933, by Miss Jessie M. Crosby and Mrs. May T. Crosby

WOODLAWN CEMETERY
INDEPENDENCE, MISSOURI

At the request of the Independence Pioneers Chapter, Daughters of the American Revolution, the records of Woodlawn Cemetery, one of the oldest burying grounds in the County are not entered here, as these records and those listed in the Independence Court House are to be published later by the Independence Pioneers Chapter.

SMALL BURYING GROUNDS

ALLEN CEMETERY
Section 32, Township 50, Range 31 W
Data contributed by Mr. J. M. Allen

Allen, Amos, died 1882 or 1883; age, 89 years
Allen, wife of Amos Allen
Allen, Martin
Allen, Annie

Copied by Miss Jessie M. Crosby

BAKER GRAVE
Section 19, Township 50, Range 31 W

Baker, Eleanor, wife of Joseph Baker, died 1885; buried in the orchard on the Baker farm

BUTTS CEMETERY
Section 19, Township 50, Range 31 W

Butts, Salathiel, died 1856
Butts, Mernervia, wife of Salathiel Butts
Butts, George, son of S. and M. Butts
Butts, William, son of S. and M. Butts

CAL THOMPSON BURYING GROUND
Section 36, Township 50, Range 32 W

The family of Cal Thompson had a burying ground on their farm, located on the old Lexington Road, just a little west of the Hedrick cemetery.

HEDRICK CEMETERY
Section 36, Township 50, Range 32 W

Hedrick, Andrew E., born April 7, 1876, died May 14, 1903
Hedrick, George F., died May 13, 1927; age, 81 years
Hedrick, Hannah Elizabeth, born April 26, 1857, died March 31, 1907
Hedrick, Harvey A., died April 6, 1875; age, 22 years, 3 months, 22 days
Hedrick, Granville, died August 22, 1881; age, 66 years, 11 months, 20 days
    Eliza Ann, born September 8, 1833, died April 6, 1910
Hedrick, John H., died May 11, 1872; age, 52 years, 7 months, 13 days
    E. A., wife of John H. Hedrick, born 1825, died 1885

JOHNSTON CEMETERY
Section 4, Township 49, Range 32 W
Contributed by Miss Jessie M. Crosby

Anderson, Amanda Johnston, wife of A. F. Anderson, born August 15, 1829, died April 22, 1867
Johnston, Dorothy, born December 14, 1800, died October 21, 1846
Johnston, Jacob, born July 16, 1796, died July 25, 1851; he went to California during the gold rush and when he returned to Jackson County, Missouri, he was called "Gold" Johnston
Johnston, Larinda, born February 12, 1834, died July 25, 1851
Woodall, Dan C., born February 22, 1802, died October 6, 1872
    These remains have been removed to the Woodlawn cemetery in Independence, Missouri.

MOON BURYING GROUND
Section 16, Township 49, Range 32 W

Moon, William, died July 10, 1859
Moon, Sarah Catharine Mann, wife of Wm. Moon, died March 6, 1868
Noland, Sarah Catharine, died May 20, 1867
    These bodies were removed to Woodlawn cemetery in Independence, Missouri.

MOORE CEMETERY
Section 32, Township 50, Range 31 W

Meador, A. A., died April 21, 1863; age, 55 years, 5 months, 18 days
Meador, Rachel, wife of A. A. Meador, died September 23, 1866; age, 60 years
Moore, John, died October 9, 1866; age, 55 years, 2 days
Moore, Isabella, died July 4, 1886; age, 74 years, 10 months, 7 d
Moore, T. D.

NOLAND CEMETERY
Section 3, Township 49, Range 32 W
Data contributed by Allan Kincade, Independence, Mo.

Kincade, Hickman
Kincade, Nellie
Kincade, Mary Noland, died about 1890
Noland, Barnett
Noland, Sena, wife of Barnett Noland
Noland, Pitcher
    The above mentioned remains were removed to the Woodlawn cemetery, Independence, Missouri.
Noland, B. M., died December 25, 1889; age, 71 years, 1 month, 24 days
Noland, William (School Teacher)
Noland, Susie

Copied by Miss Jessie M. Crosby

CEMETERIES—BLUE TOWNSHIP

OLDHAM BURYING GROUND
Section 14, Township 49, Range 32 W

There was a burying ground on the John R. Oldham farm, but the bodies of those buried there have been removed to the Woodlawn cemetery in Independence, Missouri.

PARKER CEMETERY
Section 24, Township 50, Range 32 W

Parker, Robert, died about 1877; age, 40 years
Parker, Hiram, died before 1877; age, 16 years
Parker, infant

There were a number of other graves in this cemetery but this cemetery was destroyed when Kentucky Road was built. The road passes over the site of the cemetery and all of the tombstones were destroyed.

QUIGLEY GRAVE
Section 27, Township 50, Range 32 W

"In Memory of Robert Quigley
Died on his way to California
1848 from Ohio"

REED CEMETERY
Section 32, Township 50 Range 32 W
Data contributed by Miss Lydia Reed and Jesse Reed

This land was entered by Mathias Reed in 1831. The first person buried in the Reed cemetery was Mike Kelley, who died in 1835.

Benson, Elizabeth
Benson, Nettie
Davis, Mr. Davis
Hall, Irene, an infant, died 1876
Reed, Mathias, born 1782, died May, 1865, a fifer in the War of 1812 in Virginia
Reed, Mahala Harper, wife of Jasper Reed
Stevens, Rettie
Smith, Grandma, died, age 88 years
Webster, two children
Webster, Perry Green, a small boy

These bodies have never been moved but all trace of the graves is obliterated.

RENICK CEMETERY
Section 19, Township 49, Range 32 W
Data contributed by A. L. Renick

Renick, George A., removed to Brooking cemetery
Renick, Maggie
Renick, Melvina Reed, wife of Abe Renick
Howell, Melissa
Howell, William, removed to Independence, Missouri
Howell, Francis
Howell, John
Thomson, Mary Eliza Howell, wife of William Thomson

SCHOLL BURYING GROUND
Section 16, Township 49, Range 32 W

A Mr. Himes and several members of the Scholl family are buried on the old Scholl farm. All traces of the graves have been obliterated.

SMILEY CEMETERY
Section 24, Township 50, Range 32 W

Smiley, Edward T., born February, 1844, Union Soldier, killed in the battle at Independence, Missouri, during Civil War.
Smiley, Nancy Simmons, wife of Edward T. Smiley, born 1822, died about 1888
Smiley, Hugh, died during the Civil War; age, 12 years
Smiley, Thomas, son of John G. and Mary S. Smiley, born 1867, died about 1869

TWYMAN GRAVES
Section 5, Township 49, Range 32 W
Data contributed by John H. Twyman

William H. Twyman, born 1824, died March 14, 1873, was buried on the Twyman farm. His wife, Sarah Elizabeth Hale Twyman, born January 15, 1839, died February 16, 1920, was buried in Mt. Washington Cemetery. Later the body of Mr. Twyman was removed from the farm and buried beside hers. William H. Twyman's parents died about 1838 and were buried in the Leeds Bottoms.

UNNAMED CEMETERY
Section 18, Township 50, Range 31 W

Baker, Joseph, died before the Civil War
Baker, Cord, daughter of Joseph Baker; age, 12 years
Fann, James, came to Missouri from Columbia Gap, Tenn.
Fann, Lucy, wife of James Fann

There were several others buried in this cemetery but there are no inscriptions on the native headstones.

WIGFIELD BURYING GROUND
Section 18, Township 49, Range 32 W
Contributed by Charles Stewart

Johnson, Jacob
Johnston, Reuben
Johnston, Reuben, Jr.

KAW TOWNSHIP

Organized May 22, 1827

BURYING GROUND ON THE BRADLEY FARM
KANSAS CITY, MISSOURI

Information concerning the Bradley Family furnished by Mrs. Virginia Duck Baker, Grandview, Missouri

Isham Bradley and his wife, Catherine Hudgens Bradley, with their two small children, Lucy Bradley (who married Willis Steele), and Martha Bradley (who married James Noland), together with Finnius Scruggs, his brother-in-law, came to Westport from Virginia in 1831.

Finnius Scruggs and family remained in Westport; Isham Bradley settled on a farm of 640 acres at what would now be located as Cleveland Avenue on the west, Jackson Avenue on the east, 26th Street on the south, and St. Mary's Cemetery on the north.

Mrs. Virginia Duck Baker of Grandview, Missouri, states that her mother, Catherine Bradley, daughter of Isham Bradley and wife (Catherine Hudgens), was born in Westport in 1832, and married Benjamin Duck of Williamsburg, Pennsylvania, who came to Lexington, Missouri, in 1843, and to Jackson County in 1848, and was the Superintendent of the Sunday School in the first Methodist Church organized in Kansas City, of which Mr. and Mrs. Duck were charter members. Mr. Duck was the grandson of Jake Duck, a soldier of the American War of the Revolution, who married Nancy Norris, a daughter of Henry Norris, who laid out Norristown, Pennsylvania.

On this old Bradley Farm was a Family Burying Ground in which were buried:
Isham Bradley, buried about 1868
Catherine Bradley, wife of Isham Bradley, buried July 4, 1866
Robert Hudgens, brother of Catherine Hudgens Bradley, died about 1875
Several slaves of the family

This Burying Ground was vacated in 1885. The bodies of Mr. and Mrs. Bradley were removed to West Line, Cass County, Missouri.

EARLY CATHOLIC CEMETERIES

Contributed by Mrs. Nathan W. Buzby

The first Catholic cemetery in Kansas City was a plot in the ten acre tract bought by Father Roux. It extended from Pennsylvania Avenue on the west to Jefferson Street.

Father Donnelly said of an earlier cemetery:

"There is reason to believe that the first Christians who died in the vicinity of Kansas City were buried at the summit angle of the bluff, just east of the foot of Grand Avenue. I saw the rude cross there in 1848."

The cemetery site at Thirty-first and Jefferson Streets, the present St. Joseph's Orphan Home, was never used for burial purposes, because of its rocky soil which made it unsuitable. When Father Donnelly purchased the forty acres comprising Mount St. Mary's Cemetery in 1876, burials ceased in the old cemetery. Eventually all the bodies were transferred to Mount St. Mary's cemetery, where the records are kept in a fireproof vault by its superintendent.

The St. Peter's and St. Paul's Cemetery situated at Twenty-fourth and Brooklyn Avenue was established in 1876 by the German speaking Catholics of Kansas City and abandoned in 1920, when most of the bodies were transferred to Mount St. Mary's Cemetery.

> REV. BERNARD DONNELLY, *resident Catholic Pastor in Jackson County, Missouri, kept the records in his own handwriting. The following summary was written by him in the year* 1873, *on the completion of Volume* 1 *of these records and the beginning of Volume* 2. *Copied from the original by Dorothy E. Buzby.*

May 14, 1873

RECORDS OF THE DEAD, VOLUME 2

"This Book commences the second volume of the Records of the Dead in the Catholic Congregations of the city of Kansas, Jackson County, Missouri. All the records of the dead since the end of the year 1845 are contained in one single volume up to the foregoing date, a period of over twenty-seven years and four months. It is a long time to witness, by one pastor, the Lamentations uttered and the tears shed by friends and relatives over the graves of fourteen hundred and about six persons since the end of the year 1845 up to May 14, 1873.

"I am now about commencing a volume after having finished one—but who will finish this one? Will my own name be written in this volume amongst the names of the departed, by some friendly pastor? Who will he be? When will the time of Record come? Where shall be my burying place? Of these things I am ignorant. He who created me—who conducted me to this place,—whose love and providence I have experienced up to this date—He alone knows and foresees all these—He who said, 'Quae est enim vita vestra? Vapor est ad modicum parens, et deinceps exterminabetur. Plange quasi virgo plebs mea; ululate sacerdotes in cinere et   ; quia venit *dies* Domini magna et amara valde.'

"I desire here to say that I wish to be interred in the midst of my flock—in the present old cemetery of Kansas City—in the spot which I have already pointed out to my friends—where the cross was planted by Father DePointe, and around which are interred the mortal remains of those who first invoked and professed the name and doctrines of my Divine Redeemer in this portion of the world, and whose remains I officially consigned to the dust during twenty-eight years of my pastoral life. I am unable to state how many were buried in our old cemetery previously to the year 1845, but the first volume in my own handwriting has recorded in it the names of all those who died in Kansas City, Westport and the country around since January 1, 1846. Many were brought for interment from Clay and Wyandotte and from more distant parts—about fourteen years ago, three corpses were hauled in from southern Kansas, a distance of one hundred and fifty miles from Kansas City; the three were in one wagon.

"The spot where the first Catholics of Westport Landing were buried, was the summit of the bluff south of Sherman house and east of the foot of Grand Avenue. The remains of at least one Hunter were removed from there in my own memory and reinterred in the Laliberte Lot in our present old cemetery.

"The original graveyard was but a small one fenced by oak pickets, dressed by the axe, sharpened at the upper end and stuck close together uprightly in the ground and enclosing less than half an acre. About the year 1858 the property in the neighborhood was laid off in lots and streets extended. At this period I extended the cemetery on all sides—so as to be bounded on the north by Eleventh Street and on the east by Pennsylvania Avenue, on the west by Jefferson Street, and on the south by Twelfth Street, making a square of 270 feet free of street and sidewalks. I was obliged to put up new fences on all sides at this period. I sold a few family lots at $2.50 each, a few more at $5.00 each, and more recently a few ten dollar lots. The sale of these secured me the means of putting up the new fences. About three years ago I introduced the custom of charging two dollars for each grave lot from which I derived a portion of the means to enable me to pay the interest on money borrowed to purchase land for a new cemetery, 40 acres.

"At length the long expected Railroads reached Kansas City, the bridge across the Missouri was completed, the city was built up rapidly, property became very valuable in city and vicinity, the Catholic population was numerously increased and funerals became much more frequent than previously. Now I commenced to reflect more seriously on the necessity of securing more ample territory for the interment of the dead. To accomplish this many difficulties presented themselves. Firstly, owners of land beyond the city limits were unwilling to sell land at *any price* for cemetery purposes,—secondly, the prices asked were high, and thirdly, I had not a dollar in my possession. At length I secured a ten acre lot directly south of the old cemetery on the level summit of the hills south of McGee Creek and one-eighth of a mile west of the line of Broadway. One corner of the lot joined the land of Mobillon McGee.

"These ten acres cost me two thousand two hundred dollars. I found my new purchase heavily and finely timbered. I now considered that I had a good tract of well located land for a new cemetery. I had also purchased a few years before a tract of 20 acres from Mr. Guinotte, and also the adjoining ten acres from Mr. Bingham. These 30 acres I intended to use as my fire wood tract but finding that I had brick clay on my church lot and brick materials in great demand, and that I had two kinds of wood usually employed in the making of brick, I conceived the novel idea of brick and —— the wood on both tracts to aid in paying for the land. I undertook the job and succeeded beyond my calculations, in two seasons of fatiguing labor and constant attention I had sixteen hundred thousand bricks manufactured. I sold a portion to pay expenses, and donated the remainder to Convents and Churches. The extension of the city limits in the direction of the ten acres now began to alarm me. I began to foresee the danger of again having our cemetery within the city bounds. Impelled by this idea I bought a tract of forty acres from Mr. Levi Owings, S. E. of McGee's addition which has cost me up to this date (July 1, 1873) $8,175—principal, interest, taxes, fencing and roadmaking. I have had a great desire to save the ten acres,—but I have been compelled to mortgage them for four thousand dollars in order to make the final payment on the forty acres and in order also to save the new church at Westport from sheriff's sale at the suit of the mechanics. In a few days I hope to have the debt on the ten acres reduced to three thousand dollars: but where shall this sum be found? I have but a small parish—a scanty support—I am 63 years old today—I have not had an entire day of rest for thirty years—I am very tired—weary with watching, loaded with cares—perplexed by my own worthlessness, desponding yet hopeful—baffled but determined to persevere, 'desiring to be dissolved and to be with Christ,' but if He has any more work for me to do 'non recuso laborem.'

"The kind citizens of Kansas City have generously tolerated our graveyard up to the present although it has been in the power of the authorities to interdict interments. For this tolerant forbearance I feel exceedingly grateful."

ST. MARY'S CEMETERY

The original records of deaths, kept in the vault of St. Mary's Cemetery, Kansas City, Missouri, were translated from the Latin by the courtesy of Rev. John Doyle, and copied by Miss Dorothy E. Buzby.

RECORD OF DEATHS IN THE CATHOLIC CONGREGATION FOR THE YEARS 1846-47 AND THE SUCCEEDING YEARS:

Entries made in the handwriting of Rev. B. Donnelly

Edward Petelle, died January 1, 1846; age, 40 years

Mary Dripps, Otto Nata, died June 1, 1846; age, 36 years

Virginie Philibert, died July 15, 1846; age, 2 months; infant daughter of Gabrelio and Mario Philibert

Julie Philibert, died August 15, 1846; age, 6 years

Charles Gerrier, died August 17, 1846; age, 63 years

Marie Q. Belmarre, died August 7, 1846; age, 15 months; infant daughter of Maysi and Adelio Belmarre

L. Felix Canville, died August 4, 1846; age, 4 months; infant of Andred B. and Louisa Canville

James Grey, died February 10, 1847; age, 14 years

Victor Lagoutrie, died April 18, 1847; age, 11 years

Maurice Le Duc, died January 4, 1847; age, 64 years

Rose Etu, died December 20, 1847; age, 1 year, 20 months; daughter of Rosa Maria Etu and Marita Theodoro Etu

Marie Calice Montredie, died June 18, 1847; age, 49 years

Bertrand, died November 10, 1847; age, 51 years

Solomon Revard, died March 9, 1848; age, 23 years; son of Ludovici; moved to cemetery July 24

Andrew Petit Roy, died February 3, 1848; age, 34 years

Celeste Bowers, died August, 1848; daughter of Calixti Montredie
    Philibert, died Aug. 17, 1848; age, 15 days

Teresa Jarboe, died November 6, 1848; age, 8 years; moved from Platte County 14 years after death

Mary Judson, died January 6, 1849; age, 12 days; born to George Judson and Agnes Gray Judson

Philomele Vertfenille, died January 20, 1849; age, 1 year; born to Joseph and Elisabeth Novolette

Olive Mellanger, died February 23, 1849; age, 1 year; daughter of Pierre and Adeline Montardi Mellanger

Mary Cunjeon, died February 19, 1849; born to Curjeon and Marguerita

Joseph Deslories, died March 17, 1849; born to Antonie and Louise Roy

Jean Baptiste Bernard, died April 22, 1849

Mary Adeline Curyeon, died April 22, 1849; age, 3 years; died of cholera

Josephine Gouin, died April 24, 1849; age, 7 years; died of cholera

Leonard Mesmoit, died April 27, 1849; age, 26 years; removed May 1881 to lot 284 11-B
Mary Elizabeth Gouin, died April 24, 1849; age, 2 years
Mary Chouteaus, married, died July 1, 1849; age, 44 years; died of cholera
Auguste Janio, died July 11, 1849; age, 23 years
Julie Lessert, died August 2, 1849; age, 12 years; daughter of Clement and Julie Roy
Agnes Judson, died August 27, 1849; wife of George
   Lesage, died June, 1850; age, 1 year, 4 months; son of John Lesage and Frances Roy
Frances Farrier, died June 10, 1851; age, 21 years, wife of Louis Farrier, daughter of Francis Mangeon and Constance Bainville
Jane Waller, died July 24, 1851; age, 18 years
Elizabeth Vertfeuille, died July 20, 1851; age, 27 years
   Her child, died July 21, 1851; age, 1 year, 11 months
Samuel Geer, died August 4, 1851; age, 13 months; infant son of Samuel Geer and Emily Roler
La Croix, died April, 1850; age, 9 years
Julius Olivet, died June 5, 1851; age, 1 year
Julius Whittaker, died March, 1851; age, 3 years
Lydia Anne Jarboe, died August 6, 1851; age, 49 years; wife of Joseph Jarboe
Sara Roy, died August 22, 1851; age, 30 years; relict of Peter Roy
George Hudson, died December 24, 1851; age, 40 years; George Hudson of Kansas, formerly of Canada
George W. DeRome, died July 10, 1852; age, 23 years; formerly of Fort Wayne, Indiana
Louis Barada, died July, 1852
Charles Hunt, died August 19, 1852; age, 6 months; infant son of Mary Hunt
Olivier Crete, died August 22, 1852; age, 52 years; native of St. Ange near Quebec, L. C.
Henry Henri, died December, 1852; age, 44 years, native of France
Margaret Prudhomme, died April 26, 1853; age, 57 years
Bridget Lehan, alias Hawkins, died February 3, 1853; age, 26 years; wife of William, native of Co. Clare, Ireland
Edward Geseau Chouteau, died February 9, 1853
   Guinot, died April 3, 1853
Letitia Mary Blatman, died April 6, 1853; age, 35 years; wife of Frank Blatman
Gabriel Philibert, died May 1, 1853; age, 52 years
Joseph Ed. Olovoet, died 1853; age, 1 month
Pierre Laliberte, died September 28, 1853; age, 61 years; of Kansas
Clement Lessert, died July 20, 1854; age, 58 years; native of Canada
Louis Marier, died September 20, 1854; age, 2 years, 6 months; son of Prospere Marier
Josephine Turgeon, died September 21, 1854; age, 2 years, 10 months; daughter of Louis Turgeon
William Turgeon, died September 22, 1854; age, 4 years; son of Louis Turgeon
John O'Halligan, died May 6, 1855; age, 2 years
Joseph M. Knight, died May 5, 1855; age, 35 years
John Baurleine, died April 8, 1855; age, 6 months
   McCarthy, died May 11, 1855; age, 8 months
James A. Blatman, died May 12, 1855; age, 6 years
   Hopkins, died May 18, 1855
Mary Connenny, died June 1, 1855; age, 26 years
Joseph McKnight, died June 2, 1855; age, 38 years
Henry Krey, died June 3, 1855; age, 32 years
Mrs. Cooley, died July 12, 1855; age, 35 years
   O'Halligan, died September 26, 1855; daughter of Patrick O'Halligan of Westport
   O'Halligan, died September 26, 1855; son of Patrick O'Halligan
   Moore, died September 28, 1855, of Westport; died of cholera
Henry G. Neile, died October 1, 1855; formerly of Baltimore, Maryland
Theodore Persin, died January 29, 1856

Mary Houston, alias Lesage, died 1856
Frank Houston, son of the above
Joseph Bisson, died April 19, 1856; age, 30 years
Isabella View, died January 12, 1857; age, 11 years, daughter of Peter View
Michael Connolly, died July, 1856; age, 33 years
Edmund Turgeon, died March 1, 1857; age, 14 years
Mary Martha Godier, died April 16, 1857; age, 26 years; wife of Joseph
Joseph Hunot, died June 2, 1857; age, 40 years
Adam Cassimir, died July 19, 1857; age, 37 years
Bernard L. Olovoet, died August 20, 1857; age, 8 months
James Tracy, died August 20, 1857; age, 14 months
    Bannon, died August 20, 1857; age, 14 months
John Lackney, died July 26, 1857; age, 63 years
Mary Cassidy, died September 5, 1857; age, 14 months
Eliza Jane Burke, died September 8, 1857; age, 21 days
John Spencer, died September 5, 1857; age, 32 years
Mary Frances Steward, died September 8, 1857; age, 1 year
Daniel Early, died September 9, 1857; age, 40 years
Patrick McMahon, died September 21, 1857; age, 32 years
Mary Celestine Mulchy, died September 26, 1857; age, 4 months
William Selman, died September 26, 1857; age, 20 months; German
Michael Starrs, died October 2, 1857; age, 30 years
Mary Ellen Shannon, died October 1, 1857; age, 2 years
John Rollins, died October 11, 1857; age, 35 years; Wyandotte County
John Webber, died October 14, 1857; age, 18 years
Mary Tracy, died October 19, 1857; age, 7 months; Quindaro
John McCabe, died October 22, 1857; age, 24 years; native of Canada
Joseph Steiart, died November 2, 1857; age, 6 years
Helena Francisca Schmees, died November 27, 1857; age, 2 years, 1 month
Dennis Griffin, died December 7, 1857; age, 2 years, 8 months
John Harrington, died December 19, 1857; age, 1 year, 17 days
William Ryan, died December 20, 1857
Mrs. Mary Ryan, died 1857; age, 42 years; Wyandotte City
Michael Kelly, died January 7, 1858; age, 28 years; native of Court Brown Co., Limerick, Ireland
Geoso Chouteau, died February 23, 1858; son of Menard Chouteau and Mary Polk
Daniel Fitzmaurice, died February 24, 1858; age, 18 years
Terence Maguirk, died March 5, 1858; age, 41 years
    Howard, died March 24, 1858
Dennis Shay, died March 24, 1858; age, 15 months
Michael Francis Tracy, died 1858; age, 5 years; of Wyandotte
Roger McMennomen, died April 24, 1858; age, 3 years
Bryan McCormick, died April 29, 1858; age, 27 years; native of Co. Sligo, Ireland
Patrick Kelly, died May 12, 1858; age, 40 years
Mary Ellen Burns, died May 13, 1858; age, 4 years, 6 months
John Herman Vincent, died May 14, 1858; age, 4 years, 6 months
B. Bradish, died June 1, 1858; age, 40 years
    Barbour, died 1858
George Lanehardt, died June 27, 1858; age, 2 years, 8 months
Margaret Coghlan, died June 27, 1858; age, 16 months
Mary Ann Coghlan, died June 27, 1858; age, 5 years
Patrick Molloy, died July 5, 1858; age, 28 years
John McCluskey, died July 5, 1858; age, 22 years
John Thomas Kelly, died July 7, 1858
John Thomas Moroney, died July 25, 1858; age, 2 years, 5 months
Otho Schwarzkopf, died August 1, 1858; age, 9 months

CEMETERIES—KAW TOWNSHIP

Michael Ryan, died August 4, 1858; age, 1 year
Daniel David O'Brien, died August 5, 1858; age, 7 months, 11 days
Daniel Magrath, died August 8, 1858; age, 40 years
Michael Kennedy, died August 11, 1858; age, 4 months
Joseph Long, died August 12, 1858; age, 28 years
Timothy Sullivan, died August 13, 1858; age, 38 years
John Henry Schmees, died August 13, 1858; age, 5 months
Bernard Kernan, died August 14, 1858; age, 30 years
John Lysaight, died August 15, 1858; age, 35 years
John Gibbon, died August 17, 1858; age, 48 years
Mary Ellen Lynch, died August 18, 1858; age, 20 days
Elizabeth Ellen Whelan, died August 19, 1858; age, 1 year
Peter Tracy, died August 22, 1858; age, 26 years
George Feehan, died August 23, 1858; age, 15 months
Patrick Clancy, died August 23, 1858; age, 15 months
Francis Evans, died August 24, 1858; age, 32 years
        Whelan, died August 25, 1858
Christopher Cassidy, died August 28, 1858
        Scanlon, died August 30, 1858
Joseph Bushmire, died August 31, 1858; age, 1 year
John Sullivan, died September 4, 1858; age, 32 years
Bridget McNamara, died September 9, 1858; age, 22 years; Wyandotte
Nicholas Smith, died September 11, 1858
Mary Liker, died September 12, 1858; age, 6 days
Francis Bradish, died September 13, 1858; age, 2 years, 3 months
Anne Kane, died September 13, 1858; age, 64 years; wife of James Kane, native of Butters
    Bridge, Co. Cavan, Ireland
Eliza Mansfield, died September 13, 1858; age, 4 months, 4 days
Francis Larkin, died September 13, 1858; age, 6 weeks
Mathew William Yauch, died September 13, 1858; age, 2 months, 21 days
Kate Cassidy, died September 15, 1858; age, 6 months, 21 days
        Bradish, died September 15, 1858
Catherine Anne Meanny, died September 16, 1858; age, 2 months
Stephen Russell, died September 16, 1858; age, 2 years, 2 months
John Fennelly, died September 18, 1858; age, 28 years
Ann Jacobine, died September 19, 1858; age, 5 years
Francis Peter, died 1858; age, 5 years
Mary Morrissy and infant, died September 22, 1858; age, 35 years
Pauline Klassen, died September 23, 1858; age, 3 days
        Dolan, died September 23, 1858; age, 1 month
Rosa Smith, died September 28, 1858; wife of John Smith, native of Ireland
        Olovoet, died September 29, 1858; age, 1 month; infant son of Ed. Olovoet
Bridget Connor, died September 30, 1858; age, 1 week
Mary McCarthy, died October 4, 1858; age, 1 week
William Kennedy, died October 3, 1858; age, 1 year
Mrs. Ann Madden, died October 4, 1858; age, 65 years
Charles Haghn, died October 5, 1858; age, 28 years; Westport
Peter Leizer, died October 7, 1858; age, 64 years
Dennis Collins, died October 9, 1858; age, 9 months
        Burke, died October 8, 1858
Louise Vasquier, died October 9, 1858; age, 4 years, 8 months
Dominick Zeizer, died October 15, 1858; age, 6 months
Michael Killeen, died October 16, 1858; age, 1 day
Michael Russell, died October 16, 1858; age, 28 years
Mary Russell, died October 21, 1858; age, 9 weeks
John Griffin, died October 22, 1858; age, 8 years

Elizabeth Charley, died October 23, 1858; age, 1 year
Elizabeth Bushmire, died October 29, 1858; age, 2 weeks
John O'Dea, died October 31, 1858; age, 25 years
Thomas Smith, died October 30, 1858; age, 56 years; native of Co. Cavan, Ireland
Dennis O'Brien, died November 20, 1858; age, 1 day
Philip Donohoe, died November 3, 1858; age, 12 years; Parkville, Clay Co.
Annie Halloran, died November 16, 1858; age, 4 years
Mary Ann Sheehan, died January 5, 1859; age, 1 year
Mary Sullivan, died January 5, 1859; age, 1 year, 8 months
Thomas Melvin, died January 8, 1859; age, 23 years
Henry Fox, died January 13, 1859; age, 36 years
Henrietta Fox, died December 29, 1858; buried January 13, 1859; age, 4 months
Peter McKeon, died October 3, 1858; buried January 13, 1859; age, 50 years
Johanna McNamara, died January 18, 1859
John Ostermeyer, died January 22, 1859; age, 36 years
John Shea, died February 10, 1859; age, 45 years; Wyandotte City
Dr. Benoist Troost, died February 11, 1859; age, 72 years
Sara Gorman, died February 17, 1859; age, 18 months
Emily Jane Jarboe, died February 18, 1859; age, 18 months
John Farrelly, died February 19, 1859; age, 21 months
    O'Hallihan, died February 19, 1859; infant of Patrick O'Hallihan
Herman Henry, died February 23, 1859; age, 15 months
    Lanehardt, died 1859
William Carroll, died February 25, 1859; age, 32 years; Wyandotte
James Lynch, died February 26, 1859; age, 1 day; Wyandotte
Michael McNamara, died February 27, 1859; age, 35 years; Wyandotte
Charles W. Heins, died February 28, 1859; age, 5 months
Crescentia Claus, died March 26, 1859; age, 62 years; native of Hewhlengen, Wurtenberg
Patrick Sheeran, died March 29, 1859; age, 25 years
Thomas Molloy, died March 1, 1859; age, 7 years
Margaret Torpey, died March 29, 1859; age, 26 years
Andrew Gessler, died April 4, 1859; age, 56 years; Wyandotte
Baptist Lambert, died April 8, 1859; age, 20 years
William Collins, died April 12, 1859; age, 29 years
Aleida Maria Wertz, died April 17, 1859; age, 3 years; Shawneetown
John Francis Durerney, died April 20, 1859; age, 11 days
Thomas Grey, died May 7, 1859; age, 19 years
Alice McEnnenny, died May 12, 1859; age, 5 weeks
James Riel, died 1859
Henry Davis O'Connor, died June 29, 1859; age, 3 months
Henry Jacob, died June 30, 1859; age, 4 months
Leon Lemoine, died July 24, 1859; age, 10 months
Annie Eliza Curran, died July 25, 1859; age, 7 months
Mary Gertrude, died July 26, 1859; age, 14 months
Henry Schoutte, died September 1, 1859; age, 1 day
Mary Ann Wesner, died August 11, 1859; age, 69 years; native of Readsals, Alsace, France
Mary Whelan, died August 14, 1859; age, 35 years
Margaret Christopher, died August 16, 1859; age, 28 years
Mary Enright, died August 18, 1859; age, 7 months
James Heally, died August 24, 1859; age, 5 months
James Kane, died August 25, 1859; age, 71 years
Mary Gosser, died September 13, 1859; age, 10 weeks
Patrick Gleason, died September 13, 1859; age, 15 years
Redmond Keating, died September 22, 1859; age, 75 years; Gardner, Johnson Co., Kansas Territory
    David, died September 23, 1859

Mary Waller, died September 24, 1859; age, 2 days; Wyandotte
Mary Christopher, died September 25, 1859; age, 68 years
Mary Ward, died September 26, 1859; age, 13 months
Daniel Francis Boland, died September 28, 1859; age, 3 weeks
Mary Cummings, died October 2, 1859; age, 11 months
James Kelly, died October 2, 1859; age, 24 hours
Margaret Dowd, died October 12, 1859; age, 13 months
Joseph Tam, died October 26, 1859; age, 26 years
Thomas Quinlan, died October 31, 1859; age, 2 months
Mary O'Connor, died October, 1859; age, 30 years
Edward Aspell, died November 29, 1859; age, 35 years; lately of New Auburn, Minnesota
Timothy Lynch, died December 6, 1859; age, 32 years
James Antoin Schoen, died December 16, 1859; native of Bavaria
Mary Anne Schouett, died December 16, 1859; age, 27 years

ELMWOOD CEMETERY
KANSAS CITY, MISSOURI

Elmwood Cemetery comprises fifty acres of beautifully shaded land between Elmwood Avenue and Van Brunt Boulevard, Twelfth and Fifteenth Streets.

According to the records in the office of the Secretary of the Elmwood Cemetery Society, the first lots were sold in the year 1872. At that time it was a private enterprise and it was so conducted until taken over by this Society. The first interment recorded is that of "Infant Ayres." The block number and lot are indicated, but further information is not obtainable for the record is not complete and there is no marker at the grave.

Elmwood Cemetery Society was incorporated under the laws of Missouri in 1896, and a charter granted for nine hundred and ninety-nine years. Because of the rapid growth of Kansas City, various small cemeteries and family burying grounds were abandoned. The lists show that in the eighties many families made the change to Elmwood Cemetery.

The name of the pioneers of Jackson County and of the State of Missouri who are buried there are too great in number to be fully given in this book. Those desiring further information are referred to the files in the office of Elmwood Cemetery.

The following list of those who purchased lots in Elmwood Cemetery up to the year 1876, has been copied from those files:

Purchaser, date of purchase, lot description and block letter

Lyman O. Chapin, lot S ½ 110, block L
John Baneolin, lot 18, block L
Sans W. Bonton, lot S W ¼ 67, block L
J. P. Weller, May 22, 1873, lot N W ¼ 38, block L
Martha M. Hicks, October 2, 1874, lot 29, block L
C. C. Clemons, May 29, 1873, lot S E ¼ , block L
Mrs. Marion West, June 12, 1873, lots 85-86, block K
Louis Dauzer, June 17, 1873, lot E ½ 66, block L
Frederick Eitilgeorge, June 17, 1873, lot E ½ 24, block L
A. G. Trumbull, June 17, 1873, lot W ½ 26, block L
Henry Meyer, October 10, 1873, lot N ½ 110, block L
Henry N. Ess, October 11, 1873, lot 117, block K
Robert H. Drennon, October 13, 1873, lot E ½ 67, block K
Dr. A. B. Taylor, October 13, 1873, lots 23-24, block K
C. Wertz and son, November 11, 1873, lot E ½ 64, block L
Mrs. Louis King, November 14, 1873, lot 66, block J
Geo. W. Evington, February 11, 1874, lot N W ¼ 17, block L

D. W. Wells, June 30, 1874, lot 119, block K
Robert J. Holmes, July 11, 1874, lots 2-3-4, block N
Carl Spengler, August 26, 1874, lot E ½ 33, block L
E. A. Axtel, September 29, 1874, lot E ½ 36, block L
Thomas M. Speers, September 29, 1874; lot ½ 112, block K
E. L. Patch (canceled), October 2, 1874, lot N E ¼ 167, block L
Mrs. I. P. Weeks, April 1, 1875, lot S W ¼ 106, block K
J. W. Dunlop, April 17, 1875, S E ¼ 32, block L
A. W. Allen, April 17, 1875, lot W ½ 36, block L
Kansas City Kranken Schutz, May 25, 1875, lot 69, block L
Mrs. Tripp, September 1, 1875; lot N E ¼ 112, block K
Charles Brooke, September 25, 1875, lot W ½ 32, block L
John E. Jewett, September 25, 1875, lot N ½ 103, block K
Stephen P. Twiss, September 25, 1875, lot E ½ 12, block L
Jane P. Skinner, November 12, 1875, lot 118, block K

Compiled and copied by Mrs. Max A. Christopher, Regent Kansas City Chapter, D. A. R. 1931-34

THE McGEE CEMETERY
The McGee Cemetery was located on Twentieth Street between Broadway and Wyandotte Streets, and was in use in the early 1830's

This cemetery, which was one of the earliest burying grounds in what is now known as Kansas City, Missouri, was on the farm owned by James H. McGee, who came to Missouri from Shelby County, Kentucky, with his wife, Eleanor Frye McGee, and little family, in 1827, and to Westport Landing, Jackson County, in 1828. He was one of the first white men to own land in this locality, taking out his land patent November 14, 1828. The history of this early pioneer family is inseparably woven with the history of Kansas City, Missouri.

James McGee purchased land which was afterwards intersected by 16th and Grand Avenue; later he purchased the greater portion of the land lying between the "levee" and Westport and built a log cabin near the corner of Twentieth and Central Streets, Later he opened a brick yard, the first in Jackson County, and of the brick burned by himself and sons he built the first brick house erected in the County, at Baltimore Avenue and Twentieth Street. From the first brick kiln burned by Mr. McGee, Father Donnelly, the pioneer Catholic Priest, obtained the brick with which he built the chimney of the little log church at the corner of Eleventh and Penn. Following are the names of the children of James H. and Eleanor Frye McGee; all are buried in Elmwood Cemetery except A. B. H. McGee, the eldest son, who is interred in Union Cemetery:

Amelia McGee (Evans-Steen), born 1813
Allen B. H. McGee, born 1815
Frye P. McGee, born 1816
Mobillon W. McGee, born 1817
Elijah Milton McGee, born 1819
Catherine McGee (Johnson), born 1821
Eleanor McGee (Campbell), wife of John S. Campbell, born November 14, 1825, died December 9, 1889; buried on Campbell lot in Elmwood Cemetery
Angeline McGee, died early
Thomas McGee, died early
Francis Manor McGee, born 1831
Mary McGee, died early
James McGee, born 1837

The brown granite monument which stands on the McGee lot in Elmwood Cemetery and which stood for many years in the old McGee Burying Ground, was purchased by E.

Milton McGee, Mayor of Kansas City in 1870, and his name, "E. M. McGee," appears across the base of the shaft.

The old McGee Cemetery was vacated in 1881 and the McGee monument was moved to the lot in Elmwood Cemetery, and was at that time the first tall shaft in Elmwood Cemetery.

The following inscriptions were copied from the stones on the McGee lot in Elmwood Cemetery, and are for those whose bodies were removed from the old McGee Burying Ground:

Chiles, Mary Ann, wife of Joseph B. Chiles, died January 19, 1836; age, (not decipherable)
Evans, Anna, born November 10, 1852, died May 27, 1857
Evans, Elizabeth, born July 5, 1836, died May 19, 1851
Evans, Ellen, born January 18, 1835, died August 8, 1847
Evans, John W., son of Wm. B. and Amelia Evans, died December 25, 1864; age, 21 years
Evans, Wm. B., died January 27, 1855; age, 48 years, 1 month, 27 days
Harris, Bertha A., born August 13, 1864; died July 25, 1865
Johnson, Catherine McGee, born January 21, 1821
Johnson, James, born March 6, 1802, died August 31, 1867
Johnson, Rebecca, wife of James Johnson, died July 29, 1838, in her 28th year
Johnson, Benjamin, son of J. and R. E. Johnson, born Nov. 6, 1841, died Aug. 27, 1844
Johnson, Eleanor, daughter of James and Rebecca Johnson, born March 28, 1834, died November 4, 1867
Limes, Ida May, daughter of Charles and Mary Limes, born March 19, 1869, died November 9, 1869
McGee, James H., died May 26, 1840; age, 54 years, 4 months, 25 days
McGee, Eleanor F., wife of James H. McGee, born October 10, 1793, died November 22, 1880
McGee, Angeline T., daughter of James H. and Eleanor F. McGee, died September 13, 1845; age, 15 years, 10 months, 7 days
McGee, Mary, daughter of James H. and Eleanor F. McGee, born and died December 6, 1832
McGee, Thomas, son of James H. and Eleanor F. McGee, born and died March 5, 1856
McGee, Francis Manor, son of James H. and Eleanor F. McGee, born March 6, 1831; killed at the Battle of Franklin, Tenn., November 30, 1864
McGee, Frye P., born May 27, 1816, died September 17, 1861
McGee, Martha E. (wife of Frye P. McGee), born April 16, 1820, died August 31, 1867
McGee, James H., III, born September 15, 1862, died April 30, 1863
McGee, J. Hyatt, born June 27, 1866, died November 23, 1867; children of James H. McGee, Jr., and wife, Ruth T. McGee
McGee, Samuel C., son of F. P. and Martha McGee, born Oct. 26, 1842, died April 26, 1843

Among the other members of this early pioneer family buried on this lot are:
Bales, William, born December, 1834, died December, 1924
Bales, Hattie Evans, wife of Wm. Bales, born February 19, 1848, died July 4, 1887
Harris, Wm. D., died January 2, 1883; age, 65 years
Harris, America E., wife of Wm. D. Harris, died October 7, 1882; age, 41 years, 6 months, 6 days
Holmes, Mary C., wife of L. D. Holmes, born July 14, 1854, died January 1, 1884
McGee, James H., born 1837, died 1895
McGee, Ruth, wife of James H., born 1839, died 1909
McGee, Mobillon W., born December 25, 1817, died June 11, 1888
McGee, Mary E., wife of M. W. McGee, born August 12, 1826, died November 3, 1900
McGee, E. Milton, born May 30, 1819, died Feb. 11, 1873; Mayor of Kansas City 1870
McGee, Sarah Adeline DeMoss, wife of E. Milton McGee, died February 22, 1883; married in Texas
*Steen, Amelia (McGee) Evans, born June 17, 1813; died July 28, 1885

*Amelia McGee, oldest child of James H. McGee and Eleanor McGee, married (first) William B. Evans, who owned and built the first ferry on the river, which was put into service in 1830.

Vincent, Charles and wife Gertrude McGee Vincent the only child of E. M. McGee and wife Sarah McGee

Vincent, seven children of Charles and Gertrude Vincent

Vineyard, members of the Vineyard family

Allen B. H. McGee, born May 21, 1815, the eldest son of James H. and Eleanor Frye McGee, chose Union Cemetery as the burying place for the members of his family, and to this cemetery he moved the bodies of members of his family who had been interred in the old McGee Cemetery.

Mr. Allen B. H. McGee was one of the fourteen men who bought the "original" Kansas City. The land belonging to the heirs of Gabriel Prudhomme was sold at auction by his father, James H. McGee, who was the guardian of the heirs. The price ranged from $5000 to $7000.

Mr. McGee married (first) Melinda Frey, daughter of Henry Frey of Shelby County, Kentucky, in 1837. His wife died September 19, 1846. He then married Christiana Frey, a sister of his first wife. His second wife died March 19, 1867. In 1869 he married Susan B. Gill, who died May 9, 1901. Mr. A. B. H. McGee died October 8, 1903, at the age of eighty-eight years, and his body was placed in the vault which he built in 1884 in Union Cemetery.

The foregoing data pertaining to the McGee family was given Mrs. Max A. Christopher by Mrs. Nellie McGee Nelson, Miss Eleanor McGee and Mr. Milton McGee Vincent

PORTER CEMETERY

Twenty-sixth Street and Troost Avenue, Kansas City, Missouri

This cemetery contained the remains of one of Jackson County's most notable connections with the Revolutionary War,—Mrs. Elizabeth Porter, who spent one year of the Revolutionary War a prisoner of the British forces at Fort Niagara.

After her marriage to Samuel Porter, in Ireland, she with her husband emigrated to Richmond, Virginia. Later, Samuel Porter, with his young wife and his slaves, penetrated the wilderness of Tennessee, and set up their home near Franklin, far removed from Bunker Hill and Brandywine. Their home was in the "farthest West." Across the Mississippi River was the unexplored wilderness of "Upper Louisiana." But it was not far enough from the battlefields to escape the Indians, who were British allies.

One day, when Mr. Porter was away from home, an Indian band captured Mrs. Porter and her few neighbors. It is thought there must have been British soldiers present or the settlers' scalps would have been taken. The prisoners were marched, day after day, through the wild expanse of country that stretched away between Franklin, Tennessee, and the British Fort,—Niagara,—in Canada. After months of marching, fording rivers, and suffering incident to such a march, they arrived at the fort. There they spent the winter, but were returned the next spring to their Colonial adherents.

Mrs. Porter, in 1829, then a widow, came with her son, the Rev. James Porter, to Jackson County. In 1833 they settled on the old Porter Farm, which surrounded what is now the intersection of 28th Street and Tracy Avenue. At her death in 1845, she was buried in the Porter private cemetery on the farm.

The following were buried in the Porter Cemetery:

Porter, Elizabeth, wife of Samuel Porter, died April 11, 1845, in the 95th year of her age

Porter, Rev. James, born October 28, 1786, died October 31, 1851

Porter, Jane, wife of Rev. James Porter, born May 11, 1786, died November 25, 1873
Porter, Jesse L., son of James and Jane Porter, born July 30, 1827, died May 15, 1868
Sutton, Mr. and Mrs. Samuel

When the widow of Jesse L. Porter gave the land for the Troost Avenue Methodist Church (26th St. and Troost Ave.), the bodies in the Porter Cemetery were removed to the Union Cemetery.

Compiled and copied by Miss Jessie M. Crosby

SHELLEY PARK CEMETERY
Located between Missouri Avenue and Independence Avenue; Oak and Locust Streets, Kansas City, Missouri

The Old Town company about the year 1837 gave to the town organization this tract of land, the purpose for which the land was to be used being that of a burying ground. It was a rough tract then and was considered, when compared with other lands, almost unsalable. The land was about a mile from the steamboat landing, over hills, hollows and ravines, and through forests of trees and great tracts of "underbrush." In the southeastern part of the tract was then a great ravine, but the whole piece is now level. The first person buried there was an unknown woman, and the second person was William M. Chick, who died April 7, 1847. As the years passed by and the town grew, the graveyard filled up rapidly, and hundreds of new graves were made during the prevalence of the cholera epidemic in the years 1848 and 1849, when Captain Suter's discovery of the little shining particles in his mill race in California caused emigrants by the thousands to land at Kansas City and take the overland route for the land of gold.

In this graveyard the lots were free to all who wished to enter, and although there were several marble monuments and many tombstones the graves were not arranged in rows, and the palings surrounding the resting places of the dead were not systematically placed, but presented a singular ghostly, erratic appearance. The McDaniel, the Eldridge, the Jackson and the McDowell families had lots in this graveyard, and here rested the remains of Dr. Andrew Fulton, a physician of wide repute in early days, and near him John W. Bayne and Elijah Jackson were buried.

The city council in 1857 passed an ordinance declaring it illegal for any more interments to be made in this cemetery and consequently burials ceased. For many years the graveyard was unused for any purpose, the fences were torn down, many of the dead were removed to other cemeteries. Nearly all the graves were upon a high ridge running north and south, parallel with Oak Street, the summit of which was about forty feet east of Oak Street, and few, if any, were as far east as the middle of the square, but many were in Oak Street and Missouri Avenue. This ridge has been graded off to a depth of from 8½ feet to the south to 17 feet at the north, an average of about 11 feet, necessitating, of course, the removal of all remains. The removal of earth from the square aforesaid was begun about 1868, and the entire surface was leveled off in 1878. The city did the grading; the place was planted in trees, enclosed by a fence and called Shelley park, after Mayor Shelley.

The records of the city council:

"Resolution December 30, 1872" City Engineer to make arrangements for disinterring and reinterring remains."

"Resolution May 12, 1872" Report of City Engineer Marvin on same. Contracts with Undertaker Welden to remove remains to Union Cemetery referred to."

Compiled by Miss Jessie M. Crosby

SOME SMALL EXTINCT CEMETERIES

Once located within the present city limits of Kansas City, Missouri

Data and records concerning these old cemeteries have been collected and compiled by Miss Jessie M. Crosby. They are:

BALES BURYING GROUND
Data contributed by Mrs. J. E. Bales of Lee's Summit, Missouri

There was a family burying ground on the Walter Bales farm. The bodies of those buried there have been removed to the Bales lot in Elmwood Cemetery.

An interesting claim of the Bales family is that when Walter Bales settled here, he was much distressed because of the lack of schools in the locality, and to promote education, he built the first school house.

CAMPBELL CEMETERY
Cypress Avenue, between 24th and 25th Streets
Data contributed by Mrs. Samuel Hudson Laws

"The Campbell Cemetery was on the farm of John Wallace Campbell, which he bought in 1833. The cemetery would now be located on what is Cypress Avenue, between 24th and 25th Streets. John Wallace Campbell and wife, Eliza Ann Laws Campbell, were buried there, and in 1898, owing to the ground being taken into the city, the bodies were taken up and moved to the Brooking Cemetery. John Wallace Campbell was born February 12, 1810, died June 26, 1853. Eliza Ann Laws Campbell, wife of John Wallace Campbell, died May 11, 1848 (have no record of her birth)."

COLLINS CEMETERY
Twelfth Street and Hardesty Avenue, Kansas City, Missouri
Contributed by Mrs. L. W. King (nee Collins)

This land was owned by Ancel Collins and Thomas West.

Collins, Michael
Collins, Rebecca Noland, wife of Michael Collins, daughter of Ledstone Noland. Mr. and Mrs. Collins died before the Civil War.
Collins, Leander
West, Mrs.
  Wimsatt, infant daughter of Arland and Elizabeth Wimsatt.

These bodies were removed about 1888 to Elmwood Cemetery, Kansas City, Missouri. There were other graves in this cemetery which have never been removed but all record of them has been lost.

GREEN CEMETERY
27th Street and Van Brunt, Kansas City, Missouri
Data contributed by Mrs. Samuel Hudson Laws

Alfred Laws was killed on his farm by bushwhackers during the Civil War. He was buried in the Green Cemetery.

HOLLOWAY CEMETERY
Brooklyn Avenue and Thirtieth Street, Kansas City, Missouri
Data contributed by John Frank Lee Holloway

"My grandfather, James Allen Holloway, came to Jackson County from Kentucky in the year 1846. He purchased two hundred acres of land now a portion of Kansas City. A portion of the land has been set aside as the Spring Valley Park, and it was at the springs there, that Grandfather got his water for his home as well as his stock. The Burial Lot was located on the east side of Brooklyn and about 100 feet north of 30th street. This burial lot was condemned by the city some 35 years ago. My father, Ben T. Holloway, was ordered to remove the graves, which he did, after opening some 30 graves and placing what could be found of the remains of one large walnut box, he had the bodies placed in our family lot in Elmwood Cemetery.

"I have no knowledge who was buried there, outside of my Grandfather, who died at 67 years and my father's first wife, a "Cannin" (Millie Canine). She was one of the old families of Jackson County. There were a number of the children of the Holloway slaves buried in the lot, and, I judge, my father's mother, my Grandmother Holloway ("Timpy" Holloway), who died about 1850, for my father was but 9 years old at the time of her death. My father's oldest brother was named James Holloway, and he died in the Civil War, so I presume he was buried in the lot. My grandmother Holloway was a Thornburg."

HOLMES CEMETERY
KANSAS CITY, MISSOURI
Contributed by Mrs. Mattie Stevenson, daughter of Silas Holmes

Silas Holmes came to Kansas City in 1844 from Kentucky. He died August 15, 1855, and was the first one buried in this plot on his farm.

Bailey, Alfred
Bailey, Betsy, wife of Alfred Bailey
Bailey, Alice, age, 2½ years
Bailey, William, age, 2 years
Mrs. Locket and baby, died of cholera
Mr. Knight, a young man living near
Three members of a family living near died of cholera, a father and 2 daughters; Mrs. Stevenson could not remember their names
Mrs. Stevenson is a daughter of Silas Holmes.
These remains were removed to Elmwood Cemetery.

JARBOE CEMETERY
Sixth and Bluff Streets

The Jarboe family had a burying ground at Sixth and Bluff Streets. The bodies of those buried there were later removed to the Catholic Cemetery.

KNOCHE BURYING GROUND
Section 29, Township 50, Range 32 W

The farm of Philip Knoche was situated where the Blue river empties into the Missouri river. The family burying ground was on this farm. Sometime after 1890 the bodies of those buried there were removed to Elmwood Cemetery, Kansas City, Missouri.

STEELE CEMETERY

Brighton Avenue and 24th Street, Kansas City, Missouri
Contributed by Mr. Robert L. Smith (relative)

Jackson, Carrie, daughter of Isaac and Mariah Jackson
Smith, Arthur
Smith, Ann Maria, wife of Arthur Smith
Smith, Bell, daughter of Wallace and George Ann Smith
Smith, Thomas
Smith, Ruth, wife of Thomas Smith
Steele, Larkin
Steele, Cassie Owens, wife of Larkin Steele
Steele, Jennie, daughter of Richard and Lizzie Steele
Mr. Seabold

These bodies were removed to Elmwood Cemetery.

Other extinct cemeteries, in Kaw Township, see Index for: Bradley, McGee, Porter, Shelley and Smart

SMART CEMETERY

Northwest corner of Twelfth and Main Streets, Kansas City, Missouri
Contributed by Mrs. Louis E. Newman, granddaughter of Thomas Austin Smart

Mr. Smart gave the lot on this corner to the First Christian Church, where the church was built in 1859, but retained the privilege of the Smart burial grounds in the rear of the church.

Thomas Austin Smart, son of Elisha and Ann Glover Smart, was born in Campbell County, Virginia, near Lynchburg, on March 16, 1806, and died in Kansas City, Missouri, September 18, 1879. He was raised in Montgomery County, Kentucky, where he moved with his family at an early age. He, with his wife, Harriet Louise Thompson Smart, settled in Kansas City in 1839. There were nine children by this marriage.

Harriet L. Thompson Smart, first wife of Thomas A. Smart, died of cholera May 6, 1849, at the age of 40 years, 2 months

Martha Smart, a daughter, died March 10, 1861; age, 15 years, 2 months

Mrs. Newman believes that these two were buried in the Smart Cemetery, as were probably George, William, Robert, Thomas and Mary, children, who died quite young. There is no record to be found of the death of these last named children. No bodies were removed from the Smart graveyard, so far as Mrs. Newman can ascertain, except that of Mrs. Smart.

Mary A. Smart (second wife of T. A. Smart), died July 11, 1892

Thomas A. Smart was buried in Union Cemetery

Mrs. Eliza Ridge, a daughter, is buried in the Dr. I. M. Ridge lot in Union Cemetery

Mrs. Caroline Graves, a daughter, was buried in Mt. Washington Cemetery, born April 21, 1829, died 1919

Mrs. Harriet M. Bryant, a daughter, was buried in Woodlawn Cemetery, Independence, Mo., born March 4, 1850, died April 8, 1920

NOTE:—The three last named were daughters of Thomas A. Smart and wife, Harriet L. Smart

UNION CEMETERY

Entrance, 2815 Walnut Street, Kansas City, Missouri
Contributed by Mrs. Max A. Christopher

It has been said, "A history of a community is written upon the tombstones in the cemeteries of that community." It is deeply regrettable that so much of the early history of our community has been lost by the destruction of the stones of those early cemeteries. The first burials in the vicinity now known as Kansas City, were the family burying grounds. The early residents, having no other alternative, formed the habit of reserving, on their farms, from a half to an acre of ground upon which to bury their dead. Thus on the farms of the McCoy, McGee, and Smart families were found these family burying grounds, typical of many others to be seen in the neighborhood in the early 1830's.

As the community known as Kansas City grew, the same mistake was made as was made in many other parts of the country; there was no adequate provision for the protection of such burial places as already exist, hence much interesting history has been lost.

In the minds of a great number of residents of Kansas City today, Union Cemetery, established in 1858, remains the oldest of all the urban cemeteries. As a matter of fact, a great number of burial places such as those mentioned above, have either been vacated or erased by the rapidly growing city with its tall buildings and paved streets.

In fact, Union Cemetery was not established until after the cemetery at Fifth and Oak Streets, established in 1847 as the first City Cemetery, was found to be inadequate. The location for the new cemetery was halfway between the town called Kansas (Kansas City), and the community known as Westport, so placed that it might meet the needs of both places. We are told that when this cemetery was established, "Away out beyond O. K. Creek," its forty-nine acres would solve the problem of the community for all time to come. It must be remembered that Kansas City was, at that time, a village of about three thousand persons. It is interesting to note, also, that at this time the south "city limits" were Twelfth Street, while the north line of the forty-nine acres selected for Union Cemetery was what we know today (1933) as Twenty-seventh Street.

The remains of many of the early pioneers of the community were removed to this cemetery as is evidenced by the number of stones found there which have dates showing that death occurred years before there was a Union Cemetery. Tradition says that there are more than one thousand soldiers of the Civil War buried in this cemetery, and less than four hundred of them are marked with permanent markers. It is a well-known fact that there are hundreds of other graves there which are unmarked.

The late Mrs. Beverley Tucker Thompson, mother of Mrs. Nettie Thompson Grove, secretary of the Missouri Valley Historical Society of Kansas City, attended the first funeral in Union Cemetery. This was the funeral of a child who was a patient of Dr. Thomas B. Lester, uncle of Mrs. Thompson, nee Miss Heron, at whose home she was visiting.

In more recent years, there have been removals from Union Cemetery to Elmwood (1872), Forest Hill (1888), Mount Washington (1900), and to others of the more recently established cemeteries. At this date, however, there are yet occasional burials in this historic cemetery, which a few years ago was reduced in acreage. The entrance, which for many years was at Twenty-eighth and Main Streets, was changed to Twenty-eighth and Walnut Streets, when Walnut Street was cut through the cemetery property and a large block of the ground was taken for business property.

Great care has been taken in copying for this publication, a list of the early lot owners, together with the block and lot number.

UNION CEMETERY

These records were copied from the original cemetery records loaned through the courtesy of Mr. Louis W. Shouse and Mr. Walton H. Holmes, members of the Union Cemetery Association.   Mrs. Max A. Christopher

KNOW ALL MEN BY THESE PRESENTS That we, James M. Hunter, Edward G. Peery, Joseph C. Ransom, William R. Bernard, Milton J. Payne and Robert J. Lawrence have this day associated ourselves and by these presents do associate ourselves upon equal terms as Members of the "UNION CEMETERY ASSOCIATION" and agree to be governed in all things pertaining or touching the premises which a majority of the association may determine in a formal meeting, the ground purchased for our purpose being of James M. Hunter by his deed to the President and Secretary of this association of even date herewith.

Given under our hands and seals this 19th day of May, 1857.

In the presence of Ch. C. Spalding,

(Signed) D. M. Boland (Seal), M. J. Payne (Seal), Jos. C. Ransom (Seal), W. R. Bernard (Seal), E. T. Peery (Seal), Jas. M. Hunter (Seal), Daniel L. Shouse (Seal).

Union Cemetery Association of Jackson County, Missouri, was incorporated by act of Missouri Legislature approved November 9, 1857.

James M. Hunter, Edward T. Peery, Joseph C. Ransom, William R. Bernard, Robert J. Lawrence, Milton J. Payne, corporators.

D. L. Shouse bought R. L. Lawrence's interest.

J. C. Ransom's interest bought by the Company.

C. T. Peery's interest bought by Mary J. Bernton, who sold to Mary Clarke, she to M. J. Payne.

LIST OF LOTS SOLD IN UNION CEMETERY 1858-1873

W. R. Bernard, block 30, lots 6 and 5
Joseph C. Ransom, block 31, lot 10
A. M. Eisley, block 35, lots 35 and 10
R. S. Thomas, block 31, lot 13
James M. Hunter, Block 33, lot 1, and block 33, lot 10
E. T. Peery, block 3, lot 18
Samuel S. Rolls, block 3, lot 25
Thomas I. Wilson, paid by J. W. Summers, Adm., Sept. 24, 1862, block 1, lot 21
Henry Morlack, block 3, lot 24
Joseph Wicksale, block 11, lot 15
John Hyer, block 29, lot 10
M. J. Payne, block 1, lot 20
Samuel L. Arnold, block 35, lot 11
J. A. Boggs, block 31, lot 1
C. D. Caldwell, block 7, lot 9
A. Street, block 31, lot 9
J. N. Bradney, block 71, lot 7
J. Robert Erekel, settled with F. W. Barnes, block 7, lot 8
R. T. Van Horn, block 30, lot 2
Louis Schoen, block 35, lot 9
F. A. Gross, block 39, lot 2
Alex. S. Harris, block 32, lot 6
John Richardson, block 7, lot 3
Carl Crumleigel, block 7, lot 2
Chalfant and Barcus, block 15, lot 5
Peter Schneitzable (?), block 37, lot 6
Wm. Lyman, south ½ to Saml. J. Platt, block 31, lot 6
M. B. Hedges, block 33, lot 3
R. S. Symington, block 34, lot 3
L. P. Wills (or Mills), block 35, lot 13
Corbin, block 38, lot 9
Wm. Petrie, block 31, lot 7
Sol. Bidwell, block 32, lot 9
Matthew Rule (paid by Mrs. McDonnell), block 1, lot 15
Jacob Stiles, block 1, lot 12
Jacob Leurbough, block 35, lot 12
Eugene Quinon, block 35, lot 7
G. M. B. Maughs—½ sold to T. B. Lord, this includes Mrs. Wordsgrovee (?), block 3, lot 23
H. S. Word or Ward, Thos. R. Lord
T. M. James, block 30, lot 3
G. D. Foglesong, block 35, lot 14
David McGee, block 3, lot 22
D. M. Ross, block 35, lot 6
W. R. Porsley, block 35, lot 5
D. L. Shouse, block 1, lot 18
W. P. Allen, block 1, lot 28
Dr. George B. Wood, condemned and used for single graves, block 35, lot 22
N. C. Clairborne, transferred to Robert Adams, block 30, lot 1
Geo. M. Tod, used for single graves, block 35, lot 2
Aaron S. Raub, block 3, lot 20
Wm. S. Chick, block 3, lot 19
Joshua Norton, block 2, lot 2
John Paus, north ½ sold by Paus to block 39, lot 3
P. Smith, block 35, lot 36
Geo. W. See, block 29, lot 4
Dr. J. T. Morris, block 31, lot 12

J. L. Ashbaugh, used for single graves, block 35, lot 23
T. H. Rosser, block 30, lot 2
J. G. and G. A. Baker, block 31, lots 11 and 8
A. Waskey and Jno. Purdom, block 35, lot 40
Richard T. Ferguson, used for single graves, block 7, lot 1
Owen C. Steward, used for single graves, block 3, lot 21
March 20, John J. Curd, block 1, lot 3
April 18, William Long, block 28, lot 1
April 26, J. B. Higgins, block 32, lot 7
May 6, Hugh Brown, block 35, lot 21
May 18, J. E. McKenkie, block 35, lot 26
May 18, W. C. Cook, block 7, lot 6
June 19, W. Beencher, block 35, lot 8
July 2
Henry Helmerich, block 28, lot 2
Richard Everingham, block 27, lot 6
E. C. McCarty, block 1, lot 18
Anthony Richter, block 3, lot 14
F. H. Booth (widow), block 3, lot 15
Francis Cunningham, block 35, lot 20
J. B. Moxcey, block 35, lot 4
William B. Poteet, paid Sept. 24, 1862 by J. W. Summers, Adm., block 35, lot 16
Thomas I. Wilson (twice entered), block 1, lot 21
Aug. , J. H. Ruckel, block 31, lot 5
Aug. 10, Lot Coffman, block 11, lot 3
Aug. 10, R. B. Nelson, block 11, lot 6
Sept. , Mrs. Margaret Botts, block 11, lot 7
Oct. 5, Reuben H. Dickinson, block 31, lot 4
Oct. 12
E. J. Frazier, block 7, lot 6
Byron E. Dye, block 15, lot 2
R. M. Salisbury, block 28, lot 3
Nov. 24, Hy. L. Hahn, block 28, lot 13
Nov. 29
Charles F. Smith, block 1, lot 17
Geo. Weideman, sold by Bernard, block 10, lot 5
S. G. Truett, block 10, lot 6
1861
Jan. 29
C. Caniume, block 1, lot 29
(W. Griffith) P. Horton, block 15, lot 1
J. Enders, block 31, lot 3
April 3, Asa Maddox, block 30, lot 9
Aug. 8, Mrs. Sarah Luck, block 6, lot 4
Aug. 8, B. A. James, block 1, lot 7
Dec. 28, John C. Hodgen, block 3, lot 12
1862
March 18
R. H. Nelson, block 33, lot 4
H. B. Holman—David C. Gillette, block 32, lot 8
Henry Grosshopf, block 15, lot 6
I. O. O. F., block 16, lot 7
April 6, R. T. Gambrel, paid by W. J. Gambrel, Adm., block 16, lot 8
May 1
Elizabeth York, block 2

D. Hindman, paid by W. Peacock, Adm., block 16, lot 9
July, Simeon B. Kerr, canceled, block 35, lot 3
July, Thos. R. Lord, part, block 3, lot 23
Aug. 2, Fritz Hollinghausen, block 28, lot 12
Aug. 9, Jordan O. Waldron, block 1, lot 6
Sept. 24, Joseph Haefner, block 28, lot 4
1861, January, Nancy L. Simpson, block 28, lot 9
1862
Oct. 5, W. W. Talley, block 29, lot 6
Nov. 4, Mrs. Julie E. Simpson, block 35, lot 18
Nov. 13, James A. Hutcheson, block 35, lot 17
Dec. 18, R. G. Stevens, block 1, lot 25
Dec. 28, C. W. Fairman, block 34, lot 7
1863
Jan. 10, S. W. Kelley, block 37, lot 7
Jan. 10, R. S. Hale, block 34, lot 6
March 1, J. T. Quarles, block 27, lot 9
March 8, F. Langsenkamp, block 28, lot 5
March 8, J. C. McCoy, block 32, lots 5 and 4
March 8, Dr. J. Lykins—T. S. Case, block 34, lot 1
May 26, J. R. Babbitt, block 28, lot 10
1862
Aug. 12, C. E. Kearny, block 1, lot 13
Aug. 12, Ed. Price, block 1, lot 14
Nov. 6, Golden Square Lodge A. T. M., block 26, lot 4
1863
J. W. Parker, block 11, lot 2
Feb. 13, George A. Horning, block 3, lot 26
April 17, Mrs. Kate McGee, block 6, lot 5
April 29, Lewis Vogle, block 3, lot 13
May 30, Frederick Klaber, block 3, lot 11
June, H. B. Connell, block 1, lot S. ½ 27
1864
T. C. Patton, block 31, lot 2
Jan. 15, Michael Windolph, block 28, lot 6
Jan. 22, Robert Dunbar, block 27, lot 8
Jan. 30, Thomas James, block 7, lot 6½
Feb. 10, E. F. Rogers, block 29, lot 1
Feb. 23, Atchison Campbell, block 33, lot 44½
March 10, A. R. Sinclair (S. ½), block 1, lot 12
March 19, D. G. Blair, block 6, lot 6
March 23, A. P. Haller, block 6, lot 3
April 16, Mrs. Ann Chick, block 3, lot 17
1863
May 2, Annual Meeting
July 8, Rev. Alexander Machette, block 6, lot 5
Aug. 1, T. P. Boteler, block 10, lot 4
Nov. 11, John J. Delashmutt, block 1, lot 2
1864
June 12, Wm. Hooks, block 1, lot 16
June 12, L. and T. B. Bullene, block 1, lot 26
June 18, George Debus, block 39, lot 4
July 25, Christ. Heintzelman, block 28, lot 11

Aug. 9, Hiram Cooper, block 1, lot 10
Aug. 2, P. W. Ditsch, block 29, lot 9
Aug. 26, Gertrude Rucker?—Charles Long, block 55, lot 12
Aug. 28, Capt A. J. Lloyd, block 53, lot 11
Sept. 3, F. Esslinger, block 29, lot 3
Sept. 18, John W. Black, block 43, lot 3
Sept. 26, Mrs. Sarah Mehaffey (?), block 3, lot 29
Sept. 28, J. C. Wilhite (Sold back to cemetery), block 53, lot 2
Oct. 15, A. Fernald, block 55, lot 4
1865
Feb. 4, B. M. Genette (Jenette?), block 3, lot 16
Feb. 4, S. Smith, block 1, lot 11
March 1, N. Holmes, block 1, lot 24
March 14, Charles Long, block 3, lot 9
March 14, J. W. Summers, paid Susan A. Summers, block 3, lot 27
March 7, Dr. J. H. Bennett, paid by B. L. Riggins, Fraction, block 54, lot 12
March 23, America A. Walker, block 35, lot 1
April 17
Mrs. Robert Laish, block 6, lot 8
A. Ellenberger, block 29, lot 7
W. J. Huckett, block 52, lot 10
May 1, 1865—Annual Meeting
May 17, Major H. H. Williams (This lot purchased by Cemetery Co., Nov., 1870), block 37, lot 2
June 9, J. R. Ham, block 52, lot 9
June 14, J. A. Walker, block 32, lot 2
June 14, Mrs. Salina Ackerman and John E. Meily, block 52, lot 11
June 20, Robt. A. Shore, block 6, lot 2
June 22, R. J. Lewis, block 36, lot 4
July, T. D. Thatcher (Simeon Kerr), block 35, lot 3
Oct. 2, J. W. McDonald, block 32, lot S ½
Nov. 9, Henry D. Gillett, block 42, lot 5
Dec. 5, R. C. Crowell (?), block 37, lot 8
Dec. 11, Anton Schurlein, block 3, lot 5
1866
Joseph Chew, block 17, lot 5
Jan. 6, Peter Partonner, block 5, lot 5
Jan. 22, S. B. Bell, block 17, lot 6
Feb. 15, Mrs. Carrie M. Stevens, block 43, lot 5
Jan. 29, Oliver Marsh, block 34, lot 2
March 2, William Culver, block 35, lot 15
April 14, T. B. Lester, block 52, lot 2
April 14, Frank Duncan, F. M. & J. S., block 53, lot 6
Reported all of the above at the Annual Meeting, May 7, 1866
May 16, Christian Myer, block 3, lot 32
Sept. 26, Philip Becker, block 3, lot 31
Nov. 7, Moses Wolf, block 29, lot 8
Nov. 27
Wilhelmine Hedding, block 1, fr. lot 1
Cyrus Rice, block 30, lot 10
John McCornish, block 6, lot 1
Christian Glanz, block 35, lot 34
Robert Boggs, block 7, lot 6
Chris W. Widerman, block 10, lot 7
Sam Rucker, block 35, lot 46
May 24, R. A. Bagly, block 36, lot 61
May 24, Wm. Douglass, block 35, S ½ lot 23
May 29, Benjamin F. Allen, block 38, lot 8
July 14, Matthias Marty, block 34, lot 4
Aug. 6, R. C. Walpole, block 10, lot 8
Aug. 12, P. Schneitzgabel, block 29, lot 2
Aug. 14, K. Coates, block 51, lot 4
Aug. 25, John M. Wise, block 39, lot 5
Sept. 1, W. E. Whiting, block 26, lot B
Sept. 8, W. O. Booher, block 45, lot 4
Sept. 14, Mrs. Permelia Engles, block 40, lot 2
Sept. 15
George Leasch and John Moss, block 26, lot 2
Mrs. Sarah Gossett, paid by Dr. Porter, block 40, lot 3
W. U. Wiley, block 40, lot 1
J. E. McKenzie, block 59, lot 4
G. W. Toler, block 54, S ½ lot 14
J. W. Brothers, block 54, lot 15
Oct. 27, Mrs. M. Dowling, block 52, lot 5
Oct. 26, Benjamin Yelton, block 53, lot 12
Nov. 20, S. H. Estabrook, block 59, lot 3
Nov. 20, A. F. Bidwell, block 59, lot 2
Nov. 20, Jesse Ray, 3 single graves
Nov. 30
Geo. W. Branham, block 52, lot 3
C. J. Thompson, block 53, lot 13
M. Dively, block 52, lot 4
Dec. 13, Madison M. St. Clair, block 52, lot 7
1867
Jan. 11, Frederick Schoelten, block 38, lot 9
Jan. 9, John Taylor, block 14, lot 2
Feb. 4, F. P. and E. Flagler, block 52, lot 8
Feb. 1, W. M. Rogers, block 55, lot 1
Feb. 7, John Campbell, block 51, lot 3
April 18, Alexander Majors, block 52, lot 6
May 6, Thomas Haslett, block 25, lot 1
May 6, Sol. Smith, block 52, lot 15
June 15, Dr. A. C. Woodard, block 52, lot 12
June 15, R. Arendorff, block 52, lot 12
June 15, J. Q. Watkins, block 51, lot 5
June 10, Henry Borgstede, block 46, lot 2
June 11, Louis Deardorff, block 53, lot 15
June 13
Ernst Hempel, block 38, lot 12
D. S. Twitchell, block 53, lot 16
J. A. J. Chapman, block 35, lot 45
F. Hez, block 38, lot 11
E. A. Phillips, block 68, lot 4
June 10, Wm. Sower, block 16, lot 6
June 21, August Neil, block 38, lot 13
June 24, Heirs of Wm. A. Hopkins, block 54, lot 3
Sept. 12, B. F. Smith, block 5, lot 4
Sept. 19
Wilson Askew, block 25, lot 4

CEMETERIES—KAW TOWNSHIP

Rev. Frazier, donated, block 53, lot 5
Mrs. Mary Clinton, block 14, lot 3
J. Strimple, block 5, lot 6
Oct. 8, Benjamin Simpson, block 1, lot 22
Nov. 22, Misses Emma and Sarah Allen, block 55, lot 2
Nov. 28, Mrs. May Vipond (?), block 56, lot 12
Nov. 28, Benjamin F. Hewitt, block 19, lot 8
Nov. 28, James Swaney, block 19, lot 9
Dec. 30, H. Tobener, block 52, lot 13
Dec. 30, R. A. Ball, block 28, lot 7
1868
Jan. 29, Jacob Bernard, block 27, lots 4 and 5
Feb. 1, Joseph S. Chick, block 37, lots 1 and 10
Feb. 18, John S. Allen, block 40, lot 5
March 14, Mrs. Kate Thayer, block 41, lot 8
March 15, Henry E. Brown, block 55, lot 3
March 17, Mrs. Kate Simpson, block 52, lot 14
April 14, Henry Topping, block 41, lot 7
April 21, H. J. Clark, block 39, lot 1
April 29, Catherine E. Brammel, block 41, lot 6
1868
May 18, David Kendall, block 25, lot 6
May 29, Edith Black, block 14, lot 1
May 11, James W. Cook, block 54, lot 4
May 26, Thos. A. Smart, block 55, lots 13 and 14
June 1, S. Noyes, block 40, lot 4
July 18, William Townsend, block 54, lot 16
Aug. 19, Mrs. Mary Messersmith, block 54, lot 17
Sept. 25, Mrs. C. Birkley, block 39, lot 6
Oct. 6, Wm. Garrett, D. Ellison, block 54, lot 1
Oct. 6, L. A. Garrett, J. A. Garrett, block 54, lot 2
Sept. 14, Mrs. Bouton, block 54, lot 5
Sept. 10, John Kimmons, block 53, lot 12
Oct. 4, E. H. Gregg, block 38, lot 14
Oct. 19, Geo. W. Rarens and Augustus Staunch, block 9, lot 8
Oct. 23, Elias H. Gregg (Crossed out), block 38, lot 14
Nov. 24, August Hoffmeister
Nov. 24, D. R. Wilson
Dec. 14, S. B. Cauliflower
1869
Jan. 15, M. Bailey, block 55, lot 5
Jan. 15, J. S. Ambrose, block 55, lot 7
Feb. 1
P. S. Gidley, block 42, lot 8
Mary Harmon, block 54, lot 18
George Threlkeld, block 39, lot 8
April 17
R. W. Quade, block 39, lot 7
Mary Mumms, block 52, lot 16
G. H. Smith, block 4, lot 5
Mrs. Jane Jarboe, block 53, lot 14
Henry Jobes' heirs, block 4, S ½ lot 5

July 13, Walbridge and Mitchell, block 53, lot 17
July 19, William Gilliss, block 51, lot 2
July 29, A. G. Bodwell, block 4, lot 6
July 30, T. W. Letters, block 39, lot 9
Aug. 5, Luther H. Wood, block 55, lot 15
Aug. 11, G. E. Pitkin, block 53, lot 4
Aug. 23, W. P. Winner, block 4, lot 7
Sept. 10, E. J. Eby, block 55, lot 6
Sept. 14, J. R. Balis, block 51, lot 6
Sept. 15, H. N. Smith, block 52, lot 17
Sept. 17, T. K. Hanna, block 54, lot 6
Sept. 27, Wm. Evans, block 4, lot 4
Oct. 18, Jesse Riddlesbarger (see note)** block 15, lot 35
Oct. 18, Mrs. L. C. Dennison and others (E. Latimore), block 55, lot 18
Oct. 4, T. T. Arerly (Marked out), block 54, lot 21
Oct. 13, Chas. Thomas, block 4, lot 3
Oct. 13, Wm. P. Cunningham, block 32, lot 1
Dec. 17, Dr. John T. Lock, block 26, lot 5
Dec. 9, A. L. Charles, block 27, lot 1
Dec. 29, Heroine Lodge A. F. M., block 35, lot 49
1870
Feb., Mrs. E. Boult, block 53, lot 17
Feb. 11, F. A. Tappan, block 53, lot 17
Feb. 14, M. Muehlschuster, block 54, lot 7
Feb., F. D. and B. F. Jones, block 35, lot 19
March 17, W. H. Sutton, block 15, lot 4
March 26, Alvah Mansur, block 53, lot 18
April 11, H. J. Latshaw, block 41, lot 2
April 16, F. H. Liscum, block 53, lot 19
April 9, Mrs. A. J. Warren, block 37, S ½ lot 3
April 5, L. C. Smith, block 56, lot 19
April 23, Wm. W. Bissell, block 59, lot 1
April 28, H. L. Burnham, block 52, lot 1
1869 (Reported May 1870)
June 11, Hamilton Finney, block 40, lot 13
June 22, Solomon Houck, block 16, lot 55
July 28, Jas. G. Hamilton, block 4, lot 30
Sept. 25, F. H. Booth, block 3, lot 15
Dec. 7, John F. Locke, block 26, lot 5
May 6, William Sechrest, block 36, N ½ lot 1
June 29, Edward Masuch, block 57, lot 7
June 6, J. P. Hamblin, block 53, lot 8
June 30, Wallace Pratt, block 54, lot 10
June 30, Wm. Todd, block 53, lot 7
July 11, David Craig, block 53, lot 10
July 4, J. M. Smith, block 53, lot 9
July 15, Warwick Hough, block 54, lot 8
July 24, Robertson Bros., block 35, lot 24
July 24, Z. Culbertson, block 54, lot 20
July 25, A. and J. E. Fisher, block 55, lot 8
July 30, John S. Harris, block 1, lot 23
**(This note found at bottom of page) Jesse Riddlesbarger has deed for lot 35, block 15, bought Oct. 18, 1869, and deed issued. Where is his lot? Must be lot 14, block 35.

July 30, Joseph L. Norman, block 23, lot 3
Aug. 8, T. B. Bullene, block 2, lot 3
Aug. 23, John Phillips, block 55, lot 10
Sept. 10, M. B. Napton (Crossed out), block 35, lot 48
Sept. 23, John C. Warnecke, block 55, lot 9
Sept. 23, Nancy Minners, block 19, S ½ lot 10
Sept. 5, J. H. Gillin, block 19, N ½ lot 10
Sept. 7, H. S. Millett, block 54, lot 22
Sept. 9, Frederick Frank, block 37, lot 9
Sept. 17, B. A. Bailey, block 19, S ½ lot 11
Oct. 4, R. S. Brown, block 5, lot 11
Oct. 19, Joseph Miller (Crossed out)
Oct. 22, P. G. Wilhite, block 2, lot 1
Nov. 7, Lucy R. Rule (Vacated 3-25-71), block 35, lot 43
Nov. 21, A. C. Dyas, block 25, lot 5
Nov. 14, George Long, block 3, lot 10
Nov. 30, T. B. Bullene, block 2, lot 4
Dec. 9, D. A. James, block 25, lot 3
1871
Jan. 3, R. Hausing, block 55, S ½ lot 10
Jan. 3, Virgil C. Wood, block 41, N ¼ lot 8
Feb. 3, Mrs. Martha Welsh, block 40, lot 12
Feb. 20, Robert Irwin, block 54, S ½ lot 19
March 11, Mrs. Robert Skinner, block 38, S ½ lot 15
March 3, Wm. M. Clark, block 19, S ½ lot 12
March 4, Wm. Holmes and C. W. Bryan, block 35, lot 43
March 21, Mrs. Anna S. Drury, block 54, N ½ lot 19
April 8, F. L. McHenry, block 56, lot 1
April 17, John Kinnar, block 56, N ½ lot 19
April 27, Isaac F. Lawler, block 1, N ½ lot 3
April 29, Susie Paine, block 15, N ½ lot 4
May 12, Chas. Whitehead, block 1, S ½ lot 3
May 23, J. E. Chambers, block 57, lot 1
June 24, E. Lynde, block 55, lot 20
June 28, R. A. Hoffman, block 56, lot 22
June 5, James Ford, block 56, S ½ lot 20
June 5, B. S. Henning, block 55, lot 22
June 8, Dean S. Kelley, block 54, lot 9
June 8, A. L. Hosmer, block 24, lot 4
June 16, C. O. Tichenor, block 53, lot 20
June 18, E. Lynde (Crossed out), block 55, lot 20
June 26, G. W. Mapes, block 3, S ½ lot 33
June 26, R. A. Hoffman (Crossed out), block 56, lot 22
June 29, J. Feld, block 57, lot 21
July 6, Mrs. James D. Nelson (?), block 56, N ½ lot 20
July 20, Geo. B. Wheeler, block 37, lot 2
July 27, J. W. Keefer, block 16, lot 5
July 31, John Elliot, block 56, N ½ lot 21
Aug. 10, John R. Griffin (Crossed out)
Sept. 10, Mrs. Eliza Carpenter, block 55, lot 11
Sept. 22, A. A. Goodman, block 54, lot 11
Sept. 29, John P. Withers, block 37, N ½ lot 3
Sept. 4, J. W. Byers and J. L. Kelley, block 10, lot 3
Sept. 6, Ermine Case, block 55, lot 19
Sept. 7, Frederick A. Eckhard, block 56, N ½ lot 18
Sept. 8, A. D. Madeira, block 14, lot 5
Sept. 19, A. L. Mason, block 44, lot 1
Sept. 22, Albert F. Allen, block 3, N ½ lot 33
Sept. 25, G. W. Lovejoy, block 57, lot 8
Oct. 11, Henry H. Bedgood, block 56, S ½ lot 18
Oct. 14, George P. Olmstead, block 4, lot 8
Oct. 23, F. H. Kump, block 3, lot 8
Oct. 26, Minor T. Graham, block 53, lot 1
Nov. 3, C. F. Quest, block 3, lot 1
Nov. 8, H. C. Train, block 57, lot 10
Dec. 4, L. S. Cady, block 16, lot 3
Dec. 9, E. Schwanenfeldt, block 5, lot 7
Dec. 21, James Thayer, block 56, S ½ lot 21
1872
Jan. 2, W. M. Runnelly, block 3, N ½ lot 35
Jan. 11, L. C. Slavens, block 55, lot 21
Jan. 22, Wm. A. Benton, block 7, lot 9
Jan. 27, R. M. Quarles, block 45, N ½ lot 19
Feb. 1, Richard Melville, block 57, N ½ lot 9
Feb. 8, A. G. Nugent, block 16, lot 5
Feb. 17, N. C. Scoville, block 40, lot 11
Feb. 19, Mrs. Maggie Buckly, block 4, lot 2
Feb. 22, Mrs. Lettia Raulins, block 3, S ½ lot 35
March 4, Dr. Geo. Halley, block 1, lot 19
March 11, J. S. Martin, area 222 feet, block 41, lot 1
March 23, J. Riordan, block 44, S ½ lot 2
March 28, G. W. Mitchell, block 4, lot 10
April 3, Wm. Lackman, block 4, lot 1
April 8, F. R. Allen, block 35, S ½ lot 44
April 12, E. W. Pierce, block 37, lot 4
April 25, J. R. Cline, block 38, lot 5
April 26, A. G. Nugent, block 16, lot 4
April 26, Mary Ann Lee, block 40, S ½ lot 11
May 20, R. B. Woodson, block 35, lot 47
June 1, J. C. Howell, block 57, S ½ lot 9
June 3, Wm. Lackman, block 4, lot 1
June 27, D. M. Eaton, block 42, S ½ lot 6
June 20, Wm. Allender, 10x12, block 24, S ½ lot 6
July 1, S. D. and J. N. Irwin, block 24, lot 5
July 5, Estate of S. B. Wade
Aug. 2, Joseph Thayer, block 5, S ½ lot 1
Aug. 11, E. W. Pattison, block 56, lot 11
Aug. 16, W. C. Newcomb, block 38, lot 7
Aug. 16, F. M. Black, 10x12, block 24, N ½ lot 6
1871
Aug., John Archer, block 45, S ½ lot 3
Aug. 21, J. Brumback, block 14, lot 7
Aug. 14, Blake L. Woodson, block 54, N ½ lot 14

Aug. 28, James Port, block 16, lot 2
Sept. 9, Louis Kraus, block 27, S ½ lot 2
Sept. 17, R. W. Hillicker, block 56, lot 2
Sept. 22, Wm. Haltzell, 200 feet, block 36, lot 8
Oct. 8, T. J. Anders, block 5, N ½ lot 30
Nov. 2, Alex Eagle, block 42, N ½ lot 6
Dec. 3, J. P. Anderson, block 23, lot 4
Dec. 11, C. Q. Follett, block 14, lot 8

1873
Jan. 2, D. M. Keys, block 3, S ½ lot 30
Feb. 11, William Lewis, block 38, lot 40

A MONUMENT FOR FIFTEEN CONFEDERATE SOLDIERS
UNION CEMETERY
KANSAS CITY, MISSOURI

The following inscriptions have been copied from the two Bronze Tablets which are found on a Granite Shaft in Union Cemetery:

"ERECTED BY
THE
UNITED STATES
TO MARK THE BURIAL PLACE OF
FIFTEEN CONFEDERATE SOLDIERS WHO DIED
AT KANSAS CITY, MISSOURI, WHILE PRISONERS OF WAR
AND WHOSE REMAINS WERE BURIED
IN THE CITY CEMETERY AND SUBSEQUENTLY REMOVED
TO THIS CEMETERY, WHERE THE INDIVIDUAL GRAVES
CANNOT NOW BE IDENTIFIED."

Jacob W. Blackenship, Co. A, Love's Mo. Reg.
Abram W. Blythe, Co. A, Smith's Ark. Reg.
Alexander Cates, Co. L, Love's Mo. Reg.
Jos. G. Hopkins, Co. G, Nichol's Mo. Reg.
Wm. K. McConnell, Co. H, McGehee's Ark. Reg.
Andrew S. Medley, Co. I, Green's Mo. Reg.
Francis Mitchell, Co. —, Mo. Reg.
Daniel F. Pitts, Co.   ·, Ark. Reg.
Alexander Rodgers, Co. —, Nichol's Mo. Reg.
Jefferson Self, Co. —-, Coleman's Mo. Reg.
Josiah Smith, Co. E, Nichol's Mo. Reg.
Walter Smotherman, Co. H, McGehee's Ark. Reg.
Seward Taylor, Co. C, McGehee's Ark. Reg.
John A. Turner, Co. E, Wood's Battn., Mo. Cav.
Charles Yarbough, Co. C, Nichol's Mo. Reg.

LIST OF INTERMENTS IN UNION CITY CEMETERY, KANSAS CITY, JACKSON COUNTY, MISSOURI, AS RECORDED IN ROLL OF HONOR, VOL. 10, PAGES 34, 35 and 36

The following list sent to Mrs. Hale Houts by the War Department, Washington, D. C.

Number, Name, Rank, Regiment and Company

1, Able, Jos., 43rd Mo.
2, Baling, Christian, Private, 13th Mo. Cav., Co. A
3, Blankernst, J. W., Private, Kansas Cav., Co. A
4, Bransin, Levi T., Private, 3rd M. S. M. Cav.
5, Cate, Jno., Private, 43rd, Co. H
6, Chase, Jno. H., 17th Ind.
7, Cooper, Thos., Private, 6th Kans. Cav., Co. E
8, Filly, Jno., Private, 23rd, Co. H

9, Gilpatrick, E., Private, 43rd Mo.
10, Hannegan, Jno., Private, 2nd Colo. Cav.
11, Hardner, W.
12, Harkner, Frank
13, Heath, Wm., Private, 13th M. S. M. Cav., Co. D
14, K——, J. W., 3rd Wis.
15, Kea, J. S. A., Private, 4th M. S. M. Cav.
16, Johnson, Jno., Private, 4th ——, Co. A
17, McMurray, Robt., Private, 1st Kans. Cav.
18, Mollzie, Jas., —— Kans.
19, Moore, Thos., Private, 43rd ——
20, Rivers, D., Private, 5th Kans. Cav., Co. I
21, Smith, Jas. A., Private, M. S. M. Cav., Co. C
22 through 139 Unknowns
140, Woodburn, Jas., Private, 7th Kans. Cav., Co. C

UNION CEMETERY

Copied from the tombstones by Mrs. Max A. Christopher and Mrs. Hale Houts

A

Ackers, Paulina, b. in Berlin, Germany, June 20, 1838, d. Feb. 5, 1907
Ackerman, Henry, b. 1830, d. 1865
Ackerman, Sabina, b. 1831, d. 1902
Ackerson, Andrew, b. Feb. 25, 1837, died April 9, 1884; age, 47 years
Adams, Bertha Porman (mother), d. June 19, 1901; age, 68 years
Adams, Mary A., b. April 7, 1818, d. Jan. 22, 1882
Adams, John Q., of Action C. H., d. May 6, 1819; age, 21 years, 10 months, 15 days
Adams, John W., b. May 2, 1840, d. Aug. 12, 1869
Adams, Green A., b. 1845, d. 1919
Adams, Jeff (Government marker)
Adams, Harriet, d. March 12, 1892; age, 83 or 63 years
Addington, J. A., Co. "A" 147 Ind. Inf. (Gov. marker)
Addington, Nancy, b. in Virginia in 1830, d. May 6, 1917
Addington, Carrie, b. in Virginia, dates not readable
Ailor, William P. (husband), b. April 10, 1848, d. Dec. 20, 1899
Akers, Frank W., d. Nov. 22, 1899; age, 38 years
Albery, Martha A., wife of Richard Albery, b. July 30, 1829, d. Nov. 3, 1896
Alexander, Annie E., b. Feb. 5, 1855; d. Nov. 10, 1897
Alexander, James Albert (father), d. May 3, 1892; age, 57 years
Alexander, S. J., no dates
Allen, George, b. May 17, 1800, d. Nov. 17, 1867
Allen, Sarah H., d. January 24, 1887; age, 57 years
Allen, Corporal, Amos W., Co. "K" 26 Ill. Inf. (Gov. marker)
Allen, Franklin R., d. Feb. 19, 1897; age, 72 years
Allen, Edwin A., d. Jan. 8, 1893; age, 69 years
Allen, Jude (father), d. Nov. 30, 1872; age, 77 years, 3 months, 26 days
Allen, Caroline Wells, b. 1833, d. 1910
Allen, John Stewart, b. 1829, d. 1879 (Acting Asst. Paymaster, U. S. Navy—Gov. marker)
Allaire, Jas. P., b. in New York City; age, 83 years
Allaire, Susan M., wife of J. P. Allaire, b. in New Jersey; age, 86 years
Allis, William, d. Nov. 2, 1866; age, 21 years, 10 months, 29 days
Alton, Richard Arley, d. July 19, 1900; age, 35 years
Ambrose, Hannah, wife of Eld. Joseph Ambrose, d. April 1, 1870 (?) D. A. R. Marker as Daughter of a Revolutionary Soldier

Anders, Jennie E. Fegus, b. Aug. 30, 1845, d. Oct. 5, 1872
Anders, Alwilda J. Roach, wife of Thomas J. Anders, b. Feb. 23, 1851, d. Aug. 11, 1905
Andre, Karl, d. Nov., 1869; age, 42 years
Andrews, Grace Hope, no dates
Anderson, Henry, b. 1856, d. 1899
Anderson, A., b. 1818, d. 1907
Anderson, May A., b. May 1, 1848, d. Oct. 9, 1911
Angell, Lena M., d. March 9, 1910; age, 55 years (mother)
Andrus, Loomis, d. Oct. 1, 1848; age, 32 years
Andrus, William L., d. Dec. 23, 1872; age, 23 years
Anton, John A., d. May 20, 1883; age, 54 years, 1 month, 21 days
Arnold, Ida J., wife of S. H., b. April 9, 1857, d. March 25, 1894
Arnott, Bertram, b. in Edinburgh, 1850, d. 1902
Asashe, Chas., b. 1864, d. 1893
Ashley, J. G., b. Aug. 18, 1834, d. Jan. 10, 1924
Ashley, Minerva, wife of J. G. Ashley, b. May —, 1839, d. May 29, 1898
Atkinson, Margaret A. (mother), b. 1814, d. 1897
Atkinson, Joseph, b. 1814, d. 1885
Atwater, Delia, d. July 20, 1895; age, 27 years
Austin, Fanny, wife of Edward Austin, b. in North Wales, d. in Kansas City May 9, 1888
Austin, J. C., Gunner, U. S. Navy—Government marker
Averitt, Nathaniel O., b. Sept. 21, 1846, d. March 6, 1909

B

Babcock, Mrs. N. M., d. April 8, 1870; age, 66 years
Baer, Agnes, wife of Jacob Baer, b. Sept. 21, 18—, d. (too worn to read)
Baerman, Friedrich, b. April 9, 1822, d. Dec. 1, 1891
Baerman, Amela, b. Aug. 9, 1822, d. April 28, 1901
Bagly, Mrs. Mary E., d. June 3, 1866; age, 25 years, 7 months, 10 days
Baggs, Dr. H. W., d. Jan. 18, 1897; age, 61 years
Bailey, Eddie, son of Joseph and Emma Bailey, b. July 3, 1872, d. Nov., 1876
Bair, Fanny B., d. May 14, 1897 (no age given)
Baker, John F., b. Dec. 5, 1816, d. Nov. 26, 1885 (Soldier)
Baker, Elizabeth A., b. July 7, 1824, d. Jan. 10, 1902
Baker, Isabella J., wife of Isaac G. Baker, and daughter of Joseph C. and Margaret K. Davis, b. Oct. 1, 1830, d. Aug. 22, 1859
Baldwin, Sylvester P., b. April 19, 1849, d. Sept. 18, 1904
Bales, Walter Muretree, b. Dec. 15, 1869, d. Sept. 26, 1873
Bales, John B., d. April 22, 1893; age, 33 years
Ball, Anna Maud (mother), b. 1833, d. 1891
Ballintine, Eustasiah, wife of M. R. Ballintine, d. April 29, 1885; age, 34 years
Bankart, Kesia W., wife of Percy Bankart, b. in Columbus, Ohio, Jan. 15, 1844, d. March 25, 1885
Banta, Levis, d. Dec. 25, 1881; age, 46 years, 3 months, 29 days
Barber, Charles V. (father), b. 1849, d. 1925
Barber, Mary M., b. Dec. 3, 1833, d. March 28, 1922
Barber, William R., b. Oct. 20, 1831, d. Feb. 5, 1895
Barger, Cora Bell, b. April 21, 1876, d. Sept. 10, 1897
Barnum, Frank, d. Oct. 6, 1876; age, 44 years
Barnes, Ella, wife of J. J. Barnes, b. Jan. 26, 1853, d. Aug. 17, 1895
Barnett, Jonathan, b. Oct. 11, 1825, d. April 25, 1878
Barnett, Sarah Covell, b. Nov. 16, 1829, d. Jan. 1, 1913
Barker, Samuel, d. Dec. 4, 1871; age, 66 years
Barker, Elizabeth, wife of Sam'l Barker, d. March 21, 1865; age, 62 years
Barrett, Adaline, b. 1822, d. 1903
Barron, Charles F., b. March 13, 1832, d. April 24, 1882
Bass, children of R. T. and Juliet M. Bass

Baum, Jacob, d. Aug. 7, 1877; age, 75 years
Bavens, George H. C., b. March 15, 1809, d. Aug. 3, 1860
Bavens, —— (probably wife, name not readable), b. May 15, 1801, d. Feb. 15, 1859
Beamer, Emily J., wife of W. S., d. Aug. 5, 1872; age, 36 years
Becker, Mrs. Annie, d. Nov. 13, 1894; age, 50 years
Becker, Nickles, d. Oct. 25, 1906; age, 62 years
Becker, Margaret, d. Oct. 26, 1909; age, 62 years
Belinder, Hannah Cecilia, daughter of A. G. and Hannah Belinder, d. June 7, 1891; age, 7 years, 11 months
Bell, C. N. (Soldier), b. 1841, d. 1900
Bell, Margaret (mother), b. 1827, d. 1909
Bell, Joseph Edgar, son of W. H. and Mary R. Bell, d. June 26, 1863; age, 13 months
Bell, Thomas O., b. Nov. 25, 1859, d. July 16, 1898
Bell, Lt. Clayton H., Co. "C" 14th Kentucky Cav. (Government marker)
Bell, D. H. L., b. 1823, d. 1894
Bell, Frances V., b. 1822, d. 1872
Bell, Hannah L., b. 1825, d. 1899
Bell, Frances D., b. 1850, d. 1874
Bethmann, Julius, b. Aug. 10, 1830, d. June 8, 1900
Betzer, Emma L., b. 1858, d. 1900
Belts, Jane, wife of Mark Belts, d. Sept. 30, 1886; age, 55 years
Bender, Elizabeth E., b. July 17, 1834, d. June 10, 1905
Bendon, Richard, Co. "D" 13th Indiana Cavalry, b. in Ireland 1838, d. Aug. 13, 1885; age, 38 years
Benjamin, George A. (M. D.), b. Jan. 8, 1828, d. March 13, 1891
Bender, Melvin, son of J. H. and Kate Bender, d. Sept. 2, 1872; age, 1 year, 5 days
Bennett, Mary, b. Aug. 4, 1849, d. Oct. 11, 1905
Bennefeld, Alfred, b. Nov. 18, 1854, d. May 21, 1900
Benney, W. F., d. Oct. 29, 1893; age, 48 years; Co. "L" 2nd Regiment Wisconsin Vol.
Berkley, Benjamin F., b. Aug. 7, 1828, d. Sept. 25, 1868
Berkley, Nancy C., wife of Benjamin Berkley, b. May 28, 1825, d. Jan. 19, 1908
Bernard, Margaret Elizabeth, b. Dec. 27, 1830, d. May 30, 1851
Bernard, William R., b. Dec. 8, 1823, d. Nov. 25, 1906
Bernard, Susan H., b. June 27, 1834, d. April 9, 1895
Bernard, Joab, b. July 12, 1800, d. April 30, 1879
Bernard, Bell, d. Dec. 17, 1851, d. Jan. 27, 1868
Beroth, James O., b. Jan. 4, 1853, d. May 6, 1899
Bickel, J. P. (stone broken and only name visible)
Bicking, Valentine, d. July 26, 1905; age, 75 years
Bicking, Jane, d. April 7, 1880; age, 47 years
Biddle, Edgar M., b. Dec. 13, 1857, d. Dec. 17, 1891
Bidwell, Emily A., b. 1846, d. 1902
Bidwell, Frank L., b. Sept. 24, 1856, d. Sept. 14, 1931
Bidwell, Alonzo, d. Nov. 17, 1870; age, 47 years, 5 months, 16 days (Soldier)
Bidwell, George, died 1861
Bierley, Daniel Eckman (father), b. Oct. 17, 1839, d. June 24, 1910 (G. A. R. marker)
Bierley, Caroline Harriet (mother), b. June 27, 1842, d. April 29, 1927
Bigger, Katie Boyd, d. July 22, 1873; age, 5 years, 10 days
Bigger, Sam. W., b. Oct. 6, 1857, d. March 16, 1883
Bigger, Elizabeth E., wife of Dr. D. P. Bigger, b. Sept. 12, 1833, d. Aug. 17, 1873
*Bingham, George C. (Captain), b. March 20, 1811, d. July 7, 1879
Bingham, Henry W., b. —— 1847, d. Nov. 8, 1868
Bingham, Mattie L., b. 1824, d. 1890
Bird, J. P., b. 1855, d. 1894
Bishoff, John, b. Dec. 16, 1857, d. Feb. 10, 1908

*A painter of note

CEMETERIES—KAW TOWNSHIP

Bishoff, Henry, d. March 27, 1899; age, 49 years
Bischoff, Emma, b. March 10, 1852, d. July 26, 1891
Black, B. F., b. 1824, d. 1866
Black, Edith, wife of B. F. Black, b. 1825, d. 1901
Black, Edith (mother), b. 1787, d. 1868
Blackledor, J. M., Co. "A" 47th Indiana Infantry (Gov. marker)
Blackburn, Nellie M., b. Nov. 10, 1845, d. May 11, 1901
Blair, George D., son of D. C. and M. J. Blair, d. Sept. 13, 1857; age, 10 years
Bliss, Darwin H. (M. D.), b. June 20, 1852, d. Sept. 20, 1882
Blankens, Alice E., b. Nov. 2, 1851, d. May 4, 1900
Bloys, Mrs. Roxana A., b. June 6, 1835, d. July 16, 1880
Bloom, Peter, b. Nov. 16, 1841, d. July 7, 1902
Bluford, James G. (husband), d. April 29, 1893; age, ——
Boardman, Carrie E., wife of H. A. Boardman, d. June, 1884; age, 65 (?) years
Boese, John Henry, d. Feb. 21, 1895; age, 46 years
Boggs, Louisa A., b. April 17, 1851, d. Aug. 7, 1892
Boggs, Frederick G., son of J. R. and M. Boggs, d. ——, 1866
Boggs, Mary H., daughter of D. W. and T. J. Boggs, d. 1855; age, 20 years
Bolen, Samuel W., b. May 2, 1831, d. Sept. 16, 1889
Bolen, Harriet Ann, wife of John Bolen, b. Sept. 29, 1861, d. Jan. 5, 1886
Bolen, James A., b. 1846, d. 1921
Boles, Elam F., Co. "L" 2nd Nebraska Cavalry (Gov. marker)
Bombeck, Julius D., b. March 8, 1841, d. Sept. 19, 1884
Bombeck, A. Caroline, b. in Hamburg, Germany, Aug. 12, 1845, d. Aug. 9, 1876
Bombeck, A. A., b. March 25, 1839, d. Nov. 23, 1897
Bomgardner, Peter F., b. 1836, d. 1898 (father)
Borgstede, Henry, b. May 11, 1835, d. March 26, 1888
Boone, Mary, daughter of Jane Boone, b. May 1, 1870, d. July 18, 1876
Borchert, Emilie Y., b. July 5, 1844, d. June 29, 1897
Boullt, Emeline, b. Jan. 6, 1809, d. April 26, 1900
Boullt, Harry, d. Jan. 31, 1870; age, 20 years
Bouton, Henry B., d. Sept. 12, 1858; age, 53 years, 5 months, 19 days
Boyer, Effie, daughter of W. C. and Effie Boyer, b. Dec. 23, 1860, d. Jan. 18, 1883; age, 23 years, 26 days
Bowen, Carrie, d. March 10, 1896; age, 21 years
Bower, Catherine (mother), b. 1841, d. 1906
Bower, Merric B. (father), b. 1832, d. 1913
Bowman, Ellen, wife of N. B. Bowman, b. March 4, 1841, d. March 4, 1901
Bowker, Dr. Seth D., b. Feb. 10, 1830, d. June 8, 1901 (soldier)
Bodell, Fidelia, d. Sept. 21, 1902; age, 32 years
Brady, Henry, b. 1821, d. 1889
Brady, Rebecca, wife of Henry Brady, b. 1823, d. 1909
Bradley, Owen, d. June 7, 1888; age, 33 years
Braeunert, Emilie B. Geb., 10 Marzt 1806, Gest, 20 Marzt 1882
Braeunert, Unsere (mother)
Bramwell, Dr. H. V., d. April 27, 1868; age, 64 years
Bramwell, Catherine, wife of Dr. H. V. Bramwell, d. Oct. 21, 1892
Brand, Sarah E., d. Jan. 27, 1890; age, 36 years, 2 months, 23 days
Brand, Sarah Ann Brand, wife of John Kell, b. Feb. 5, 1831, d. Feb. 29, 1904
Brande, Caroline, wife of R. H. Brande, d. Sept. 28, 1896; age, 45 years
Brandt, H. C. (M. D.), b. in Christiana, Norway, in 1814, d. in Kansas City, Mo., April 8, 1893
Brandenburger, Julia, wife of A. Brandenburger, d. March 18, 1874; age, 36 years, 10 months, 10 days
Brandenburger, Lizzie, wife of A. Brandenburger, d. April, 1879

Branham, Margaret S., d. 4:30 p. m., April 2, 1882, at 1652 Madison Ave., Kansas City, Mo.; age, 23 years, 10 months, 4 days
Branham, William C., Co. "I" 137 Indiana Infantry (Gov. marker)
Branham, George W., b. Dec. 8, 1812, d. Aug. 1, 1885
Branham, Mary M., b. Oct. 5, 1818, d. Feb. 1, 1911
Brasington, Sarah A., b. 1845, d. 1903
Brice, Rev. J. C., b. 1800, d. 1889
Brice, Eliza P. True, wife of Rev. J. C. Brice, b. 1809, d. 1885
Bridges, Eliza, b. Aug. 18, 1848, d. March 20, 1893
Brigham, William A., b. 1840, d. 1929
Brigham, Lucinda, b. 1811, d. 1885
Bronson, Laura A. (mother), b. Jan. 19, 1831, d. July 31, 1897
Brooks, Elizabeth, wife of E. H. Brooks, b. July 11, 1829, d. March 11, 1877
Brown, Eunice J. (mother); age, 45 years (stone broken)
Brown, Amil Carl (father), b. 1831, d. 1899
Brown, Edward, b. 1840, d. 1913
Brown, Rhoda, b. 1847, d. 1922
Brown, John, dates invisible
Brown, Franklin B., d. March 23, 1869; age, 26 years, 6 months, 11 days
Brown, Sarah (mother), b. 1844, d. 1900
Brown, Paul R., d. July 8, 1909; age, 42 years
Brown, Harmore, son of Robert and Matilda Brown, b. April 16, 1850, d. July 7, 1926
Brown, Anna Nelson, wife of Harmore Brown, b. in Hjenarp, Sweden, Nov. 25, 1853, d. Nov. 20, 1928
Brown, Hugh, d. Oct. 14, 1905; age, 78 years
Brown, Ann Elizabeth, wife of Hugh Brown, d. March 7, 1899; age, 68 years
Brown, Cordelia, d. May 6, 1860; age, 7 years
Brown, H. C., b. March, 1836, d. October, 1875
Brown, Sarah Long, wife of H. C. Brown, b. May, 1833, d. April, 1876
Brown, Sarah Mehaffy, wife of Gideon Brown, b. 1816, d. 1890
Browne, Belinda C., b. 1809, d. 1886
Browne, Laura Booth, b. July 22, 1841, d. March 14, 1876
Brumback, Catherine Fullerton, wife of Jeff. Brumback, b. Oct. 29, 1834
Brunn, Hans, d. July 7, 1899; age, 66 years
Braun, Jacob, b. Dec. 13, 1847, d. Sept. 23, 1920
Bryant, Carrie, daughter of E. and M. Bryant, b. June 7, 1859, d. 1879
Bryant, Euphamia, d. March 31, 1888; age, 76 years
Brhrem, Frank, d. March 1, 1889; age, 62 years
Buck, Charles Mansfield, d. Dec. 18, 1901; age, 59 years, 10 months
Buchanan, Rebecca A., d. April 7, 1893; age, 40 years
Bucher, Samuel, b. 1825, d. 1879
Bucher, Margaret, wife of Samuel Bucher, b. 1827, d. 1915
Bucher, Lizzie, b. 1847, d. 1887
Bucher, Jennie Erwin, b. 1849, d. 1908
Buckle, Jno. (Gov. marker)
Budd, Barney, b. Jan. 25, 1827, d. March 22, 1875
Bugsch, Samuel, b. Feb. 17, 1851, d. Oct. 28, 1894
Bullock, George W., b. June 4, 1839, d. Dec. 5, 1909 (father)
Bulyar, Adam, b. July 12, 1817, d. Nov. 1, 1895
Bulyar, Mary, b. Jan. 1, 1819, d. Oct. 6, 1899
Bundy, Solon S., d. Feb. 4, 1901; age, 54 years, 9 months, 16 days
Bunz, Jacob, d. March 5, 1886; age, 46 years
Bunz, Augustine (mother), b. 1853, d. 1930
Burden, George W. (brother), d. Nov. 19, 1897; age, 48 years
Burton, Josiah H., b. March 12, 1831, d. Dec. 6, 1918; Co. "F" 1st Ill. Art. (Gov. marker)
Burton, Alice T., b. Feb. 7, 1833, d. July 19, 1923

CEMETERIES—KAW TOWNSHIP

Burton, Jessie G., wife of A. Roundy, d. May 29, 1888; age, 29 years
Burham, Horace L., (Major) 50th Ill. Inf. (Gov. marker)
Burtis, J. M. (Gov. marker)
Butts, Samuel J. (father), b. 1847, d. 1923
Byers, William, b. Jan. 1, 1845, d. June 11, 1902
Byrne, Lottie, wife of T. F. Byrne, b. Aug. 3, 1863, d. 1883

C

Calley, Benjamin, b. Nov., 1832, d. April 4, 1900
Calhoon, Susan E., d. March 7, 1899; age, 58 years
Calkins, Frank (Soldier), d. Dec. 6, 1877; age, 39 years
Cameron, Robert, d. Feb. 13, 1896; age, 66 years
Camp, Z. M., b. Dec. 22, 1844, d. Aug. 20, 1890
Campbell, Lizzie, b. Aug. 11, 1860, d. April 16, 1876
Campbell, John J., b. Oct. 26, 1858, d. Aug. 27, 1886
Campbell, Charlotte, b. Dec. 14, 1832, d. June 6, 1907
Campbell, William Lee, b. Oct. 21, 1855, d. April 26, 1919
Campbell, William, b. Oct. 23, 1818, d. Dec. 5, 1852
Campbell, John, b. Aug. 8, 1820, d. March 11, 1900
Campbell, G. W., b. 1828, d. 1878
Canine, Loucinda M., wife of R. B. Canine, d. Oct. 13, 1900; age, 50 years
Cardwell, Maria M., d. 1899
Carley, Mora, d. May 29, 1896; age, 36 years
Carman, Mary, b. April 15, 1849, d. March 13, 1898
Carney, J. C., b. Aug. 18, 1857, d. Jan. 18, 1896
Carlen, Andrew, b. Sept. 16, 1847, d. Feb. 3, 1899
Carter, Rosa L., wife of Lucian D. Carter, d. May, 1896 (?)
Carothers, James B., d. Dec. 5, 1905; age, 50 years
Carter, Martha Ann, d. Dec. 3, 1895; age, 67 years
Cartright, C. D., d. Feb. 6, 1887; age, 69 years
Carson, W. H., b. April 13, 1832, d. Nov. 26, 1905
Carson, Clara J., wife of W. H. Carson, b. May 26, 1833, d. Aug. 16, 1874
Craig, Lizzie, wife of Dr. J. T. Craig, b. Dec. 16, 1856, d. Feb. 14, 1887
Crawford, Frankie F., son of W. R. and A. Crawford, d. March 4, 1873; age, 2 years
Casten, Melisa, b. 1848, d. 1896, (sister) evidently of James Griffin
Cass, Mary (mother), b. 1841, d. 1896
Cass, A. L. (father), b. 1835, d. 1907
Castron, Herman H., b. Oct. 19, 1826, d. Feb. 23, 1902
Caswell, Elizabeth, wife of Newport Caswell (dates worn)
Castello, James Q., d. July 31, 1881; age, 37 years, 9 months, 20 days
Causey, Katie, b. July 14, 1854, d. March 20, 1887
Chadwick, Alonzo E., b. Nov. 25, 1840, d. June 28, 1908 (Soldier)
Chadwick, Sarah M., d. Aug. 15, 1888; age, 48 years
Chalfont, D. Y.*(Gov. marker)
Chalfont, Sarah E. (mother), b. 1836, d. 1932
Chapel, Mary E., d. April 29, 1873; age, 63 years
Chapman, Fannie (mother), b. 1855, d. 1907
Charles, Augustus Lutz, b. 1820, d. 1908
Charles, Anna E. (mother), b. 1811, d. 1878
Charles, Aug. (father), b. 1824, d. 1880 (Gov. marker) 3rd U. S. Infantry
Chaudes, Auroea, d. Dec. 13, 1898; age, 80 (?) years
Cheatham, Susan A. Summers, wife of W. T. Cheatham, b. 1832, d. 1903
Cheese, Belle, wife of S. E. Cheese, d. May 3, 188— (stone broken and other dates invisible)
Chew, Henry, b. June 28, 1848, d. April 22, 1873
Chew, John W., b. Dec. 31, 1857, d. Dec. 10, 1865

Chesney, John, b. in County Antrim, Ireland, Dec. 15, 1850, d. May 9, 1893
Chick, Ann ("Our Mother"), b. Sept. 25, 1796, d. July 24, 1876
Chick, William Sidney, d. April 10, 1895; age, 76 years
Chick, Frances, daughter of W. S. and M. C. Chick, b. Feb. 18, 1857, d. Dec. 28, 187-
Chick, William M., Jr., son of W. S. and Margaret Chick, b. July 8, 1848, d. Sept., (?) 1859
Chick, Margaret C., wife of W. S. Chick, b. May, 1823, d. Jan. 11, 1890
Christ, Jacob, b. Nov. 7, 1830, d. April 30, 1915
Christie, Mary, wife of W. H. Christie, d. Jan. 21, 1892; age, 45 years
Church, Sarah (Grandma), b. 1793, d. Sept., 1879 (see Pattison)
Church, Albert N., b. Sept. 15, 1855, d. July 14, 1908
Church, Anna M., b. 1855, d. 1931
Churns, Jos. W., Co. "K" 11th Pa. Inf. (Gov. marker)
Coleman, Miss Cinny U., daughter of John M. and Fannie Coleman (no dates)
Clements, Baby, b. 1871, d. 1873
Clifton, Samuel L., father of J. Clifton, b. Jan. 4, 1833, d. Aug. 27, 1894
Cline, James R., b. Jan. 18, 1847, d. April 24, 1872 (Soldier)
Clinton, Thomas F., d. Oct. 31, 1867; age, 17 years
Clinton, P. F., d. Dec. 19, 186-; age, 35 years (G. A. R.)
Clinton, Thomas, d. Oct. 31, 1867; age, 17 years
Clair, Mary A., wife of M. W. Clair, b. June 21, 1855, d. Dec. 11, 1896
Clark, Issachar, b. Dec. 2, 1820, d. Sept. 1, 1885
Clark, Sarah (mother), b. 1828, d. 1917
Clark, Laura O. A., d. May 8, 1902; age, 49 years
Clark, Joseph Harrison, b. 1843, d. 1921
Clark, Mary H., d. July 8, 1933; age, 78 years, 28 days
Clark, Abraham, b. 1843, d. 1910
Clark, Sarah (very old stone, dates impossible to read)
Clarke, Mary S., wife of H. E. Clarke, b. Sept. 9, 1831, d. Feb. 1, 1897
Clipper, August, d. June 28, 1888 (Soldier)
Close, Andrew J., d. Jan. 15, 1883; age, 46 years, 11 months (Gov. marker)
Cobb, Nelson, b. April 28, 1811, d. June 15, 1894
Cobb, Susan Z., b. June 14, 1833, d. Dec. 27, 1930
Coe, William D., b. Aug. 20, 1834, d. Sept. 27, 1898
Coe, May J., b. Jan. 24, 1836, d. May 8, 1909
Coe, Abigail C., b. 1833, d. 1912
Coe, John P., b. 1828, d. 1909
Coffman, Almeda, daughter of Lot and Nancy J. Coffman, d. March 6, 1858; age, 8 years, 2 months, 19 days
Coffman, Mary C., daughter of Lot and Nancy J. Coffman, d. Aug. 11, 1860; age, 1 year, 3 months, 24 days
Cole, Harriet C., d. Sept. 3, 1891; age, 55 years
Cole, Peter J., b. Dec. 26, 1831, d. Nov. 9, 1904
Coleman, Martha A., wife of D. B. Kyley, daughter of John and Fannie U. Coleman
Collins, Caroline, d. Oct. 6, 1896; age, 68 years
Coloflower, Rebecca, b. April 27, 1823, d. Dec. 13, 1868
Coloflower, Samuel, b. Feb. 7, 1819, d. Sept. 30, 1886
Compton, Robert W., b. Aug. 15, 1820, d. Aug. 4, 1895
Compton, C. W., b. Jan. 26, 1820, d. July 30, 1904
Conklin, Addie (mother), b. June 14, 1850, d. July 1, 1904
Connor, Daniel, d. Sept. 28, 1908; age, 60 years
Conrad, John A., b. May 25, 1852, d. June 12, 1898
Conway, Virginia Lee, wife of Jos. L. Conway, d. May 10, 1884; age, 34 years
Conkling, Matilda Withers Dodge, b. 1826, d. 1906
Conwell, Henry Leftwich, son of H. B. and J. S. Conwell, b. Aug. 22, 1862, d. June 11, 1863

Cook, Eliza A., wife of Jas. W. Cook, b. May 8, 1825, d. Nov. 15, 1880
Cook, William P. (Lieut.), d. Sept. 28, 1900; age, 67 years (Gov. marker)
Cook, Cassandra C., wife of William P. Cook, b. Dec. 31, 1835, d. April 16, 1883
Cook, Cora E., b. 1847, d. 1895
Cook, Peter L., b. 1848, d. 1912
Cooley, Mary F., b. 1844, d. 1920
Cooley, Dr. F., b. 1817, d. 1911
Cooper, Clark Osband, b. 1832, d. 1918
Cooper, Susan Elizabeth, b. 1841, d. 1901
Cooper, Ann, d. March 22, 1888; age, 56 years
Cooper, Hiram W., b. Oct. 6, 1834, d. April 8, 1900
Cooper, Julia E., wife of H. W. Cooper, b. Feb. 3, 1829, d. May 13, 1897
Copeland, Charles C., b. at Dexter, Maine, Jan. 23, 1847, d. June 26, 1893; age, 46 years, 5 months, 3 days
Cox, Eliza, no dates
Crabtree, Henry E., son of Tillman and Lorinda V. Crabtree, d. July 11, 1874; age, 12 years, 7 months, 8 days
Crabtree, William E., d. Feb. 7, 1883; age, 29 years
Crabtree, Tillman, d. Feb. 27, 1889; age, 56 years, 1 month, 2 days
Crafton, J. D., d. March 3, 1907; age, 88 years
Cramer, Nancy P. (mother), b. May 29, 1823, d. Nov. 11, 1896
Craig, Benjamin F., b. May 15, 1820, d. May 8, 1884
Craig, Elizabeth A., wife of B. F. Craig, d. Sept. 3, 1896
Cravens, E. B., b. March 17, 1807, d. Dec. 15, 1881
Creek, Fanny F. (our mother), wife of W. W. Creek, b. Oct. 28, 1822, d. June 20, 1873; age, 51 years, 8 months, 3 days
Cresap, Anna Jane, b. June 29, 1854, d. Aug. 18, 1893
Crews, Maris, b. June 12, 1857, d. Aug. 7, 1895
Crocker, Minnie C., b. 1851, d. 1896
Cronover, Willie, son of G. A. and J. M. Cronover, b. Feb. 11, 1871, d. March 7, 1872
Crooks, Adie Vernige (mother); age, 52 years (Buried in section of cemetery where burials varied from 1898 to 1906)
Cross, F. L. C., Co. "D" E. N. H. Infantry (Gov. marker)
Crow, John M., b. Sept., 1860, d. Nov. 16, 1901
Crowell, Robert C., b. 1832, d. 1899
Crowell, Elizabeth Leedy, b. 1843, d. 1928
Crowell, Maria H., wife of Robert R. Crowell, d. Nov. 19, 1867; age, 31 years, 9 months, 10 days
Crowell, Major R. C., 25th Missouri Infantry (Gov. marker)
Culley, James S., d. June 18, 1896; age, 66 years
Cummington, Ella M., daughter of J. and E. A. King, b. Sept. 17, 1857, d. March 14, 1884
Cummings, Lucy (mother), b. 1840, d. 1891
Cummings, William, Co. "E"   (Gov. marker)
Cunningham, C. L., b. March 5, 1849, d. Jan. 4, 1898

D

Daggett, Mary G., d. Dec. 4, 1869; age, 70 years
Daly, George W. (my son), b. Sept. 24, 1846, d. June, 190-
Daly, Hester E., b. April 5, 1825, d. ———, 1913
Dancy, N. L. (father), b. Feb. 2, 1826, d. Dec. 30, 1895
Dancy, Sarah J. (mother), b. April 11, 1835, d. July 28, 1901
Dannenberg, Franz, b. Feb. 24, 1846, d. March 16, 1903
Darrow, Jennie M., wife of J. M. Darrow, d. July 23, 1868; age, 26 years, 5 months, 21 days
Davis, Rossanna Brayton, b. July 12, 1815, d. March 27, 1896
Davis, George Woodson (M. D.), b. Dec. 7, 1851, d. Sept. 21, 1927

Davis, Solomon Jackson, b. Feb. 12, 1847, d. Aug. 10, 188-
Davis, Mary Ann, b. July 1, 1855, d. April 7, 1887
Davis, Corpl. G. S., Co. "R" 26th Mass. Inf. (Gov. marker)
Davis, Frank, d. March 18, 1904
Davies, Harvey (wooden marker, no dates)
Davies, Mary D., d. May 30, 1889; age, 63 years
Davies, John D., d. Nov. 13, 1888; age, 62 years
Davidson, G. W., d. Feb. 8, 1893; age, 77 years
Davison, Caroline, b. 1823, d. 1900
Davenport, Dora (mother), b. Aug. 6, 1843, d. March 13, 1903
Dawson, Mary, b. Jan. 28, 1851, d. Jan. 16, 1899
Deaton, Leona Everetta, daughter of W. P. and L. J. Deaton, d. Aug. 29, 1869; age, 8 years, 8 months, 5 days
Deaver, Tillie S., b. 1839, d. 1919
Deck, Florien, d. Jan. 6, 1889; age, 64 years
Defosse, Elizabeth Philomene Anne (nee a Maline Belgeque), b. July 22, 1842, d. March 1, 1887
DeHart, Elizabeth M., wife of Reuben DeHart, b. May 19, 1830, d. Feb. 7, 1902
Dehmer, Sebastian, d. May 22, 1890; age, 38 years, 10 months
Delahay, Samuel Uriah, b. Oct. 4, 1847, d. Dec. 11, 1924
Denslow, John H., d. July, 1880; age, 43 years
Denslow, Elizabeth, d. July 8, 1908; age, 64 years
Deweese, Catherine; age, 79 years
Deweese, Arthur A., b. March 15, 1872, d. Feb. 18, 1899
Dexter, Allmeda E., d. Aug. 28, 1877; age, 77 years
Dickerson, infant son of Dr. D. E. and M. E. Dickerson, d. Feb. 14, 1871; age, 15 days
Dickinson, P. S. (Soldier, Gov. marker)
Dickinson, W. G. (Soldier, Gov. marker)
Dietz, Elizabeth, b. in Germany, Sept. 14, 1827, d. April 25, 1899
Dillon, Charlotte L., b. June 23, 1854, d. May 8, 1872
Dixon, John, b. July 3, 1831, d. May 1, 1885
Dixon, Emma, beloved wife of John Dixon, b. Nov. 29, 1831, d. Sept. 23, 1885
Diveley, William M., b. June 30, 1837, d. Nov. 18, 1908
Diveley, Mary, b. April 1, 1841, d. Sept. 30, 1879
Diveley, Menine M., b. June 22, 1866, d. May 27, 1873 (sister)
Diveley, Merty, b. April 5, 1874, d. Oct. 7, 1874 (sister)
Diveley, William B., d. Dec. 7, 1906; age, 45 years
Diveley, Eliza, wife of Edward Diveley, d. Aug. 14, 1867; age, 48 years, 4 months, 1 day
Diveley, Michael, b. Dec. 8, 1828, d. Nov. 19, 1901
Diveley, Cornelia L., wife of Michael Diveley, b. 1843, d. 1920
Diveley, Hattie E., d. March 17, 1880; age, 40 years
Diveley, Edward, d. June 14, 18-7; age, 48 years, 11 months, 1 day
Dobbins, B. O., d. Sept. 2, 1897; age, 43 years, 7 months, 11 days
Dobler, Jacob Frederick, b. June 25, 1821, d. June 8, 1902
Dockweiler, Sophronia, wife of J. B. Dockweiler, b. March 28, 1835, d. Dec. 22, 1903
Dodge, Charles Edwin, b. 1810, d. 1875
Donnelly, Louisa C., daughter of D. M. Putman, b. 1837, d. 1929
Doolin, Claiborn, d. Feb. 2, 1901; age, 47 years
Dornseif, John, b. July 25, 1831, d. Feb. 26, 1924
Dornseif, Cecilia, wife of John Dornseif, b. April 23, 1835, d. Jan. 11, 1903
Dowling, W. H., no dates
Dowling, Mary, no dates
Douglas, Henry, d. Feb. 7, 1870; age, 49 years
Douglas, children of William S. and Florence W. Douglas
    Ruth, d. July 26, 1869
    Mark, d. Aug. 26, 1865

CEMETERIES—KAW TOWNSHIP

Douglas, Henry, d. Feb. 7, 1870; age, 49 years
Douglas, Ria Sutherland, b. 1840, d. 1918
Downs, Augusta M., wife of Frank E. Downs, b. Oct. 1, 1827, d. Nov. 10, 1880
Downs, Frank F., d. Aug. 16, 1897; age, 70 years (Gov. marker)
Drury (Geo. or Bro.), b. Feb. 28, 1819, d. May 19, 1874 (Soldier)
Dudley, John Boyd, b. March 7, 1827, d. April 21, 1908
Dudley, Pamelia Ann Palmer, wife of John Boyd Dudley, b. Feb. 17, 1835, d. Aug. 28, 1914
Duff, Helen M., wife of John E. Duff, d. Feb. 6, 1887; age, 56 years
Duff, John E., d. Nov. 4, 1891; age, 73 years, 3 months, 7 days
Duckett, Mabel, wife of Walter M. Duckett, d. Sept. 8, 1888; age, 25 years
Dunlop, Marcelina T., b. 1848, d. 1890
Dunlop, Mathew, b. 1839, d. 1897
Duncan, Eliza Mount, b. 1848, d. 1892
Duncan, Francis M., b. 1836, d. 1914
Duncan, Rachel, d. April 2, 1897; age, 70 years
Dunn, E., d. July 10, 1896; age, 53 years
Dunn, Naomi, wife of E. Dunn, d. Dec. 10, 1881; age, 45 years
Durkop, Hans Christian, d. Dec. 17, 1908; age, 77 years, 7 months
Durkop, Marie, d. Jan. 8, 1920; age, 79 years
Durnell, George B., d. July 11, 1889; age, 44 years, 9 months
Duvall, Jos. M., Co. "E" 43rd Ind. Inf. (Gov. marker)

E

Ealey, Lizzie, wife of David C. Ealey, d. Aug. 29, 1898; age, 40 years
Eanghanel, Daniel A., b. 1825—rest of inscription invisible
Eason, George W., b. 1844, d. 1922
Eason, Sarah Ann, his wife, b. 1842, d. 1884
Ebersold, Charles, b. Feb. 9, 1841, d. Feb. 15, 1876; Lt. of Co. "G" (Gov. marker)
Ebersold, H. G. (Gov. marker)
Eby, Laura, wife of Noah Eby, d. Sept. 3, 1887; age, 65 years
Eckert, Conrad, b. 1812, d. 1898
Eckert, William C., b. 1860, d. 1918
Eckert, Minnie, wife of Conrad Eckert, b. 1835, d. 1907
Eckert, Jessie Lyman, wife of Herman Eckert, b. Jan. 2, 1878, d. July 26, 1900
Eddington, John, d. Oct. 29, 1887; age, 48 years, 8 months
Egelhoff, John M., b. Aug. 20, 1803, d. Dec. 29, 1885; a native of Dorndurkheim, Rheim, Province Hessen
Eggles, David, b. Dec. 18, 1817, d. July 16, 1874
Eggleston, Arthur, b. Sept. 23, 1830, d. Jan. 29, 1896
Egossard, Jasper (Gov. marker)
Ehlert, Theodore, b. April 23, 1853, d. Aug. 16, 1893; age, 40 years, 3 months, 24 days
Eichholz, Lebrecht, b. Jan., 1823, d. Feb. 21, 1888
Eisele, Andrew M., b. Sept. 30, 1815, d. Aug. 27, 1884
Eisele, Rosena E., wife of Andrew M. Eisele, b. Jan. 14, 1820, d. Jan. 24, 1896
Eisele, Margaret A., d. 1850 (Children of A. M. and R. E. Eisele)
Eisele, Andrew M., d. 1853
Eisele, Emmet W., d. 1864
Elkins, John T., b. Jan. 23, 1843, d. Aug. 2, 1886
Elkins, Adah H., wife of John T. Elkins, b. Oct. 15, 1852, d. Oct. 5, 1908
Ellenberger, Corp. A., b. Aug. 15, 1817, d. Nov. 12, 1883 (Gov. marker)
Ellenberger, Catherine A., wife of A. Ellenberger, b. 1817, d. April 12, 1885
Elrod, Nora J., daughter of G. E. and H. L. Elrod, d. June 10, 1876; age, 10 months, 15 days
Embree, Thos. J., b. April 1, 1835, d. April 28, 1909
Emmack, C. H., b. 1832, d. 1912; Co. "D" 160 Reg. Ohio Vol.

Emmert, Barbara, b. March 15, 1834, d. Dec. 13, 1910
Emmert, Johanas (son), b. Sept. 30, 1859, d. May 22, 1904
Emmert, Frank, b. Sept. 13, 1849, d. Oct. 24, 1906
Emmons, Luthena M., wife of L. Emmons, daughter of J. and M. Rubey
Endres, John, d. April 18, 1886; age, 40 years (Soldier)
Endres, George P., d. July 17, 1869; age, 22 years, 9 months, 27 days
Enders, Jacob, d. Feb. 13, 1876; age, 56 years, 6 days
Enders, Rudolf, son of Jacob and Philahma Enders, b. Sept. 21, 1854, d. June 9, 1857
   Enders on same lot with Endres
Engle, George B., no dates
Engle, Permelia, no dates
Erllich, Louis (Gov. marker)
Estes, Martin, Co. "F" U. S. Cavalry (Gov. marker)
Estep, Sarah (mother), b. 1830, d. 1914
Estep, Elizabeth, b. 1858, d. 1914
Estep, Andrew Smith, b. Jan. 1, 1864, d. June 17, 1901 (Estep burials upon Perviance lot)
Evans, James G., b. 1843, d. 1919
Evans, Mrs. Mary E., d. March 12, 1932; age, 77 years, 4 months, 1 day
Evans, John, b. Nov. 29, 1825, d. Jan. 31, 1887
Evans, T. W., b. Feb. 24, 1855, d. Jan. 28, 1884
Evans, Elizabeth, b. Dec. 22, 1832, d. Aug. 8, 1888
Evans, James H., b. April 9, 1850, d. Nov. 27, 1902
Evans, Kittie M., wife of G. W., d. Aug. 9, 1881; age, 27 years, 5 months
Evans, Hannah J., wife of William Evans, d. 187-
Evans, William D., d. Nov. 29, 1874; age, 19 years
Evernghim, William T., 1st Lt. (Gov. marker), b. Feb. 24, 1834 in New York, d. Nov. 16, 1903
Ewing, Robert Finis, son of Robert C. and Mariah C. (?) Ewing, d. Dec. 9, 1878; age, 19 years, — months, 13 days

F

Fapp, Catherine, wife of Donald Fapp, d. March 9, 1879; age, 34 years
Fapp, Donald, d. Oct. 2, 1893; age, 63 years
Falker, Frisbie, no dates
Falker, Mary Boteler, wife of Frisbie Falker
Fallet, Mary A., b. 1858, d. 1893
Fairman, Jane A., d. April 24, 1875; age, 40 years
Fairman, Susie, d. Dec. 28, 1862; age, 1 year, 3 months
Farrar, Alfred O., b. 1849, d. 1907
Farrow, W. F., b. Jan. 20, 1854, d. March 4, 1885 (husband)
Feamore, Lawrence, b. 1845, d. 1928
Fearn, Caroline Barron, b. April 9, 1835, d. May 31, 1903
Ferguson, Elizabeth R., b. March 18, 1801, d. Dec. 27, 1890
Ferguson, Richard T. (our father), b. Dec. 10, 1818, d. Dec. 23, 1898; age, 80 years, 13 days
Ferguson, Minerva A., wife of Richard T. Ferguson, b. Hartford Co., Maryland, May 3, 1818, d. Nov. 29, 1882
Ferguson, Clarence E., b. Jan. 13, 1859, d. Feb., — 1869
Ferris, Sarah J., b. 1837, d. 1900
Fernald, Almon, b. Nov. 23, 1829, d. Nov. 4, 1903
Fernald, Mary O., wife of Almon Fernald, b. Feb. 14, 1832, d. Jan. 10, 1895
Fernald, Samuel H., b. Nov. 12, 1833, d. Oct. 12, 1864
Foster, Charles W., d. Jan. 9, 1906; age, 62 years
Finchers, Robert, d. Oct. 28, 1909; age, 80 years
Fincke, Charles W., b. Aug. 23, 1823, d. April 28, 1890
Fincke, Julia, b. April 12, 1828, d. Aug. 1, 1896
Finley, Frank E., d. July 7, 1901; age, 48 years

Finn, Annie F., d. Nov. 1, 1906; age, 59 years
Finn, Harry A., d. March 17, 1907; age, 63 years
Finn, W. H., Sept. 15, 1839, d. May 29, 1903
Finnie, Walter Benedict, b. July 1, 1850, d. Oct. — 1886
Finney, Fide, b. April 8, 1849, d. June — 1870
Finney, Frank Lowther, b. May 25, 1861, d. June, 1869
Finney, Catherine Margaret, b. Nov. 28, 1823, d. Feb. 15, 1896
Finney, Hamilton, b. May 12, 1818, d. March 7, 1902
Fisher, A. C., Co. "C" Van Horn's Co. U. S. R. C. Mo. Cav. (Soldier)
Fisher, C. C., Co. "H" 28th Ohio Inf. (Soldier)
Fisher, Ranson G., son of A. and R. C. Fisher, b. April 5, 1839, d. July 25, 1876, Co. "H" 23rd Regt. Ohio Vol. Inf. (Soldier)
Fisher, Abel, b. Oct. 15, 1831, d. July 17, 1877
Fisher, Rachel, wife of Abel Fisher, b. Oct. 6, 1837, d. Nov. 18, 1892
Fisher, Joseph Selden, b. May 2, 1820, d. Aug. 25, 1908
Fisher, Martha Duvall, wife of M. R. Fisher, b. Jan. 1, 1817, d. May 29, 1894
Fisher, Merritt R., b. Dec., 1807, d. May 1, 1887
Fisher, Florence R., b. May 14, 1848, d. July 13, 1905
Fischer, Ernstine, b. 1851, d. 1887
FitzRandolph, Joseph, b. Bridgetown, Nova Scotia, Feb. 9, 1848, d. Aug. 27, 1906
Flatter, Oswald, b. Feb. 24, 1829, d. July 20, 1892
Flagler, Frances Harriet, wife of Philip Flagler, b. June 20, 1805, d. March 2, 1867
Flagler, Philip, b. Oct. 16, 1802, d. Feb. 8, 1874
Fleming, Esther, b. 1840, d. 1910
Forcade, Jacob, d. Feb. 8, 1876; age, 45 years (Masonic Emblem)
Forbes, Mattie, d. Aug. 8, 1903; age, 63 years
Forbes, Corp'l J. W., Co. "K" 25 Ohio Infantry (Soldier)
Ford, Alice, wife of George Ford, d. Nov. 30, 1901; age, 41 years, 10 months, 26 days
Ford, William T., b. May 26, 1850, d. July 31, 1921
Ford, Albert, no dates, very old stone
Ford, John H., d. May 25, 1865; age, 25 years, 6 months, 17 days
Foreman, Lucretia H., wife of Emos Foreman, b. Jan. 8, 1822, d. Dec. 21, 1891
Folliemus, Dr. William, b. 1829, d. 1902
Forrester, Thomas, b. July 31, 1856, d. Oct. 25, 1890
Foster, Mary, wife of Charles W., d. Jan. 24, 1898; age, 42 years
Forsythe, James, Co. "H" 11th Kansas Cavalry (Soldier)
Fox, Martin, Co. "B" 10th Ill. Inf. (Soldier)
Fradenburg, Charles E., b. 1834, d. 1887
Fradenburg, Elnora E., b. 1838, d. 1917
Frame, Lizzie, wife of James A., d. March 21, 1869; age, 34 years
France, Sanford, b. Jan. 16, 1848, d. Feb. 1, 1903
Fraser, John, b. June 15, 1843, d. March 9, 1881
Fraser, Fannie T., wife of John Fraser, daughter of Judge Beverly of Dodge City, Kansas, d. Oct. 23, 1879; age, 22 years
Fraser, Mary Robertson, wife of the late William Fraser, b. in Dreehess, Scotland, d. Jan. 28, 1874; age, 64 years
Frazier, Elizabeth (mother), b. Jan. 15, 1830, d. March 7, 1879
Frazier, John (father), b. July 26, 1819, d. April 17, 1900
French, Lydah F., b. March 7, 1814, d. Aug. 7, 1890
French, Moses S., b. Aug. 15, 1811, d. Jan. 20, 1886
Frey, Theodore, d. Aug. 31, 1890; age, 34 years
Fry, George (S. G. T.), 32nd Ohio Inf. (Soldier)
Frye, America E., b. Oct. 20, 1816, d. April 27, 1902
Frick, Constantin, d. June 23, 1878; age, 54 years
Friedrichkruger, Kuni, wife of   Friedrichkruger, b. Feb. 21, 1848, d. July 18, 1903
Fritz, Joseph A., b. Nov. 24, 1829, d. June 13, 1881

Frost, Lee, b. December 17, 1849, d. March 3, 1898
Fularczik, John S., b. Dec. 28, 1835, d. March 16, 1891
Fuller, Nelson W., d. April 25, 1907; age, 69 years
Fulkerson, Mary J., wife of J. M. Fulkerson, d. Feb. 20, 1881; age, 41 years, 8 months, 24 days
Fulkerson, children of J. M. and Mary J. Fulkerson
    Alpha, d. 1870
    Mary Luella, d. 1873
    Cora Lee, d. 1878
Furgason, Dissie C., d. Nov. 29, 1866; age, 29 years, 8 days
Furgason, Edgar N., d. Aug. 14, 1867; age, 1 year, 1 month, 1 week

G

Garberson, H., Co. "D" 4th Ohio Infantry (Gov. marker)
Gardner, Robert (father), b. April 10, 1821, d. Aug. 14, 1893
Gardner, Sarah (mother), b. April 5, 1825, d. March 26, 1903
Gardner, Samuel (brother), b. Sept. 6, 1844, d. Nov. 3, 1900
Gardner, Samuel, Co. "H" 91 Indiana Infantry (Gov. marker)
Gardner, Amelia, d. Sept. 13, 1893; age, 81 years
Gardner, James W., b. Oct. 9, 1849, d. Feb. 6, 1910
Garley, Janet, d. Nov. 12, 1902; age, 50 years
Garnett, Reuben, b. 1812, d. 1897
Garnett, Susan, b. 1812, d. 1898, same stone as Reuben Garnett
Garrett, Emma, d. Aug. 22, 1871; age, 28 years
Garrett, William, d. April 23, 1890; age, 91 years
Garrett, Mary D., wife of William Garrett, d. July 7, 1881; age, 80 years
Gates, Horatio, Co. "M" (Serg't)
Gaugler, Barbara, wife of John Gaugler, b. Jan. 2, 1848, d. Feb. 7, 1897
Garver, S., 1st Lieut. (Gov. marker)
Gay, Jane, mother of John G. Gay, b. ——shire, Scotland, May 9, 1815, d. May 30, 1882
Garnett, Newton Gordon, 5th son of Dr. J. W. and M. J. Garnett, b. Sept. 1, 1856, d. April 13, 1880
Gammon, Thomasena M. Bagbett, wife of James S. Gammon, d. Oct. 23, 1879; age, 34 years
Geary, Daniel, b. 1835, d. 1924
Geary, Emma Salisbury, wife of Daniel Geary, b. 1834, d. 1923
Gebhardt, William, "The Friend and Benefactor of the German Hospital of Kansas City, Missouri"
Gerard Stephen, b. Nov. 15, 1835, d. Jan. 19, 1898
Gerard, Lydia S., b. Dec. 19, 1836, d. Nov. 28, 1891
Gerling, Reca M., wife of Henry G. Gerling, d. March 30, 1893; age, 34 years, 10 months
German, George B., d. May 14, 1885; age, 22 years, 8 months, 29 days
Gibbs, George N. (brother), b. Nov. 25, 1851, d. Nov. 20, 1897
Gibbs, Enoch O. (father), b. Feb. 9, 1818, d. Feb. 9, 1893
Gilson, Mary Park, wife of S. Gilson, b. 1846, d. 1868
Gibson, William C., b. 1816, d. 1873
Gibson, William F., b. 1855, d. 1873
Gibson, Mary E., b. 1843, d. 1915
Gibson, Sarah J., b. 1841, d. 1905
Gibson, Nancy, b. 1820, d. 1872
Gibson, Amanda E., b. 1848, d. 1895
Gidley, Phillip S., b. 1836, d. 1916
Gidley, Maria, b. 1838, d. 1907
Gilbert, Byron, son of Byron E. and Mary L. Gilbert, d. Oct. 28, 1860
Gillen, James, d. Sept. 3, 1870; age, 58 years
Gillis, William, d. July 18, 1862; age, 72 years

Gillett, Jerome B., b. 1822, d. 1899
Giles, Peter D., b. May 23, 1823, d. Nov. 17, 1904
Giles, Matilda C., wife of Peter D. Giles, b. July 26, 1832, d. July 9, 1915
Gile, H. G. (dates invisible), Gov. marker
Gilham, Virginia Dellon, b. 1849, d. 1899
Gingry, Joseph A., born in Juniata County, Pa., Nov. 28, 1830, d. Nov. 15, 1856 (?)
Glaskey, Sarah M., d. Aug. 20, 1884, in the 78th year of her age
Glasner, D., Sr., b. Sept. 28, 1807, Braunschwerg, Germany, d. June 6, 1890
Glasner, Daniel, d. July 30, 1895; age, 60 years; Capt. of Co. "I" 16th Ill. Infantry (Gov. marker)
Glaser, Franz, b. 1825, d. 1884
Glover, Henry Lyman, b. 1841, d. 1880
Glover, Emma L., wife of Henry Lyman Glover, d. Feb. 5, 1930
Gollady, Bronson, b. Oct. 26, 1844, d. Dec. 15, 1900
Goodman, A. A., b. Jan. 28, 1813, d. June 18, 1893
Goodman, Hannah W., wife of A. A. Goodman, b. Feb. 23, 1820, d. Jan. 21, 1873
Gouchman, Melton (father), b. 1834, d. 1929
Gouchman, Melvine (mother), b. 1867, d. 1927
Gould, Rosa F., wife of W. S. Gould, b. Sept. 24, 1852, d. March 20, 1909
Gove, Charley, only child of H. and M. Gove, d. Jan. 14, 1880
Graeber, Caroline, no dates
Graefenstein, William, b. 1840, d. 1895
Graham, McB., Co. "C" 17th Indiana Infantry (Gov. marker)
Grant, Allen D., d. Feb. 27, 1898
Grant, "Mother," b. 1812, d. 1903
Graves, Mary P., b. Nov. 13, 1801, d. Sept. 15, 1879
Gray, Thomas, b. May 1, 1856, d. Feb. 13, 1883
Gregg, Clark (Soldier, Gov. marker)
Gregg, Villerby, b. 1849, d. 1931
Gregg, Lizzie J., b. Oct. 30, 1854, d. Nov. 9, 1898
Gregg, Philander, b. Jan. 29, 1818, d. Jan. 13, 1899
Gregg, Mary E., b. April 8, 1822, d. April 13, 1911
Gregg, Walter S., b. April 24, 1857, d. Dec. 9, 1926
Gregory, Robert Samuel, son of W. S. and E. A. Gregory, d. April 5, 1856; age, 5 years, 11 months, 14 days
Gregory, Willie, infant son of W. S. and Mary C. Gregory, d. July 12, 1855; age, 12 days
Gregory, Eliza A. (Wade), wife of W. L. Gregory, d. April 16, 1851; age, 23 years, 1 month, 6 days (Gregory inscriptions given above, removed from Wade Cemetery)
Green, Amanda, b. Feb. 11, 1848, d. Aug. 6, 1884
Green, Lewis P., of Melborn Aus., d. Oct. 14, 1899; age, 68 years; born Mercer Co., N. J.
Green, Mary Matilda, b. Sept. 11, 1871, d. Sept. 30, 1872; daughter of J. W. and M. E. Green
Green, Elizabeth Seudder, b. Feb. 14, 1876, d. May 4, 1877; daughter of J. W. and M. E. Green
Green, Margaret E., wife of John W. Green, and daughter of Wm. and Mary M. Scudder, b. at Scudders Falls, N. J., Nov. 15, 1843, d. Sept. 30, 1880
Greenwell, George, b. July 17, 1837, d. July 18, 1887
Greenwell, Charlotte, beloved wife of George Greenwell, b. June 26, 1849, d. Jan. 25, 1880
Gres, Alvis, b. July 4, 1831, d. April 18, 1874
Grieger, Anna D., d. Dec. 15, 1886; age, 63 years, 3 months, 6 days
Grubb, Frank T. (husband of M. A. Grubb), b. July 22, 1842, d. March 22, 1883
Griffin, James B. (brother), b. 1862, d. 1930
Griffin, Christina (mother), b. 1830, d. 1914
Griffin, Clara, d. Sept. 30, 1897; age, 50 years
Grove, Catherine McCall, b. Baltimore, Md., July 12, 1802, d. Oct. 16, 1889
Grover, D. A. N., b. in Campbell County, Ky., Sept. 14, 1828, d. Feb. 11, 1880

Grover, Latitia Jane, b. in Clay County, Mo., Jan. 30, 1839, d. March 15, 1902
Grover, Pliny W., b. Oct. 17, 1873, d. Feb. 15, 1876
Guenther, T. B., (Soldier), b. Feb. 10, 1839, d. July 31, 1890; age, 50 years
Guenther, Minnie (nee Joern), b. July 22, 1814, d. Oct., 1888
Guenther, Rudolph J., d. July 14, 1899; age, 50 years
Gwynne, Nat. M., Lieut. 13th Ohio Cavalry, b. July 5, 1849, d. Jan. 6, 1883

H

Haag, John, b. 1833, d. 1893
Haag, Jacob, b. 1836, d. 1898
Habhegger, Christian, b. 1847, d. 1879
Haddock, Maria, d. Sept. 19, 1882; age, 65 years
Haefner, Joseph, b. May 5, 1830, d. July 27, 1892
Haefner, Margretha, wife of Joseph Haefner, b. March 3, 1836, d. March 11, 1906
Hahner, Frances Caroline, b. Dec. 22, 1841, d. June 4, 1876
Hahn, Frederich, d. Nov. 17, 1893; age, 52 years, 9 months; Co. "A" 32nd Reg. N. Y. Inf. Vol., Co. "D" 11th Reg. N. J. Vol.
Haines, John M., b. May 6, 1841, d. Nov. 13, 1909
Hale, Thomas B., d. Feb. 8, 1863; age, 33 years, 5 months
Hall, Perry J., b. Sept. 19, 1831, d. July 17, 1901
Hall, Malinda, wife of P. J. Hall, b. April 30, 1831, d. Dec. 28, 1899
Hall, William Ewing, b. Dec. 21, 1846, d. July 6, 1906 (See Porter)
Haller, Nancy H. (mother), b. May 13, 1822, d. July 12, 1870
Ham, Julia H. Brand, b. Oct. 20, 1862, d. Dec. 6, 1927
Hamblen, George H. (husband), d. April 20, 1897; age, 63 years (U. S. Navy)
Hamblen, Lida, d. Oct. 30, 1898; age, 64 years
Hamilton, Mamie, d. Sept. 19, 1872; age, 6 years
Hamilton, James G., d. Aug. 27, 1869; age, 52 years, 9 months, 1 day
Hamilton, Cornelia O., d. Feb. 26, 1912; age, 90 years, 1 month, 2 days
Hamonn, Margaret B., b. 1815, d. 1862
Hamonn, J. M., b. 1811, d. 1874
Hammon, M., b. March 29, 1842, d. Sept. 17, 1879 (Gov. marker) (Martin Hammon)
Hammon, Rosa, infant daughter of Martin and Mary Hammon, b. 1877, d. 1881
Hampton, William A., son of T. J. and Emma Hampton, d. Feb. 13, 1885; age, 23 years, 6 months, 11 days
Hampton, John, d. Aug. 31, 1920
Hampton, Susan Mary, b. Sept. 14, 1837, d. Aug. 11, 1905
Hampton, Lydia, mother of M. E. Isaac, b. Feb. 1, 1813, d. Feb. 8, 1894
Hamilton, Jos. M. C., d. Nov. 7, 1869; age, 24 years
Hamilton, J., son of J. I. and M. J. Hamilton, d. Nov. 26, 1879; age, 22 years
Harbaugh, Mattie A., d. Jan. 25, 1904; age, 67 years
Hardy, Stephen, Co. "A" 12th Indiana Inf. (Gov. marker)
Harlan, P. Morris, b. April 10, 1823, d. Jan. 31, 1893
Harlan, Rachael Griffiths, wife of P. Morris Harlan, b. March 25, 1832, d. May 5, 1904
Harlan, Elizabeth Gertrude, daughter of P. Morris and Rachael Harlan, b. Oct. 19, 1859, d. Jan. 26, 1861
Harris, John S., b. Aug. 22, 1827, d. Feb. 16, 1897
Harris, Virginia, b. March 28, 1873, d. Feb. 17, 1874
Harris, John, b. Dec. 4, 1795, d. Aug. 7, 1874
Harris, Henrietta, wife of John Harris, b. Feb. 2, 1804, d. April 24, 1881
Harris, Alexander L., b. Oct. 9, 1820, d. Aug. 27, 1898
Harris, Kate A., d. Jan. 25, 1906
Harris, William W. (M. D.), b. 1834, d. 1922
Harris, Nellie McCoy, b. 1840, d. 1926
Harris, Cordelia A., b. Sept. 20, 1829, d. March 8, 1898
Harris, William Warren, d. Aug. 6, 1865; age, 17 months, 3 days

Harris, Calvin McCoy, b. Jan. 31, 1866, d. Sept. 5, 1868
Harris, Thomas L., b. Oct. 17, 1868, d. June 25, 1870
Harris, William H., b. July 11, 1845, d. Feb. 6, 1895
Harris, J. A., d. March 20, 1904; age, 48 years, 6 months
Harris, Edgar E., d. June 29, 1900; age, 71 years
Harris, John B. (father), b. 1828, d. 1903
Harris, Elizabeth (mother), b. 1842, d. 1907
Harrison, John S., b. June 13, 1846, d. April 14, 1885
Harriman, —— (Soldier, Gov. marker)
Harrington, Rev. S. P., b. Nov. 27, 1827, d. Jan. 15, 1901
Harmonson, Lorinda (mother), d. July 22, 1900; age, 89 years
Harmony, Capt. J. H., Co. "L" 22nd Pa. Cav. (Gov. marker)
Hartwell, D. M., b. April 18, 1822, d. Sept. 28, 1878 (our mother)
Harp, Mary L. (sister), b. 1844, d. 1888 (See Tapp)
Harper, James P., b. Dec. 15, 1838, d. Feb. 3, 1899
Harper, Lottie, wife of Thomas L. Harper, d. June 21, 1877; age, 27 years
Hatfield, J. M. (Soldier)
Hashingger, J. A., d. Feb. 4, 1887; age, 35 years, 5 months, 6 days
Hasenbeler, N. (Soldier)
Hasselman, Ferdinand A., b. May 14, 1834, d. Jan. 27, 1888
Hancock, G. S., Co. "E" 199 N. Y. Inf. (Gov. marker)
Hausler, Charles J., d. Oct. 12, 1892; age, 40 years
Hansborough, Lucothoe M., wife of B. E. Hansborough, daughter of J. and M. Rubey
Harwood, O'Kelly, C—— E. Frank and C. V. Harwood, b. in Petersburgh, Va., Nov. 29, 1866, d. Aug. 19, 1867
Hayden, T. G., b. July 16, 1812, d. Aug. 10, 1881
Hayter, Almira, wife of E. A. J. Hayter, d. July 12, 1879; age, 42 years
Hayes, Samuel, Sergt. Co. "K" 132 Indiana Inf.
Hays, Margaret A., b. Aug. 26, 1831, d. Aug. 1, 1900 (mother)
Hays, William R., b. July 15, 1819, d. Jan. 28, 1898 (father)
Hays, J. M., b. Dec. 23, 1848, d. Feb. 21, 1905
Hayes, Ann Elizabeth, wife of Rev. John Hayes, b. Oct. 19, 1808, d. Aug. 16, 1883
Hayes, Rev. John, b. July 1, 1810, d. April 20, 1893
Hayes, W. T., Lt. Co. "K" 8th Iowa Inf. (Gov. marker)
Hayes, Walter, b. Oct. 11, 1838, d. Nov. 7, 1906
Hay, Frederick, b. April 2, 1831, d. Aug. 18, 1874 (Masonic Emblem)
Hazlett, Leah, d. April 9, 1900; age, 53 years
Hazlep, Jacob, b. June 10, 1812, d. March 8, 1896
Hazlep, Samuel E., b. Sept. 10, 1860, d. Sept. 21, 1885
Hearn, James, b. March 31, 1856, d. May 20, 1897
Heiep, Wilhelmine, b. June, 1833, d. Dec., 1885
Hellman, Christian, b. Oct. 20, 1829, d. Feb. 5, 1882
Hempel, Josephine, b. 1842, d. 1910
Hempel, Ernest W., b. 1831, d. 1915
Hempel, Christian —, b. March, —, 1808
Hendie, Mary A., b. Aug. 13, 1833, d. Dec. 9, 1886
Henning, Ben. Campbell, d. June 21, 1874 (?)
Henshaw, B. S., July 29, 1890; age, 70 years
Hereford, Dr. Henry F., b. Dec. 7, 1827, d. July 5, 1900
Hereford, Martha A., wife of Henry F. Hereford, b. May 16, 1832, d. June 22, 1914
Hereford, Benjamin H., b. April 21, 1830, d. July 2, 1890
Heinricks, Christian (Soldier), b. March 28, 1839, d. April 8, 1892
Huebetter, General Henry M., d. July 6, 1888 (3?); age, 75 years (Gov. marker)
Heydon, Ella E., b. Feb. 9, 1850, d. Nov. 25, 1894
Heydon, Dr. George E., b. April 27, 1830, d. April 19, 1888
Heyer, John, b. June 24, 1827, d. April 9, 1865

Heyer, Reginia, wife of John Heyer, b. July 18, 1838, d. July 26, 1864.
Hickok, Frank (Gov. marker)
Hickerson, Lucy Jane, b. 1856, d. 1901
High, Joseph H., b. Aug. 15, 1832, d. Aug. 19, 1883
Highley, W. J. (Soldier, Gov. marker)
Hiersley, Louise (mother), b. March 11, 1847, d. March 3, 1914
Hiff, Leopold, Co. "F" 1st Kansas Infantry (Gov. marker)
Hilliker, Martha Welch, wife of R. W. Hilliker, d. July 13, 1899; age, 66 years
Hilliker, R. W. (husband), b. April 7, 1830, d. Nov., 1903
Himes, F. M. (father), b. April 10, 1848, d. Nov. 1, 1905 (Soldier)
Hipshire, Dan. L., Co. "K" 45th Ohio Infantry (Gov. marker)
Hoenick, Louise, b. Feb. 17, 1831
Hoenick, Charles, b. Jan. 4, 1838, d. March 5, 1903
Hofmann, Olympia, mother of Ottokar Hofmann, b. Feb. 28, 1818, d. March 31, 1900
Hoffmeister, August G., b. Feb. 22, 1831, d. Feb. 16, 1872
Hoffmeister, Elizabeth, wife of August G. Hoffmeister, b. July 7, 1837, d. 1902
Hogan, John, Co. "E" 115th Ill. Inf. (Soldier, Gov. marker)
Hogan, Janet Thayer, b. in Glasgow, Scotland, May 16, 1825, d. Aug. 12, 1894
Hogue, Susan B., d. June 29, 1900 (no other dates)
Holman, Fred Augustus Churchill, son of H. R. and A. Holman, d. June 25, 1859; age, 2 years, 11 days
Holland, Analiza, d. Jan. 24, 1888; age, 47 years, 11 months, 7 days
Hollinghouser, Fred, b. Aug. 29, 1831, d. Dec. 28, 1905 (Gov. marker)
Hollinghouser, Amelia, b. Nov. 29, 1836, d. Jan. 23, 1910
Hollenback, Dovie G. M., daughter of T. and S. Hollenback, d. Dec. 31, 1862; age, 16 yrs.
Hollingsworth, Mary L., d. Sept. 21, 1878; age, 38 years
Holmes, W. J., d. April 29, 1886; age, 51 years
Holt, James R., d. Jan. 9, 1889; age, 54 years
Holladay, B. (Soldier, Gov. marker)
Holloway, James M., b. June 24, 1811, in Danville, Ky., d. Sept. 3, 1871; age, 60 years, 2 months, 10 days
Holloway, Evelyn Byrd, b. 1851, d. 1920
Holloway, James M., b. 1847, d. 1917
Holmberg, Selma, d. Aug., 1886, born in Sweden
Hooks, William, d. Feb. 4, 1869; age, 39 years, 7 months, 9 days
Hooks, Elizabeth M. (mother), b. 1833, d. 1908
Home, Edward, husband of Mary Home, d. Sept. 2, 1829; age, 68 years
Horn, James H., d. Feb. 10, 1874; age, 24 years, 8 months, 28 days
Horner, Emilie Christiana (mother), b. in Sachsen, Germany, July 20, 1830, d. Feb. 20, 1895
Horner, Carl August Anton, b. in Sachsen, Germany (father), March 12, 1829, d. Feb. 27, 1896
Hosman, Nettie, d. July 5, 1904; age, 45 years
Hosea, Mrs. Louisa, b. Feb. 24, 1806, d. Jan. 5, 1884; age, 78 years
Hosmer, Frances E., wife of A. L. Hosmer, d. April 21, 1870; age, 23 years, 4 months, 12 days
Horsley, W. L., d. Dec. 18, 1897
Houck, Solomon, b. June 2, 1802, d. Jan. 1, 1872
Houck, Rachel, wife of Solomon Houck, b. June, 1817, d. June 21, 1869
Houtell, William Y., d. 1864; age, 37 years
Hovey, Mary Frances, b. Jan. 1, 1845, d. March 30, 1881
Hovey, Lorenzo Dow, b. Nov. 9, 1808, d. Dec. 10, 1882
Hoyt, Benjamin, b. 1832, d. 1903
Howey, Anna Elizabeth, b. March 3, 1817, d. Aug. 13, 1906
Howey, H. G., d. June 26, 1902; age, 67 years
Howe, J. P., b. June 28, 1809, d. April 3, 1893

CEMETERIES—KAW TOWNSHIP

Howell, Lillian Price, wife of Dr. E. P. Howell, d. Dec. 4, 1897; age, 36 years
Huckett, Charles E. (father), b. in London, England, Jan. 22, 1844, d. July 7, 1894
Huckett, Janet (mother), b. in Glasgow, Scotland, June 2, 1846, d. Feb. 2, 1892
Hudson, John, d. June 16, 1871; age, 59 years
Hudson, Alonza B., b. May 6, 1877, d. March 20, 1904
Hudson, Sela, d. July 14, 1861; age, 57 years, 2 months
Hudson, Ralph W., d. July 11, 1873; age, 4 years
Huffaker, infant son of C. C. and E. H. Huffaker, d. Sept. 1, 1859
Huffaker, C. C., b. Nov. 17, 1823, d. April 1-, 1873
Huffaker, Nannie, b. Nov. 19, 1872, d. May 27, 1886
Huffaker, Kate M., b. 1839, d. 1915
Huffaker, Samuel J., b. 1830, d. 1897
Hume, Sabria, wife of W. L. Hundley, b. Jan. 14, 1838, d. April 25, 1894
Hundley, William L., b. April 12, 1836, d. July 11, 1906 (Huntley?)
Hunt, Winifred, wife of Noah Hunt, b. April 27, 1839, d. Feb. 28, 1906
Hunter, Richard S., b. July 8, 1829, d. July 6, 1858
Hunter, James M., b. June 2, 1808, d. Jan. 1, 1871
Hunter, Duke William, b. 1832, d. 1913
Hunter, J. Eugene, son of T. H. and Anna E. Hunter, d. July 30, 1866
Hunteman, Conrad Henry, b. in Lee County, Iowa, Aug. 13, 1852, d. Nov. 17, 1899; age, 47 years, 3 months, 4 days
Huntemann, Adolph, b. in Peine, Germany, Aug. 16, 1834, d. March 8, 1907
Huntemann, Christian Henry, b. in Peine, Hanover, Germany, Feb. 17, 1803, d. April 15, 1884; age, 81 years, 1 month, 28 days
Huntsinger, Elizabeth, d. March 10, 1903; age, 57 years
Hursley, John H., d. June 10, 1888; age, 58 years
Hutchinson, Clyde W., son of J. C. and L. A. Hutchinson, d. May 17, 1871; age, 2 years, 5 months, 9 days
Hyre, Elizabeth, wife of Isaac Hyre, d. March 4, 1892; age, 54 years, 5 months, 15 days
Hyre, Mary E., wife of W. E. Hyre, d. Nov. 18, 1887; age, 24 years, 4 months
Hyre, Angline, daughter of I. and E. Hyre, d. March 21, 1875; age, 13 years
Hyatt, Siebie E., d. July 22, 1874; age, 23 years
Hydeman, G. S., b. April 6, 1851, d. March 2, 1901
Hyne, Frank L., d. Jan. 15, 1884; age, 51 years, 6 months, 7 days
Hyne, Mary E., wife of Frank L. Hyne, b. April 22, 1848, d. Nov. 10, 1897

I

Ingle, John, Co. "D" 2nd Kansas Cav. (Gov. marker)
Ingraham, Aylwin, d. March 4, 1871; age, 55 years, 9 months, 9 days
Inscho, Ozias J., b. Nov. 10, 1829, d. June 5, 1900
Inscho, Lydia Eaton, b. March 17, 1836, d. May 30, 1929
Irwin, Julia M. Hughs, wife of J. C. Irwin, d. Jan. 20, 1878; age, 30 years, 6 months
Irwin, Martha E., wife of Lieut. A. S. Irwin, b. Aug. 22, 1829, d. March 25, 1895
Irwin, J. C., b. April 18, 1818, d. March 31, 1909
Irwin, Mary Hamilton, b. Feb. 10, 1832, d. Jan. 6, 1915; age, 83 years
Irwin, Joseph William, son of J. C. and Mary Irwin, b. Aug. 12, 1854, d. Aug. 17, 1921; age, 67 years, 5 days
Isaac, Missouri E., wife of W. J. Isaac, b. Feb. 1, 1855, d. May 4, 1897
Ives, T. N., d. May 30, 1891; age, 55 years
Ivy, William, d. Dec. 20, 1895 (stone sunken in ground so rest of inscription cannot be read)

J

Jackson, Charles C., d. July 7, 1900; age, 75 years, 11 months (Soldier)
Jackson, Sarah, wife of Charles C., b. Aug. 17, 1828, d. July 9, 1904
Jackson, William W., son of J. M. and J. M. Jackson, b. Aug. 19, 1853, d. Sept. 12, 1866
Jackson, Margaret E., b. 1839, d. 1892, wife of Peter A. Jackson

Jackson, Peter A., b. 1835, d. 1897 (Soldier)
Jackman, Thomas A., d. Feb. 16, 1900; age, 45 years, 3 months, 11 days
Jacobs, Charles Fremont, b. 1856, d. 1890
Jaeger, Anna, b. Jan. 2, 1846, d. Dec. 30, 1904
James, Milton, b. March 22, 1842, d. Feb. 14, 1895
James, T. M., b. 1823, d. 1901
James, S. A., b. 1827, d. 1916
James, Lottie, b. June 2, 1845, d. Feb. 28, 1899
James, Howard Marshall, son of Thomas and B. A. James, b. Nov. 16, 1853, d. Jan. 29, 1864
James, John N., Co. "L" 1st Missouri Light Artillery (Gov. marker)
James, Ephraim, d. April 8, 1882; age, 82 years
Jaudon, Benjamin, b. in the State of South Carolina, Nov. 18, 1795, d. Jan. 27, 187-
Jaudon, William Huston, d. Aug. 8, 1869
Jaudon, Sarah Eva, d. July, 1875; both are children of Thos. P. and Eva N. Jaudon
Javens, Eveline T., b. Aug. 16, 1825, d. Jan. 29, 1852 (On Ragan lot)
Jay, William H., of Texas—no dates
Jewett, Callie B., wife of William A. Jewett, b. 1849, d. 1919
Jewett, B. M. (M. D.), b. Aug. 20, 1810, in Greenwich, Mass., d. Jan. 6, 1879
Jewett, Matilda, b. 1809, d. 1865
Jewett, Annie M., daughter of B. M. and —— Jewett, b. Jan. 27, 1848, d. July 24, 1867
Jewett, William A., b. Dec. 2, 1840, d. Jan. 15, 1879
Jobe, Henry, son of Henry and Elizabeth Jobe, of Martinsberg, Berkley County, Pa., d. Feb., 1819; age, 38 years, 5 months, 12 days
Johns, Phillip (father), b. 1830, d. 1906 (Soldier)
Joern, Christiana, b. Sept. 27, 1801, d. May 5, 1873 (see Guenther)
Johnson, Edward Payson, b. Oct. 2, 1835, d. Nov. 16, 1906
Johnson, Daniel W., b. March 17, 1836, d. Aug. 10, 1897, Michigan Cav. (Gov. marker)
Johnson, James W., b. Feb. 6, 1831, d. Sept. 2, 1895
Johnson, Anna B., wife of James W. Johnson, b. Aug. 14, 1840, d. Nov. 7, 1886
Johnson, Augusta, wife of F. Johnson, d. Jan. 9, 1879; age, 35 years, 8 months, 14 days
Johnson, H. P., b. March 14, 1850, d. Jan. 31, 1900
Johnson, John F., d. July 11, 1931; age, 71 years, 9 months, 19 days
Johnson, William, d. March 17, 1894; age, 93 years
Johnson, G. E., d. July 21, 1887; age, 71 years
Johnson, Gustaf, b. April 26, 1828, d. Nov. 2, 1908
Johnson, Anna, wife of F. J. Johnson, d. March 28, 1907; age, 56 years
Johnson, E. L., Co. "E" 51st Ohio Infantry (Gov. marker)
Johnson, James H., b. Aug., 1822, d. Aug. 10, 1851
Johnson, Jacob S., b. Jan. 1, 1847, d. May 7, 1849
Johnson, John W., b. April 5, 1855, d. Nov. 24, 1897
Johnson, Fanney, d. Oct. 6, 1892; age, 55 years
Johansson, Johan, b. Aug. 15, 1854, d. Aug. 10, 1901
Jones, John W., b. April 30, 1837, d. Nov. 19, 1914 (born Cardiff, South Wales)
Jones, wife of John W. Jones, b. March 6, 1842, Cardiff, South Wales, d. Jan. 15, 1904
Jones, Anne, wife of John E. Jones, d. Oct. 5, 1878; age, 54 years
Jones, John E., d. April 7, 1902; age, 77 years
Jones, Alex. A., d. Feb. 24, 1901; age, 52 years
Jones, Martha G., d. Aug. 15, 1869; age, 65 years
Jones, Margaret Anna (mother), b. 1842, d. 1898
Jones, Julia, wife of Thomas Jones, b. Sept. 5, 1833, d. Feb. 23, 1902
Jones, Thomas A., b. in Simpson County, Ky., March 25, 1825, d. March 27, 1888
Jones, William H., b. 1854, d. 1915
Jones, Lela Watkins, b. 1865, d. 1923
Jones, Thomas, d. June 20, 1883; age, 47 years
Jonkowsky, Nettie, b. Feb. 21, 1833, d. Sept. 1, 1895 (mother)
Jordon, Hannar R., b. Sept. 27, 1812, d. Sept. 6, 1874

Jorkman, Olaf B., b. March 24, 1846, d. Sept. 24, 1901
Jorkman, Anna B., b. 1843, d. 1908
Judson, Ella (Old stone impossible to read dates)
Jurgle, Mariah, b. 1856, d. 1901
Jury, Edward T. (father), b. June 10, 1824, d. July 6, 1902
Jury, Polly A. (mother), b. March 3, 1827, d. Nov. 4, 1901

K

Kail, Garagathia (mother), b. 1846, d. 1926
Kail, Alexander (father), b. Feb. 26, 1833, d. April 28, 1891
Kaneen, Robert, husband of E. Kaneen, d. April 12, 1888; age, 63 years
Kaut, Bertha, Jan. 26, 1851, d. May 26, 1897
Kearney, Hattie Drisdom, b. Dec. 25, 1844, d. Feb. 20, 1927
Kearney, Josephine, b. June 28, 1832, d. Jan. 11, 1913
Kearney, Charles E., b. March 8, 1820, d. Jan. 3, 1898
Keck, John L., b. Feb. 8, 1840, d. Oct. 5, 1875
Keefer, Luther W., d. July 26, 1871; age, 15 years, 10 months, 26 days
Keefer, Willie E., d. Sept. 25, 1864; age, 10 months, 8 days
Kell, Sarah Ann Brand (mother), b. Feb. 5, 1831, d. Feb. 29, 1904
Kelly, James, d. Jan., 1886; age, 81 years
Kelly, Mary, wife of James Kelly, d. Dec., 1855; age, 82 years
Kelly, Dean S., b. Jan. 8, 1838, d. May 1, 1906
Kelly, Dilla S. Holden, b. May 26, 1836, d. April 17, 1896
Kelly, Margaret (mother), b. 1846, d. 1910
Kelly, Rush, b. Jan. 3, 1835, d. Nov., 1903
Keeney, George M., d. March 14, 1888; age, 59 years, 3 months, 6 days
Keeney, Rhuanna, wife of George M. Keeney, d. March 17, 1888; age, 58 years, 9 months, 10 days
Keeney, Lou Ann Wade, d. Aug. 1, 1855; age, 18 years, 11 months, 10 days (moved from Keeney Cemetery)
Kempf, Elizabeth, b. 1838, d. 1918
Kiene, L. W., b. 1838, d. 1912
Kiene, Wilhelmine, wife of William Kiene, d. Sept. 7, 1894
Kiesel, George, b. March 11, 1855, d. Feb. 26, 1896
(King) Ella M. Cunningham, daughter of J. and E. A. King, b. Sept. 17, 1857, d. March 14, 1884
Kiley, William, b. March 12, 1855, d. Feb. 5, 1902
Kimmons, John, Co. "F" 47th Iowa Infantry (Gov. marker)
King, William H., d. March 4, 1893; age, 42 years, 6 months, 15 days
King, Peter, Co. "E" (Stone sunken in ground so that rest of inscription is invisible)
King, Sarah, d. March 14, 1902; age, 77 years
Kinkead, James H. (father), b. 1828, d. May 22, 1876
Kinley, no first name given (mother), b. Sept. 28, 1824, d. Jan. 12, 1884
Kinley, no first name given (father), d. Nov. 25, 1863; age, 44 years (Soldier)
Kintner, Flora M., wife of J. A. Kintner, b. July 4, 1855, d. March 25, 1887
Kirk, Thomas, husband of Margaret Kirk, b. in Crawford, Scotland, May 16, 1849, d. Dec. 28, 1891
Kirkpatrick, Alexander, b. March 2, 1809, d. Feb. —, 1867
Kirk, John, Co. "A" (Gov. marker)
Klaber, Mary Louise, d. 1877; age, 19 years
Klaber, Eugenia, b. May 12, 1861, d. Dec. 28, 1867
Klayber, Eliza L. Price, b. Sept. 2, 1811
Klayber, Frederick, d. 1865; age, 85 years
Klayber, Frederick, d. Dec. 11, 1866; age, 36 years, 8 months, 3 days
Knight, John M., b. Nov. 24, 1851, d. May 8, 1908
Knight, Amelia, b. 1847, d. 1917

Knauber, Marie Anna, b. June 14, 1798, d. June 6, 1884; age, 85 years, 11 months, 22 days (Becker name on same monument)
Koons, Mary Ann (mother), wife of Daniel Koons, d. July 18, 1892; age, 48 years, 5 months, 11 days
Kreanzlein, Margaret, b. April 20, 1815, d. March 4, 1875
Kretchmar, Anna, b. March 14, 1830, d. Jan. 3, 1912
Kretchmar, F. E., b. 1848, d. 1914
Kretchmar, Elizabeth, d. Jan. 30, 1933; age, 81 years, 11 months, 19 days
Kohlmeyer, Elizabeth B., wife of G. Kohlmeyer, d. Sept. 23, 1878; age, 42 years
Knoche, Emma, wife of Daniel Knoche, nee Kraenzlein, b. Nov. 17, 1854, d. July 26, 1882
Knowlden, Annie, wife of Offei, b. Aug. 16, 1847, d. Oct. 28, 1903
Kranzlein, John G., b. Nov. 19, 1811, d. May 22, 1903 (Gov. marker)
Kranzlein, Louise, b. April 20, 1819, d. May 8, 1907
Kroos, Henry, son of F. H. and Minnie Kroos, d. 1879; age, 17 months
Kroos, Frank H., d. Sept. 5, 1878; age, 35 years, 11 months, 9 days (Gov. marker)
Krueger, Albert H. E., b. May 10, 1846, d. Nov. 15, 1907
Knackstedt, Louis, b. Oct. 21, 1834, d. Dec. 11, 1902
Kuehne, L. C., d. Sept. 10, 1879; age, 55 years, 3 months, 10 days
Kuehne, Mary, wife of L. C. Kuehne, d. April 4, 1885; age, 59 years, 2 months, 2 days
Kuge, August, b. Aug. 16, 1822, d. April 22, 18—
Kump, Lillian A., d. April 29, 1893; age, 18 years, 5 months
Kump, Lucretia (mother), b. 1841, d. 1925
Kunz, Jacob, b. Aug. 18, 1804, d. Oct. 28, 1886
Kunz, Rossina, wife of Jacob Kunz, b. Jan. 16, 1814, d. Aug. 16, 1886
Kyley, Martha A. (Coleman), wife of D. B. Kyley and daughter of John and Fannie U. Coleman
Kyrk, Isaac H., d. Dec. 2, 1897; age, 88 years

L

Lach, Frederich, b. June 17, 1823, d. Oct. 23, 1889
Laemmle, Christian, b. May 10, 1858, d. April 16, 1897
LaHines, Dennis, b. Oct. 25, 1836, d. May 15, 1897 (Gov. marker)
LaHines, Elizabeth, wife of Dennis LaHines, d. Dec. 14, 1889; age, 46 years
Lakey, Anne Wilcox, d. Dec. 3, 1895; age, 89 years (Erected by her children, W. H. Gregg and Julia E. Cooper)
Lambert, Florence, no dates
Lambert, Benjamin, no dates
Lambert, Frederick, no dates
Lambert, Mary, no dates
Lamphere, George E., d. Dec. 30, 1895; age, 48 years
Landon, Mattie A., d. Sept. 18, 1846, d. Nov. 7, 1907
Langdon, Marietta, b. 1824, d. 1897
Largent, Charles T., d. Jan. 27, 1902; age, 46 years
Larson, Peter M., b. 1842, d. 1908
Larson, Johanna, b. 1839, d. 1914
Laugum, Stephen, d. April 10, 1933; age, 78 years
Laundy, Fletcher, b. Sept., 1830, d. Oct. 18, 1911
Laundy, Catherine, wife of Fletcher Laundy, b. Feb. 12, 1838, d. Sept. 12, 1896
Lantz, Elizabeth, b. in Shenandoah Co., Va., Sept., 1787, d. Jan. 11, 1876; age, 89 years, 4 months, 12 days
Lattimore, Col. R., d. March 11, 1876; age, 58 years
Layton, Mary L., wife of Frank Layton, b. Sept. 20, 1850, d. Dec. 7, 1885
Leach, Permelia, wife of Thomas Leach, b. Oct. 4, 1849, d. May 19, 1880; age, 30 years, 7 months, 15 days
Lee, Harry M., of Liverpool, England, d. in Kansas City, Mo., Feb. 13, 1885; age, 23 years
Lee, Emily M., b. in Plymouth, Ohio, Aug. 16, 1855, d. Feb. 10, 1881

CEMETERIES—KAW TOWNSHIP

Lee, Rev. James, d. Feb. 16, 1879; age, 63 years, 10 months, 12 days
Lee, Greene, d. March 8, 188-; age, 18 years
Leavens, William Wilshire, d. Jan. 15, 1880; age, 58 years, 10 months, 11 days
Leavens, Lucy McCutcheon, wife of William Wilshire Leavens, d. June 13, 1893; age, 53 years, 11 months, 26 days
Leininger, William (father), b. 1836, d. 1904
Leininger, Anna Mary (mother), b. 1841, d. 1908
Letzie, Augustem (father), b. Dec., 1832, in Stollberg Sachsen, Germany, d. Aug., 1895 (Inscription in German)
Letzie, Stone bearing the word "Mutter" (mother), no name nor dates
Levering, Levi L., b. Oct. 8, 1831, d. Sept. 17, 1909
Levering, Sarah M., wife of Levi L. Levering, b. June 4, 1841, d. Oct. 10, 1889
Lewis, Martha I., b. March 21, 1815, d. Oct. 7, 1890
Lewis, Rees J., b. Aug. 28, 1830, d. Feb. 25, 1907 (Lieut. Gov. marker)
Lewis, Mary Elizabeth, wife of Lt. Rees J. Lewis, b. June 27, 1839, d. Oct. 25, 1905
Lewis, Christine, b. 1843, d. 1898
Light, John, b. Feb. 4, 1790, d. Oct. 14, 1869
Light, Martha, wife of J. Light, b. Jan. 28, 1800, d. Jan. 15, 1883
Lindsay, David, b. Nov. 10, 1802, d. Feb. 21, 1890
Lindsay, Malvina O., b. Dec. 15, 1810, d. Feb. 23, 1890
Lindsley, Louisiana P., b. Aug. 27, 1816, d. April 10, 1888
Lines, Elizabeth E. (mother), d. Dec. 20, 1900; age, 64 years
Linkogel, Elizabeth, d. Dec. 29, 1917; age, 72 years, 11 months, 14 days
Linkogel, Joseph, d. Oct. 22, 1893; age, 71 years, 8 months
Little, Jane A., b. Aug. 27, 1827, d. June 18, 1903
Little, Alice, b. Dec. 28, 1852, d. May 7, 1890
Lloyd, Eulalie, youngest daughter of A. J. and A. E. Lloyd, d. Aug. 17, 1861; age, 1 year, 11 months, 17 days
Lloyd, A. J., d. Aug. 16, 1866; age, 29 years, 1 month, 19 days (Lieut. Gov. marker)
Lloyd, Adelaide E., wife of A. J. Lloyd, b. Jan. 24, 1839, d. Sept. 28, 1908
Loesch, George, b. Sept. 27, 1829, d. Sept. 13, 1866
Loesch, Saloma, wife of George Loesch, b. April 1, 1830, d. June 19, 1896
Logan, Bertha E., b. Oct. 28, 1852, d. Oct. 6, 1900
Long, William, d. Sept. 2, 1858; age, 38 years
Long, Caroline, b. Dec. 28, 1856, d. Feb. 17, 1865
Long, David S. (father), b. Oct. 28, 1836, d. April 8, 1900
Long, Mollie L., b. March, 1841, d. Dec. 12, 1897
Long, Lt. Col. John S., d. Jan. 2, 1880; age, 46 years (Gov. marker)
Long, Lt. D. S. Long (Gov. marker)
Long, Amelia, no dates
Longbenkamp, Frank, b. Oct. 1, 1830, d. Aug. 28, 1866
Loughridge, John A., d. May 7, 1887; age, 54 years
Loughridge, Cindarella E., wife of John A. Loughridge, b. Feb. 28, 1839, d. Jan. 10, 1874
Love, Ann Elizabeth, b. Jan. 5, 1821, d. Aug. 21, 1890
Love, George Louis, Jr., b. Oct. 19, 1832, d. June 17, 1890
Lowe, Hattie E., b. 1857, d. 1888
Lowe, J. H., d. Nov. 1, 1899; age, 37 years, 9 months, 9 days
Lowe, Milton M., b. Sept. 10, 1854, d. Oct. 2, 1904
Lowell, Alfred A., Co. "A", b. April 22, 1845 (Gov. marker)
Lowell, J. F., b. June 24, 1818
Lowell, Martha, no dates
Lucas, Charles D., b. 1834, d. 1903
Lucas, Laura Fisher, b. 1844, d. 1913
Lucas, John D., Co. "C" 62 Regt. Ohio Vol. Inf., b. Aug., 1834, d. Oct. 15, 1899 (Gov. marker)
Luedermann, Dora, b. Aug. 22, 1811, d. Feb. 1, 1891

Luedermann, Ludweig, b. March 24, 1815, d. Feb. 9, 1891
Lukens, Margery, d. Aug. 6, 1889
Lunau, Emma — (mother), wife of D. C. Lunau, d. Oct. 29, 1888
Lush, G. W., b. Feb. 28, 1837, d. July 10, 1901
Lykins, Dr. Johnston, b. April 15, 1800, d. Aug. 15, 1876 (Mayor in 1854)

M

Machette, Samuel (Soldier), b. Feb. 10, 1830, d. Nov. 5, 1895
Machette, infant son of S. M. and A. Machette (See inscription of Thos. Wilson, on monument with Machette)
Madeira, Rev. Addison Dashiell, b. 1828, d. 1919
Madeira, Price E., b. 1841, d. 1876
Madeira, Louise Isett, b. 1832, d. 1871
Magnuson, b. April 23, 1857, d. July 15, 1901
Mahne, John H., b. Aug. 6, 1843, d. Jan. 29, 1897; age, 53 years
Maiden, Roy I., no dates
Maiden, Grace, no dates
Majors, Alexander, b. Oct. 4, 1814, d. Jan. 13, 1900
Majors, Katerine Stalcup, wife of Alexander Majors, b. Sept. 26, 1820, d. Feb. 13, 1856
Malone, Milton A., b. 1821, d. 1895
Maltery, Charles J., d. Jan. 3, 1888; age, 26 years
Mann, William P., d. 1872; age, 40 years
Mantel, Sayab, d. Aug. 8, 1901; age, 79 years, 9 months, 2 days
Mansfield, Frankie, daughter of J. P. and L. C. (old stone)
Mansfield, Charles C., d. July 12, 1908; age, 58 years
Mapes, John, b. March 18, 1791, d. June 26, 1871
March, George, b. June 19, 1829, d. April 9, 1902
Mark, Julia S. Hood, wife of —— Mark, d. 1886
Marks, J. N. (Gov. marker)
Marks, Caroline L. Taylor, wife of John N. Marks, b. Dec. 24, 1822, d. April 15, 1910
Market, F. H., b. Sept. 29, 1832, d. July 17, 1908
Marlatt, Sophronia (mother), wife of Isaac Marlatt, Sr., b. Sept. 16, 1816, d. Sept. 23, 1886
Marrs, John B., d. July 9, 1888; age, 52 years
Marrs, Sarah J., d. March 2, 1918; age, 78 years
Martin, John S., b. Sept. 14, 1818, d. Oct. 16, 1904
Martin, Margaretta M., wife of J. S. Martin, d. Oct. 19, 1889; age, 52 years
Martin, Henry, b. Dec. 24, 1817, d. June 26, 1880
Martin, Margaret, b. Sept. 6, 1828, d. May 27, 1910
Martin, Katy M., b. April 7, 1853, d. April 6, 1890
Martin, Capt. J. W. (John), d. March 7, 1874; age, 38 years
Martyn, David E., b. Aug. 25, 1849, d. Sept. 15, 1901
Martyn, Harriet J., wife of David E. Martyn, b. June 12, 1844, d. March 30, 1902
Martyn, Jacob, Co. "B" 2nd Colo. Cav. (Gov. marker)
Marugg, Otto, b. Nov. 17, 1857, in Grausinnen Schweitz, d. Dec. 3, 1893; age, 36 years
Marsh, Timothy W., son of G. and O. A. Marsh, d. Feb. 28, 1860; age, 1 year
Marsh, "Little Jennie," daughter of W. P. and Althea Marsh, d. Oct. 11, 1869; age, 1 year, 3 months, 4 days
Marshall, L. A., b. Jan. 11, 1843, d. March 30, 1901
Marshall, Eliza, wife of M. P. Marshall, d. Oct. 24, 1898; age, 67 years
Marshall, Zilpha A., wife of Lewis Marshall, b. Jan. 27, 1847, d. March 28, 1903
Marshall, John W., b. 1848, d. 1924 (In Navy during Civil War)
Marshall, Samuel J., b. 1846, d. 1910
Max, Katherine and Baby, wife and child of G. L. Max (daughter of F. L. and K. Ludwig), d. March 20, 1870; age, 22 years
Mayer, Johanna, wife of Charles Mayer, b. July 29, 1833, d. Nov. 16, 1883

Mayer, Rudolph H., b. June 9, 1858, d. April 17, 1909
Mastin, D. G., b. 1842, d. 1899
Mastin, Mildred E., b. 1847, d. 1913
Mathias, Daniel, b. in Dowlair, Wales, July 17, 1833, d. Jan. 30, 1892
Mathias, Charlotte, wife of D. Mathias, d. Dec. 21, 1887; age, 54 years
Mathias, William, b. Aug. 10, 1856, d. June 7, 1900
Marques, Emmett O., d. April 9, 1901; age, 48 years
Masuch, C. E. (husband), b. 1824, d. 1873
Masuch, Amelia (wife), b. 1837, d. 1907
Maughs, Stephen, b. 1776, d. 1857
Muehlbach, Joe, b. Oct. 20, 1851, d. 1890
Meader, Fleming T., b. 1823, d. 1912
Medsker, D. A. (Gov. marker)
Medsker, A. M., d. March 12, 1894; age, 50 years
Mehaffy, Sarah, wife of Gideon Brown, b. 1816, d. 1890
Mehaffey, A. W., b. 1843, d. 1916
Mehaffey, George W., b. 1818, d. 1864 (Soldier)
Mehornay, Manlius D., b. 1840, d. 1903
Mehornay, Mattie A., wife of Manlius D. Mehornay, b. 1843, d. 1875
Meily, Samuel, b. June 26, 1804, d. Sept. 19, 1861
Melville, Richard, b. May 25, 1835, d. April 18, 1907
Melville, Jane, wife of Richard Melville, b. May 24, 1839, d. April 4, 1879
Melville, Annie, sister of Richard Melville, b. Oct. 12, 1839, d. June 14, 1903
Mennis, Josephine F., b. 1852, d. 1889 (On Barber lot)
Mensing, Mary A., wife of J. H. Mensing, b. April 17, 1835, d. June 22, 1883
Menop, Martha, wife of J. A. Menop, b. Feb. 7, 1845, d. Jan. 31, 1901
Merritt, William M., b. Dec. 14, 1886; age, 45 years, 1 month, 6 days
Messerschmidt, George G., b. July 14, 1826, d. Aug. 18, 1868 (Soldier)
Messerschmidt, Anna Marie, b. 1810
Mickel, Serena M., daughter of J. S. and Sarah A. Mickel, d. Oct. 22, 1884; age, 26 years, 6 months, 2 days
Middleton, Mary E., wife of A. J. Middleton, b. May 23, 1852, d. June 30, 1889
Millard, Martin Sanford, d. Jan. 4, 1912; age, 62 years, 5 months
Miller, Amalia, b. 1841, d. 1887
Miller, Ellen W., wife of John K. Miller, b. 1816, d. 1891
Miller, John K., b. 1816, d. 1902
Miller, Johan Konrad, b. June 8, 1854, d. June 1, 1903
Miller, Clara E., b. May 23, 1849, d. Feb. 15, 1891 (On Diveley Monument)
Milligan, Elizabeth H., wife of B. Milligan, b. Oct. 16, 1829, d. Oct. 30, 1896
Milligan, B., b. Aug. 12, 1826, d. April 20, 1910
Mills, N. C., b. Oct. 11, 1872, d. Jan. 27, 1873
Mills, E. G., Co. "I" 23rd Iowa Inf. (Gov. marker)
Millspaugh, Sarah Frances, wife of A. W. Millspaugh, b. Sept. 1, 1839, d. May 16, 1874
Millet, H. S., b. Feb. 14, 1834, d. July 16, 1910
Mimms, Elizabeth, b. April 29, 1821, d. June 29, 1899; age, 78 years
Mimms, David W., d. July 27, 1879; age, 65 years, 10 months, 18 days
Mitchell, Lee W., b. Aug. 23, 1840, d. May 9, 1893
Mitchell, Emeranda L., wife of F. A. Mitchell, d. June 7, 1871; age, 35 years, 8 months, 21 days
Mize, Mary, b. June 29, 1807, d. Feb. 9, 1871
Montgomery, Merand, wife of C. J. Montgomery, b. June 5, 1836, d. Nov. 7, 1890
Monroe, Sarah E., d. June 16, 1901; age, 53 years
Mooney, Joseph (father), d. Jan. 13, 1892; age, 76 years
Moran, Paul, d. May 21, 1895
Moreland, J. D. (dates too worn to read)
Moreland, Ella A., d. Dec. 8, 1929; age, 84 years, 6 months, 26 days

Moreland, W. H., Co. "B" 43rd Maryland Infantry (Gov. marker)
Morgan, Henrietta, wife of D. T. Morgan, b. Feb. 26, 1842
Morgan, Charlotte, d. March 10, 1893; age, 83 years
Morgan, A. H., b. Oct. 3, 1845, d. Oct. 27, 1907
Morgan, Ella, wife of A. H. Morgan, b. Sept. 6, 1855, d. Aug. 2, 1911
Moore, Mrs. Clara L. (daughter), b. March 27, 1850, d. Sept. 25, 1877 (On Eldridge Monument)
Moore, Charles, Co. "H" 19th Kansas Cav. (Gov. marker)
Moore, Caleb W., b. March 20, 1854, d. March 14, 1882
Moore, D. J. E., d. Nov. 20, 1891; age, 63 years
Moore, Owen H., son of Harriet and Allyn Moore, d. Aug. —, 1869; age, 19 years
Moore, Tom (Pop), b. April 8, 1819, d. Feb. 19, 1897
Moore, Sergt. A. T., Co. "F" 39th La. Inf. (Gov. marker)
Mohr, Kasper, b. in Bremen, Deutschland, March 9, 1825, d. Oct. 5, 1898
Mohr, Metta, d. Dec. 19, 1900; age, 70 years
Morris, James M., d. Feb. 1, 1894; age, 78 years
Morris, Sarah A., wife of S. Z. Morris (mother), d. April 4, 1883; age, 49 years
Morris, Silas Z. (father), b. 1832, d. 1915
Morris, Joel T., b. Jan. 26, 1822, d. Dec. 7, 1872
Morris, Robert S., b. Sept. 11, 1854, d. Oct. 7, 1855; son of J. T. and M. J. Morris
Morris, Nannie S., b. Aug. 15, 1858, d. Nov. 17, 1859; daughter of J. T. and M. J. Morris
Morrow, Willie, b. Oct. 25, 1876, d. Jan. 30, 1881
Moos, John (Soldier, Gov. marker)
Moos, Frank, b. Aug. 8, 1853, d. April 16, 1871
Moske, Emma T., d. Dec. 12, 1930; age, 73 years, 5 months, 15 days
Moseley, Minnie L., b. 1844, d. 1885
Moseley, Eliza P., b. Nov. 12, 1812, d. Oct. 21, 1880
Mosher, Catherine, daughter of George Clark and Ida Beagle Mosher
Mosher, George Stanford, b. 1836, d. 1909
Muengu, Mul., b. Aug. 29, 1851, d. March 15, 1892
Muff, Freda S., d. Jan. 28, 1908; age, 79 years
Muehlschuster, Michael, b. July 15, 1813, d. — 14, 1870
Muehlschuster, Marie, b. April 28, 1821, d. Dec. 25, 1905
Muehlschuster, Joseph, b. March 17, 1844, d. Jan. 20, 1901
Mulligan, California, wife of William Mulligan, b. Oct. 6, 1859, d. Sept. 4, 1885
Muir, Nannie E., wife of H. P. Muir, d. April 18, 1898; age, 60 years
Muir, Elbia T., b. Oct. 10, 1866, d. Feb. 17, 1896
Muir, Agnes Ella, d. May 19, 1826; age, 10 months
Murray, W., d. Dec. 4, 1886; age, 57 years
Murray, Mary Jane, daughter of William and Jane Murray, d. Nov. 20, 1882; age, 24 years, 8 months, 8 days
Murth, Bertha Marie, d. Nov. 5, 1898; age, 41 years
Murphy, Andrew E., b. 1850, d. 1921
Murphy, Margaret E., b. 1857, d. 1899
Myers, W. E., b. in Knox Co., Ohio, Aug. 26, 1848, d. May 14, 1884
Myers, Lillie, b. in Oblong, Ill., July 10, 1854, d. Oct. 14, 1902

Mc

McArthur, Jessie, wife of J. W. McArthur, d. Nov. 19, 1878; age, 37 years
McCall, Catherine (Grove), b. in Baltimore, Md., July 12, 1802, d. Oct. 16, 1889
McClain, Mary, d. Aug. 17, 1894; age, 52 years, 8 months
McCarty, Charles G., b. Oct. 4, 1821, d. July 23, 1852; age, 30 years, 9 months, 19 days
McClelland, Mervin Stuart, d. Nov. 13, 1893; age, 28 years, 1 month, 13 days; native of Greenook, Scotland
McClelland, Christiana A., wife of Rev. D. M. McClelland, d. Sept. 18, 1880; age, 39 years, 3 months, 6 days

CEMETERIES—KAW TOWNSHIP

McClelland, William (Gov. marker)
McClintock, Elizabeth C., b. April 11, 1830, d. May 20, 1901
McConnell, Louis N., b. July 25, 1840, d. Oct. 20, 1904
McConnell, E., b. June 1, 1858, d. Feb. 27, 1892
McCormack, Mary E., wife of T. C. McCormack, d. Nov. 28, 1896; age, 51 years, 2 months, 20 days
McCormack, John T., b. July 24, 1832, d. Feb. 7, 1903
McCormack, Willie F., d. Nov. 16, 1865; age, 7 years
McCormack, Baby Elizabeth, d. Sept. 3, 1867 (Children of J. F. and M. E. McCormack)
McCory, John, d. Feb. 9, 1892; age, 76 years
McCory, James H., d. Nov. 20, 1913; age, 75 years
McCoy, Virginia Chick, wife of John C. McCoy, b. May 28, 1849; died of Cholera; age, 28 years, 5 months, 6 days
McCoy, Spenser, d. Jan. 8, 1863; age, 18 years, 5 months, 14 days
McCoy, John Calvin, b. Sept. 28, 1811, d. Sept. 2, 1889; age, 79 years
McCoy, Elizabeth, wife of John C. McCoy, b. March 7, 1819, d. Aug. 7, 1896
McDill, E. B., d. Oct. 7, 1874; age, 33 years (Soldier)
McDill, C. S.; age, 47 years
McDonald, Capt. J. O., Co. "E" 43rd Ohio Inf. (Gov. marker)
McDonald, Mary S. (mother), d. Jan. 22, 1904; age, 52 years
McDonald, Lucia, wife of J. McDonald, b. in Willsborough, N. J., Jan. 22, 1834, d. Jan. 9, 1884
McDowell, Joseph, b. Dec. 25, 1814, d. Feb. 19, 1888
MacDowell, Mary E., b. 1844, d. 1897 (on McDonald lot)
McDowell, S. M., b. Jan. 6, 1836, d. March 20, 1906
McDowell, Mary E., wife of A. McDowell, b. Dec. 3, 1851, d. Nov. 10, 1900
McGee, Ruth J. (mother), b. 1842, d. 1904
McGee, A. B. H., b. May 21, 1815, d. Oct. 7, 1903
McGee, Sue B., wife of A. B. H. McGee, b. March 8, 1848, d. May 9, 1901
McGee, Adelia S., daughter of —— McGee, b. and d. March 29, 1839
McGee, Alice M., daughter of —— McGee, b. April 3, 1843, d. Dec. 6, 1856
McGee, Albert H., son of —— McGee, b. Aug. 6, 1849, d. Dec. 31, 1851
McGuire, Andrew (Gov. marker)
McLaughlin, Hugh, d. Feb. 7, 1880; age, 59 years
McLeod, George W., d. May 25, 1869; age, 39 years
McNabb, Elizabeth, no dates
McNevins, Charlotte, d. May 5, 1898; age, 48 years
McNutt, Rev. Patterson (D. D.), b. Aug. 27, 1832, d. Feb. 9, 1886
McNutt, Louise Slavens, wife of Rev. Patterson McNutt, b. Dec. 14, 1833, d. Feb. 14, 1894
McNutt, Collin, b. Jan. 7, 1802, d. July 13, 1888 (Gov. marker)
McNutt, Mary Ann, b. Feb. 1, 1811, d. Jan. 16, 1875
McNutt, Frances M., b. Nov. 20, 1845, d. July 19, 1931
McPherson, Hannah Cary, b. in Seneca Co., Ohio, Jan. 10, 1837, d. Sept. 24, 1928
McPherson, William Fitch, b. in Huron Co., Ohio, Jan. 17, 1837, d. Dec. 16, 1901
McVey, Hugh (father), b. Sept. 2, 1831, d. Jan. 18, 1907
McVey, Sarah (mother), b. June 14, 1833, d. April 3, 1903
McVey, Jerry M., d. July 25, 1928; age, 74 years, 1 month, 16 days
McWhorter, William M., b. in Cambridge, N. Y., d. Aug. 8, 1878; age, 27 years
MacDonald (father), d. April 4, 1905 (Masonic Emblem)
MacNamara, M. H., 9th Mass. Vols., d. May 8, 1897; age, 59 years

N

Nathan, H., d. 1862; age, 27 years
Neal, W. H., Government marker, no dates
Needham, Simon B., b. 1826, d. 1906
Near, Mary J., wife of Cyrus W. Near, b. Feb. 14, 1845, d. Feb. 12, 1917

Near, Cyrus W. (father), b. 1845, d. 1908 (Soldier)
Neighbors, J., no dates
Nelson, Richard H., b. July 15, 1812, d. Sept. 12, 1884
Nelson, Nancy A., wife of Richard H. Nelson, b. July 14, 1814, d. April 7, 1888
Nelson, G. R., b. Sept. 3, 1840, d. April 14, 1921
Nelson, C. W., d. Nov. 20, 1883; age, 53 years
Nelson, Lotta B., b. 1835, d. 1906
Nelson, John R., b. 1821, d. 1900
Nelson, Nellie (mother), b. 1845, d. 1886
Nelson, Embric, b. 1851, d. 1929
Nelson, Mary, b. 1854, d. 1931
Newham, Annie M., wife of William M. Newham, d. July 31, 1929; age, 83 years, 6 months, 5 days
Newham, William M., d. May 28, 1880; age, 40 years, 8 months, 28 days
Newham, John M., d. May 5, 1874; age, 38 years, 8 months, 25 days
Newcomb, Jean, daughter of W. C. and Joan Newcomb, b. April 10, 1866, d. Aug. 15, 1872
Newcomb, Missouri J., daughter of W. C. and Mary J. Newcomb, b. Aug. 10, 1858, d. Nov. 14, 1873
Newcomb, Robert, b. in Flemingsburg, Ky., Jan. 12, 1804, d. May 15, 1877
Newcomb, Salley, wife of R. C., b. in Flemingsburg, Ky., Oct. 4, 1805, d. May 13, 1872
Newkirk, Amanda B., wife of I. Newkirk, b. Feb. 16, 1835, d. Aug. 18, 1881
Neumann, Gus, d. July 14, 1895; age, 37 years, 5 months, 25 days
Nichols, Patty V. Draper, d. Jan. 7, 1881; age, 24 years, 11 months, 28 days
Nichols, Thomas S., b. March 5, 1847, d. Feb. 2, 1898
Nichols, Lt. G. G., 7th Ohio Cav. (Gov. marker)
Nichols, W. T., d. July 7, 1892; age, 76 years, 1 month, 21 days
Nichols, Mariame, d. April 12, 1895; age, 75 years, 8 months, 18 days
Nichols, Roswell, d. April 15, 1869; age, 27 years, 11 months, 10 days (Masonic Emblem)
Niedermeyer, August, b. Jan. 15, 1842, d. June 9, 1900
Niven, James, unable to read the rest
Northrope, Albert, b. Sept. 8, 1818, d. June 11, 1898
Norman, Martha Jane, b. 1846, d. 1901
Norman, Sergt. Jones (Gov. marker)
Norton, G. M., Co. "M" 5th Kansas (Gov. marker)
Norton, Dr. Joshua, d. May 7, 1860; age, 64 years
Norton, Walter (Beloved Son), d. July 9, 1883; age, 27 years
Norris, Nancy, wife of Basil Norris, b. June 30, 1827, d. Oct. 7, 1900
Noyes, Samuel, son of C. and L. Noyes, d. March 30, 1861; age, 2 years
Nuckols, infant son of Bradford and Cora Nuckols, July 8, 1859
Nye, Nancy, no dates
Nye, James A., no dates

O

Obannon, Mary A., b. April 10, 1810, d. July 23, 1868
O'Connor, Fannie, wife of L. P. O'Connor, b. March 12, 1845, d. March 5, 1893
Oglesby, Susan A., b. 1792, d. Jan., 1874 (On Lindsay Monument)
Ogden, Louis B., b. April 30, 1812, d. Aug. 19, 1879
Ogden, Isabell, wife of Louis B. Ogden, b. March 3, 1824, d. Sept. 10. 18—
Oldham, Eva S. Threlkeld, wife of W. D. Oldham, b. 1843, d. 1880
Oldham, Elias, b. March 17, 1816, d. Jan. 22, 1892
Olson, Mathias, Co. "I" 28th Ill. Infantry (Gov. marker)
Olson, Emma, b. April 3, 1864, d. Jan. 30, 1890
Opitz, Julia, b. March 27, 1821, d. March 30, 1884
Orr, Maria, b. July 6, 1835, d. Jan. 9, 1887
Ortloff, Gustav, b. July 7, 1834, d. Sept. 1, 1897, 16th Ill. Vol.

CEMETERIES—KAW TOWNSHIP

Ortloff, Constance, wife of Gustave Ortloff, b. May 26, 1843, d. June 20, 1901
Osborne, Alpheus, b. in Pass Christian, Miss., July, 1856, d. May, 1887
Osgood, M. T., d. March 17, 1887; age, 43 years, 3 months (Soldier) Co. "G"
Osgood, Samuel Morril, b. Oct. 16, 1877, d. June 1, 1904
Osgood, T. M., b. Sept. 8, 1808, d. March 27, 1875
Osgood, G., b. April 7, 1854, d. Aug. 30, 1875
Osgood, Mrs. Sarah B., d. Feb. 17, 1894; age, 77 years, 7 months, 4 days
Oster, George A., b. May, 1875
Oswald, Elizah, b. in Chillicothe, Ohio, Feb. 27, 1830, d. May 8, 1884
Otto, Emil, b. Sept. 22, 1842, d. March 19, 1914
Otto, Catharina, wife of Emil Otto, b. Oct. 12, 1847, d. Sept. 22, 1897
Ouker, Christian, b. 1850, d. 1888
Owen, C. F., b. April 4, 1846, d. June 6, 1879 (Gov. marker)
Oyer, J. W., b. May 27, 1852, d. Sept. 24, 1906

P

Pace, Anne E., d. Oct. 20, 1902; age, 56 years
Pack, George (Gov. marker)
Palmer, Elizabeth M., wife of Capt. H. E. Palmer, b. 1841, d. 1865
Palmer, Victoria C., d. Nov. 2, 1930; age, 82 years, 2 months, 16 days
Palmer, James R., b. 1831, d. 1917
Pattimore, ——, b. 1834, d. 1904
Pardonner, Elizabeth, b. June 17, 1817, d. April 4, 1896; age, 79 years
Pardonner, George, b. March 12, 1804, d. Feb., 1869
Parker, Grace, daughter of J. W. and E. R. Parker, b. March 6, 1856, d. Oct. 25, 1862
Parmelee, Lizzie S., wife of Edward L., d. Oct. 27, 1889; age, 36 years
Parnham, Effie C. (mother), b. Nov. 11, 1848, d. March 16, 1903
Parsons, William, Co. "H" 9th Mo. S. M. Cav. (Gov. marker)
Partington, Henry, b. 1821, d. 1883
Partington, Elizabeth, wife of Henry Partington, b. 1823, d. 1883
Parrish, Sergt. W. M. G., Co. "A" 13th Iowa Inf. (Gov. marker)
Pattemore, George, d. in America, Aug. 10, 1886; age, 52 years
Pattemore, Emma, wife of George Pattemore, d. in England, March 11, 1884; age, 61 years; natives of Monmouthshire, England
Patten, Dr. J. L., d. Nov. 9, 1897; age, 61 years
Pattison, E. W. (father), b. Sept. 24, 1821, d. Sept., 1885
Pattison, Tomzelle C. (mother), b. May 11, 1825, d. Aug., 1886
Pattison, E. Rolla (brother), b. May 23, 1846, d. June, 1871 (On stone with name of Sarah Church)
Patton, Tevis C., b. Aug. 28, 1821, d. March 24, 1889 (Patton and Lindsley names on monument)
Patty, John H., b. Dec. 28, 1844, d. Jan. 13, 1896
Patty, Rose Adams, b. Jan. 29, 1858, d. April 19, 1895
Pankow, Charles W., d. Feb. 8, 1882; age, 35 years, 3 months, 8 days
Payne, Mary, d. May 14, 1898; age, 58 years
Payne, Joseph (husband), b. Oct. 15, 1854, d. May 19, 1905
Payne, W. W., b. March 19, 1836, d. Sept. 20, 1908
Payne, Phoebe H., b. Feb. 1, 1841, d. Feb. 10, 1891
Peck, James, d. Feb. 13, 1877; age, 62 years, 2 months, 8 days
Peck, Theresa McCutcheon, wife of James Peck, d. Feb. 11, 1880; age, 39 years, 7 months, 23 days
Peck, William M., d. April 26, 1895; age, 52 years
Peers, Thomas G., b. April 13, 1826, d. Aug. 16, 1886
Peers, Lurinda T., b. Nov. 27, 1829, d. March 7, 1904
Peery, Margaret V., b. Dec. 18, 1833, d. Sept. 21, 1837
Peery, Martha J., b. March 15, 1834, d. Nov. 17, 1835

Peery, Virginia A., b. Feb. 18, 1838, d. Dec. 30, 1844 (Upon Peery Monument)
Peery, Mary J., wife of Rev. T. J. Peery, d. Nov. 21, 1872; age, 55 years, 4 months, 28 days
Peery, Susan T., b. Jan. 10, 1842, d. Jan. 17, 1860
Peery, Ella, b. Aug. 3, 1851, d. June 8, 1876
Peery, James A., b. Dec. 3, 1837, d. Nov. 28, 1853
Peery, Jeremiah D., b. March 20, 1846, d. Aug. 1, 1880
Peery, George W., b. June 10, 1850, d. Aug. 12, 1856
Peery, Edward T., b. Jan. 22, 1858, d. Feb. 28, 1870
Peery, F. T., b. Dec. 31, 1847, d. Jan. 4, 1923
Perry, Littleton, b. March 7, 1839, d. Dec. 3, 1897
Peery, Rev. Edward T., b. 1800, d. Nov. 28, 1864
Peery, Mary S., wife of Rev. E. T. Peery, b. March 26, 1814, d. Jan. 26, 1890 (Upon this monument, "Incorporated this cemetery in 1858")
Pennell, W. P., Co. "D" 17th Pa. Reg. Inf. (Gov. marker)
Pershall, Emma Ansley, b. 1836, d. 1886
Pershall, J. R., d. Nov. 25, 1898; age, 65 years
Peterson, George, b. Jan. 13, 1854, d. Sept. 29, 1883
Peterson, Ellen, b. April 29, 1832, d. March 10, 1895
Peterson, John A., b. Jan. 15, 1849, d. July 22, 1901
Peterson, Marie (mother), b. 1842, d. June 28, 1901
Pflager, John M., b. 1839, d. 1896
Philipp, Therese (nee Leppien), b. Sept. 21, 1843, d. Oct. 4, 1906
Phillips, Rebecca (mother), b. Sept. 26, 1846, d. April 19, 1904
Phillips, Silas (father), b. Sept. 1, 1839, d. Jan. 7, 1905
Phillips, John, b. — 17, 1800, d. Jan. 31, 1875
Phillips, Katherine, wife of John Phillips, d. April 22, 1870; age, 67 years
Phillips, Mary J., wife of E. A. Phillips, b. in Providence, R. I., Sept. 11, 1842, d. in Sedalia, Mo., Feb. 15, 1880
Phillips, Joseph R., b. in Pennington, N. J., Sept. 6, 1809, d. Jan. 18, 1874
Philips, H. T., b. 1827, d. 1880; age, 53 years
Philipber, Mary A. (mother), b. Dec. 19, 1836, d. Feb. 1, 1903
Philipber, Frederick, d. Feb. 14, 1891; age, 56 years
Philpott, Helen Mar, wife of S. M. Philpott, d. Oct. 6, 1907
Pierce, Mary, b. Dec. 24, 1842
Pigeon, Emily, b. 1825, d. Sept. 24, 1891
Pigg, Nora, daughter of P. and S. Pigg, b. — 20, 1866, d. 1878
Pitman, Elona, b. 1850, d. 1903
Pitzer, Rufus, b. Feb. 22, 1816, d. Dec. 30, 1876
Pitzer, Virginia M., b. Feb. 20, 1823, d. March 8, 1881
Plaisted, Joseph, b. April 12, 1833, d. March 25, 1886; Capt. Co. "E" 5th Ohio Infantry, 1861-1865, Gov. marker
Platt, Samuel J., b. July 28, 1827, d. Oct. 14, 1885
Plumsteel, Norman, b. March 29, 1847, d. April 10, 1903
Plumsteel, Mary, wife of Norman Plumsteel, b. May 14, 1847, d. Dec. 30, 1894
Poe, Laura Peck (Name upon monument of William M. Peck)
Polke, Henry Clay, son of John W. and Sarah A. Polke, b. Jan. 24, 1842, d. Feb. 10, 1859
Polke, S. M. M. Ivy, wife of John W. Polke, d. in Westport, Mo., Jan. 29, 1846; age, 22 years, 9 months, 22 days
Polke, Elizabeth, daughter of Thomas W. and Eliza Polke, d. July 1, 1819; age, 18 years, 1 month, 6 days
Pond, Helen E., d. Nov. 3, 1878; age, 20 years, 2 months
Pope, Martha A. (mother), b. 1844, d. 1898
Porter, W. F., b. Nov. 7, 1842, d. Dec. 21, 1899
Porter, Bettie L., wife of W. F. Porter, b. July 3, 1844, d. Jan. 10, 1894
Potter, Anna, wife of J. B. Potter, d. July 26, 1879; age, 33 years, 1 month

CEMETERIES—KAW TOWNSHIP

Potter, James B., b. Sept. 25, 1856, d. Aug. 30, 1903
Porter, Lucy A., wife of Jesse L. Porter, b. April 20, 1833, d. Jan. 9, 1893
Porter, Emily Hall, b. July 27, 1853, d. Nov. 8, 1927
Porter, Ada S., b. June 6, 1855, d. May 19, 1927
Porter, Jane, wife of Rev. James Porter, b. May 1, 1786, d. Nov. 25, 1873
Porter, Jesse L., son of James and Jane Porter, b. July 30, 1827, d. May 15, 1868
Porter, Elizabeth, wife of Samuel Porter, d. April 11, 1845, in the 95th year of her age
Porter, Rev. James W., b. Oct. 28, 1786, d. Oct. 31, 1851
Poteet, William B., d. July 10, 1860; age, 36 years, 2 months, 11 days
Poulton, Charlotte Deming, b. 1811, d. 1899 (Marker as a Real Daughter of the American Revolution)
Prevost, Samuel B., b. Oct. 16, 1844, d. July 26, 1913 (Gov. marker)
Prevost, Sarah C., wife of S. B. Prevost, b. Aug. 31, 1845, d. June 24, 1895
Price, Campbell, b. March 20, 1853, d. Feb. 1, 1911
Price, Emeline, b. 1821, d. 1874
Price, Edmund, b. 1810, d. 1870
Price, Florence, b. 1841, d. 1867
Price, William Findley, son of E. and E. A. Price, b. Oct. 22, 1848, d. Aug. 2, 1850
Probst, Elizabeth, b. 1849, d. 1902
Proctor, Sarah, b. 1833, d. 1882
Proudfoot, Alexander, b. June 10, 1801, d. Feb. 12, 1879
Proudfoot, Alice, wife of Alexander Proudfoot (Unable to read the rest of the inscription)
Pueschel, Edmund G., d. Feb. 6, 1898; age, 45 years
Purdom, Catherine, b. 1786, d. 1859 (On lot with Poteet family)
Purdom, Jane S., b. May 15, 1803, d. July 2, 1890
Purdom, Thomas W., b. May 28, 1821, d. April 14, 1868
Purviance, William A., b. Jan. 15, 1853, d. Nov. 14, 1897 (Woodmen of the World marker)
Putman, Diantha, wife of John A. Putman, d. Oct. 12, 1880; age, 72 years, 11 months, 19 days
Putman, Louisa C. Donnelly, b. 1837, d. 1929; daughter of D. M. Putman
Putman, William C., b. July 27, 1837, d. July 31, 1901

Q

Quade, Sarah E., wife of G. H. Quade, b. Oct. 28, 1851, d. March 20, 1886
Quarles, Percy, son of R. W. and A. P. Quarles, d. Oct. 9, 1874; age, 2 years
Quarles, Hattie, daughter of R. W. and A. P. Quarles, d. Oct. 19, 1879; age, 4 years
Quest, George, b. Nov. 5, 1786, d. Dec. 12, 1877 (Soldier of 1812)
Quest, Malinda, b. Sept. 1, 1804, d. May 28, 1881
Qurnie, Sarah A., d. Oct. 1, 1893; age, 48 years

R

Radley, James, Co. "H" 15th Ill. Inf., Government marker
Raels, Samuel, b. 1829, d. 1894
Raels, S. Fannie, b. 1843, d. 1915
Ralls, Sam, b. 1868, d. 1907
Ragan, Jacob, b. in Lexington, Ky., Dec. 7, 1792; removed to Jackson County, Mo., Oct. 31, 1837; he was an active member of the Old Town Co. of Kansas City, Mo.; d. Nov. 7, 1878
Ragan, Anna C., wife of Jacob Ragan, b. in Buckingham Co., Va., Feb. 6, 1797, d. March 8, 1886
Ragan, Jane P., wife of G. L. Ragan, b. Sept. 28, 1816, d. April 15, 1893
Ragan, Greenberry L., b. May 6, 1816, d. March 28, 1886
Ragan, Rane, son of G. L. and Jane P. Ragan, b. April 6, 1851, d. March 30, 1868
Ragan, Stephen C., b. 1823, d. 1909; Capt. Co. "I" 14th Texas (C. S. A. marker)
Ragan, Josephine G., wife of Stephen C. Ragan, b. 1837, d. 1915

Ragan, Rosa, wife of H. B. Ragan, d. Aug. 18, 1899; age, 27 years, 10 months, 6 days
Ragan, Joseph H., b. Dec. 23, 1834, d. Sept., 1857
Rainey, Mary A. (mother), d. Feb. 15, 1898; age, 49 years
Rams, Estella M., wife of W. C. Rams, d. April 25, 1871; age, 19 years, 6 months, 1 day
Ramsey, Samuel, d. Sept. 15, 1869; age, 39 years
Randael, M. P., d. Oct. 11, 1864; age, 41 years
Randal, Kitty (nee Atkinson), b. 1843, d. 1890
Rankins, Jean (mother), b. 1826, d. 1908
Rankin, Margaret C., daughter of William and Margaret Rankin, d. Aug. 27, 1877; age, 4 yrs.
Ranson, Joseph C., b. July 19, 1819, d. Aug. 31, 1883
Raphael, Hugh, b. June 21, 1844, d. July 22, 1902
Rasmussen, R. Paul (father), b. Sept. 13, 1816, d. July 27, 1897
Rasmussen, Marie N., b. Feb. 19, 1922, d. Nov. 23, 1901
Raub, John S. Franklin, b. July 27, 1854, d. Aug. 2, 1859
Ray, Jesse, d. May 2, 1889; age, 81 years, 5 months, 23 days
Ray, Elizabeth P., wife of Jesse Ray, d. Aug. 2, 1880; age, 60 years
Ray, Daughters of Jesse and Elizabeth Ray
    Mary A., b. in Urbana, Ohio, April 13, 1845, d. Nov. 4, 1866
    Martha E., b. in Marshall Co., Ill., July 2, 1853, d. Nov. 11, 1866
Ray, Oliver H., b. Jan. 19, 1833, d. Aug. 1, 1873
Read, William F., b. Feb. 5, 1825, d. June 22, 1903 (Soldier)
Ream, Julia A. (mother), b. Oct. 31, 1827, d. Aug. 21, 1900
Red, Oscar, b. Sept. 16, 1830, d. March 21, 1895; age, 65 years
Reddy, Andrew, d. in Chicago, Ill., March 25, 1885
Redheffer, Mary E., wife of James Redheffer, d. Feb. 12, 1876; age, 29 years
Redman, Thomas F. (husband), d. July, 1900 (rest of inscription sunken in ground)
Rodgers, Charles, b. April 5, 1842, d. April 15, 1909
Rees, William, d. June 17, 1882; age, 27 years
Reed, Caroline, b. Feb. 16, 1819, d. Feb. 19, 1884
Reed, William P., b. May 14, 1818, d. Jan. 10, 1894
Reed, Martha B., b. May 8, 1838, d. June 3, 1880
Reed, Mrs. Hester, d. Sept. 1, 1890; age, 42 years, 2 months, 1 day
Register, Stephen A., d. 1905; age, 52 years
Reimann, John C., b. 1835, d. 1912 (father)
Reimann, Gertrude M., b. 1836, d. 1903 (mother)
Reinhardt, Theobald, b. in Germania, Oct. 13, 1802, d. Nov. 21, 1873
Reinchenesker, May, wife of George T. Reinchenesker, and granddaughter of William and
    Mary Garrett, d. July 6, 1879; age, 28 years
Relee, Henry C., d. March 20, 1899; age, 62 years
Relee, Sarah Ellen, wife of Henry C. Relee, d. Jan. 23, 1901; age, 60 years
Remnitz, William J., b. Aug. 11, 1833, d. Sept. 18, 1892
Reuschlein, John, b. Feb. 12, 1832, d. May 25, 1888
Reynolds, Benjamin B., b. 1853, d. 1927
Reynolds, F. C., b. April 7, 1816, d. March 1, 1904
Reton, Theodore F., eldest son of J. T. and M. E. Reton, d. April 5, 1875; age, 22 years
Rhodes, William, d. Oct. 12, 1889; age, 69 years
Rhodes, Martha, d. March 18, 1894; age, 60 years
Richmond, David, b. Oct. 14, 1841, d. Feb. 19, 1902
Richardson, Stephen M., b. Oct. 12, 1824, d. Sept. 19, 1898
Rider, Oliver J., d. Sept. 26, 1902; age, 63 years
Ridge, James P. (Old stone, inscription cannot be read)
Ridge, Mary Ann, daughter of John G. and Mary Ann Ridge, d. June 1, 1852; age, 10
    years, 2 months
Ridge, Eliza, wife of Dr. I. M. Ridge, b. Oct. 30, 1830, d. July 22, 1878
Ridge, Children of Dr. I. M. Ridge and E. A. Ridge
    Harriet S., b. Aug. 18, 1850, d. Sept. 6, 1858

CEMETERIES—KAW TOWNSHIP

Ridge, Isaac M., b. July 26, 1868, d. April 5, 1871
Riddesbarger, Mary, wife of J. Riddesbarger, d. July 17, 1852
Riddesbarger, Jesse, son of J. and S. Riddesbarger, b. Jan. 25, 1856
Righters, Anthony, b. in Neihaus, Kingdom of Prussia, Dec. 10, 1811, d. May 21, 1860; age, 48 years
Righters, Elizabeth, d. March 23, 1899; age, 79 years, 3 months
Righter, Charles, d. April 27, 1870; age, 19 years, 10 months, 25 days
Righter, A. F., d. Jan. 2, 1870; age, 23 years, 11 months
Ring, Ransome, b. March 28, 1849, d. May 4, 1901
Rixon, Margaret A., wife of John Rixon, b. 1851, d. 1922
Robbins, Elizabeth, d. April 17, 1885; age, 68 years
Robinson, Kate Hutt, b. 1809, d. 1898 (Marker as a Real Daughter, D. A. R.)
Robinson, George A., d. June 28, 1881; age, 31 years, 3 months, 23 days
Robinson, John J., b. in Westmoreland Co., Va., Dec. 17, 1801, d. Dec. 24, 1883
Robulson, John A., d. Oct. 5, 1875
Rockey, Charles H., d. Sept. 25, 1895; age, 33 years
Rodgers, Charles, b. April 5, 1842, d. April 15, 1909
Roeder, Alvina Erdmuthe, wife of Frank Roeder, d. July 19, 1887; age, 47 years
Roeder, Frank, b. March 5, 1842, d. March 16, 1912; age, 79 years
Rogers, Luther P., b. Dec. 20, 1852, d. May 31, 1890
Rogers, William M., b. April 9, 1819, d. Dec. 19, 1893 (Gov. marker)
Rogers, Margaret J., b. June 3, 1836, d. April 16, 1914
Rogers, William Owen (son), b. April 7, 1849, d. March 30, 1867
Rogers, Elisha F. (son), b. March 11, 1868, d. Nov. 8, 1868
Rogers, Susie, b. Sept. 16, 1852, d. Aug., 1882
Rollert, Pauline, wife of Charles A. Rollert, b. Feb. 1, 1834, d. June 4, 1876
Rone, George, b. in St. Louis, Mo., Oct. 25, 1857, d. Nov. 16, 1897
Rose, Joseph, b. 1823, d. 1880
Rose, Morris E., d. May 23, 1881, Kansas City, Mo.; age, 24 years, 7 months, 3 days
Rosenburg, Herman, b. 1848, d. 1901
Rosenburg, Maria, b. 1848, d. 1891
Ross, Alice A. (sister), b. 1850, d. 1931
Ross, James H. (brother), b. 1835, d. 1899
Rothrock, Sarah Ann (mother), b. 1838, d. 1897
Routt, George E., b. June 19, 1836, d. Jan. 5, 1885
Routledge, Joseph, b. in Penrith Cumberland, England, May 1, 1814, d. Jan. 26, 1891
Roundy, Jessie G. Burton, wife of A. Roundy, d. May 29, 1888; age, 29 years
Rowlett, Andrew W., d. Feb. 1, 1901; age, 58 years
Rowell, Sarah H., b. 1821, d. 1890
Rubey, James, b. 1779
Rubey, Martha, wife of James Rubey
Rudigel, Lucy G., b. May 28, 1821, d. Nov. 24, 1898
Rugg, George B. (U. S. N.), d. March 28, 1901; age, 57 years
Runyon, Mary A., d. Aug. 8, 1895; age, 83 years
Rutter, Maggie, d. Dec. 5, 1898; age, 37 years
Rutter, John, d. May 1, 1888; age, 44 years
Rustenbach, Friedrich, b. Sept. 25, 1841, d. Dec. 6, 1898
Rustenbach, Sophia, b. Dec. 13, 1852, d. Sept. 18, 1910
Russell, Sarah Lykins, d. Dec. 16, 1901; age, 87 years ("In memory of her daughter, Theodora")
Russel, E. F., b. Aug., 1848, d. Oct. 21, 1871
Russel, W. W., b. Sept. 8, 1848, d. July 8, 1896; Co. "N" 47th Ill. Inf., Gov marker
Russell, R. H. (father), b. Oct. 11, 1815, d. July 9, 1894

S

Sager, Mary, wife of H. Sager, b. July 26, 1823, d. May 29, 1854
Sager, Henry, b. Nov. 25, 1815, d. March 30, 1886
Sager, Albert G., b. Feb. 11, 1852, d. April 12, 1886
Salisbury, Betsy, wife of Warren Salisbury, d. Nov. 18, 1860; age, 63 years
Salisbury, Mortimer E., d. Nov. 20, 1867; age, 37 years
Salisbury, Lora W., d. April 14, 1867; age, 35 years
Sames, Wenfield; age, 4 months, 6 days; son of L. P. and J. Sames
Sameson, Jane; age, 84 years, no dates, very difficult to read
Sampson, Robert, d. Aug. 9, 1887; age, 38 years
Sands, Ruth P., d. Feb., 1895; age, 59 years, 11 months, 15 days
Sanders, Ben, d. March 10, 1902; age, 24 years
Sanford, George, d. March 14, 1890; age, 55 years
Sanger, John G., b. 1857, d. 1927
Sanders, Frances M., wife of F. H. Sanders, d. Sept. 18, 1909; age, 66 years
Saltonstall, Augusta (On Dyas monument "To my wife Augusta Saltonstall")
Sayrs, Hannah M., b. 1828, d. 1906
Sauer, Anton, d. Aug. 16, 1879; age, 55 years
Sauer, Helen F., d. July 15, 1879; age, 1 year
Sauer, Marie, b. Nov. 23, 1840, d. Nov. 30, 1919
Sauer, Emil J., d. Sept. 8, 1875; age, 23 years
Schaeffer, George, b. Feb. 27, 1844, d. May 14, 1897
Schaeffer, Margaret, wife of George Schaeffer, b. June 29, 1850, d. June 11, 1924
Schaefer, Sophia, d. March 15, 1883; age, 79 years
Schaefer, Conrad, d. Jan. 9, 1884; age, 65 years
Schaefer, John, d. May 23, 1885; age, 35 years
Schaeffer, Joseph, b. March, 1857, d. Nov., 1897
Schaeffer, Mattie E., wife of W. H. Schaeffer, b. April 6, 1840, d. Aug. 9, 1876
Schmack, Charles H., d. June 29, 1880; age, 35 years, 8 months, 8 days
Schmidt, Rosina Barbara, b. 1827, d. 1904
Schmidt, M. Dorothea, d. Nov. 24, 1894; age, 54 years, 7 months, 4 days
Schneider, George, b. Dec. 12, 1845, d. Sept., 1903
Schrager, A. F., d. Feb. 14, 1886; age, 16 years
Schrager, H. F., d. May 26, 1880; age, 35 years
Schrager, Osker, b. Sept. 28, 1879, d. Feb. 3, 1917
Schrager, Lizzie, b. April 15, 1856, d. Jan. 7, 1919
Schroder, Augusta, wife of C. Schroder, d. Feb. 14, 1891; age, 66 years
Schroeder, August, b. April 13, 1821, d. May 9, 1885
Schermerhorn, Nellie Irwin, wife of B. Schermerhorn, and daughter of J. C. and Mary Irwin, d. Sept. 13, 1882; age, 32 years, 7 months
Scruggs, Martha, wife of N. H. Scruggs, d. Oct. 3, 1853; age, 57 years
Scruggs, Virginia, daughter of N. H. and M. S. Scruggs, b. Nov. 25, 1835, d. Jan. 6, 1857
Scruggs, N. H., b. March 4, 1792, d. March 16, 1864
Schock, Henrietta, wife of M. Schock, b. Feb. 9, 1841, d. June 13, 1901
Schoen, Joseph Anton, d. Dec. 25, 1859; age, 23 years, 4 months
Schoenrock, Carl, d. Aug. 20, 1878; age, 36 years
Schoenrock, Kate, wife of Carl Schoenrock, d. Oct. 9, 1896; age, 60 years
Schoeller, Christian, b. Sept. 26, 1831, d. Aug. 17, 1901 (Gov. marker)
Schoeller, Anna, b. Feb. 28, 1831, d. Dec. 4, 1899
Scotford, Rev. John, b. June 1, 1808, d. Jan. 21, 1881
Schuler, Peter (Gov. marker)
Scurlock, Elizabeth Lee, wife of George N. Scurlock, d. June 21, 1899
Schurlein, Gussie (infant), d. Jan. 10, 1874
Scupham, James R., b. in Scotland, Sept. 9, 1845
Schwitzgebel, Peter, b. Nov. 26, 1821, d. Aug. 19, 1889

Schwitzgebel, Wilhelmine, wife of Peter Schwitzgebel, b. Sept. 29, 1834, d. Oct. 14, 1871
Schevanenfeldt, Eleanor, b. 1833, d. 1912
Schustrum, Esther Aurora, wife of G. H. Schustrum, d. March 29, 1885; age, 87 years, 5 months, 22 days
Scott, Lee, son of G. and A. Scott, d. Aug. 24, 1874; age, 10 months, 4 days
Scott, Juda, b. May 12, 1835, d. July 5, 1905
Scott, Benjamin, d. March 1, 1911; age, 53 years
Scott, Margaret Ellen, b. May 16, 1817, d. April 22, 1852
Scott, Margaret Ellen, b. Oct. 16, 1848, d. Oct. 11, 1851
Scott, Robert H., b. Nov. 5, 1838, d. Aug. 17, 1839
Scott, James M., b. in Newry Co., Armach, Ireland, Dec. 25, 1817, d. March 22, 1887 (Soldier)
Sechrest, Lucy, wife of William Sechrest, d. Sept. 10, 1882; age, 46 years
Sechrest, William, b. Sept. 26, 1813, d. Feb. 26, 1892
Sedenburg, Benard, b. in Noblesville, Hamilton County, Ind., d. Feb. 25, 1882; age, 24 years
Seddon, Alfred, b. 1817, d. 1867
Seddon, Elizabeth Taylor, b. 1824, d. 1880
Selmer, Mrs. C., d. Jan. 4, 1896—no other dates
Severd, Elizabeth, d. Jan. 31, 1874; age, 63 years
Severd, Laura and Elizabeth, daughters of Jacob and Esther A. Severd, d. July 18, 1874
Severd, Jacob, b. Oct. 4, 1833, d. Dec. 27, 1902 (Gov. marker)
Sexton, James M. (father), d. July 9, 1878; age, 70 years, 23 days
Sexton, Ann B., d. March 17, 1867; age, 54 years, 9 days
Shackett, M. T., b. Oct. 3, 1843, d. Sept. 13, 1895
Shamleffer, Margie A., wife of John Shamleffer, b. Sept. 20, 1844, d. April 11, 1878
Shamleffer, John, d. Aug. 20, 1883; age, 44 years, 3 months, 21 days
Shannon, Lula A., d. Dec. 17, 1899; age, 37 years
Shannon, Chauncey, d. July 13, 1898; age, 66 years
Shea, Elizabeth, wife of John Shea, b. in Ravely, England, d. May 13, 1888
Shelly, Maggie R., wife of R. J. Shelly, b. Aug. 11, 1840, d. March 15, 1907
Shepard, Mrs. Mary, d. May 25, 1898; age, 54 years, 9 months
Sheppard, Jennie, wife of William Sheppard, b. in Lingion Co., Ohio, May 13, 1840, d. Sept. 17, 1876
Sheppard, children of N. W. and J. Sheppard
  Elinor, b. June 1, 1870, d. July 10, 1870
  Walter, b. Feb. 1, 1872, d. Jan. 27, 1873
  Wilard, b. March 1, 1875, d. July 6, 1876
Sheppard, Mary (mother), b. July 15, 1802, d. June 15, 1896
Sherlock, Joseph, Co. "E" 90th Ohio Inf. (Gov. marker)
Sherman, Charles, d. Sept. 12, 1866; age, 22 years
Shover, Delia F., d. Jan. 27, 1878; age, 48 years, 10 months, 25 days
Shook, Leola, b. Aug. 22, 1856, d. Feb. 29, 1908
Shewmaker, Mary S., b. 1846, d. 1898 (On Barber lot)
Sier, Molisa, wife of F. D. Sier, d. Nov. 13, 1881; age, 34 years, 21 days
Silver, Mary, b. 1856, d. 1918
Silver, G. W., d. Aug. 27, 1894; age, 89 years
Silver, David C., b. 1883, d. 1905
Sims, Mrs. Belinda E., b. March 9, 1844, d. April 23, 1900
Simmons, Eliza J., d. Sept. 15, 1888; age, 73 years
Simmons, Eli, d. March 13, 1907; age, 60 years
Simmonds, Lucinda, b. Aug. 6, 1821, d. May 14, 1895 (mother)
Simpson, William S., b. Sept. 21 (?), 1856, d. Dec. 3, 1899
Simpson, Marion A., wife of William F. Simpson, d. May 19, 1853; age, 40 years (?)
Simpson, George R., b. 1842, d. 1927
Simpson, Richard, b. March 3, 1770, d. July 24, 1853 (Harris Monument)

Sinclair, A. S., d. Aug. 29, 1862; age, 27 years, 11 months, 20 days
Sivewright, John, d. Nov. 22, 1910; age, 82 years
Sivewright, Mary, d. Dec. 29, 1909; age, 75 years
Sivewright, James, b. Feb. 24, 1858, d. Oct. 10, 1892
Skinner, Alice F., d. Nov. 19, 1895; age, 32 years
Slattery, Charles J., d. Jan. 3, 1888; age, 26 years
Slavens, Luther, b. Aug. 13, 1836, d. Oct. 23, 1913
Slavens, Sallie, b. March 31, 1836, d. March 5, 1911 (Slavens monument, erected by his and her daughter, Martha)
Slavens, John Heber, b. Nov. 4, 1853, d. Dec. 29, 1873
Sloan, Rev. Robert, b. May 11, 1801, d. May 27, 1868
Sloan, Margaret Davidson, wife of Rev. Robert Sloan, and daughter of Rev. Finis Ewing, b. July 28, 1807, d. Sept. 7, 1897
Sloan, James H., b. Nov. 25, 1842, d. May 23, 1898
Sloan, Allen, b. May 15, 1816, d. April 17, 1889
Slocomb, Joseph A., b. July 4, 1837, d. May 3, 1903
Slocome, Frank M., b. June 1, 1858, d. Feb. 1, 1894
Sligh, Charles, d. Sept. 5, 1901; age, 37 years
Small, Charles, d. Sept. 9, 1877; age, 23 years, 10 months, 14 days
Smart, Thomas A., b. Nov. 16, 1806, d. Sept. 18, 1879
Smart, Mary J., wife of Thomas A. Smart, d. July 11, 1892
Smart, Harriet, wife of Thomas A. Smart, d. May 6, 1849 (of Cholera); age, 40 years, 2 months
Smart, Martha A., daughter of T. A. and Harriet Smart, d. March 10, 1854; age, 15 years, 5 months, 5 days
Smith, Lt. C. S., Co. "E" 11th Kansas Cav. (Gov. marker)
Smith, James W., b. 1846, d. 1898
Smith, J. J., d. Dec. 19, 1899; age, 47 years
Smith, Fannie S., wife of W. W. Smith, b. Jan. 2, 1849, d. Aug. 29, 1888
Smith, Douglas Cooper Smith, b. 1848, d. 1905
Smith, Agnes, b. in Belfast, Ireland, no dates
Smith, H. N., b. in Belfast, Ireland, no dates
Smith, Sydney, b. in Belfast, Ireland, no dates
Smith, Henry Nelson, b. in Belfast, Ireland
Smith, Edward Coey, b. in Belfast, Ireland
Smith, Agnes Coey, b. in Belfast, Ireland
Smith, Mary V., b. 1850, d. 1931
Smith, Frank T., b. 1853, d. 1930
Smith, Laura E., b. 1846, d. 1890
Smith, Harriet, b. July 21, 1824, d. July 22, 1890
Smith, Miss Ellen, d. July 1, 1933; age, 75 years, 6 months, 16 days
Smith, C. G., d. May 4, 1876; age, 29 years, 5 months, 5 days
Smith, Eliza Davies, wife of John Smith (our mother), d. March 24, 1885
Smith, John (our father), d. Feb. 21, 1895 (Very old stone)
Smith, Harriet Eliza, b. May 31, 1831, d. April 4, 1905; age, 74 years
Smith, J. P. (father), b. 1851, d. 1885
Smith, Mrs. E. A., b. 1848, d. 1908
Smith, Mary J., d. June 24, 1901; age, 62 years
Smith, Ed., d. Feb. 13, 1901; age, 56 years
Smith, Flora E., wife of J. W. Smith, b. July 7, 1855, d. Jan. 10, 1900
Smith, Lewis, d. July 15, 1891; age, 57 years
Smith, Julia A., d. Nov. 3, 1906; age, 69 years
Smith, Miles E., b. March 9, 1848, d. Dec. 25, 1860
Smiley, Charles H., d. July 17, 1877; age, 34 years
Smithson, H. D., b. Oct. 20, 1845, d. Oct. 1, 1897
Smithson, Mary C., b. May 14, 1845, d. Jan. 20, 1913

Snell, Thomas Harold, b. Sept. 12, 1836, d. July 11, 1883
Snow, Margaret, d. Feb. 28, 1860; age, 75 years
Snyder, Corpl. D. C. (Gov. marker)
Sobbe, Anna M., wife of Theo. Sobbe, d. June 9, 1897; age, 64 years, 4 months, 15 days
Sobbe, Theo., b. April 25, 1824, d. March 12, 1882 (Gov. marker)
Soles, Isaac W., b. Aug. 4, 1830, d. Aug. 9, 1907 (husband and father) (Soldier)
Solie, Andrew, d. April 7, 1888; age, 48 years
Sommer, August, Co. "I" 6th Reg. of Kansas Cav. Vol. (Gov. marker)
Sounson, John, b. July 6, 1835, d. Nov., 1898
Sonnschein, William, b. 1811, d. 1887
Sonnschein, Maria, b. 1810, d. 1881
Spalding, Sergt. Alonzo, Co. "K" 102 N. Y. (Gov. marker)
Spangler, F. C., b. Feb. 24, 1816, d. March 18, 1898
Sparks, Delbert, d. Feb. 14, 1901; age, 34 years
Spencer, Mary J., b. March 17, 1837, d. Jan. 8, 1900
Springer, Johann Georg, b. April 24, 1828, d. Dec. 10, 1890
Springer, Karoline, b. Oct. 4, 1838, d. April 4, 1907
Sprague, Corpl. P. T., Co. "C" 7th Iowa Inf. (Gov. marker)
Spuhel, Conrad (father), b. May 6, 1850, d. Feb. 16, 1901
Spuhel, Henry (Old stone, no dates)
Squires, Susan O., wife of William H. Squires, b. March 9, 1843, d. May 10, 1893
Stamp, Christopher, d. June 19, 1892; age, 76 years
Stanberry, Rev. Albert G., b. Sept. 5, 1837, d. Jan. 12, 1890; Co. "C" 3rd Tenn. Inf. (Gov. marker)
Stanley, Ann, b. 1855, d. 1904
Stains, S. H., b. 1846, d. 1908 (Soldier)
Stansch, Amelia, wife of August Stansch, d. Nov. 24, 1875; age, 39 years, 5 months, 18 days
Starr, Martha, b. July 4, 1842, d. Nov. 20, 1905
Stearns, Emery, d. April 13, 1895; age, 45 years
Stearns, Benjamin (father), b. 1813, d. 1887
Stearns, Sarah (mother), b. 1823, d. 1898
Steenburgh, Martha A., b. May 17, 1850, d. Feb. 16, 1902
Steinegle, Adolph (impossible to read dates)
Sterner, Geo. (Gov. marker)
Stillwell, W. H., Co. "B" 19th Mo. Inf. (Gov. marker)
Strayer, Anna R., wife of J. W. Strayer, b. Sept. 16, 1856, d. Oct. 24, 1888
Streeter, Maria J., b. Dec. 25, 1838, d. Sept. 4, 1901
Stremmel, Jacob, b. Jan. 23, 1841, d. March 17, 1881
Stevens, Mrs. Eliza J., d. Feb. 27, 1883; age, 72 years
Stevenson, Norris H., b. July 2, 1858, d. June 25, 1897; age, 38 years ——
Stephenson, John, b. Dec. 23, 1845 (?), d. Sept. 4, 1893
Stewart, Jehu G., b. Jan. 18, 1840, d. Feb. 15, 1904
Stewart, Mary E., wife of Jehu G. Stewart, b. Aug. 15, 1846, d. Dec. 24, 1903
Stewart, Thomas K., b. Nov. 11, 1848, d. Oct. 8, 1879
Stewart, Mary Anne (mother), wife of H. Stewart, d. Jan. 29, 1897; age, 85 years
Stuart, Samuel H., b. 1850, d. 1924
Stewart, Thirza, b. July 20, 1813, d. Jan. 22, 1865
Stewart, John and Martha A. Stewart, "Soulmates and companions for over 50 years." Martha Stewart, d. Nov. 25, 1907; age, 70 years
Stolte, Susanna, b. 1822, d. 1898
Stone, James E., b. Sept. 30, 1842, d. Aug. 11, 1887
Stone, Mary T. (mother), b. Sept. 9, 1838, d. Nov. 9, 1888
Stump, Hannah, b. Aug. 1, 1833, d. March 18, 1908 (mother)
St. Bingfield, Sergt. G. W., Co. "F" 37th Ill. Inf. (Gov. marker)
Sullivan, Nancy, d. Aug. 17, 1894; age, 53 years
Summers, Susan A., wife of W. T. Cheatham, b. April 28, 1832, d. March 24, 1903

Summers, John W., d. February 20, 1866; age, 42 years, 2 months, 15 days
Summers, children of J. W. and S. A. Summers
    Mary E., d. Sept. 10, 1853; age, 2 years, 1 month
    Thomas, d. Aug. 10, 1854; age, 1 year
Summers, William H., b. Aug. 27, 1844, d. June 20, 1896
Summers, Sadie A. (mother), b. 1859, d. 1891
Sutton, W. H., d. May 16, 1876; age, 35 years
Sutton, Nellie, daughter of W. H. and L. M. Sutton, d. March 11, 1876; age, 10 years
Sutton, Samuel, b. Feb. 24, 1783, d. Oct. 4, 1868 (Stone very old and worn)
Sutherland, Flora, b. 1822, d. 1914
Sutherland, Ria Sutherland Douglas, b. 1840, d. 1918
Sutherland, Neil, b. 1856, d. 1923
Swachbach, Henry, b. Oct. 15, 1821, d. Sept. 15, 1851
Swain, Sophia, b. May 19, 1837, d. Sept. 17, 1891
Swaney, Katie, daughter of James and Harriet Swaney, d. Nov. 24, 1867; age, 14 years
Swanson, Johanna, wife of P. Swanson, b. March 8, 1839, d. Aug. 17, 1885
Swanson, Gustave, b. 1851, d. 1906
Swayne, daughter of L. P. and Fannie Swayne, d. April 11, 1876; age, 3 years, 9 months
Sweeney, Elder James, b. Aug. 20, 1815, d. June 11, 1893
Sweetser, Josephine W., wife of Albert H. Sweetser, b. July, 1840, d. Nov. 25, 1886
Swetzgebel, Katherine, b. 1845, d. 1923
Swygard, John R., b. Oct. 7, 1843, d. March 1, 1881

T

Talley, Katherine, b. 1810 (?), d. 1876
Tapp, Martha N. (mother), b. 1804, d. 1882
Tapp, Mary L. Harp (sister), b. 1844, d. 1888 (On Tapp lot and evidently Mary L. Tapp Harp)
Tapp, George (brother), b. 1843, d. 1923
Tappan, Hugh, d. Feb. 11, 1870; age, 62 years
Tappan, Laura McCoy, wife of Hugh Tappan, d. Sept. 27, 1870; age, 59 years
Tappan, James A., d. Aug. 9, 1863; age, 19 years
Tappan, Arthur Rex, son of Dr. Francis and Celia Partholomew Tappan, no dates
Tate, George W., b. Jan. 5, 1790, d. Nov. 12, 1863
Taylor, Isaac, d. Jan. 29, 1895; age, 42 years
Taylor, James, b. Feb. 18, 1829, d. May 18, 1887
Taylor, Mary, wife of James Taylor, b. Feb. 22, 1830, d. May 1, 1879
Taylor, Jennie E., wife of Benjamin A. Taylor, b. April 14, 1857, d. Dec. 6, 1882
Taylor, Edward Charles, son of Edwin C. and Emily Taylor, b. Aug. 15, 1855, d. Nov. 2, 1904
Taylor, Serg't. O. T., Co. "I" 51st Ohio Inf. (Gov. marker)
Taylor, George, b. April 23, 1854, d. Aug. 20, 1883
Taylor, John (Gov. marker)
Teed, Eli, b. 1831, d. 1908
Terrill, Emma, wife of W. L. Terrill, d. May 1, 1900; age, 42 years
Tew, G. W., of New York; age, 53 years
Tew, S. F. (father), d. May, 1877; age, 79 years
Thayer, William, native of England, d. June 22, 1875 (On same lot with Hogan)
Thayer, Isaac, b. Feb. 15, 1818, d. March 12, 1868
Thelen, Catherine, wife of William F. Thelen, d. Jan. 19, 1882; age, 32 years
Thoes, Mrs. Mary, d. July 14, 1905; age, 72 years
Thomas, Anna, d. July 27, 1896; age, 46 years
Thomas, Arthur B., d. Oct. 25, 1901; age, 47 years
Thomas, Jesse, b. Nov. 7, 1803, d. Dec. 12, 1887
Thomas, Maria, wife of Jesse Thomas, b. Dec. 10, 1808, d. Nov. 15, 1839
Thomas, Eva H., wife of David P. Thomas, d. April 10, 1887; age, 29 years
Thomas, N. B., b. Jan. 28, 1823, d. Feb. 7, 1872

Thomas, Julia A., b. Aug. 4, 1826, d. Aug. 4, 1878
Thompson, Joseph, b. April 20, 1805, d. Feb. 1, 1870
Thompson, Margaret O., wife of Joseph Thompson, b. Feb. 2, 1818, d. Jan. 31, 1890
Thompson, John Wesley, d. Aug. 2, 1867; age, 38 years, 9 months, 13 days
Thompson, Lee Longstreet, son of John M. and A. E. Thompson, b. Dec. 11, 1864, d. Sept. 21, 1866
Thorne, Joshua, Asst. Surgeon (Gov. marker)
Thornton, John F., d. May 17, 1908 (Soldier)
Thornbury, Anna M., wife of William Thornbury, d. Dec. 30, 1878; age, 48 years
Threlkeld, George O., no dates
Threlkeld, Belle Ringo, no dates
Threlkeld, Sallie R., b. 1839, d. 1917
Thurston, John, b. Feb. 22, 1835, d. May 30, 1892
Thurston, Mary A., b. July 15, 1820, d. March 31, 1894
Tiffany, Otis E., b. Feb. 23, 1827, d. May 14, 1885
Tilton, W. A., 11th Kansas Cav., Co. "K" (Gov. marker)
Tomlinson, Jennie, daughter of S. A. and C. A. Tomlinson, b. February 18, 1888, d. Sept. 30, 1896
Todd, John, d. Feb. 18, 1880; age, 58 years
Todd, George B., d. July 8, 1907; age, 52 years
Todd, Mary, wife of John Todd, d. Nov. 24, 1884; age, 52 years
Todd, Mrs. E. L. (mother), d. Sept. 29, 1871; age, 72 years, 9 months
Todd, George H., d. Oct. 13, 1867; age, 6 years, 3 months, 14 days
Toler, Judge George W., b. in Goochland Co., Va., April 23, 1816, d. Sept. 27, 1866
Tollman, Sophie, wife of G. Tollman, b. Dec. 25, 1829, d. Aug. 21, 1874
Tollman, George, b. Sept. 11, 1808, d. May 25, 1885
Tonkinson, H. F., no dates
Topping, children of Henry and May Topping
    Kate, May, Charles, and Amy—no dates
Trafz, John, no dates
Train, Marie, wife of H. C. Train, d. Nov. 7, 1871; age, 52 years, 7 months
Travis, John (father), b. 1820, d. 1905
Trenley, William M., b. 1841, d. 1896 (father)
Trendell, Charles, d. June 28, 188- (Soldier)
Trimble, M. M., b. April 2, 1821, d. Dec. 13, 1883
Trimble, M. E., b. Jan. 9, 1831
Troutman, Samuel, Co. "F" 7th Mo. Cav. (Gov. marker)
Trowbridge, James (Gov. marker)
Turner, T. J., b. June 26, 1839, d. Nov. 13, 1914
Turner, Mary Virginia, wife of T. J. Turner, b. July 28, 1845, d. Dec. 30, 1900
Turner, Maude Hughes, daughter of T. J. and M. V. Turner, d. Feb. 28, 1870; age, 1 year, 1 day
Turner, Marcus Tolman, son of T. J. and M. V. Turner, d. June 28, 1874
Trusdell, John Henry, d. Oct. 3, 1887; age, 27 years, 11 months, 21 days
Tucker, Jennie, wife of A. T. Tucker, b. May 10, 1852, d. Aug. 12, 1883
Turnage, James, b. 1811, d. 1908 (Soldier)
Turnage, Mary, b. 1827, d. 1924
Turner, Lizzie A., b. May 31, 1844, d. June 8, 1894
Turner, James P., b. Oct. 16, 1835, d. July 20, 1879
Tunison, John C., d. April 20, 1891; age, 81 years
Tunison, Julia C., d. Nov. 2, 1902; age, 87 years
Twyman, Lucy A. Bryant, wife of William Twyman, d. Dec. 8, 1875; age, 32 years
Tyree, Mary C. (mother), d. Feb. 12, 1904; age, 55 years

U

Underwood, H. Q., d. June 5, 1903; age, 71 years
Uttech, child of Charles and Clara, name and date too worn to read
Urban, Clara V. Henkle, wife of Morris G. Urban, d. July 11, 1879; age, 20 years
Urton, Lydia W., wife of L. V. Urton, b. June 17, 1827, d. Aug. 31, 1889
Unsworth, William, b. Feb. 3, 1816, d. Sept. 25, 1888
Unsworth, Elizabeth, wife of William Unsworth, b. Aug. 19, 1815, d. Jan. 29, 1879

V

Vanderpool, J. C., Co. "B" 14th Ill. Inf. (Gov. marker)
VanDyke, Mary Jane, b. Jan. 3, 1829, d. Jan. 30, 1901
VanVoorhees, Isaac S., d. Dec. 12, 1888; age, 44 years
Vaughn, Sarah E., b. 1838, d. 1929
Vaughn, J. Francis (Gov. marker)
Veatch, Jennie S., wife of Harmon Veatch, b. July 4, 1845, d. Oct. 15, 1899
Vest, Jefferson, no dates
Vest, Emaline, no dates—old stone
Vest, Thomas M., Co. "D" 35th Mo. Inf. (Gov. marker)
Vindice, Deo, C. S. A. marker
Vichmann, Katherina, b. in Germany, Feb. 25, 1809, d. Sept. 21, 1869
Viel, Hanna, b. Stoellzing, Feb. 2, 1830, d. Jan. 11, 1881
Vincent, T. R., son of A. B. and N. G. Vincent, b. July 11, 1868, d. Sept. 24, 1892
Viers, E. W., b. April 8, 1847, d. June 18, 1907
Vochatzer, Joseph Lewis, U. S. Navy, b. in Marlsruhl, State of Baden, Germany, Dec. 15, 1845, d. May 3, 1895 (Gov. marker)
Vogel, Cathern, wife of G. W. Vogel, b. Jan. 15, 1847, d. June 23, 1901
Vogel, Susan, b. Oct. 1, 1819, d. Feb. 24, 1853
Vogel, Louis, b. March 11, 1806, d. May 6, 1879
Vogel, Louis, son of Louis and Susan Vogel, b. April 9, 1841, d. April 27, 1863
Vogel, George W., Jr., b. 1874, d. 1913
Vork, Edwin, native of Bristol, England, d. Dec. 21, 1861; age, 47 years
Vork, Mary, d. Aug. 19, 1877

W

Wachsmann, Capt. A., d. Jan. 10, 1883; age, 49 years, 1 month, 10 days; Capt. Co. "A" 2nd Mo. L. A. (Gov. marker)
Walbridge, Amaryllis, d. Jan. 8, 1872; age, 42 years
(Wakely) Mrs. Matilda Brown, wife of George Wakely, daughter of Edward and Mary O'Brien Pryce, Baronet, b. in London, England, May 1, 1814, d. Sept. 4, 1888
Waldron, Elijah, d. April 27, 1888; age, 63 years
Waldhier, John A., d. Aug. 23, 1887; age, 33 years, 2 days
Waldhier, Jane E., b. 1838, d. 1897
Walrond, Wilson M., d. July 20, 1851; age, 40 years
Walrond, Granville J.
Walrond, Jordon O., d. July 12, 1890; age, 68 years (Soldier)
Walrond, Louisa G., d. Aug. 5, 1862; age, 4 years
Wallace, William, b. March 8, 1842, d. Sept. 16, 1890
Wallace, Lt. Joseph, d. April 14, 1866, Co. "I" 1st Kansas Inf. (Gov. marker)
Walker, Dr. Eldon, b. Nov. 28, 1820, d. March 21, 1865 (Soldier)
Walker, W. W., Co. "F" 2nd Iowa Inf. (Gov. marker)
Walker, Julia Ann, b. June 30, 1829, d. Dec. 1, 1904
Walker, Charles, unable to read dates
Walker, Sarah (sister), b. 1841, d. 1922; George Tapp (brother)
Watkins, Thomas, b. Nov. 14, 1853, d. April 17, 1907
Watkins, Louisa A., wife of John Q. Watkins, b. Aug. 20, 1839, d. June 2, 1867
Walton, Mary, d. March 1, 1908; age, 69 years, 11 months, 17 days
Walton, Eli (father), b. 1846, d. 1908

Walton, W. W., d. Feb. 21, 1899; age, 65 years, 9 months, 3 days
Wanziqua, P. F. Z., d. July 13, 1897—no dates
Ward, Francis M., b. Jan. 7, 1838, d. Oct. 27, 1916
Ward, Sarah, b. Aug. 5, 1829, d. Oct. 25, 1906
Ward, Charles B., b. in Lafayette Co., Mo., Feb. 18, 1849, d. March 27, 1891
Warner, J. L., b. Dec. 19, 1814
Warner, Sarah B., wife of J. L. Warner, d. Oct. 1, 1888; age, 71 years, 4 months, 14 days
Warner, Frank E., d. April 12, 1901; age, 47 years
Warner, ——, d. Feb. 9, 1888; age, 49 years (Soldier) (on loose stone on right name Ely)
Warren, Samuel T., b. March 15, 1842, d. Feb. 26, 1901
Waskey, Alexander, b. Nov. 22, 1814, d. June 1, 1879 (father)
Waskey, Nancy B. (mother), b. Oct. 19, 1815, d. Aug. 9, 1903
Waskey, Kate B., daughter of A. and N. B. Waskey, b. June 9, 1852, d. Dec. 30, 1855
Watson, George, d. Sept. 23, 1871; age, 54 years
Watson, Emma, wife of George Watson, b. in England, March 9, 1821, d. Aug., 1882
Way, Charles S., son of J. W. and Elvina Way, b. Jan. 5, 1862, d. Nov. 6, 1872
Wear, Abram W., b. March 10, 1820, d. July 8, 1899
Webb, Maria, d. Feb. 11, 1905; age, 76 years
Weber, Johann Chis, son of F. and M. Weber, b. Sept., 1868, d. Feb. 18, 1870
Webber, Henry, b. Dec. 25, 1851, d. May 20 (rest invisible)
Wreckstrom, O. M., d. June, 1882
Weichert, Clara B., wife of George P. Weichert, b. Jan. 1, 1852, d. Dec. 15, 1897
Weir, Samuel, d. Oct. 27, 1900; age, 78 years
Weir, Catherine H., wife of Samuel Weir, d. July 14, 1900; age, 75 years, 8 months
Weis, Willie Anna, b. 1851, d. 1929
Weis, John M., b. March 6, 1818, d. Oct. 1, 1891 (father)
Weis, Margarettha, b. Nov. 16, 1832, d. July 6, 1874 (mother)
Welch, J. H., d. July 3, 1871; age, 45 years (Masonic Emblem)
Weller, John Roher, b. May 3, 1825, d. Dec. 10, 1895
Weller, C. W. (Gov. marker)
Weltman, John, b. Sept. 16, 1826, d. March 5, 1900
Welsh, Nona, d. Aug. 11, 1887; age, 16 years, 11 months, 23 days
Wenzel, Eliza J., wife of G. G. Wenzel, b. Feb. 6, 1847, d. March 30, 1887
Werner, Gustave (father), b. 1842, d. 1893
West, Edward, b. June 9, 1824, d. Oct. 11, 1883
West, Susan M., wife of Edward West, b. Aug. 12, 1836, d. Jan. 19, 1904
West, Richard James, son of Tillman Howard and Elizabeth James West, b. in Simpson County, Ky., June 22, 1843, d. June 8, 1886
West, Ann Penelope Bryan, wife of R. J. West, and daughter of Frederick Barfield and Holland Bush Bryan, b. in Marengo County, Ala., Feb. 12, 1847
Westhoven, George C., b. 1851, d. 1907
Wezstein, Fr.; age, 42 years (Soldier)
Wilson, Thomas G., b. Jan., 1839, d. Aug., 1848
Wheeler, Leanah Jackson, b. May 3, 1842, d. April 14, 1917
Wheeler, daughters of George and Leanah Wheeler
    Sarah E., b. Sept. 1, 1859, d. Jan. 30, 1860
    Hattie, b. Dec. 14, 1861, d. July 25, 1862
    Roma Booth, b. Jan. 13, 1871, d. July 18, 1871
Wheeler, James J., b. March 22, 1830, d. May 6, 1895 (Gov. marker)
Wheeler, T. E., b. May 23, 1856, d. Nov. 26, 1892
Whitager, Adelia A., wife of Cyrus Whitager (stone badly defaced)
Whitaker, Birdie R., daughter of I. and S. Whitaker, b. Dec. 2, 1869, d. March 14, 1871
Whitaker, Fred R., son of I. and S. Whitaker, d. July 1, 1875; age, 2 years
Whitelaw, Louisa J., b. 1831, d. 1922
White, Mary F., b. 1849, d. 1927
White, Margaret, d. Dec. 20, 1881; age, 56 years

White, Mary G., b. July 24, 1844, d. Dec. 11, 1891
White, James P., b. 1854, d. 1926
White, Joseph O. F., b. July 7, 1834, d. Feb. 2, 1905
White, Eliza, b. Nov. 4, 1832, d. Feb. 25, 1907
White, Rachel, d. March 11, 1882 (?); age, 63 years
Whiting, Mary Elizabeth, wife of William E. Whiting, b. Dec. 22, 1835, d. Sept. 8, 1866
Whiting, William E., b. Dec. 25, 1837, d. Dec. 31, 1885
Whredon, Charles H., b. Feb. 21, 1849, d. Dec. 9, 1904
Wiederman, Juliene (?), wife of Wilhelm, b. 1819, d. 1872
Whyte, Ebenezer, b. Jan. 22, 1837, d. April 25, 1901
Widmer, John A., d. May 10, 1879; age, 49 years
Widmer, Kunigunda, b. May 28, 1839, d. Feb. 12, 1891
Wikoff, Lucinda, d. Jan. 27, 1907; age, 73 years
Wikoff, Reuben, d. Feb. 16, 1902; age, 81 years
Wild, Mary Burbara, b. in Switzerland, Sept. 11, 1829, d. Oct. 4, 1903
Wilkerson, John and Rose (father and mother), no dates
Wilhite, Presley G., b. 1833, d. Aug. 1, 1880
Wilhite, Mary Louise Price, wife of Presley G. Wilhite, b. 1834, d. 1919
Wilson, Alexander, Co. "E" 136 Ill. Inf. (Gov. marker)
Wilson, Mary Jane, d. Oct. 3, 1929; age, 76 years
Wilson, Samuel S., b. Jan. 22, 1858, d. Dec. 3, 1883
Wilson, Hugh G., d. May 25, 1886
Wilson, Clara and Charlie, daughter and son of David R. and Catherine Wilson, d. Nov. 28, 1861; ages, 6 and 4 years
Wilson, Daniel, b. 1845
Wilson, Thomas, b. Feb. 18, 1796, d. July 25, 1860
Wilson, Deborah, wife of Thos. Wilson, b. June 28, 1811, d. Jan. 31, 1852
Wilson, William, son of Thos. and D. Wilson, b. April 7, 1848, d. May 13, 1849
Wilson, Amelia, d. Feb. 19, 1895; age, 42 years
Wilson, James D., d. July 5, 1871; age, 40 years
Wilson, Ann, b. March 17, 1817, d. Feb. 1, 1899; age, 80 years
Wilson, John E., b. Jan. 1, 1855, d. Aug., 1906
Wilson, Lilly, no dates
Will, A. H., Co. "A" 43rd Ohio Infantry (Gov. marker)
Willson, George, of North Carolina, b. Feb. 12, 1812, d. July 24, 1856 (Reinterred by the Odd Fellows of K. C., Sept. 12, 1897)
Williams, John E., d. Jan. 1, 1905; age, 70 years
Williams, Clara A., d. July 10, 1909; age, 56 years
Williams, Clara B., daughter of Samuel and Mary Williams, d. Oct. 18, 1878; age, 18 years
Williams, Owen T., b. April 24, 1841, d. Jan. 26, 1872
Williams, Ada J., b. 1845, d. 1896
Williams, Corporal C. T., Co. "A" 2nd Kansas Inf.
Williams, Lydia A., b. Feb. 22, 1827, d. Sept. 22, 1891
Wiedenmann, G., b. Jan. 30, 1807, d. March 21, 1890; age, 83 years
Winchester, Sarah, d. Feb. 6, 1897; age, 60 years
Winn, John W., b. April 22, 1844, d. April 9, 1904
Winter, Louis (Gov. marker)
Winterhalter, N. J. (mother), b. June 30, 1839, d. Oct. 21, 1905
Winterhalter, ―― (father), b. Aug. 12, 1819, d. March 29, 1901
Wintsh, Helena, wife of Henry Wintsh, d. Jan., 1876
Wirz, Barbara, other names invisible except Von Stromberg
Wishropp, Charles F., b. Nov. 28, 1842, d. Oct. 17, 1910
Windolph, Michael J., b. Feb. 24, 1833, d. July 14, 1889
Windolph, Julia S., wife of Michael J. Windolph, b. Dec. 7, 1843, d. Feb. 6, 1903
Wolfrum, Margaret, b. March 9, 1853, d. Jan. 23, 1901
Wood, Martin, b. in Middlebury, Vt., Sept. 22, 1843, d. April 5, 1904 (Soldier)

Woods, Ren., b. May 30, 1858, d. May 8, 1895
Woods, Georgia Ann (mother), d. May 27, 1901; age, 58 years
Woodson, Edward C., b. 1855, d. 1898
Woodson, Robert Everard, b. Jan. 18, 1817, d. May 19, 1872
Woodson, Isaac Barnett, b. 1845, d. 1881
Woodson, Sarah Waddle, b. 1862, d. 1875
Woodward, Lovina, b. Dec. 12, 1828, d. March 17, 1897
Woodward, Nancy B., d. April 15, 1889; age, 74 years
Woodsworth, M. A., b. Feb. 26, 1821, d. April 21, 1896
Woodsworth, Col. H. D., d. Jan. 15, 1882; age, 60 years, 4 months, 15 days
Woolworth, Richard P., b. Jan. 17, 1837, d. Jan. 16, 1903
Woodsworth, Mary Kate, wife of H. D. Woodsworth, b. April 29, 1836, d. Dec. 3, 1862
Wren, Mary, wife of P. Wren, b. in Co. Kerry, Ireland, d. May 19, 1885
Wright, Mrs. Emma, d. March 5, 1880; age, 82 years
Wright, R., d. April 1, 1894; age, 38 years
Wuerz, Ida, b. Oct. 9, 1825, d. Feb. 26, 1880
Wuerz, August (Civil War Soldier)

Y

York, Wilhelmine, b. 1838, d. 1907
York, Anna, b. 1869, d. 1888
York, Ida, b. 1877, d. 1898
Young, Sergt. William (Gov. marker)
Young, Mary E., b. 1844, d. 1916
Young, Amanda A., wife of Riley Young, d. July 6, 1891; age, 62 years
Young, Jacob (father), b. May 20, 1842, d. May 9, 1900
Youngclause, George, b. 1842, d. 1909
Youngclause, Emma H., b. 1853, d. 1926

Z

Zacharias, Cecilia, d. April 29, 1890; age, 41 years
Zahn, Martha, — August 30, 18— (Unable to read more)
Zahner, Emily J., d. March 21, 1900; age, 57 years
Zimmerschild, John Ferdinand, b. Dec. 11, 1849, d. Jan. 27, 1930
Zweig, Johanna, d. April 18, 1907; age, 72 years

(The words—Government marker—appearing so often in this record contain the information that the individual was a soldier or sailor in some department of the U. S. forces and the tombstone is the regulation one provided by the Government for its men.)

The above names and dates were copied from the tombstones in Union Cemetery, September, 1933, by Mrs. Max A. Christopher and Mrs. Hale Houts

SNI-A-BAR TOWNSHIP

Organized May 5, 1834

BLUE SPRINGS CEMETERY
Copied by Miss Julia Kinney

Adams, Jonathan, died June 8, 1877; age, 44 years, 2 months, 14 days
Andrews, Andrew J., born 1835, died 1916
Andrews, Susan Frances, born 1844, died 1912
Armstrong, Thomas, born February 18, 1830, died May 22, 1899
Boardman, H. J., born May 15, 1838, died March 21, 1909
Bolm, William, born March 10, 1832, died August 1, 1908
Bolm, Mary, wife of William H. Bolm, died February 17, 1877; age, 33 years, 8 months, 13 days
Branton, Moses, born 1842, died 1923
Branton, Sarah A., born 1841, died 1903
Brezendine, Orville F., born December 26, 1829, died January 27, 1897
Bridges, Silas, born 1845, died 1926
Brown, Henry, born September 18, 1839, died November 15, 1904
Bruce, Henry J., born 1847, died 1924
Bruce, Elvira F., born 1847, died 1915
Burnett, Jeremiah, died June 28, 1848; age, 99 years
Burrus, George W., born August 13, 1843, died May 16, 1861
Burrus, James M., died October 9, 1893; age, 74 years, 4 months, 16 days
Burrus, James W., born 1847, died 1919
Burrus, Virginia A., born 1847, died 1925
Burrus, William T., born January 22, 1811, died November 2, 1858
Cummings, John M., born February 14, 1806, died March 24, 1871
Cummings, Eliza A., born September 28, 1810, died July 18, 1834
Campbell, George W., born July 31, 1838, died February 15, 1905
Campbell, Patsie R., born January 6, 1844, died June 9, 1920
Carlat, Claude, born April 13, 1805, died February 22, 1892
Carson, William, born May 5, 1847, died October 25, 1880
Casey, Robert, born 1838, died 1917
Casey, Amanda, born 1843, died 1923
Cash, Thomas B., born March 4, 1839, died November 1, 1907
Caswell, Martha J., wife of J. Caswell, born January 15, 1837, died October 4, 1904
Chapman, Madison, born 1804, died 1902
Chapman, Sallie E., born 1829, died 1904
Clark, John W., died August 19, 1900; age, 77 years
Clark, Sarah A., born 1780, died 1863
Clark, Mary Jane, died June 16, 1929; age, 71 years, 22 months, 16 days
Clark, Thomas P., born 1811, died 1874
Cox, William R., born June 28, 1825, died July 13, 1910
Cox, Sarah A., wife of W. R. Cox, born February 10, 1831, died April 16, 1923
Crawford, Jyslithah M., died January 29, 1863; age, 50 years, 12 months, 12 days

Dillingham, Joshua, born March 29, 1816, died December 16, 1875
Dillingham, Susan, born September 18, 1826, died June 26, 1911
Dillingham, Cillins J., born 1847, died 1924
Dillingham, Sarah E., born 1850, died 1910
Dillingham, Morgan V., born 1843, died 1925
Dillingham, Anslvina E., born 1850, died 1928
De Long, Emanuel, born October 16, 1848
Donahue, Caroline D., wife of Patrick Donahue, born August 14, 1843, died May 7, 1909
Duncan, William, died August 17, 1888; age, 85 years, 5 months
Dunham, Royal, born September 1, 1815, died October 29, 1902
Dunham, Sarah, wife of Royal Dunham, born April 7, 1828, died March 2, 1902
Fields, Frederic R., born November 27, 1812, died March 6, 1896
Fields, Mary R., born 1826, died 1900
Furnish, Jeremiah, born 1843, died 1910
Furnish, Mary L., wife of Jeremiah Furnish, born 1850, died 1898
Gill, Sarah M., daughter of G. W. and S. M. Gill, died June 25, 1872; age, 23 years, 9 months, 24 days
Gill, George W., died June 8, 1895; age, 74 years, 10 months, 14 days
Gillespie, R. A., born 1847, died 1921
Hamilton, George W., born May 29, 1849, died December 25, 1915
Hamilton, Mary E., born February 22, 1861, died January 20, 1904
Harris, William, died March 28, 1847; age, 50 years, 11 months, 14 days
Harris, Rhoda, died September 9, 1878; age, 78 years, 2 months, 18 days
Harris, Columbus W., son of William Harris, died June 13, 1852; age, 19 years, 6 months, 11 days
Harris, Icom B., died April 6, 1852; age, 28 years, 4 months, 14 days
Harris, Samantha J., born January 29, 1850, died March 1, 1930
Hayes, Rev. Leander Fields, born January 19, 1836, died June 5, 1907
Hayes, Susan Katherine, wife of Rev. Leander Fields Hayes, born January 1, 1837, died June 19, 1922
Holloway, R. J., born July 6, 1826, died April 2, 1902
Holloway, Sarah E., born November 7, 1833, died August 18, 1887
Holloway, James, born May 26, 1798, died September 22, 1876
Holloway, Mildred, wife of James Holloway, born February 1, 1803, died September 11, 1874
Inlow, William T., born August 4, 1848, died August 18, 1924
Jessee, Catherine, born November 18, 1844, died August 13, 1876
Johnson, Larkin J., born June 6, 1843, died November 29, 1910
Johnson, Samaria, wife of Larkin J. Johnson, born February 10, 1848, died October 22, 1921
Jones, W. H., born December 20, 1840, died February 16, 1912
Jones, ——, wife of W. H. Jones, born December 29, 1844, died February 10, 1914
Jones, Mother, born December 29, 1844, died February 14, 1914
Ketterman, Martha E., died August 8, 1881; age, 48 years
Ketterman, Z. David, born 1846, died 1921
Kimberlin, Samuel, born January 1, 1809, died November 9, 1862
Kimberlin, Eliza, wife of Samuel Kimberlin, born February 27, 1814, died October 9, 1895
Kirby, J. T., born May 2, 1830, died September 10, 1905
Kirby, Barbara A., wife of J. T. Kirby, born November 4, 1828
Kirby, William R., born May 6, 1831, died January 17, 1905
Kirby, Susan Capelle, born April 29, 1841, died January 25, 1918
Knight, Thurston, born June 20, 1819, died July 10, 1910
Knight, Martha A., wife of Thurston Knight, born February 14, 1823, died March 29, 1908
Lane, S. J., born 1850, died 1931
Lear, A. J., died April 24, 18—
Lear, Sarah, wife of A. J., died August 20, 1879; age, 61 years, 9 months, 17 days
Ledge, John Watson, born April 18, 1850, died February 25, 1930

Lewis, John Harvey, born June 1, 1825, died May 24, 1903
Lewis, Elizabeth Kelso, wife of John Harvey Lewis, born February 21, 1831, died September 16, 1908
Ligon, Elias L., born August 29, 1822, died August 15, 1926
Lilly, Nancy, born April 1, 1816, died November 30, 1901
Mann, Robert ———
Mann, Louisa, wife of Robert Mann, died 1880; age, 70 years
Marr, Benjamin F., born October, 1847, died November, 1930
Martin, John B., born 1849, died January 12, 1931
Mauzey, J. H., born 1822, died 1909
Mauzey, Margaret, wife of J. H. Mauzey, born 1837, died 1910
Mayes, J. G., born 1818, died 1889
Mayes, H. Clinton, born 1845, died 1927
Mock, Dr. D., born 1823, died 1897
Mock, George, born 1834, died 1907
Mock, Sarah, born 1831, died 1910
Moore, Theany A., wife of J. H. Moore, born November 19, 1844, died August 2, 1917
Moore, J. Henry, born December 28, 1843, died February 22, 1923
Morris, John W., born 1841, died January 12, 1931
Morrison, Gabriel, born November 7, 1839, died July 16, 1903
Morrison, Keziah J., wife of Gabriel Morrison, born February 25, 1844, died November 18, 1876
Mungy, David P., born 1836, died 1910
Mungy, Maranda, born 1837, died 1915
Nave, Cinderrilla, born May 31, 1829, died July 11, 1909
Neal, Lucy, wife of Felden Neal, died May 2, 1875; age, 78 years
Newman, T. J., born October 25, 1836, died July 26, 1905
Newman, Rebecca, wife of T. J. Newman, born April 12, 1826, died September 17, 1898
Owsley, Harve, born 1847, died 1915
Parr, Hannah, born August 20, 1816, died September 4, 1910; age, 94 years, 14 days
Parr, J. K., born 1844, died 1913, Company "B" 16th Illinois Volunteer Infantry
Parr, Nancy, born November 29, 1837, died September 21, 1915
Parr, William S., born September 19, 1832, died July 25, 1909
Parr, Amos, born 1845, died 1914
Pope, J. A., born 1838, died 1919
Pope, Mary E., wife of J. A. Pope, born 1840, died 1916
Prewitt, George W., born 1836, died 1917
Prewitt, Fannie E., wife of George W. Prewitt, born 1850, died 1878
Pruitt, Albert J., died October 14, 1894; age, 61 years, 8 months, 27 days
Pruitt, Mary A., wife of Albert J. Pruitt, born 1836, died 1923
Pruitt, John, born February 22, 1802, died May 7, 1870
Records, Thomas W., born May 13, 1841, died February 28, 1931
Records, Stella, wife of T. W. Records, born September 3, 1842, died January 1, 1919
Rice, Polina, wife of C. J. Rice, died February 7, 1877; age, 67 years, 4 months, 3 days
Rice, Amanda, wife of T. C. Rice, died December 1, 1868; age, 19 years, 8 months, 8 days
Robertson, Samuel, born 1833, died 1914
Robertson, Judith L., born 1842, died 1917
Reid, Joseph K., born 1843, died 1912
Robertson, George, born December 19, 1835, died July 22, 1882
Robertson, Julia J., born January 12, 1844, died March 1, 1911
Roof, Reuben, born May 9, 1823, died August 13, 1905
Roof, Nancy, wife of Reuben Roof, born March 17, 1825, died January 3, 1911
Rowe, Moses T., born June 3, 1841, died May 13, 1914
Rowe, Caroline M., born January 21, 1839, died May 6, 1920
Rowe, William E., born 1839, died 1924
Rowe, Violet E., born 1851, died 1923

Saunders, J. W., died January 29, 1863; age, 49 years, 10 months, 16 days
Scott, Emma S., wife of G. W. Scott, born 1844, died 1908
Selvey, Edna, wife of M. N. Selvey, born November 28, 1843, died November 23, 1898
Seymour, Josiah (father), born February 19, 1836, died February 12, 1921
Seymour, Martha (mother), born January 2, 1842, died July 14, 1916
Shrout, John H., born July 8, 1830, died February 6, 1912
Shrout, Mary E., born August 25, 1850, died November 8, 1926
Shrout, David W., born 1830, died 1894
Shrout, Mary A., born 1837, died 1917
Smith, Noah, born November 18, 1818, died April 23, 1906
Smith, Lucinda, wife of Noah Smith, born May 10, 1823, died August 6, 1888
Smith, Thomas D., died January 15, 1854; age, 32 years
Snodgrass, Bartley A., born 1849, died 1916
Snodgrass, Dovie A., born 1854
St. Clair, Charles E., born June 5, 1835, died November 3, 1923
St. Clair, Mary L., wife of Charles E. St. Clair, born July 8, 1846, died February 28, 1903
Stanley, James W., born 1839, died 1915
Stanley, Priscilla J., born 1837, died 1894
Stillwell, William, died July 14, 1925; age, 80 years, 6 months, 15 days
Stillwell, Mary F., wife of William Stillwell, died February 3, 1889; age, 86 years, 8 months
Stokes, Bethena (mother), born 1843, died 1930
Stratzman, Elder William M., born February 18, 1850, died July 20, 1905
Stratzman, Cornelia Bowen, born February 9, 1849, died July 2, 1925
Tatum, David F., born 1842, died 1907
Tatum, Lizzie A., born 1843, died 1930
Tatum, John W., born 1834, died 1918
Thompson, William M., born March 7, 1809, died September 21, 1889
Thompson, Lucinda, born March 13, 1821, died February 27, 1915
Thompson, Rev. J. D., born November 15, 1847, died February 17, 1911
Thompson, Isabella J., born September 4, 1845, died March 29, 1903
Weatherford, John, born June 20, 1814, died February 2, 1892
Weatherford, Adeline M., wife of John Weatherford, born November 10, 1817, died May 13, 1904
Webb, Thomas, born July 3, 1839, died October 21, 1928
Webb, Larkin M., born February 24, 1826, died March 1, 1908
Webb, Sicily J., wife of Larkin M. Webb, born April 6, 1825, died December 23, 1915
Wiley, James A., born February 16, 1843, died December 2, 1923
Wiley, Sarah C., wife of James A. Wiley, born October 13, 1845, died December 26, 1928
Williams, A. G., born 1835, died 1913
Williams, Amanda A., wife of A. G. Williams, born 1838, died 1918
Williams, John W., born November 23, 1816, died February 26, 1895
Williams, Sarah Frances, born October 31, 1838, died December 4, 1880
Witt, Thomas H., born May 12, 1850, died January 26, 1907
Witt, Nancy Elizabeth, wife of Thomas H. Witt, born April 13, 1847, died April 25, 1930
Worley, F. M., born September 15, 1847, died April 24, 1903
Worley, Adaline, born February 19, 1849
Wood, Jeremiah, born 1792, died November 17, 1847
Wood, Elizabeth, born December 20, 1795, died April 3, 1884
Wood, George W., born June 5, 1841, died August 9, 1872
Wood, Jennie Y., wife of George W. Wood, born February 6, 1847, died February 3, 1910
Woof, Robert T., born 1849, died 1922
Young, Charles, born March 7, 1830, died February 24, 1880
Young, Rebecca J., died November 19, 1875; age, 41 years, 10 months, 2 days
Zimmerman, Phillips, born January, 1850, died November, 1931

Copied April, 1933, by Miss Julia Kinney

BRIDGES CEMETERY
Section 12, Township 49, Range 30 W
On farm now owned by Mrs. W. R. Randall and Mrs. A. J. Randall

Bridges, Annie Powell, died 1879; wife of James Bridges
Bridges, James, died about 1881
Bridges, Elmira, daughter of James Bridges and wife, Annie Powell Bridges
Harris, Jane, wife of Samuel Harris, born June 12, 1814, died August 19, 1893 (A granddaughter of John Burnett, Rev. soldier of Virginia)
Harris, William H., died February 6, 1868; age, 25 years, 8 months, 22 days
Powell, Hannah Jewson, 3rd wife of Joseph Powell (Rev. Soldier)
Riley, Delia, daughter of J. T. and Mary E. Riley, died June 30, 1884; age, 1 day
Riley, Mary E., wife of J. T. Riley, died April 27, 1887; age, 26 years, 2 months, 15 days

(This was a family cemetery, upon the farm of James Bridges, who came to Jackson County, Missouri, in 1832 from Claiborne County, Tennessee. There are here buried 4 sons, 2 daughters, 2 daughters-in-law and several grand children of James Bridges, as well as members of the Harris family and neighboring families of Ragland, Mahurin, Riley and others. Information relative to the families supplied by Mrs. A. J. Randall, of Independence, Missouri.)

Copied August 14, 1933, by Mrs. Hale Houts

BROWN CEMETERY
Section 32, Township 48 N, Range 29 W

Austin, Joseph, born January 1, 1820, died May 31, 1889
Austin, Martha, wife of Joseph Austin, born May 21, 1818, died February 3, 1896
Austin, Richard F., born July 9, 1853, died December 26, 1911
Brown, Elizabeth, wife of James Brown, born November 27, 1790, died 1860
Brown, T. H., died August, 1872; age, 58 years, 4 months, 21 days
Brown, Kizcah, wife of T. H. Brown, died March 8, 1874; age, 57 years, 8 months, 6 days
Brown, William A., died February 15, 1898; age, 66 years, 2 months, 1 day
Corn, Solomon A., born October 8, 1827, died September 21, 1860
Duncan, Charles T., born November 23, 1836, died August 31, 1919
Hudson, J. W., born May 23, 1848, died December 29, 1928
Hudson, Cora A., wife of J. W. Duncan, born October 11, 1867, died January 16, 1907
Hudson, Mary E., wife of J. W. Hudson, died February 1, 1895; age, 47 years, 5 months, 14 days
Patterson, Henrietta and infant, wife of Joel P. Patterson, died July 23, 1866; age, 32 years, 4 months, 9 days
Patterson, Jesse, son of J. P. and S. P. Patterson, died August 22, 1881; age, 14 years, 10 months, 18 days
Peerson, Thomas W., born 1849, died 1881
Peerson, Elizabeth Gardner, born 1848, died 1924
Robinson, Mattie A., wife of J. J. Robinson, born December 21, 1862, died May 22, 1885
Scott, A. C., born February 7, 1844, died February 25, 1921
Scott, N. R., wife of A. C. Scott, born November 12, 1845, died April 15, 1911
Scott, Harmon H., born 1880, died 1930
Scott, Susan O., wife of G. W. Scott, died July 9, 1886; age, 81 years, 6 months, 27 days
Temple, John S., born June 18, 1827, died August 16, 1862
Temple, Marcella Dean, wife of John S. Temple, born May 9, 1827, died March 29, 1892

Copied September 3, 1933, by Miss Julia Kinney and Miss Ethel Merwin

CHIDDIX (or Johnson) CEMETERY

Sections 2 and 4 (across the line), Township 49, Range 30

Located on the farm of Nellie G. Adams

Chiddix, Mary, daughter of Eli and Olley Chiddix, died July 10, 1882; age, 70 years, 2 months, 22 days
Chiddix, Perlie, daughter of A. G. and R. C. Chiddix, died June 25, 1887; age, 4 months
Chiddix, Robert, son of A. G. and R. C. Chiddix, died September 11, 1884; age, 9 months
Chiddix, Samuel H., died August 25, 1880; age, 66 years, 3 months, 4 days
Chiddix, John, died February 2, 1884; age, 66 years, 1 month, 2 days
Chiddix, Rachel, wife of John Chiddix, died July 18, 1887; age, 53 years
Chiddix, Samuel, born July 30, 1846, died May 16, 1902
Chiddix, Manerva, wife of Samuel Chiddix, died October 28, 1878; age, 22 years
Duff, Robert A., born February 11, 1842, died August 29, 1925
Duff, Margaret, wife of Robert A. Duff, died January 4, 1908; age, 54 years
Graham, Georgia H., daughter of A. M. and — M. Graham, died December 6, 1879; age, 3 years, 2 months, 9 days
Hilt, Edward T., born February 25, 1839, died July 22, 1928
Hilt, John R., son of Edward and Elizabeth G. Hilt, died November 22, 1882; age, 21 years, 6 months, 21 days
Jessee, Stephen, died March 18, 1880; age, 69 years
Johnson, David, died March 18, 1882; age, 44 years, 3 months, 8 days
Johnson, Frances Elizabeth, died January 7, 1884; age, 59 years, 3 months, 20 days
Johnson, H. A., born May 17, 1846, died December 18, 1927
Johnson, Permelia Jane, wife of H. A. Johnson, born April 7, 1845, died November 11, 1922
Johnson, James R., son of H. A. and P. J. Johnson, died January 10, 1904; age, 3 years, 2 months, 8 days
Johnson, James H., born May 10, 1842, died March 15, 1932
Johnson, Melissa E., wife of James H. Johnson, born March 15, 1845, died December 5, 1900
Johnson, Sarepta, daughter of D. D. Johnson, died May 14, 1877; age, 26 years, 9 months, 2 days
Johnson, Nancy Woody, wife of Lee J. Johnson, born October 25, 1849, died November 25, 1903
Johnson, Tony P., son of L. J. and W. J. Johnson, died August 26, 1878; age, 1 year, 9 months, 2 days
Johnson, Rosy E., daughter of Lee J. and N. J. Johnson, died September 11, 1895; age, 11 years, 7 months, 8 days
King, Delaney (mother), born 1847, died 1899
Kirby, John A., died November 8, 1883; age, 40 years
Mack, James, died April 24, 1889; age, 31 years, 5 months; almost obliterated
Mack, Auda, born August 31, 1887, died July 15, 1908
McGraw, Minnie, daughter of Dan and A. J. McGraw, died September 10, 1883; age, 10 months, 10 days
Majors, Sarah A., wife of B. S. Majors, died October 10, 1890; age, 40 years, 10 months, 15 days
Necessary, S. P., born January 18, 1840, died October 1, 1922
Necessary, Margaret, wife of S. P. Necessary, died February 15, 1884; age, 39 years, 10 months, 5 days
Necessary, Wesley; age, 75 years
Necessary, Annie, wife of Wesley; age, 92 years
Necessary, Henry, born November 2, 1849, died January 12, 1906
Necessary, Louisa, wife of Henry Necessary, born July 18, 1858, died August 27, 1899
Phillips, Virginia, wife of J. T. Phillips, died August 19, 1907; age, 85 years, 3 months, 19 days

Phillips, James W., died October 16, 1872 (age obliterated)
Phillips, Alice M., daughter of J. W. and S. E. Phillips, died August 16, 1879; age, 24 years, 10 months, 2 days
Phillips, Carrie, daughter of J. W. and S. E. Phillips, died December 21, 1873; age, 8 years, 6 months
Phillips, Sarah Eletha, wife of J. W. Phillips, died July 17, 1908; age, 79 years, 6 months, 8 days
Wyatt, Crittenden, died March 1, 1901; age, 82 years, 2 months, 14 days
Wyatt, Winnyford D., wife of Crittenden Wyatt, died February 29, 1884; age, 50 years

Copied May 18, 1933, by Miss Julia Kinney and Miss Ethel Merwin

CORN CEMETERY
Section 17, Township 48, Range 29 W

Adams, John O, d. April 12, 1882; age, 64 years, 3 months
Adams, Phebia J., died January 23, 1905; age, 77 years
Ashcraft, Sudie Cobb, wife of P. C. Ashcraft, born March 5, 1850, died December 26, 1899
Axene, Permelia, born August 1, 1839, died September 25, 1881
Bateman, Barbara C., wife of Joel Bateman, born January 27, 1849, died May 13, 1885
Bridges, Thomas, died July 4, 1851; age, 32 years
Browne, Arlandes A., son of W. H. and E. Browne, died April 3, 1820; age, 17 years
Brown, John H., born 1854, died 1922
Brown, Mary T., wife of John H. Brown, born 1856, died 1922
Corn, John S., died February 4, 1892; age, 80 years, 4 months
Corn, Saleta, wife of John S. Corn, died January 27, 1894; age, 75 years, 6 months
Corn, John Henry, born 1847, died 1930
Corn, Rhoda E., wife of J. H. Corn, died February 19, 1883; age, 38 years
Corn, Thomas J., born September 25, 1840, died May 3, 1921
Corn, Nancy E., born March 30, 1845, died September 9, 1920
Corn, infant daughter of John and Susan, born and died May 20, 1856
Husted, Bettie, born 1848, died 1920
Husted, Chancy, born 1842, died 1892
Newman, A. W., died August 5, 1907; age, 60 years, 1 month, 7 days
Newman, Mattie A., born May 20, 1855, died January 6, 1915
Nivens, Thomas, born September 15, 1818, died July 26, 1883
Nivens, Annie I., wife of Thomas Nivens, born May 21, 1827, died February 8, 1900; age, 81 years, 8 months, 17 days
Nivens, David L., born 1849, died 1925
Nivens, Mary A., wife of David L. Nivens, born 1852, died 1885
Pike, Samuel P., husband of Levina A. Pike, died August 11, 1885; age, 31 years, 5 months, 23 days
Quick, Ola, daughter of John and Lizzie Quick, died January 12, 1834; age, 1 year, 3 months, 21 days
Seitz, John Henry, son of John P. and Deborah Seitz, died March 9, 1875; age, 13 years, 16 days
Smith, Keziah, wife of John Smith, died December 13, 1869; age, 71 years, 11 months, 5 days
Steel, J. D., born August 6, 1833, died December 20, 1898
Steele, Mary J., born May 25, 1833, died April 14, 1925; age, 85 years, 10 months, 30 days
Wallin, William B., died August 16, 1862; age, 25 years, 6 months
White, Ephram, died January 1, 1906; age, 83 years
White, A. H., born March 4, 1855, died September 6, 1904
White, Mattie L., wife of A. H. White, born February 23, 1862, died July 28, 1887
White, Sarah, wife of Ephram White, born April 17, 1822
Gorm, Lenora F., daughter of W. E. and M. C. Gorm, died December 15, 1871; age, 8 years, 19 days

Copied July 25, 1933, by Mrs. Hale Houts

DUNCAN CEMETERY
Section 6, Township 48 N, Range 29 W
Located on the C. D. Capelle Farm at Oak Grove

Duncan, Thomas J., born September 25, 1808, died December 19, 1875
Duncan, Susan, daughter of T. J. and E. B. Duncan, died April 22, 1852; age, 5 months, 23 days
Duncan, Ann B., daughter of T. J. and E. B. Duncan, died October 12, 1845; age, 2 years, 7 months, 1 day
Duncan, Altie E., wife of G. T. Duncan, died July 29, 1890; age, 38 years, 8 months, 19 days
Duncan, George N., died December 6, 1861; age, 22 years, 11 months, 3 days
Duncan James, died about 31 years ago when about 70 years old; body removed to Carrolton, Missouri, 11 years ago
Capelle, infant daughter of J. O. and B. M. Capelle, died November 24, 1886
Smith, Leonides, son of G. E. Smith and J. Mizner, died May 24, 1873; age, 17 years, 3 months, 7 days

Copied September 3, 1933, by Miss Julia Kinney and Miss Ethel Merwin

GARDNER CEMETERY
Located on the Fred Wyatt Farm, (a grandson of Elias and Sally Gardner)

Gardner, Elias H., born April 18, 1816, died February 24, 1869
Gardner, Sally, wife of Elias H. Gardner, born December 24, 1814, died May 15, 1869
Gardner, B., son of S. and E. H. Gardner, born February 9, 1847, died July 3, 1865
Gardner, Franklin L., son of S. and E. H. Gardner, born September 25, 1856, died October 28, 1856

Copied September 3, 1933, by Miss Julia Kinney and Miss Ethel Merwin

GEORGE CEMETERY
South of Oak Grove

Bowman, Mary A., born July 25, 1828, died September 27, 1872; married J. L. Bowman, October 16, 1845
George, David C., son of David C. George and Nancy George, born April 17, 1843, died January 22, 1862
George, N. E. Bass, wife of David C. George, born January 10, 1808, died April 15, 1882
George, J. H., born March 24, 1838, died January 29, 1926
George, Lavisa A., wife of J. H. George, born June 18, 1841, died April 22, 1920
George, H. J., born April 7, 1834, died October 22, 1911
George, Mary T., wife of H. J. George, born August 30, 1839, died April 19, 1875
George, Maggie E., wife of H. J. George, born May 23, 1849, died January 22, 1888
George, Sarah J., born May 31, 1838, died January 21, 1901
Gorrell, J. G., born August 23, 1836, died April 9, 1877
Kabrick, Francis F., born June 4, 1841, died February 22, 1922
Owings, Joshua, born July 8, 1820, died November 26, 1879
Owings, Martha E., wife of Joshua Owings, born September 13, 1829, died January 27, 1926
Roselle, E. A. Kabrick, wife of E. H. Roselle, born March 29, 1836, died January 20, 1915
Tyer, Amanda L., wife of J. W. Tyer, died March 16, 1879; age, 31 years, 1 month, 11 days

Copied June, 1933, by Miss Julia Kinney and Miss Ethel Merwin

GORE CEMETERY

Section 6, Township 48 N, Range 30 W

Located on the old Louis Gore Farm, now owned by Levi Gore

Adams, Arthur W., son of H. A. and S. M. Adams, born January 11, 1882, died February 2, 1899

Adams, Sarah M., born February 11, 1859, died March 31, 1902

Adams—grave unmarked

Cash, Joseph F., son of T. R. and D. S. Cash, born July 30, 1872, died July 30, 1873

Gore, Louis, born October 29, 1821, died January 18, 1905

Gore, Hannah, wife of Louis Gore, born October 26, 1820, died January 13, 1909

Stith, Frances Ann, wife of R. M. Stith, born July 15, 1817, died May 22, 1843

Stith, William Argus, son of R. M. and F. A. Stith, born March 28, 1839, died December 6, 1842

Stith, Bryan Y., son of R. M. and F. A. Stith, born March 7, 1841, died March 8, 1842

Stith, Richard Lee, son of R. M. and H. G. Stith, born February 14, 1847, died November 26, 1847

Wilson, Thomas, Co. "G" 53rd Ohio Infantry, Civil War; no dates on stone

Copied September 22, 1933, by Miss Julia Kinney and Miss Ethel Merwin

HERRINGTON CEMETERY

Section 26, Township 49, Range 30 W

Banks, Joseph, died May 3, 1930; age, 79 years, 7 months, 20 days; Company "I" 19th Kansas Cavalry

Costigan, Dennis, born 1849

Costigan, Martha, wife of Dennis Costigan, born 1855, died 1927

Costigan, Maggie May, born 1894, died 1916

Douglas, W. I., father, born 1840, died 1929

Douglas, Nancy, wife of W. I. W. Douglas, born 1841

Graham, Alfred N., born February 15, 1843, died July 22, 1922

Graham, Elizabeth M., wife of Alfred N. Graham, born February 2, 1847, died April 27, 1911

Herrington, M. M., born April 24, 1836, died January 12, 1927

Herrington, Sarah F., born December 27, 1841, died November 14, 1915

Hosler, Daniel, born July 28, 1825, died March 10, 1907

Hosler, Elsie A., wife of Daniel Hosler, born June 29, 1830, died January 2, 1927

Hosler, Henry Hiram, born 1846, died 1920

Hosler, Sarah Jeanette, wife of Henry Hiram Hosler, born 1850, died 1933

Kabrich, George H B., died March 10, 1932; age, 74 years, 9 months, 21 days

Kershaw, Hannah E., wife of P. F. Kershaw, born April 1, 1840, died December 21, 1903

Kiff, Florence E., born 1850, died 1931

Williams, John, born August 25, 1846, died November 2, 1906

Williams, Lavina, born November 19, 1826

Copied July 22, 1933, by Miss Julia Kinney and Miss Ethel Merwin

LOBB CEMETERY
Section 12, Township 49, Range 31

Cumberland Presbyterian Church—Sometimes called Shakerag Church

Copied April 17, 1933, by Mrs. C. M. Uhlig and Mrs. Hale Houts

Bault, Mary E., wife of Thomas Bault, died August, 1877; age, 39 years
Baumeister, August, died October 18, 1888; age, 64 years, 10 months, 5 days
Boyd, Robert M., died January 30, 1868; age, 56 years, 9 months, 14 days
Bourman, Lucy Jane Parr, died January 14, 1928; age, 68 years, 11 months, 14 days
Bowlin, James R., born July 13, 1820, died September 18, 1913
Bowlin, Julia A., wife of James R., born January 22, 1847

Capelle, Mary M., born December 24, 1843, died March 22, 1916
Capelle, Trusten P., born August 1, 1854, died April 12, 1883
Capelle, Britton M., born October 2, 1809, died February 12, 1889
Christison, William M., son of J. M. and A. L. Christison, died January 26, 1879; age, 5 years, 1 month, 17 days
Crenshaw, John T., born 1847, died 1922
Crenshaw, Sallie A., wife of John T. Crenshaw, born 1854, died 1932
Crenshaw, A. L. H., born April 18, 1805, died March 23, 1890 (stone broken)
Crenshaw, Eliza, wife of A. L. H. Crenshaw, died July 9, 1872; age, 54 years, 8 months, 11 days
Crenshaw, E. N., died March 22, 1876; age, 30 years
Crenshaw, Thomas L., born 1843, died 1922
Crenshaw, Nancy J. (mother), born 1849, died 1916
Cook, Mary M., born January 28, 1869, died September 21, 1871
Crow, Jacob Crow, died January 19, 1892; age, 94 years
Crow, Agnessa, wife of Jacob Crow, born April 22, 1810, died July 8, 1884
Crow, John P., son of J. and A. A., born November 20, 1838, died January 6, 1844
Crow, Benjamin G., son of Jacob and Agnes A. Crow, died February 8, 1879; age, 29 years, 10 months, 26 days
Crow, Sarah A., daughter of Jacob and Agnes A., died November 25, 1871; age, 19 years, 3 months, 19 days
Crump, Elizabeth, wife of Daniel Crump, died August 22, 1849, in 62nd year of her age
Crump, Daniel, died November 15, 1858, in the 71st year of his age
Crump, Jane, died March 5, 1873; age, 74 years, 8 months, 12 days
Crump, Samuel T., born May 1, 1820, died September 16, 1854
Crump, Perlina A., wife of S. T. Crump, born August 26, 1822, died July 15, 1862
Crump, Susana Frances, daughter of Samuel T. and Perlina A. Crump, born June 17, 1848, died March 10, 1851
Crump, Lucy Ann, daughter of D. and E. Crump, died September 22, 1840; age, 16 years, 10 months, 27 days
Crump, wife of John T. Crump, born 1852, died 1914
Cummins, Laura E., died November 12, 1869

Dalton, Rev. James C., died April 9, 1910; age, 85 years, 10 months
Dalton, Lucy J., wife of Rev. James C. Dalton, died November 19, 1931; age, 89 years, 9 months
Davis, William B., son of J. and L. Davis, died July 8, 1888; age, 29 years, 5 months, 7 days
Dewitt, Margaret O., daughter of Daniel and O. S. Dewitt, born June 9, 1850, died December 28, 1859
DeWitt, Daniel, died April 30, 1888; age, 71 years, 9 months, 23 days
DeWitt, S. Caroline, born December 7, 1830, died December 11, 1921
DeWitt, John D., born 1856, died 1859
Dukes, M. A. Fisher, wife of R. S. Dukes, born December 7, 1819, died October 26, 1875
Dyer, Bennette, wife of D. P. Dyer, died September 30, 1890; age, 54 years, 7 months, 11 days
Etzenhouser, Henry, born January 13, 1824, died March 7, 1903

CEMETERIES—SNI-A-BAR TOWNSHIP

Etzenhouser, Hannah M., born November 9, 1826, died September, 1876
Etzenhouser, Daniel (their son), born November 10, 1858, died September, 1877
Etzenhouser, Magdalena St. M., born May 1, 1834, died February 10, 1884
Fisher, Mary E., wife of G. W. Fisher, died May 19, 1863; age, 32 years, 6 months, 7 days
Fisher, Elizabeth A. Crump, wife of G. W. Fisher; age, 65 years, 6 months, 6 days (no date of death)
Fisher, Adam, died February 22, 1860; age, 77 years, 8 months, 8 days (N. S., U. S. D., 1812)
Fisher, Letty, wife of Adam Fisher, died August 27, 1866; age, 80 years, 5 months
Fisher, Jeremiah C., son of G. W. and M. E. Fisher, died October 18, 1850; age, 1 year, 10 months, 9 days
Fisher, Sarah A., wife of William A. Fisher, born March 5, 1857, died October 1, 1920
Frisby, George P., born March 17, 1834, died February 14, 1919
Frisby, Evaline, wife of George P. Frisby, born October 26, 1836, died January 28, 1911
Frisby, Lucinda, wife of George P. Frisby, died October 21, 1868; age, 28 years, 8 days
George, Julia H., daughter of B. T. and V. George, died January 28, 1872; age, 1 year, 9 months, 24 days
George, Susanna, daughter of B. T. and V. George, died November 6, 1874; age, 6 months, 15 days
Gibson, S. H., died February 28, 1896; age, 59 years, 10 months, 4 days
Gibson, Elizabeth M., wife of S. H. Gibson, died March 23, 1890; age, 51 years, 5 months, 11 days
Gibson, J. F., died June 10, 1871; age, 67 years, 6 months, 5 days
Gibson, Martha, wife of J. F. Gibson, died December 25, 1878; age, 65 years, 9 months, 2 days
Gonner, Elizabeth, died May 8, 1872; age, 46 years, 5 months, 29 days
Hanna, Salley T., wife of James A. Hanna, died November 28, 1874; age, 71 years, 8 months, 7 days
Hedrick, Jeremiah, born February 15, 1833, died September 17, 1926
Herral, Ellen R. Lowe, wife of J. Herral, born August 10, 1848, died October 28, 1892
Karr, William A., son of J. J. and J. M. Karr, died 1878 (stone broken)
Keck, Sarah, wife of H. Keck, died December 2, 1876; age, 30 years, 2 months, 15 days
Keck, Robert T., son of H. and S. E. Keck, died May 21, 1871; age, 2 years, 9 months, 2 days
Keck, W., son of H. and S. E. Keck, died January 13, 1871; age, 7 months, 9 days
Key, Virginia Agnes, wife of Allen Key, born January 25, 1816, died March 21, 1866
Key, Allen, died March 1, 1877; age, 35 years, 1 month, 1 day
King, Mary E., wife of M. V. King, died March 23, 1875; age, 33 years, 2 months, 14 days
King, Sarah, daughter of Mary E. and M. V. King, died 1875; age, 11 years, 4 months, 13 days
King, Flora, daughter of Mary E. and M. V. King, died January 15, 1875; age, 2 months, 29 days
Kirby, John G., son of M. B. and S. R. Kirby, died April 30, 1871; age, 1 year, 8 months, 13 days
Little, John, died October 7, 1857; age, 58 years, 10 months, 10 days
Little, Susannah F., wife of John Little, died July 27, 1849; age, 36 years, 4 months, 16 days
Lobb, Mary E. Yager, wife of J. A. Lobb, d. May 8, 1870; age, 54 years, 4 months, 18 days
Lobb, Anthony, born March, 1826, died March, 1911
Lobb, Mary A., wife of Anthony Lobb, born February 23, 1835, died January 21, 1905
Lobb, James Madison, born December 5, 1817, died April 21, 1891
Lobb, children of A. and Mary A. Lobb
    Lobb, —— daughter, died July 26, 1875
    Lobb, George, son, died May 16, 1869
    Lobb, Ella, died April 30, 1875
Lobb, J. A., died July 5, 1894; age, 75 years, 6 months, 9 days
Lobb, James C., died October 6, 1908; age, 73 years, 6 months
Lobb, Mary E., daughter of J. A. and M. T. Lobb, born March 7, 1858, died July 31, 1858

Lobb, William W., born May 5, 1842, died August 23, 1906
Lobb, Manson L., died January 22, 1853; age, 28 years, 5 months
Lowe, Margaret, wife of John Lowe, died April 7, 1868; age, 64 years, 4 months
Lowe, John, died June 10, 1881; age, 80 years, 3 months, 11 days
Lowe, Eliza C., wife of John M. Lowe, died October 16, 1881; age, 39 years, 12 days
Lowe, infant son of J. M. and E. C. Lowe, died February 13, 1869
Lowe, Mary E., wife of A. W. Lowe, died April 16, 1882; age, 31 years, 8 months, 10 days
Lowe, Henry R., son of A. W. Lowe, died December 31, 1874; age, 1 year, 2 months
Lowe, Calvin V., born December 5, 1832, died July 14, 1908
Lowe, Mary E., wife of Calvin V. Lowe, born March 5, 1839, died March 10, 1919

Mayers, Ollie, daughter of W. S. and E. Mayers, died June 27, 1873; age, 7 years, 2 months, 24 days
Montgomery, Levi S., born August 17, 1805, died December 6, 1891
Montgomery, Elizabeth, wife of Levi S. Montgomery, born March 1, 1828, died July 25, 1898
Montgomery, E. A., died November 22, 1867; age, 24 years, 8 months
Montgomery, S. G. O., died January 19, 1863; age, 21 years, 7 months, 28 days
Montgomery, Isaac N., born May 17, 1834, died April 26, 1911
Montgomery, Eliza S., wife of I. N. Montgomery, died August 3, 1888; age, 47 years, 8 months, 10 days

Navlin, James F., born June 29, 1832, died June 5, 1905
Navlin, Sharlotte F., wife of James Navlin, born October 18, 1839, died November 26, 1873

Orchard, James, died February 21, 1883; age, 71 years, 1 month, 24 days
Orchard, Alexander, born July 23, 1855, died February 12, 1875

Paradige, J. W., born 1852, died 1926
Parr, Jemima, born April 3, 1779, died August 13, 1857
Parr, Gabriel C., born 1848, died 1919
Parr, Lucy J., wife of Gabriel, born 1859, died 1928
Prewitt, Fisher, born 1838, died 1913
Pinkard, Jane, wife of Robert Pinkard, born 1809, died August 4, 1879
Pinkard, Robert, born February 11, 1807, died November 18, 1881

Rider, George, born May 16, 1807, died December 26, 1876; age, 69 years, 7 months, 10 days
Rimble, O. D., died January 28, 1866; age, 56 years, 8 months, 6 days
Robinson, Sarah E., daughter of G. M. and E., died March 8, 1870; age, 18 years, 8 days
Robinson, Martha Jane, daughter of C. M. and E. Robinson, died May 13, 1856; age, 6 years, 2 months, 12 days
Roberts, Robert, died April 5, 1880; age, 62 years
Roberts, Marcia, wife of Robert Roberts, died March 13, 1885; age, 62 years
Rodgers, Mariah, wife of John Rodgers, born in Greenfield, Ohio, May 17, 1802, died April 13, 1878
Rodgers, Bennie, son of J. B. and M. E. Rodgers, died December 11, 1872; age, 2 years, 11 months, 5 days
Rowe, William H. B., son of M. B. and G. E. Rowe, died February 6, 1870; age, 13 years, 9 months, 8 days
Russell, John, son of N. and M. Russell, died September 12, 1876; age, 46 years, 9 months, 3 days

Scott, Mathew, died March 10, 1870; age, 54 years, 1 month
Scott, John W., born June 25, 1848, died October 25, 1878
Seevers, Thompson E., born August 8, 1827, died April 30, 1901
Seevers, Margaret J., his wife, born March 12, 1837, died April 21, 1919
Seevers, Margaret A., wife of John W. Seevers, born 1858, died 1920
Seevers, Margaret, wife of Jacob Seevers, died August 16, 1859; age, 70 years
Stanley, Lucy A., wife of Daniel Stanley, died February 12, 1865; age, 23 years, 9 days
Steele, Mary E. Watkins, wife of James A. Steele, died March 30, 1833; age, 28 years, 5 months, 26 days

Steele, Mary Jane Lowe, wife of J. A. Steele, died July 29, 1850

Steele, John W., son of J. A. and M. J. Steele, died August 27, 1852; age, 4 years, 7 months, 28 days

Stewart, Anna, wife of Samuel Stewart, died December 4, 1875; age, 5- (some) years

Thomas, Letha, wife of J. R. Thomas, born October 31, 1836, died December 3, 1878

Thomas, Abner Edwin, born 1836, died 1917

Thomas, Lucinda Ellen, wife of Abner Edwin Thomas, born 1853, died 1904

Thomas, James H., died July 24, 1856; age, 45 years, 5 months, 20 days

Thomas, Sallie E., born March 10, 1817, died January 21, 1897

Thompson, Charles, died March 7, 1867; age, 65 years, 5 months, 6 days

Thompson, Margaret, wife of C. Thompson, died September 16, 1873; age, 76 years, 16 days

Tracey, Liberty S., born January 5, 1820, died May 9, 1906

Vandyke, B. W., born May 19, 1812, died July 23, 1873

Walker, Collins, died January 21, 1858; age, 33 years, 2 months, 24 days

Walker, Eliza F., wife of A. J. Walker, died March 24, 1879; age, 33 years, 1 month, 1 day

Walker, John R., died March 2, 1871 (stone broken)

Warren, David D., son of N. A. and M. A. Warren, died November 10, 1865; age, 10 months, 9 days

Warren, Jemima Hunn, wife of N. A. Warren, died February 12, 1860; age, 28 years

Warren, Thomas H., son of N. A. and J. H. Warren, died April 18, 1858; age, 7 months, 5 days

Warren, Margaretta A., wife of N. A. Warren, born June 12, 1842, died November 11, 1879

Warren, Margaret A. Shore, wife of N. A. Warren, died November 12, 1879 (two stones erected to wife of N. A. Warren)

Warren, Lucinda Robertson, wife of N. A. Warren, died November 12, 1856; age, 40 years, 7 months, 26 days

Waterman, H. H., died February 27, 1870; age, 53 years

Waterman, M. J., died February 21, 1870; age, 48 years

White, Peter, born February 10, 1819, died February 11, 1899

White, Martha S., daughter of W. N. and Eliza White, died February 25, 1854; age, 8 years, 3 months, 21 days

Wilson, Harriet L. Thomas, wife of S. B. Wilson, died November 14, 1894; age, 50 years, 7 months

Williams, W. J., born November 15, 1844, died February 24, 1902

Williams, Mary E., died March 17, 1879; age, 30 years, 21 days

Wright, John T., born January 29, 1840, died April 19, 1887

Wright, Martha J., wife of John T. Wright, born February 16, 1848, died August 9, 1916

Young, Daniel G., born January 15, 1839, died December 24, 1898

Young, Maranda J., wife of D. G. Young, died December 27, 1895; age, 58 years, 7 months, 3 days

MECKLIN CEMETERY

Section 8, Township 49 N, Range 29

Ayres, John T., born March 26, 1822, died September 3, 1905

Ayres, Priscilla, wife of John T. Ayres, born August 26, 1832, died August 29, 1906

Calhoon, William, born July 7, 1815, died July 11, 1884; age, 69 years, 4 days

Calhoon, Nannie, wife of William Calhoon, died January 1, 1888; age, 51 years, 8 months, 23 days

Hawes, Alcinda, wife of Oliver Hawes, born May 15, 1834

Hawes, Oliver, born February 14, 1822, died September 27, 1907

Hulse, Ariste, born May 14, 1838, died October 26, 1910

Hulse, Elizabeth, wife of Ariste Hulse, born April 7, 1848, died October 20, 1927.

Hulse, G. W., born 1835, died 1901

Hulse, Nancy, wife of G. W. Hulse, born 1839, died 1923

Hulse, Ida, wife of Grenville Hulse, born June 2, 1848, died September 30, 1908
Hulse, Samuel D., born February 3, 1817, died July 8, 1884
Klotz, John M., born November 16, 1847
Klotz, Jennie M., wife of John M. Klotz, born October 14, 1856, died March 25, 1913
Martin, Robert H., born October 11, 1844, died January 20, 1929
Martin, Sarah A., wife of Robert H. Martin, born April 18, 1846, died March 28, 1884; age, 37 years, 11 months, 10 days
Martin, E. E., father, son of Robert H. and Sarah A. Martin, born 1872, died 1913
Martin, J. M., mother, wife of E. E. Martin, born 1880, died 1912
Morgan, Robert, died November 5, 1932; age, 89 years, 3 months, 21 days
Morgan, Susan M., born September 13, 1854, died June 18, 1892
Newel, M. T., age, 52 years; very old stone, no dates given
Pallette, Margaret A., wife of J. P. Pallette, born October 12, 1829, died February 13, 1906
Perkins, William H., born 1848, died 1928
Perkins, Loucretia E., wife of William H. Perkins, born 1849, died 1932
Perry, Albert C., born December 1, 1840, died June 14, 1909
Perry, Almeda, wife of Albert C. Perry, born August 2, 1841, died March 26, 1917
Simmons, Jeremiah, born 1844, died 1917
Simmons, Margaret C., wife of Jeremiah Simmons, born 1849, died 1917
Snider, W. S., born February 3, 1833, died March 12, 1921; age, 48 years, 1 month, 9 days
Stone, James P., born November 9, 1840, died July 26, 1910
Surface, Michael, born November 24, 1809, died December 4, 1889
Surface, Rachel, wife of Michael Surface, born September 4, 1820, died January 22, 1889

Copied July 22, 1933, by Miss Julia Kinney and Miss Ethel Merwin

OAK GROVE CEMETERY*
OAK GROVE, MISSOURI
Copied April 27, 1933, by Miss Julia Kinney, Miss Ethel Merwin, and Mrs. Arthur Hills

Alford, Charlie L., born 1840, died 1900
Armstrong, William A., born May 7, 1822, died February 1, 1882
Armstrong, Vilanda, wife of William A. Armstrong, born January 31, 1833, died April 8, 1910
Ashcraft, J. E., born February 6, 1819, died April 12, 1882
Ashcraft, S. H., wife of J. E. Ashcraft, born December 16, 1827, died September 1, 1902
Ashcraft, Louisa A., wife of Aler Ashcraft, died June 4, 1874; age, 39 years, 9 months, 8 days
Barnes, Eldridge, born November 9, 1839, died May 12, 1924
Barnes, Mary F., wife of Eldridge Barnes, born March 4, 1857, died January 17, 1929
Bedsaul, Peter, born 1845, died 1932
Bell, Joseph G., born 1839, died 1919
Bell, Sarah, wife of Joseph G. Bell, born 1852, died 1914
Borland, Samuel, born February 1, 1838, died June 18, 1914
Borland, Mary E., died July 13, 1912; age, 73 years, 10 months, 21 days
Bram, Charles E., born January 15, 1837, died May 30, 1914
Brannan, Samuel, born 1848, died 1926
Brannan, Nancy, wife of Samuel Brannan, born 1847, died 1923
Bowman, Elizabeth, wife of Hiram Bowman, died April 9, 1896; age, 83 years, 8 months, 13 days
Catlin, John, born 1834, died 1896
Catlin, Margaret, wife of John Catlin, born 1840, died 1915
Church, William H., born July 18, 1828, died July 2, 1919
Colvin, J. W., born February 14, 1828, died April 8, 1908
Conrad, Jonathan T., born 1838, died 1898
Conrad, Elizabeth E., born 1842, died 1925
Corn, George W., born 1849, died 1926

Crews, Catherine, born April 4, 1822, died January 9, 1890

Downey, David L., born 1850, died 1932

Downey, Matilda J., wife of David L. Downey, born 1849, died 1920

Dungan, A. T., born 1841, died 1920

Eastwood, Sarah J., born 1839, died 1912

Ferguson, Phillip, born July 18, 1843, died November 26, 1910

Ferguson, Narcisca, wife of Phillip Ferguson, born December 1, 1847, died February 16, 1932

Fishback, Whitsitt Porter, born 1849, died 1928

Foster, Theodore, died December 9, 1928; age, 52 years, 9 months, 22 days

Foster, Elizabeth, died May 16, 1927; age, 85 years, 4 months, 3 days

Foster, Elizah, died June 16, 1894; age, 60 years, 5 months, 23 days

Frick, William, born May 4, 1791, died May 25, 1875

Frick, Margaret, wife of William Frick, born September 25, 1801, died July 27, 1876

Frick, Dr. William, born 1828, died 1889

Frick, Ellen J., wife of Dr. William Frick, born 1829, died 1913

Gauldin, G. W., born March 2, 1836, died April 14, 1918

Gauldin, Annie, died February 26, 1907; age, 67 years, 9 months, 19 days

George, James O., died May 25, 1894; age, 75 years, 4 months, 5 days

George, Robert M., born 1839, died 1929

George, Anna, born 1850, died 1928

Gillard, William, born 1843, died March 21, 1903

Gregg, George S., born December 24, 1842, died May 13, 1901

Gordon, Sarah H., wife of Dr. W. S. Gordon, died December 11, 1848; age, 35 years

Gozby, W. A., died March 2, 1891; age, 67 years, 2 months

Grubb, John, born November 4, 1809, died August 17, 1892

Grubb, B., born 1843, died September 22, 1902

Gundiff, D., born May 4, 1844, died November 15, 1909

Gundiff, Lucy A., wife of D. Gundiff, born April 23, 1845, died July 25, 1925

Harrelson, Desta M., born October 22, 1817, died April 20, 1906

Harding, John M., born October 20, 1843, died May 21, 1911

Harding, Mare E., wife of John M. Harding, born March 24, 1843, died February 16, 1909

Harding, G. P., died December 5, 1868; age, 58 years, 1 month, 5 days

Harding, B. F., born 1842, died 1924

Harding, Parthena J., 1st wife of B. F. Harding, born 1844, died 1873

Harding, 2nd wife, born 1846, died 1926

Hellberg, Joseph J., born 1850, died 1913

Helm, Sallie, wife of Hiram Helm, born June 13, 1820, died November 23, 1894

Herman, John H., born 1821, died 1906

Houston, P. D., born 1839, died 1919

Howe, J. P., born 1847, died 1919

Howe, E. J., wife of J. P. Howe, born 1851, died 1916

Huffman, Abraham, born January 17, 1830, died March 6, 1907

Huffman, Sarah, wife of Abraham Huffman, born August 13, 1840, died October 17, 1920

Hufford, Georgie, wife of J. R. Hufford, born November 1, 1846, died October 20, 1908

Johnson, Nancy, wife of W. M. Johnson, died September 10, 1888; age, 45 years, 6 months, 25 days

Jones, Josiah D., born November 2, 1827, died January 11, 1885

Jones, Sarah H., wife of Josiah D. Jones, born April 11, 1856, died October 13, 1906

Karrick, Sarah G., wife of Joseph E. W. Karrick, died February 4, 1823; age, 24 years, 8 months, 3 days

Kemper, Valentine, died February 23, 1887; age, 75 years, 1 month, 3 days

Knobelsdorff, G. A., died July 6, 1891; age, 69 years, 4 months, 21 days

Lane, M. C., born July 13, 1833, died November 24, 1903

Lane, Virgil, born 1845, died 1926

Latimer, S., died February 15, 1887; age, 64 years, 1 month, 23 days
Lewis, Finetta, wife of J. Lewis, died April 5, 1895; age, 76 years, 10 months, 21 days
Locke, J. W., died December 12, 1894; age, 56 years 1 month, 9 days
Long, Davis E., born March 19, 1826, died March 3, 1890
Long, Sarah N., wife of Davis E. Long, born December 13, 1844, died June 15, 1909
Love, Granville, died September 26, 1871; age, 56 years, 5 months, 19 days
Lefholz, Herman, born 1842, died 1932
Lefholz, Josephine, wife of Herman Lefholz, born 1849, died 1891
Mabry, R. C., born February 13, 1849, died May 8, 1915
Mabry, Dora, wife of R. C. Mabry, born October 8, 1851, died March 14, 1926
Marksbury, Catherine, born March 11, 1811, died September 12, 1893
McCowen, Eleanor, born January 23, 1845, died July 27, 1926
McCowen, Samuel, born June 8, 1845, died March 10, 1929
McGowen, Lucinda, wife of Noel McGowen, died April 28, 1858; age, 49 years, 2 months, 15 days
McQuerry, Mary F., died June 7, 1914; age, 81 years, 8 months, 25 days
McQuerry, Joseph, died April 5, 1893; age, 72 years, 5 months, 17 days
Merritt, J. K., born 1847, died 1921
Miller, William H., born February 10, 1839, died April 11, 1915
Minter, James W., born 1847, died 1928
Moore, Elisha, born July 27, 1837, died November 4, 1915
Moore, Mary S., born October 7, 1835, died April 10, 1924
Morris, William, born June 27, died November 17, 1907
Morris, Rhoda, wife of William Morris, born November 20, 1836, died April 21, 1920
Mullis, Elizabeth, wife of J. Mullis, died July 1, 1867; age, 67 years
Nerley, Neta, daughter of B. R. and A. A. Nerley, born July 1, 1825, died Jan. 21, 1895
Newburn, Thomas J., born 1848, died 1930
Ogle, Elden R. M., born 1839, died 1932
Ogle, Martha, born 1844, died 1925
Owings, J. H., died January 12, 1880; age, 63 years, 10 months, 24 days
Owings, Virginia J., wife of J. H. Owings, died May 25, 1856; age, 44 years
Owsley, Joshua S., died November 10, 1899; age, 77 years, 3 months, 8 days
Owsley, Martha, wife of Joshua S. Owsley, died December 29, 1898; Age, 56 years, 4 months, 1 day
Owsley, George W., born 1849, died 1918
Pallette, Erasmus J., born April 11, 1844, died July 3, 1929
Pallette, Harriet F., wife of Erasmus J. Pallette, born April 29, 1844, died June 7, 1921
Parrent, Eli, husband of Amanda E. Parrent, died December 9, 1882; age, 48 years, 9 months, 24 days
Paslay, William, born September 22, 1834, died February 9, 1880
Paslay, Eliza J., wife of William Paslay, born January 14, 1845, died March 28, 1905
Patterson, Jesse P., born November 13, 1818, died September 21, 1875
Patterson, Sarah, wife of J. Patterson, died August 23, 1890; age, 76 years, 11 months, 26 days
Payne, Rev. T. D., born May 20, 1839, died May 22, 1918
Payne, Eliza Baxter, born March 4, 1844, died October 19, 1904
Perkins, Rodolph, born 1847, died 1916
Peerson, D. F., died October 11, 1892; age, 66 years, 11 months, 6 days
Phillips, Hester Ann Elizabeth, wife of G. H. Phillips, born March 4, 1844, died August 14, 1907
Phillips, G. H., born March 24, 1844, died June 25, 1909
Philpott, Arnelia G., wife of S. B. Philpott, born August 6, 1829, died December 3, 1901
Pigg, Charles E., born 1848, died 1928
Pigg, Evaline, wife of Charles E. Pigg, born 1849, died 1924
Prewitt, Thomas R., born December 28, 1847, died July 27, 1930

Reeves, Nelson, born March 20, 1847, died November 12, 1925
Richardson, George W., born 1841, died 1906
Robinson, A. J., born February 1, 1841, died February 10, 1907
Robinson, ——, born December 13, 1838, died August 5, 1919
Rodgers, Martha A., died January 2, 1892; age, 83 years, 1 month, 8 days
Round, Wilson D., born 1833, died 1920
Round, Mary J., wife of Wilson D. Round, born 1837, died 1920
Sharp, Benjamin, born March 26, 1830, died January 31, 1920
Sharp, Euphamy, wife of Benjamin Sharp, born March 9, 1836, died September 16, 1921
Shrock, Andrew, born 1836, died 1915
Shrock, Julia A., wife of Andrew Shrock, born 1842, died 1912
Simpson, Walter G., born 1823, died 1892
Smith, William T., born December 11, 1839, died July 11, 1925
Smith, Susannah, wife of William T. Smith, born April 12, 1845, died December 25, 1907
Tevis, Mary, died October 28, 1903; age, 66 years
Tines, Francis, died August 5, 192-; age, 72 years
Turjon, Thomas J., born March 4, 1830, died January 5, 1897
Vastal, B. T., born 1846, died 1932
Vastal, Ella, wife of B. T. Astal, born 1858
Vermillion, Thomas W., died November 7, 1932; age, 85 years, 7 months, 24 days
Warking, Jacob, died August 14, 1862; age, 59 years, 8 months, 10 days
Webb, George, born 1829, died 1857
Webb, Andrew J., born July 23, 1832, died July 11, 1906
Webb, Sarah A., wife of Andrew Webb, born June 4, 1836, died March 19, 1909
Webb, John P., born September 22, 1832, died February 4, 1913
Webb, Susan E., wife of John P. Webb, born October 1, 1843, died August 30, 1925
Webb, Lewis J., born 1849, died 1900
Webb, Mary E., born 1837, died 1898
Webb, James H., born 1837, died 1930
Webb, Larkin W., born October 27, 1834, died March 12, 1899
Webb, Sarah E., wife of Larkin W. Webb, born Dec. 14, 1834, died Feb. 22, 1901
White, Joseph W., born January 31, 1837, died March 12, 1910
Williamson, Mary A., born July 9, 1826, died November 19, 1906
Womacks, Ulysses G., died October 20, 1895; age, 64 years, 1 month, 17 days
Wood, Robert H., died May 9, 1885; age, 64 years, 2 months, 17 days
Wood, Cinderella G., wife of Robert H. Wood, died August 21, 1890; age, 66 years, 6 months, 7 days
Woolery, Isaac H., died May 17, 1897; age, 59 years, 11 months, 14 days
Youree, Jesse R., born 1841, died 1881
Youree, Frances, wife of Jesse R. Youree, born 1843, died 1928
Youree, F. A., died February 4, 1877; age, 60 years, 1 month, 20 days
Youree, Martha A. D., wife of F. A. Youree, died 1875
Youree, David S., son of Martha and F. A. Youree, died August 26, 1873; age, 24 years, 10 months, 10 days

*Oak Grove Cemetery was originally the Addison C. Philpott Cemetery, started in 1835. The son of Mr. Philpott was the first person buried there.

OAKLAND CEMETERY
Section 9, Township 49, Range 30

Alderson, Dorcas A., wife of William Alderson, born 1835, died 1927
Campbell, James, born November 26, 1834, died April 7, 1923
Campbell, Sarah J., wife of James Campbell, born Sept. 6, 1836, died Nov. 10, 1923

Chiles, Lizzie B., wife of Franklin Chiles, born July 4, 1831, died June 26, 1910

Daniel, James H., born March 4, 1834, died March 4, 1898

Daniel, Martha A., wife of James H. Daniel, born March 12, 1844, died June 25, 1921

Dysart, Eliza, born April 13, 1813, died June 10, 1909

Ewing, James N., born 1825, died 1913

Frazier, Stephen, born 1839, died 1924

Frazier, Lucy J., wife of Stephen Frazier, born 1857, died 19—

Hagan, R. N., born May 31, 1834, died May 23, 1907

Hagan, Josephine, wife of R. N. Hagan, born October 22, 1837, died June 19, 1911

Harris, Silas T. (father), died September 21, 1839; age, 46 years, 9 months, 20 days

Harris, Barbara A., wife of Silas T. Harris, died April 9, 1921; age, 78 years

Harris, Parlee, daughter of S. T. and B. A. Harris, died August 11, 1888; age, 2 years, 11 months, 3 days

Hodges, Nicholas G., born April 10, 1850, died April 7, 1925

Hodges, Mary E., wife of Nicholas G. Hodges, born August 11, 1860, died December 2, 1931

Hodges, Nicholas N., born 1877

Hodges, Ella, wife of Nicholas N. Hodges, born 1878, died 1918

Hodges, Eliania J., wife of W. C. Hodges, born January 24, 1823, died August 15, 1889

Holloway, William S., born July 18, 1815, died April 19, 1898

Holloway, Letha J., wife of William S. Holloway, born October 12, 1838

Holloway, James W., son of William and L. J. Holloway, died May 13, 1885; age, 18 years, 8 months, 24 days

House, James, born 1836, died 1911

House, Mary I., wife of James House, born 1853

Johnson, Carroll, born 1846, died 1924

Johnson, Sallie, wife of Carroll Johnson, born 1850, died 1929

Kirby, J. O., born 1848, died 1922

Kirby, ——, wife of J. O. Kirby, born 1861, died 1930

Marlow, John, born September 3, 1834, died June 18, 1912

Marlow, Nancy, wife of John Marlow, born October 20, 1848, died December 3, 1906

Mendenhall, Sallie L., mother, born 1835, died 1920

Necessary, William, born February 22, 1845, died October 1, 1912

Necessary, Eli, father, born October 22, 1843, died January 20, 1886

Necessary, Margaret, mother, born December 29, 1839, died March 23, 1918

Necessary, Margaret A., wife of J. W. Necessary, born Jan. 10, 1843, died Jan. 28, 1899

Phillips, Virgil A., father, died September 27, 1882; age, 47 years, 2 months, 15 days

Phillips, Mary J., mother, died January 24, 1908; age, 66 years, 4 months, 18 days

Powell, Sarah M., wife of A. W. Powell, born December 19, 1846, died May 1, 1913

Rannells, Mary E., born September 7, 1835, died July 14, 1901

Rice, Jason, born November 11, 1845, died January 12, 1916

Rice, Lizzie A., wife of Jason Rice, died February 1, 1899; age, 47 years, 3 months, 5 days

Steinhauser, John, born January 27, 1830, died April 21, 1901

Steinhauser, Margaret, wife of John Steinhauser, born June 15, 1844, died March 14, 1924

Tucker, Thomas A., died 1887; age, 56 years, 6 months, 24 days

Tucker, Elizabeth M., died 1906; age, 74 years, 2 months, 18 days

Tucker, J. H., born January 9, 1837, died November 3, 1909

Tucker, Mary J., wife of J. H. Tucker, born July 18, 1847, died March 1, 1892

Wample, Jacob, died June 27, 1884; age, 45 years, 1 month, 2 days

Way, Samuel, born 1843, died 1905

Way, Nancy C., wife of Samuel Way, born 1853, died 1917

Way, Freddie, son of S. W. and N. C. Way, died August 12, 1885; age, 1 year, 12 days

Weir, Martha, died January 29, 1892; age, 73 years, 8 months, 7 days

Wolfe, Eliza H., born March 5, 1820, died December 17, 1893

Copied May 11, 1933, by Miss Julia Kinney and Miss Ethel Merwin

PERDEE CHAPEL CEMETERY
Section 9, Township 48, Range 30 W
Near Grain Valley, Missouri

Beornson, Nelse, born August 2, 1843, died April 27, 1888
Beornson, Mary, wife of Nelse Beornson, born April 13, 1846
Brenner, Anna A., born February 6, 1807, died August 21, 1878; age, 71 years, 6 months. 15 days; wife of John Brenner
Bowmay, Hiram, died January 30, 1877; age, 80 years, 6 months, 28 days
Bowmay, Isabell N., wife of Hiram Bowmay, died June 2, 1854; age, 57 years, 8 months, 5 days
Boothe, Samuel A., son of C. B. and E. Boothe, died August 1, 1870; age, 16 years, 3 months, 21 days
Butt, Eleanor, daughter of R. H. and M. Butt, died February 8, 1875; age, 27 years, 9 months, 6 days
Campbell, Fannie, wife of B. A. Campbell, born August 27, 1843, died January 25, 1889
Corder, Thomas M., born August 24, 1848, died November 14, 1904
Corder, Mary A., wife of Thomas M. Corder, born June 14, 1846, died October 6, 1931
Faulconer, Jenetta, wife of James Faulconer, died January 24, 1879; age, 29 years, 19 days
Foster, Jonathan (Masonic Emblem), born September 17, 1798, died January 10, 1869
Foster, Clarinda C., daughter of J. and A. Foster, born Dec. 18, 1830, died March 13, 1869
Francis, Roda, wife of J. H. Francis, died August 17, 1886; age, 70 years, 8 months, 13 days
Gibson, son of A. H. and D. E. Gibson, born January 18, 1869, died July 20, 1885
Gore, John, husband of Louella Gore, born December 23, 1851, died February 21, 1899
Goodridge, Elizabeth, wife of M. Goodridge, died September 18, 1871; age, 19 years
Harden, Mattie, wife of W. H., died August 30, 1886; age, 54 years, 1 month, 28 days
Haukenbury, Addie, wife of J. M. Haukenbury, born August 26, 1850, died January 28, 1902
Hunter, Ellen, wife of James Hunter, born November 16, 1832, died April 27, 1908
Hunter, Mary E., died July 6, 1888; age, 28 years
Kimerplin, Nannie E., wife of R. K. Kimerplin, died October 16, 1872; age, 20 years, 2 months, 14 days
King, America, wife of W. J. King, born August 12, 1847; age, 61 years, 2 months, 18 days
Knotts, Harvey T., born October 23, 1866, died 1867
Lewis, Martha A., wife of Wilson Lewis, died February 12, 1875; age, 55 years, 8 months, 21 days
Litchford, Mary A., wife of A. J. Litchford, born November 8, 1822, died January 26, 1884
Little, Elizabeth, wife of B. G., born October 13, (?) 1826, died December 31, 1869; age, 43 years, 2 months, 13 days
Montague, Mary A., wife of J. Montague, died October 7, 1855; age, 31 years, 11 days
Moyers, J. R., husband of F. C. Moyers, born November 29, 1852, died December 10, 1897
Perdee, Sarah A., wife of W. A. Perdee, died Oct. 25, 1870; age, 42 years, 8 months, 27 days
Perdee, Nellie G., died February 10, 1875; age, 2 years, 9 months, 28 days
Perdee, Melba L., died May 23, 1873; age, 6 weeks
    (Twin children of W. A. and M. A. Perdee)
Peterman, Allen (father), born 1850, died 1918
Peterman, Salina (mother), born 1848, died 1921
Ryan, John, died March 15, 1892; age, 69 years, 1 month, 9 days
Ryan, Lucinda, died June 24, 1924; age, 91 years, 8 days
Sharp, Leatha A., born October 4, 1830, died March 18, 18-3 (?)
Shrout, James M., born November 25, 1853, died February 12, 1929
Snodgrass, Sarah F. (mother), born 1855, died 1929
Snodgrass, Parmer (father), born 1856, died 1930
Snodgrass, America, born 1847, died 1921
Snodgrass, Ephriam, died December 20, 1876; age, 34 years, 9 months, 24 days
Snodgrass, Bartley, died June 18, 1881; age, 83 years, 8 months, 24 days

Snodgrass, Lucy A., wife of Bartley Snodgrass, died November 13, 1890; age, 76 years, 11 months, 17 days

St. Clair, Caroline E., wife of George St. Clair, died July 17, 1884; age, 67 years, 1 month, 10 days

St. Clair, Alice G., born April 2, 1856, died April 17, 1897

St. Clair, J. V., born 1844, died 1918

St. Clair, William G., died September 3, 1881; age, 56 years, 5 months

St. Clair, Mary A., born 1826, died 1911

St. Clair, George, born October 10, 1808, died September 23, 1887

St. Clair, John W., born January 19, 1853

St. Clair, Mary Katherine, wife of John W. St. Clair, born September 19, 1857, died March 13, 1911

Thompson, Rufina J., wife of Henry L. Thompson, born Feb. 1, 1855, died Dec. 8, 1911

Thompson, Nancy, born April 11, 1806, died May 7, 1888

Yookey, Edna E., daughter of J. J. and Q. L. Yookey, died August 25, 1878; age, 5 years

Copied July 28, 1933, by Mrs. Hale Houts and son, Lee Houts

ROBERTSON CEMETERY
Section 18, Township 49, Range 30 W
Located on the R. H. Elrod Farm

De Witt, Dan; no stone left; information supplied by Mrs. Sheley, wife of Dr. O. C. Sheley of Independence, and granddaughter of John and Nancy Cox Robertson

De Witt, wife of Dan, and sister of Nancy Cox Robertson

M. D., no further information or dates

Robertson, John, born May 21, 1788, died July 8, 1859

Robertson, Nancy Cox, wife of John Robertson, born June 15, 1799, died April 25, 1855

Robertson, A. H., born March 8, 1833, died September 6, 1908

Robertson, Melinda, wife of A. H. Robertson, born March 6, 1852, died February 6, 1907

    Children of A. H. Robertson and Melinda

Cora B., wife of W. S. Angel, born January, 1870, died April, 1894

    Infant daughter, 1882

John and Nancy Cox Robertson were among the first settlers of Jackson County, coming to Missouri from Kentucky. A. H. Robertson was the son of John and Nancy Cox Robertson. Information supplied by Mrs. O. C. Sheley of Independence.

Copied September 22, 1933, by Miss Julia Kinney and Miss Ethel Merwin

ROBINSON-MOORE CEMETERY
Located on the Charles Morgan Farm, between Oak Grove and Mecklin

Moore, Sarah J., wife of R. R. Moore, died January 12, 1858 or 3; age, 27 years, 12 days

Moore, H. B., son of R. R. and S. J. Moore, died November 3, 1850; age, 7 months, 1 day

Moore, W. S., daughter of R. R. and L. W. Moore, died November 7, 1859; age, 16 years, 8 months, 19 days

Moore, N. A., son of R. R. and L. W. Moore, died October 30, 1866; age, 25 years, 8 months

Henry, no further name or dates

M. R., no further name or dates

R. J., no further name or dates

B. R., no further name or dates

Robinson, Martha A., born September 21, 1844, died —— date obliterated

    Part of the cemetery has been plowed up and stones lost or removed.

Copied September 3, 1933, by Miss Julia Kinney and Miss Ethel Merwin

SLAUGHTER CEMETERY
On the corner of the Wallace Montgomery Farm

Chism, Nancy, born 1806, died 1881
Chism, Eliza, born 1843, died 1922
Chism, Malinda, born 1845, died 1921
Dooley, Sarah, died April 11, 1891; age, 55 years, 1 month
Gibson, Elizabeth, wife of Silas Gibson, born March 28, 1798, died April 13, 1881
Gosner, Rachel, wife of A. Gosner, died September 10, 1870; age, 56 years, 11 days
Gosner, Mary A., wife of A. Gosner, died August 21, 1872; age, 21 years, 4 months, 10 days
Hutchings, Thomas C., born October 13, 1833, died March 20, 1900
Hutchings, Dora M., wife of Thomas C. Hutchings, born July 19, 1868, died Feb. 11, 1896
King, Robert, died February 2, 1891; age, 80 years, 11 months, 21 days
King, Malinda, wife of Robert King, died January 18, 1880; age, 70 years
King, Francis M., born 1845, died 1916
King, Eveline, wife of Francis M. King, born 1847, died 1912
Lacy, Eddie, son of G. W. and R. A. Lacy, died Oct. 20, 1871; age, 2 years, 4 months, 14 days
Potts, Levi, born October 3, 1828, died September 26, 1913
Potts, Sinia E., wife of Levi Potts, born January 25, 1832, died April 27, 1904
Slaughter, John H., died December 28, 1872; age, 40 years, 9 months, 27 days
Slaughter, Mary J., wife of John H. Slaughter, died April 5, 1905; age, 64 years, 8 months, 11 days
Slaughter, James R., son of John H. and Mary J. Slaughter, died October 26, 1868; age, 1 year, 1 month
Slaughter, Sarah A., daughter of J. H. and Mary J. Slaughter, died February 1, 1874; age, 1 year, 10 months, 16 days
Slaughter, Josiah, died December 10, 1873; age, 68 years, 6 months, 18 days
Slaughter, Elizabeth, wife of Josiah Slaughter, died February 16, 1892; age, 90 years, 2 days
Webb, Glarborn, born January 24, 1815, died August 22, 1905
Webb, Elizabeth L., wife of Glarborn Webb, died September 10, 1880; age, 53 years, 16 days

Copied July 24, 1933, by Miss Julia Kinney and Miss Ethel Merwin

STANLEY CEMETERY
Section 24, Township 49 N, Range 31 W

Bowlin, Nancy E., daughter of J. G. and M. E. Bowlin, born February 5, 1863
Cole, Joseph, died September 16, 1888; age, 80 years, 22 days
Dickson, Margaret L., wife of J. T. Dickson, born October 8, 1849, died February 5, 1898
Dickson, William, died July 17, 1879; age, 68 years
Greenville, T., born 1820, died 1906
Greenville, Elizabeth, wife of T. Greenville, born 1827, died 1867
Greenville, Martha E., wife of T. Greenville, born 1836, died 1897
Hall, J. D., born 1838, died 1924
Hall, Sarah Jane, wife of J. D. Hall, born 1851, died 1927
Hall, Isham, died September 29, 1874; age, 72 years, 7 months, 16 days
Hall, Rachel B., wife of Isham Hall, died June 15, 1870; age, 65 years, 8 months, 18 days
Johnson, Elizabeth, wife of G. T. Johnson, died January 6, 1867; age, 39 years, 6 months, 6 days
St. Clair, Mattie J., wife of George St. Clair, died February 4, 1886; age, 26 years, 1 month, 26 days
Tucker, R. B., born 1818, died 1883
Tucker, Eliza, wife of R. B. Tucker, born 1824, died 1897
Tucker, Mary E., died November 8, 1886; age, 40 years, 7 months, 8 days

Copied June, 1933, by Miss Julia Kinney

ST. CLAIR CEMETERY
Located on the farm of Mr. Charles Campbell of Independence, Mo.

Clarkson, Alfred E., born 1847, died 1931
McFarland, Mary E., wife of James M. McFarland, died October 11, 1833; age, 24 years, 10 months, 20 days
St. Clair, Elmira H., mother, born September 25, 1808, died July 19, 1865
St. Clair, Robert, father, born April 18, 1807, died April 10, 1869
St. Clair, Charles W., son of E. and M. A. St. Clair, born Sept. 8, 1868, died Oct. 21, 1868
St. Clair, Mary A., died January 20, 1926; age, 84 years
Several unmarked graves

Copied July 22, 1933, by Miss Julia Kinney and Miss Ethel Merwin

TATUM CEMETERY
Section 25, Township 48, Range 31

All markers in this cemetery are now buried underground.

Information regarding burial secured from Mrs. Bill Clark of Blue Springs, Missouri, a granddaughter of Thomas Jefferson Tatum.

Tatum, Thomas Jefferson, born about 1805, died June 26, 1875 (Came to Missouri in 1838 from Patrick County, Virginia)
Tatum, Elizabeth Clark, wife of Thomas Jefferson Tatum
Salley, daughter of above, married Bridges, died 1862
Jimmie, son of above, died August 16, 1862
Martha
Priscilla, died young

Information given to Mrs. Hale Houts, September 29, 1933

WALKER CEMETERY
Section 24, Township 49, Range 30 W

Located on the Hershel Strode Farm, ¼ Mile North of Blue Springs

Franklin, Sarah Jane, daughter of John R. and Lucy Ann Franklin, born October 21, 1837, died January 5, 1840
Walker, James M., died September 7, 1866; age, 72 years, 3 months, 14 days
Walker, Polly, wife of James M. Walker, died October 26, 1876; age, 74 years, 6 months, 26 days
Walker, Dudley, son of J. M. and P. Walker, died December 18, 1839; age, 6 months
Walker, Jefferson D., son of J. M. and P. Walker, died Dec. 18, 1840; age, 8 years, 8 days
Three names on one stone. Unable to make out except the word "sister." Dates obliterated also.

Copied September 3, 1933, by Miss Julia Kinney and Miss Ethel Merwin

WEBB CEMETERY
Section 9, Township 48, Range 29

Holman, Elzira Webb
Webb, Jane
Webb, Mary, died September 11, 1854
Webb, Thomas L., died August, 1852
Webb, Margaret C., wife of Thomas L. Webb, died March 11, 1894; age, 86 years
Webb, William

WEBB CEMETERY
Section 11, Township 49 N, Range 30 W
Located on the Farm of Dr. and Mrs. Perry

Only one date given. Approximate dates supplied by Mrs. Mollie Williams of Grain Valley, granddaughter of John and Susan Barnett.

Barnett, John, died about 1893, over 70 years old
Barnett, Susan, wife of John Barnett, died about 1879; age, about 55 years
Carson, John, husband of Susan Carson, died April 1, 1877; age, 63 years
Graham, Elizabeth, daughter of John and Susan Barnett, died 1888; age, about 48 years
Graham, Billie, son of Elizabeth
Graham, R. J.
Graham, S. E.
Graham, J. H.
Owings, Richard, died 1899; age, 59 years
Owings, Mattie, wife of Richard Owings, and daughter of John and Susan Barnett, died about 1920; age, 73 years
Owings, Delly, son of Richard and Mattie Owings, died 1915; age, 35 years
Owings, Leona Ellan, died 1878; age, 3 weeks
Owings, Johnnie, died 1873; age, 2 years

WILLIAMS CEMETERY
E Half of SW Quarter, Section 26, Township 50, Range 30

Family by the name of Williams is buried on the Frank Harra Farm.
The stones have been laid flat and covered up.

Webb Cemeteries and Williams Cemetery copied by Miss Julia Kinney and Miss Ethel Merwin

YOUNG CEMETERY
Section 7, Township 48, Range 31
On the old Polk Thomas Farm

This cemetery has long been abandoned, now in a corn field.
The parents of Mr. Charles Young are known to have been buried on this farm.

WASHINGTON TOWNSHIP
Organized February 9, 1836

All of the history and records of Washington Township were compiled and copied by Mrs. Max A. (Sue Hargis) Christopher, except those records copied by Miss Jessie M. Crosby. Mrs. Christopher is a granddaughter of the late Marcus Gill, an early resident of the Township.

THE BARTLESON BURYING GROUND
Section 32, Township 47, Range 33 W

Near Holmes Road and the Cass County Line

This old community cemetery, known as the Bartleson Burying Ground, is on the farm now owned by W. T. Kemper of Kansas City, Mo. From information gathered this was at one time a rather large burying ground. All that remains today is four stones which Mr. Kemper has carefully protected with a stone wall.

Bartleson, Andrew, died November 15, 1857; age, 66 years, 3 months, 10 days
Bartleson, Fanny, wife of John Bartleson, died October 10, 1848; age, 54 years, 9 months, 15 days
Bartleson, John, died October 7, 1848; age, 61 years, 11 months, 22 days
Bartleson, S. S., died January 25, 1859; age, 34 years, 4 months, 1 day

BLUE RIDGE CEMETERY
Section 14, Township 47, Range 33 W

Abston, Stephen, died January, 1861
Abston, Eliza, wife of S. Abston, died September 20, 1859; age, 48 years
Abston, John B., born September 17, 1838, died October 31, 1855
Adams, Mary C., wife of A. M. Adams, born January 4, 1819, died October 13, 1859
Adams, James H., son of A. M. Adams
    Marie J., daughter of A. M. and M. C. Adams, born May 13, 1844, died Nov. 24, 1859
    Barzillal L., son of A. M. and M. C. Adams, born Jan. 8, 1841, died Dec. 10, 1859
    Myrtilla S., daughter of A. M. and M. C. Adams, born October 20, 1855, died December 28, 1859
Bohn, Robert, born May 2, 1820, died June 30, 1897
    Louisa, born February 18, 1822, died April 12, 1905
Clements, J. Ambrose, born January 16, 1829, died June 21, 1904
    Hannah A., wife of J. A. Clements, born December 26, 1838, died January 29, 1887; married March 6, 1855

Clements, Milton, born September 30, 1832, died December 16, 1902
Connely, L. D., born April 1, 1836, died June 17, 1894
    Caroline N., wife of L. D. Connely, born October 13, 1843, died May 27, 1902
Connely, Daisy, daughter of L. D. and C. N. Connely, born January 21, 1870, died August 12, 1894
Connely, Charlie, son of L. D. and N. C. Connely, born March 9, 1869, died March 1, 1871
Connely, Anna, daughter of L. D. and N. C. Connely, died October 28, 1868; age, 1 year, 2 months, 16 days
Davidson, Walter A., born January 23, 1831, died June 27, 1864
    Sarah J. Kennedy, wife of W. A. Davidson, born December 16, 1838, died April 8, 1909
Evans, Nancy E., wife of W. N. Evans, died February 8, 1869; age, 28 years, 5 months, 1 day
Foree, Sarah F., wife of Joel Foree, died Oct. 14, 1870; age, 36 years, 10 months, 13 days
Gambill, W. J., died February 14, 1867; age, 40 years, 3 months, 14 days
Gore, Ella V., wife of W. J. Gore, "Farewell," born Sept. 25, 1844, died March 1, 1887
Gray, Edward, born March 24, 1810, died June 22, 1869
Gray, Nancy, wife of Edward Gray, died May 20, 1886; age, 72 years
Gray, J. I., born November 24, 1838, died April 4, 1893
Hackler, Martin, born September 18, 1815, died October 17, 1901
    Sarah, wife of M. Hackler, born January 27, 1821, died March 12, 1855
    Agnes E., wife of Martin Hackler, born December 23, 1826, died April 11, 1902
Harper, Sarah, born February, 1812, died July, 1866
Harris, mother of J. H. Harris, born September 27, 1800, died December 4, 1865
Harris, Caroline, wife of J. H. Harris, born November 27, 1831, died August 6, 1884
Hill, Cyrene V., wife of W. A. Hill, born May 27, 1844, died September 22, 1894
Jones, J. R., born October 5, 1823, died March 18, 1913
Jones, Mary A., born June 10, 1841, died March 18, 1911
Jones, infant son of J. R. and M. A. Jones, died October 5, 1859; age, 29 days
Jones, James W., died July 20, 1910; age, 82 years, 7 months
    M. J., wife of J. W. Jones, died September 8, 1889; age, 47 years, 7 months, 21 days
Jones, Willie B., son of J. W. and M. J. Jones, died March 9, 1861; age, 1 month, 16 days
Lacy, H. S., died November 16, 1874; age, 29 years, 6 months, 9 days
Lacy, Leonidas S., son of H. S. and M. A. Lacy, born October 29, 1871, died February 7, 1871
Mathews, Elliott, born September 1, 1829, died August 31, 1858
Maxwell, Lucy E., daughter of E. C. Maxwell, died November 1, 1864; age, 14 years, 2 months, 19 days
Muir, Amelia A., wife of John S. Muir, died March 14, 1874; age, 69 years, 11 months, 18 days
Pendleton, M. G., M.D., died July 4, 1878; age, 79 years, 5 months, 20 days
Pendleton, Emily, wife of M. G. Pendleton, died September 1, 1887; age, 79 years, 10 months, 17 days
Poindexter, Thomas M., born May 5, 1815, died October 1, 1855
Poindexter, John G., son of T. M. and M. A. Poindexter, born April 10, 1845, died August 25, 1856; age, 11 years, 4 months, 15 days
Riner, Andrew, born April 17, 1817, died Sept. 10, 1878; age, 61 years, 4 months, 23 days
Rule, Elizabeth J., wife of Rev. T. R. Rule, died February 5, 1869; age, 27 years, 1 day
Scrivner, Parmela, wife of Martin Scrivner, born May 6, 1804, died March 3, 1872 (D. A. R. marker)
Shelton, Green M., born April 15, 1823, died March 15, 1912
    Anna T., wife of G. M. Shelton, born January 12, 1829, died June 27, 1901
Shelton, Mary C., daughter of G. M. and A. T. Shelton, born January 21, 1857, died March 11, 1857
Shelton, Martha V., daughter of G. M. and A. T. Shelton, born January 23, 1858, died March 4, 1860

Shelton, William S., son of G. M. and A. T. Shelton, died March 4, 1874; age, 21 years, 1 month, 9 days
Smith, J. P., died October 11, 1857; age, 36 years, 9 months, 7 days (Mason)
    Eliza J., wife of J. P. Smith, died October 31, 1857; age, 31 years, 9 months, 20 days
Talley, William B., born December 26, 1792, died May 7, 1864
Talley, Sarah, wife of William B. Talley, born December 3, 1802, died April 12, 1874
Vivion, Harrison S., born July 18, 1813, died August 2, 1855
Vivion, Elizabeth H., daughter of H. S. and C. Vivion, born April 23, 1848, died July 28, 1856
Wyatt, Alson, died June 17, 1863; age, 22 years, 6 months, 7 days
Wyatt, Elizabeth L., wife of A. Wyatt, died December 1, 1864; age, 20 years, 5 months, 17 days
Wyatt, Burgess, born August 4, 1812, died March 2-, 1875
Wyatt, Elizabeth Hackler, wife of B. Wyatt, born January 27, 1821, died June 7, 1857
Wyatt, Solomon, born June 1, 1809, died July 10, 1900
    Caroline, wife of Solomon Wyatt, died July 1, 1824
Wyatt, W. M., born June 7, 1836, died May 26, 1903
Wyatt, William, died August 25, 1856; age, 74 years, 8 months
Wyatt, Mary, wife of William Wyatt, died February 21, 1861; age, about 67 years
Wyatt, Esther, wife of L. Wyatt, died March 18, 1862; age, 36 years, 3 months, 23 days
Yost, C. J., died September 17, 1875; age, 60 years, 5 months, 26 days
Yost, Elizabeth, died July 26, 1869; age, 57 years, 6 months, 23 days
Young, Elizabeth F., daughter of S. and H. L. Young, born March 30, 1818, died May 3, 1852

    Copied May 6, 1933, by Mrs. May T. Crosby and Miss Jessie M. Crosby

THE DAVIS BURYING GROUND
Section 29, Township 47, Range 33 W

    About one and one-half miles south of Martin City, Missouri, on the farm now owned by Mr. Sparks of St. Louis and Kansas City, is what is known as the Davis Burying Ground. This cemetery is quite near the Missouri-Pacific Railroad tracks and covers a block of ground fifty feet square which is walled in by a high stone fence.

    The following inscriptions were copied June 20, 1933:

Davis, Mary Ann E., wife of J. E. Davis, born April 22, 1838, died March 26, 1882; age, 43 years, 11 months, 4 days
Davis, James E., born in Bath County, Ky., March 18, 1827, died September 26, 1900
    "Sleep on, dear Father, and take thy rest,
      God called thee home, He thought it best."
Davis, William O., son of J. E. and M. E. Davis, born August 21, 1857, died October 30, 1857
Davis, infant daughter of J. E. and M. E. Davis, died November 25, 1861; age, 13 days
Davis, Nathaniel K., son of J. E. and M. E. Davis, died August 10, 1864; age, 1 year, 11 months, 7 days
Davis, Oliver P., son of J. E. and M. E. Davis, died October 28, 1869
Davis, Mary A., daughter of J. E. and M. E. Davis, born April 16, 1871, died October 25, 1871
Estus, Nancy, died April 29, 1885; age, 57 years, 10 months, 26 days
Estus, Elizabeth, wife of S. Estus, born August 22, 1862, died August 22, 1887
Robinson, infant daughter of J. T. and P. A. Robinson, died August 4, 1854; age, 10 days
Robinson, Permelia, wife of J. T. Robinson, died May 18, 1876; age, 39 years, 10 months, 22 days
Robinson, John T., son of J. T. and P. A. Robinson, died September 30, 1875; age, 4 months, 13 days
Robinson, infant son of J. T. and P. A. Robinson, died April 12, 1867; age, 12 days

Wells, Mary, died April 11, 1886; age, 78 years, 2 months, 7 days
Wells, Moses T., born January 8, 1804, died June 16, 1872
Wells, Julia A. F., wife of J. D. Wells, born July 19, 1861; died April 2, 1887

FLANERY CEMETERY
Section 27, Township 48, Range 32 W

Flanery, John, died February 9, 1893; age, 83 years, 4 months, 4 days
    Rebecca, wife of J. F. Flanery, died December 28, 1896; age, 78 years, 5 months, 27 days
Frost, George W., born June 17, 1839, died March 31, 1920
Frost, Martha J., wife of G. W. Frost, died May 10, 1906; age, 57 years
Frost, Sampson, born 1845, died 1925
Moore, In Memory of Jeremiah Moore, born September 15, 1826, died July 26, 1907
Moore, Arrimint, wife of J. Moore, born October 5, 1826, died September 18, 1889
    The following data copied from a Flanery Bible—no dates of death recorded:
Flanery, Lucinda, born May 15, 1816
Flanery, Mary Ann, born April 14, 1838
Flanery, Levi T., born March 3, 1842
Flanery, Mary A., born July 28, 1843
Gault, Rebecca J.

                                          Copied by Miss Jessie M. Crosby

GANZER CEMETERY
Section 33, Township 48, Range 32 W

Ganzer, Andrew, born January 3, 1819, died April 18, 1893
Ganzer, Elizabeth, wife of A. J. Ganzer, born July 24, 1819, died April 23, 1898
Ganzer, Fred, born January 27, 1851, died November 28, 1909
Ganzer, Albert, born August 26, 1856, died March 29, 1891
Hartman, Ann Marie Ganzer, wife of Gottlob Hartman, born November 2, 1860, died March 23, 1932
Laskawski, Christian, born November 25, 1820, died March 17, 1896
Laskawski, Augustie, born 1825, died 1904
Paul, Friedrich W., born September 10, 1827, died June 29, 1898
    Caroline, wife of F. W. Paul, born March 6, 1829, died April 5, 1901
Sohn, Emanuel, died February 15, 1906; age, 80 years, 1 month, 11 days
    Mary S., wife of E. Sohn, died November 26, 1894; age, 62 years, 11 months, 2 days

                     Copied June 12, 1933, by Miss Jessie M. Crosby and Mrs. May T. Crosby

THE GILL FARM
Section 7, Township 47, Range 33 W

    Mr. Allen B. H. McGee, a grandson of the late Marcus Gill, owns a part of the farm which his grandfather purchased from Dabney Lipscomb in 1854 at $25.00 per acre, and which was known in the early days as the Gill Farm. The location of this farm today would be about One Hundred and Twenty-third Street, between State Line and Wornall Road. Mr. and Mrs. McGee, in remodeling the old house, with its log walls and narrow

CEMETERIES—WASHINGTON TOWNSHIP

stairway, kept so much that was original in the plan of the house that it is one of the most attractive country homes in the county. Before the old fire place in the "parlor" of this house the five daughters of Marcus Gill were married.

On this farm is found another old cemetery. From all information obtainable this was one of the earliest burying grounds in that neighborhood. It must be borne in mind that in those early days there were no incorporated cemeteries or burying grounds in a community, but on almost every farm was what was called a "family burying ground." Later came the neighborhood burying ground which was one of the family burying grounds of the community used by the families in the neighborhood; and later still came the little church cemeteries.

The cemetery on the Gill Farm was in use in 1846, long before the school and church at the little town of New Santa Fe were started, in the days when New Santa Fe was a Trading Post. For years there have been only a few stones on the farm to mark the site of this family and community burying ground which was in use as late as 1883. There are those living who can remember seeing the big farm wagons as they came down the road and across the field up to the Gill Cemetery on the hill. These give us the picture of one of the funeral processions, in the days of the family burying grounds when the horse-drawn wagon was used as the vehicle for carrying the dead to the grave.

It is impossible to gather all of the names and dates of the early pioneers who lived in this section of Jackson County and who were laid to rest on the Gill Farm. The following list has been carefully gathered by Mrs. Max A. Christopher, from those still living who remember either attending the funeral on this farm or who recall having heard the names of their neighbors buried there, and from the inscriptions on the few tombstones found on the farm:

*Baxter, four children of P. H. Baxter who is buried in Mount Pleasant Cemetery and his wife, Martha McCraw Baxter (living):
  Perry Rippeto Baxter, born 1871, died 1873
  Louella Gill Baxter, born 1872, died 1873
  Harry Ridge Baxter, born 1875, died 1879
  Mary Edith Baxter, born 1883, died 1883 (One stone bears the names and dates of these four children)
Foster, James Sanford, son of Mary Jane (Foster) Gill and first husband, Sanford Foster, born April 17, 1844, died September 3, 1858
Gill, Marcus, son of Marcus Gill and wife, Mary Jane, born September 28, 1854, died November 23, 1857
Grimsley, Kate, wife of Lowry Grimsley, a Baptist Preacher
Kerr, Lemuel, son of Thos. J. and Catherine M., died Sept. 8, 1872; age, 22 years
Kerr, America Jane, daughter of Caleb D. and Pauline Kerr, died September, 1874; age, 13 months
*Lipscomb, Dabney (came to Jackson County before 1839, entered the land on which he was buried and which he sold to Marcus Gill; platted the town of New Santa Fe), born December 5, 1800, died July 16, 1854; dates copied from tombstone
*Lipscomb, Susan D., wife of Dabney Lipscomb, died June 18, 1849; age, 36 years, 5 months, 7 days (copied from tombstone)
*Lipscomb, Nathan, son of D. and S. D. Lipscomb, died September 13, 1846; age, 5 months, 28 days (copied from tombstone)
Lipscomb, Wm. W., son of D. and S. D. Lipscomb, died September 8, 1849 (copied from tombstone)
*Neeley, W. S., died March 20, 1879; age, 47 years, 3 months (copied from tombstone)
Pasley, Mrs.
Sharp, Demarius, wife of Tilman B. Sharp who is buried in Mount Pleasant Cemetery, died August 15, 1870

Wilcox, Mr. ——, and son, George Wilcox (no dates)

*Senter, Margaret, wife of N. M. Senter, died February 25, 1870; age, 55 years, 9 months, 21 days (copied from tombstone)

*Moved to the New Santa Fe Christian Church Cemetery November, 1933. All trace of this community burying ground is now erased.

EARLY RECORDS OF THE FAMILY OF MARCUS GILL

In the year 1854 Colonel Marcus Gill sold all his property at Gill's Mill, near Owingsville, Kentucky, and came, by boat, to Jackson County, Missouri, landing at Blue Mills, about six miles from Independence. Col. Gill was a grandson of Captain Thomas Gill who served in the War of the American Revolution. The following data, pertaining to this early Jackson County family, has been copied from Bible and Cemetery records.

Gill, Marcus, born April 9, 1814, in Bath County, Kentucky, the son of Samuel Chriswell Gill and wife, Sarah Malone Gill; died December 9, 1886. Married, first, Sarah A. Bruton, February 23, 1839; second, Mary Jane Bruton (Foster), January 5, 1847. Buried in Elmwood Cemetery.

Sarah Ann Bruton Gill, born in Madison County, Kentucky, June 22, 1820, died March 29, 1846. (The ashes of Sarah Gill and the old stone which marked her grave at the Gill Burying Ground in Gill's Mill, Kentucky, were removed to Elmwood Cemetery, Kansas City, Missouri.)

Mary Jane Bruton (Foster) Gill, born in Clark County, Kentucky, August 27, 1822, died September 1, 1894. Buried in Elmwood Cemetery.

Children: (First Marriage)

Enoch Bruton Gill, born in Bath County, Kentucky, December 14, 1839, died September 23, 1916. Married, first, Mary L. Lane, March 19, 1860, buried in Liberty, Missouri; second, Vina McCrum, June 22, 1880. Buried in Elmwood Cemetery.

Turner Anderson Gill, born in Bath County, Kentucky, December 8, 1841, died July 18, 1919. Married, first, March 9, 1871, Lizzie Campbell; second, July, 1909, Mrs. Ella Sites Kercheval. Was Mayor of Kansas City in 1875 and 1876. Buried in Elmwood Cemetery.

Leah O. Gill, born in Bath County, Kentucky, September 22, 1843, died March 16, 1908, in Ogden, Utah. Married, April 4, 1861, Jesse R. Noland in Independence, Missouri.

Sarah Ann Gill, born in Bath County, Kentucky, died July 11, 1848. Buried in the family burying ground at Gill's Mill, Kentucky.

(Second Marriage)

Susan Bruton Gill, born March 8, 1848, died May 9, 1901. Married, January 11, 1869, Allen B. H. McGee. Buried in Union Cemetery, Kansas City, Missouri.

Henrietta Catherine Gill, born June 30, 1850, died January 29, 1852

Sally Ann Malone Gill, born May 12, 1852, died December 17, 1887. Married, May 11, 1871, John E. George. Buried in the Cemetery at Belton, Missouri.

Marcus Gill, Jr., born September 28, 1854, died November 23, 1857

William Kibby Gill, born September 24, 1856, died March, 1888, in Duvall's Bluff, Arkansas, and was buried there. No stone marks his grave or those of his two children, Marietta and Thomas, who were buried there. Married Ella Duckworth.

Mary Edith Gill, born January 19, 1859. Married, first, January, 1884, Nicholas T. Eaton; second, Milton McGee Vincent.

Louella Gill, born November 27, 1860. Married, December 22, 1880, John C. B. Hargis.

Mrs. Mary Jane Bruton (Foster) Gill; married, first, September 2, 1840, Sanford Foster of Clark County, Kentucky, and had two children:

Jemima Foster, born January 24, 1842, died October 14, 1926. Married Fleming B. Rice. Buried in St. Peter's Cemetery, St. Louis, Missouri.

James Sanford Foster, born April 17, 1844, died September 3, 1858

Sanford Foster died May 25, 1844

GRANGE CEMETERY
Sometimes called Douglas Cemetery
Section 28 - 29, Township 48, Range 33
92nd and Troost Avenue

Agers, Moses, born 1837, died 1890

Agers, J. R., son of Moses Agers, born 1871, died 1893

Agers, S. A., son of Moses Agers, born 1878, died 1890

Amidon, Hattie D., daughter of M. L. and Sarah C. Amidon, died May 27, 1889; age, 20 years, 5 months

Amidon, Mamie, daughter of M. L. and Sarah C. Amidon, died May 2, 1884; age, 12 years, 1 month

Arn, Cornelius, born August 15, 1841, died July 21, 1880; age, 41 years, 11 months, 6 days
(N. B. Inscription on head stone copied exactly as it appeared. Age and dates do not coincide.) The monument has the following:—
Cornelius Arn, born August 15, 1841, died July 2, 1880

Arn, Albert, died November 12, 1900; age, 20 years

Arn, Emma, born April 6, 1846, died February 13, 1904

Douglas, Albin, born December 28, 1841, died June 27, 1916

Douglas, Amanda, wife of Albin Douglas, born September 5, 1843, died March 14, 1880; N. B. The second burial in the cemetery

Douglas, J. D., son of Albin and Amanda Douglas, died March 11, 1883; age, 3 years, 3 months

Douglas, William, died March 20, 1886; age, 72 years, 4 months, 11 days

Douglas, Emily Dooley, wife of William Douglas, buried by the side of her husband but no stone (Information by a grandson)

Jones, Rachel, wife of James Jones, born February, 1814, died November 30, 1881

Lee, M. B., husband of Lizzie Lee, born November 28, 1861, died February 20, 1899

Lee, Lizzie E., wife of M. B. Lee, born February 22, 1861, died October 24, 1904

Lee, George R., son of W. R. and Hattie Lee, born March, 1894, died March 3, 1902

MacDonald, Mary, born March 15, 1812, died March 10, 1888

Ricketts, William, died May 25, 1881; age, 76 years, 6 months, 19 days

Spruill, Dr. A. B., died September 8, 1889; age, 65 years

Spruill, Martha E., wife of Dr. A. B. Spruill, died July 2, 1903; age, 80 years

Spruill, James B., son of A. B. and M. E. Spruill, died October 6, 1889; age, 37 years

Spruill, Willie Alvah, child of C. B. and Anna Spruill, died August 9, 1897; age, 1 year, 2 months, 9 days

Smith, R. H., born January 13, 1849, died January 4, 1910

Smith, A. C., born 1856, died 1918 "Mother"

Stukesberry, Nancy, died September 7, 1877; age, 29 years, 6 months, 9 days

Tidwell, Sarilda, born June 2, 1834, died April 28, 1906 "Mother"

Watts, Jasper, son of LaFayette and Harriet Douglas Watts, buried by the south fence. No stones. N. B. Information given by a cousin.

N. B. A number of removals from this cemetery have been made to the Belton Cemetery, Belton, Cass County, Missouri.

HALL GRAVE
Section 25, Township 47, Range 33

On a farm owned and occupied by —— Taylor, who came to Missouri from Ohio before the Civil War, was a community burying ground. There is only one little stone left to mark the spot where, we are told, were buried a number of early pioneers. The inscription on the stone is:

John T. Hall, born December 18, 1871, died March 15, 1873

HICKMAN CEMETERY
Section 30, Township 48, Range 32 W

Information furnished by Mrs. Henry Chick. Thomas Isaac Hickman came from Kentucky to Jackson County, Missouri, in 1844 and settled on a farm, where later he set aside a family burying ground. The members of the family buried there are:

Hickman, Thomas Isaac, died in April, 1866
Hickman, Harriett Brooking, wife of Thomas I. Hickman, died in March, 1874
Hickman, Elizabeth Frances, a daughter, died in 1846
Fletcher, Waller, a son-in-law
Fletcher, William, son of Waller Fletcher
Fletcher, Martha, daughter of Waller Fletcher

Inscriptions taken from other tombstones in this cemetery are:

Briant, Martha H., died February 7, 1848; age, 2 years, 2 months, 13 days
Briant, Robert S., died December 24, 1847; age, 16 years, 3 months, 17 days
Ragan, Archibald H., son of S. C. and J. G. Ragan, born November 5, 1873, died February 22, 1875

N. B. There were a few slaves buried in the east side of the cemetery on the west side of the present road.

Copied by Miss Jessie M. Crosby

KEENEY FAMILY BURYING GROUND
Section 32, Township 47, Range 33 W

On land in the southwest part of the county, entered by Michael Keeney, who emigrated from Tennessee to Lafayette County, Missouri, in 1827 and to Jackson County, Missouri, in 1829, was located a burying ground for the members of the Keeney family.

Michael Keeney, the son of Thomas Keeney and Mary Reeves Keeney, married Nancy Wiley, and to them were born eight sons and one daughter. The daughter was Mary Ann, who married Isaac J. Holloway, and is buried in the Bryant Cemetery near Belton, Cass County, Missouri.

While the old Keeney farm was located partly in Jackson County and partly in Cass County, the burying ground was on that part of the farm which was in Jackson County. All trace of the old family burying ground is erased, but the following inscriptions were copied several years ago by Mr. J. R. Keeney, a grandson of Michael Keeney, from the stones which he found piled in a corner of a corn field:

Michael Keeney, died July 26, 1849; age, 60 years
Nancy Keeney (wife), died May 19, 1857; age, 60 years
Fountain Keeney (son), born June 25, 1829, died May 26, 1857
David Keeney (son), died May 25, 1857; age, 25 years
J. Keeney, born March 8, 1818, died September 25, 1883
Eliza Keeney, died May 4, 1855; age, 20 years, 4 months, 6 days
Julia Ann Keeney, wife of J. Keeney, born March 18, 1818, died February 18, 1863
Margaret J., daughter of J. and J. A. Keeney, died April 18, 1851; age, 1 year
Mary Keeney, daughter of J. and J. A. Keeney, born August 22, 1847, died October 15, 1868; age, 21 years, 1 month, 23 days

Miss Frances Keeney, Belton, Missouri, contributed the following information regarding several members of the family of Michael Keeney not buried in the old family cemetery:

Thomas Keeney, born March 10, 1824, died October 28, 1900; buried in Belton, Missouri
Isaac Keeney, born November 10, 1833, died April 20, 1906; buried in Belton, Missouri
Elija Keeney, born February, 1827, died June 13, 1893; buried in Bryant Cemetery, Cass Co.
Mary Ann, born March 5, 1836, died January 4, 1917; buried in Bryant Cemetery, Cass Co.

THE KERBY BURYING GROUND
THE ERVIN BURYING GROUND
Sections 4 - 5, Township 47, Range 33 W

About a quarter of a mile from Holmes Street on what is now Red Bridge Road, the highway passes over what was once a part of the cemeteries or burying grounds on the farms of "Dick" Kerby and John H. Ervin. Only a fence separated these early burying grounds. Like so many of the others, all traces of these cemeteries have disappeared.

THE KERBY BURYING GROUND

The Burying Ground on the Kerby Farm was the largest, being in use as early as 1835. There were probably as many as seventy-five to one hundred graves in this rural cemetery, which included that part of the highway which crosses that section of the farm on which this cemetery was located, and back from the highway on the south as far as one hundred feet or more. Only a small number of the bodies and stones were ever removed. What has become of those stones which once marked the spot where many of the early pioneers of that community were buried, is not known. Near the site of this burying ground stands a Santa Fe Trail marker.

Among those whose ashes were removed from this community cemetery, were ten of the Kerby family which were taken to the little cemetery at New Santa Fe, Missouri. Only four of this family had stones at their graves, and these four stones were moved and placed in the "Little Santa Fe" Church Cemetery, at New Santa Fe, Missouri. The bodies of "Dick" Kerby, owner of the farm, and that of his wife, were placed, at the time of their death, in a vault on the top of the ground and when their bodies were moved, no stone was placed at their graves in the Santa Fe Cemetery. Col. Richard Kerby was born in Greene County, Kentucky, June 16, 1820; his wife, Mary J. Johnston of Kentucky, died September 29, 1870.

Among others who were buried on this farm were twenty-two members of the Stewart family, one of the pioneer families of the community. Archie Stewart owned a large farm just south of the little town of New Santa Fe.

"Billy" Gray

—— Morton, son-in-law of "Billy" Gray

Mrs. —— Morton, daughter of "Uncle Billy" and "Aunt Betsy" Gray, died 1882

America Ann Wilson, first wife of I. J. Holloway

Josh Stewart (Steward), died December, 1891; married Leanna Kerr, daughter of Caleb Kerr, Independence, Missouri

Samuel Bartlett, born July 18, 1809

Mahala Bartlett, wife of Samuel Bartlett, born March 31, 1811

> Dates sent by granddaughter of Samuel and Mahala Bartlett, Mrs. S. J. Wyatt, Girard, Kansas.

THE ERVIN BURYING GROUND

This family burying ground was separated from the one on the Kerby farm by a fence, and was on the farm owned by John H. Ervin. Among those interred on this farm were:

The first wife of J. H. Ervin, died 1850

Bill Ervin, son of J. H. Ervin and first wife

Thomas B. Rippeto, born April 8, 1795, died May 20, 1850

Ann McW. Nielson, wife of Thomas B. Rippeto, born September 4, 1806, died January 3, 1840; age, 33 years, 3 months, 29 days (The stones for Mr. and Mrs. Rippeto were moved to Linwood, Kansas, west of Watts' Mill)

—— Riggs, son of Mr. Riggs, who built a house at the Trading Post on the Santa Fe Trail, which was only a short distance from these cemeteries. The father went West in 1849. The son's grave is by the side of the highway and is unmarked

Thomas B. Rippeto and Ann McW. Nielson were married May 17, 1825

N. B.—The above information concerning the Kerby and the Ervin Burying Grounds was furnished Mrs. Max A. Christopher by Mrs. Henry Klapmeyer, Mr. Urial Holmes and Mr. Edward Watts, residents of that community for many years; also Mrs. S. J. Hamilton (Nannie Kerr) of Harrisonville, Missouri.

THE KLAPMEYER BURYING GROUND
Section 20, Township 47, Range 33 W

Directly south of Martin City, Missouri, less than a quarter of a mile, is this old Family Burying Ground on the homestead of J. H. Klapmeyer who came to Missouri in 1826, and to Westport in 1832. The site reserved on this farm for burial purposes is about twenty-five feet square and is enclosed by a stone wall. The following inscriptions were copied from the stones and the granite monument found there:

In Memory of Our Father and Mother

J. H. Klapmeyer, born February 26, 1801, died January 9, 1879

E. C. Klapmeyer, born December 30, 1813, died March 11, 1862

Losa, William, son of Wm. and Mary Losa, born May 25, 1861, died August 18, 1861

Klapmeyer, Lizzie K., wife of Wm. Klapmeyer, born May 3, 1859, died January 21, 1890

Losa, Mary, wife of Wm. Losa, and daughter of J. H. and A. C. E. Klapmeyer, born April 13, 1837, died August 9, 1861

Reinsch, infant son of F. and A. Reinsch, born and died February 20, 1890

Reinsch, Bertha, daughter of F. and A. Reinsch, died July 18, 1872; age, 8 months, 17 days

Information given by Mrs. Henry Klapmeyer (Mollie McKinney), Martin City, Mo.

THE KNOCHE BURYING GROUND
Township 47, Range 33 W

The head of this family who came to America and to Jackson County, Missouri, a few years prior to the Civil War, was Johannes Franz Knoche, who with his wife, Elizabeth Strochbine) Knoche, were born, reared and married in Prussia. Franz (Frank) Knoche was a soldier in the Prussian army before coming to America. In sections 28 and 29 in Washington Township the Knoche family purchased farm land in the locality known today as 140th and Holmes.

On this farm was a Family Burying Ground. This land was in the path of the fast-growing demand for smaller acreage and this old Knoche farm was sold. About the year 1916 "Jim" Knoche, a descendant of the immigrant ancestor, helped to remove all of the bodies which had been interred there, to the cemetery at Belton, Cass County, Missouri.

The following inscriptions were copied from the stones of members of this Jackson County family, which are found on the lot at the cemetery in Belton, Missouri:

Chandler, Elijah, born January 11, 1821, died November 15, 1906

Chandler, Jane, wife of E. Chandler, died July 10, 1890; age, 64 years, 9 months, 18 days

Knoche, Johannes Franz, born November 8, 1796, died October 10, 1865

Knoche, Elizabeth, born October 12, 1804, died June 9, 1891

Knoche, Henry, born February 24, 1839, died August 26, 1918

Knoche, Amalie, born Feb. 7, 1855, died Dec. 20, 1891; age, 36 years, 10 months, 21 days

Knoche, George Ludwig, born May 19, 1850, died September 5, 1897

Knoche, Julia, born May 20, 1883, died June 1, 1884

Knoche, Ch. Enoch, born March 20, 1876, died November 18, 1877
Knoche, John, born September 7, 1828, died October 29, 1915
Knoche, Anna E., born January 17, 1846, died October 24, 1919
Knoche, Louis, born December 9, 1834 (No dates for death)
Knoche, Katherine, wife of Louis Knoche, born April 30, 1843, died December 8, 1909
Knoche, Daniel, born November 10, 1852, died August 18, 1917
Knoche, Mary, wife of D. Knoche, born April 21, 1868, died August 7, 1883
Kuntz, John, born May 9, 1855, died March 12, 1908
Rector, Bennett, born 1870, died 1925
Wallace, Charlie, son of T. W. and E. Wallace, born January 9, 1874, died February 10, 1880

THE LIPSCOMB FAMILY BURYING GROUND
One Hundred and Tenth Street and State Line
Section 7, Township 47, Range 33 W

Joel Lipscomb was born in Madison County, Kentucky, October 21, 1813, rode horseback to Jackson County, Missouri from Kentucky in 1839, and soon after arriving married Henrietta Simpson Harris, daughter of Jack Harris and wife, Henrietta Simpson, of Westport. His brother, Dabney Lipscomb, had married Susan Simpson, an aunt of Henrietta Harris, and had come to Jackson County, Missouri, a short time before. Louisa Lipscomb, a sister, married Duke Simpson. Joel Lipscomb and his brother entered land in Washington Township, south of the town of Westport. Dabney Lipscomb sold his farm to Marcus Gill who came to Jackson County in 1854 from Bath County, Kentucky, and that farm became known as the Gill Farm, while the farm entered by Joel Lipscomb, known as the Lipscomb Farm remained in the family until a few years ago. The home place is now owned by E. M. Ridenour of Kansas City.

Mr. and Mrs. Joel Lipscomb had ten children:
Frances, (Mrs. William Hickman), is the only child living and resides in Independence, Mo.
Rodney Bernard and James are buried in Liberal, Missouri
Harris is buried in Mount Washington, Kansas City, Missouri
Nathan is buried in Forest Hill, Kansas City, Missouri
Lou (Mrs. J. E. Watson) is buried in Albuquerque, New Mexico
Lieut. W. S. Lipscomb was killed at Vicksburg, Mississippi, June 25, 1863, and is buried there. A government marker marks his grave
Three children died and were buried on the farm.

The Family Burying Ground was directly north of the old house and garden and today is located less than one hundred yards from 110th Street, and less than a quarter of a mile from State Line. (In the days of the family burying ground there was no 110th Street.) Four old-fashioned headstones are to be found lying on the ground where it is remembered were the graves of the family. A wire fence crosses the site of this old burying ground; one can see there today the footstones with the initials of the deceased upon them, withstanding as they have for over eighty years, many destructive forces. Nearby are found several large native stones standing to mark the graves of persons buried there. One of these stones is thought to be that marking the grave of Joel Lipscomb who died December 27, 1893, and was interred there by the side of his wife and three children. No doubt there were other pioneers of that community buried on this old farm, of whom we have no record.

The following inscriptions were copied from the stones found there:
Henrietta S., wife of J. Lipscomb, born May 18, 1823, died March 24, 1859
Charles H. Lipscomb, son of J. and H. Lipscomb, born May 17, 1853, died Sept. 2, 1854

Joel Lipscomb, Jr., son of J. and H. Lipscomb, born May 11, 1851, died August 8, 1854

Henrietta H. Lipscomb, daughter of J. and H. S. Lipscomb, born March 19, 1859, died March 20, 1859

It must be remembered that on almost every farm there were buried the slaves of the family.

MONROE
Section 30, Township 47, Range 33 W

Near the Kansas-Missouri State Line, about two miles southwest of the little town of Martin City, Missouri, is to be seen a stone shaft or monument about twelve feet high, in the middle of a cornfield. This monument has been carefully protected by a fence which is made of galvanized pipe and four stone corner posts. This fence encloses a little burying spot about ten feet square. On this monument is found the following inscription:

JAMES H. MONROE
Died December 10, 1872
Age, 33 years, 6 months, 1 day

ELEANOR, daughter of J. H. and AMANDA MONROE
Died September 24, 1872
Age, 1 year, 8 months, 24 days

In the silent tomb we leave thee
Till the morn when Christ appears
Then with joy we hope to greet thee
Far beyond this vale of tears

MOUNT PLEASANT CEMETERY
THE KING BURYING GROUND
Section 17, Township 47, Range 33 W

Near 130th Street, between Holmes Street and Wornall Road, on the old King Farm, is located this community burying ground. Mr. Urial Holmes, who came to Missouri from Tennessee with his parents in 1853, relates the fact that this site had been used for burials many years prior to the time his parents came to Missouri. About 1878 Mr. Holmes and Dr. J. E. Watson platted the ground into lots and named this community burying ground, "Mount Pleasant Cemetery." The following inscriptions were copied from the stones in this old cemetery, by Mrs. Milton McGee Vincent and Mrs. Max A. Christopher.

Bart, Faldine (No stone)

Baxter, Peter Howard, born 1837, died 1898

Barger, Elizabeth, born April 15, 1830, died January 9, 1894

Barger, James, son of H. and E. Barger, born May 22, 1867, died March 6, 1870

Barger, Marietta, wife of Henry Barger, died September 12, 1864; age, 36 years, 4 months, 2 days

Barager, Henry, died June 19, 1878; age, 65 years, 3 months, 2 days (Note the difference in spelling the name of members of the same family)

DeLong, Martha K., died November 19, 1860; age, 28 years, 6 months, 2 days

Harris, ("Granny") Phoebe, wife of Richard Harris, born 1799, died 1887. No stone at her grave. Information given by Urial Holmes, grandson. Her maiden name was Harris also. Her husband, Richard Harris, went to Tennessee from Virginia in 1827 and died in Hawkins County, Tennessee.

CEMETERIES—WASHINGTON TOWNSHIP

Holmes, Urial, born October 5, 1811, died July 27, 1855; age, 43 years, 22 days

Holmes, Sallie E. J., wife of U. Holmes, born January 26, 1821, died March 1, 1870; age, 49 years

Holmes, Mary V., daughter of H. H. and R. M. Holmes, died September 25, 1899; age, 1 year, 2 months

Hays, Albert E., son of W. L. and Mary Hays, born Sept. 15, 1886, died Oct. 8, 1888

Hays, William L., and wife, Mary Hays, died in 189-, and buried in this cemetery. No stones

King, William, died April 3, 1857; age, 69 years, 6 months, 8 days

King, J. L., husband of Dora King, born October 18, 1846, died December 27, 1891

Knoche, Louis, son of E. and G. Knoche, born July 29, 1860, died October 1, 1871

Lee, Earl E., son of G. W. and Dora Lee, died July 8, 1906; age, 15 years, 9 months, 26 days

Lee, Geo. W., died June 18, 1907; age, 49 years, 8 months, 14 days

Miller, David S., born May 4, 1805, died February 17, 1879

Manion, James W., born January 5, 1804, died November 2, 1856

McCraw, Thomas W., born 1839, died 1930

McCraw, Jane, wife of Thomas W. McCraw, born 1845, died 1893

McCraw, Alonzo, born 1872, died 1889

McCraw, Thomas, born 1880, died 1897

McPherson, Edward, born December 20, 1809, died August 27, 1889

McPherson, Angeline, wife of Edward McPherson

McPherson, Lydia Bartlett, (first) wife of Albert McPherson, died 1877. No stone. Was buried by the side of Almeda Treadway (Information given by Roy McPherson, a son)

Parsons, Baldwin, husband of Elizabeth Parsons, born May 12, 1803, died April 23, 1862

Townsley, Oma, daughter of Theo. and Sallie Townsley, died September 28, 1885; age, 4 years, 11 months, 14 days

See, William M., son of J. and N. See, died July 5, 1849; age, 21 years (This young man died while enroute west with his parents in 1849. This cemetery is a short distance from the old Santa Fe Trail and the Oregon Trail. After eighty-four years, the marble head stone and the stone vault, above ground, are in excellent condition.)

Savage, Nellie May, daughter of F. C. and S. Savage, died January 29, 1890; age, 1 year, 4 months, 14 days

Shelton, John, born October, 1788, died April 25, 1854

Shelton, Mary, wife of John Shelton, died December 18, 1878 (Stone broken)

Shelton, John E., son of J. and M. Shelton, born December 14, 1835, died March 30, 1840

Shelton, Alvis H., son of J. and M. Shelton, born April 23, 1824, died January 21, 1859

Sharp, Moses T., born July 28, 1846, died March 19, 1887 (N. B. Body moved to the Belton Cemetery, Cass County, the old stone not moved)

Sharp, T. B., born November 9, 1806, died February 18, 1889 (N. B. His wife, Demarius Sharp, died August 15, 1870; buried on the Gill Farm)

Sharp, Bonnie, daughter of W. F. and C. Sharp, died April 20, 1890; age, 11 months

Self, John F., born November 30, 1803, died February 1, 1889

Watson, Dr. John E., born in Pennsylvania, November 26, 1834, died October 1, 1881

Wisdom, Jane, wife of G. W. Wisdom, died March 5, 1876; age, 41 years, 2 months, 11 days

---

Holmes, Nora, wife of Richard "Dick" Holmes, died May 12, 1906; age, 55 years, 10 months, 26 days (N. B. Was buried in Mount Pleasant Cemetery, and at the death of her husband the body was moved to Pleasant Valley Cemetery, Stanley, Kansas)

Holmes, Richard "Dick," born May 21, 184-, died July 15, 1926; buried at Stanley, Kansas, Pleasant Valley Cemetery

VITAL HISTORICAL RECORDS

NEW SANTA FE CHRISTIAN CHURCH CEMETERY
125th Street and State Line

Callis, Charles C., born November 27, 1855, died January 20, 1914
Elwell, David (father), born 1849, died 1918
Garten, Leviniher, wife of G. B. Garten, born August 28, 1828, died December 23, 1896
Gault, Wesley, Mrs., died 1887
Kerr, Thomas J., born April 4, 1820, died July 5, 1902
Kerr, Catherine, wife of Thomas Kerr, born February 12, 1827, died August 8, 1882
Kerr, Ida, daughter of T. and C. Kerr, born September 19, 1871, died August 23, 1875
Kerr, George T., born September 13, 1851, died August 10, 1925
Kerr, Cinderella S., born January 31, 1865, died March 4, 1914
Kernodle, Dr. James, son of Mrs. Wesley Gault (No stone)
Kerby, Jesse, died October 29, 1853; age, 66 years
Kerby, Nancy, died October 4, 1837; age, 45 years
Kerby, Hiley J., died 1868; age, 35 years
Kerby, —rew S., died August 13, 1853; age, 19 years
Klapmeyer, Henry, born 1847, died 1925 (Grave unmarked)
Lawson, Nancy G., born September 4, 1821, died March 21, 1888
Lyle, Henrietta, daughter of B. T. and J. E. Lyle, died September 14, 1861; age, 1 year, 3 months, 21 days
Maines, James B., son of H. D. and Nellie Maines, born January 7, 1874, died August 17, 1882
Morgan, Jeremiah (father), born August 31, 1801, died January 7, 1887
Morgan, Edith (mother), born July 29, 1804, died March 5, 1887
Morgan, Missouri J., died March, 1900; age, 60 years
McKinney, William A., died January 12, 1900; age, 72 years, 11 months, 27 days
McKinney, Eliza A., wife of W. A. McKinney, died December 29, 1885; age, 46 years, 6 months, 29 days
McKinney, Elizabeth J., daughter of W. A. and E. A. McKinney, died April 14, 1880; age, 17 years, 4 months, 21 days
Pasley, Isaac, born 1836, died 1912
Stewart, Tilman B., son of A. M. and Cinderella Stewart, born December, 1837, died February 28, 1873
Stewart, A. M., born April 5, 1812, died July 30, 1885
Stewart, Mrs. Josh, died July, 1913 (Grave unmarked)
Sweaney, Jacob, born —— 31, 1824, died January 29, 1918
Sweaney, Lydia, wife of Jacob Sweaney, born May 14, 1838, died September 8, 1901
Thompson, C. W., born 1838, died 1912
Thompson, S. I., wife of C. W. Thompson, born 1835, died 1912
Young, Johnson, born May 18, 1844, died May 8, 1907
Young, May L., wife of Johnson Young, born October 9, 1848, died January 28, 1898

The above inscriptions were copied June 18, 1933, by Mrs. Louella Gill Hargis, who was born on the Gill Farm just across the road from the little historic town of New Santa Fe, Mo., November 27, 1860. Information pertaining to a few of the unmarked graves was given by Mrs. Henry Klapmeyer of Martin City and Mrs. Ollie Sweaney Young-Scott of Hickman Mills, Mo.

NOLAND CEMETERY
Section 29, Township 48, Range 32

Bowers, A. M., died January 7, 1885; age, 35 years, 11 months, 22 days
Cox, Julia, wife of Career Cox, died February 2, 1884; age, 19 years, 8 months
Ervin, Josiah, died October 30, 1877; age, 37 years, 6 months, 27 days
Ervin, Nancy A., wife of Josiah Ervin, died March 24, 1906; age, 63 years, 9 months, 21 days

Ervin, Lafayette, M. D., died March 12, 1877; age, 31 years, 8 months, 25 days
Ervin, Nannieella, born March 8, 1868, died August 30, 1873
   Laura Jane, born April 8, 1875, died August 10, 1876
      Children of B. F. and Susane Ervin
Noland, Amos, born September 5, 1819, died December 28, 1881
   Sarah Jane, wife of Amos Noland, born January 27, 1827, died August 18, 1861
   John F., son of A. and S. J. Noland, born July 24, 1856, died November 14, 1861
   James H., son of A. and S. J. Noland, born April 13, 1858, died July 23, 1861
Noland, A. M., born August 30, 1828, died February 24, 1892
Noland, Thetis C., born August 18, 1837, died December 31, 1876
Noland, Orlena, wife of J. J. Noland, died Sept. 2, 1892; age, 66 years, 4 months, 18 days
Morris, William, born 1853, died 1905
Morris, Letha N., wife of William Morris, died April 10, 1881; age, 23 years, 2 months, 9 days
Park, Margaret A., wife of J. M. Park, died December 9, 1903; age, 62 years
   James M., died September 9, 1898; age, 62 years, 4 months, 27 days
Van Dyke, Virginia J., wife of William H. Van Dyke, died December 30, 1872; age, 18 years, 4 months, 9 days
Woodson, Malvina M., born 1847, died 1929

                Copied April 29, 1933, by Miss Jessie M. Crosby

OLDHAM GRAVES
SW Quarter Section 1, Township 47, Range 33 W

Died before 1856:
   Zera Oldham and wife
   Amanda Oldham, daughter of Zera Oldham

                Contributed by Miss Jessie M. Crosby

PALESTINE CEMETERY
Section 25, Township 48, Range 33 W

Arnett, T. J., died August 15, 1883; age, 30 years, 6 months, 5 days
Arnett, Beulah M. M., daughter of T. J. and S. Arnett, died March 2; age, 17 years, 4 months, 5 days
Bull, Mordecai, died March 23, 1885; age, 82 years, 2 months, 25 days
   Nancy, wife of Mordecai Bull, died October 5, 1885; age, 77 years
Bull, Taylor Z., born 1847, died 1914. "Farewell only for a while"
Butler, Elizabeth, died September 6, 1887; age, 57 years, 6 months, 20 days
Boggs, Adam S., born December 2, 1845, died July 5, 1906
Caudell, Mary J., wife of Andrew Caudell, born September 29, 1829, died March 27, 1900
Church, William B., died March 5, 1900; age, 60 years, 2 months, 14 days
Church, Elizabeth, born 1852, died 1919
Compton, V. S., born June 20, 1826, died July 15, 1901
Davenport, Stephen, died May 19, 1883; age, 80 years, 7 months, 3 days
Davenport, Susannah, wife of Stephen Davenport, died March 24, 1862; age, 48 years, 2 months, 23 days
Davenport, Margaret, wife of Stephen Davenport, died March 17, 1881; age, 73 years, 2 months, 10 days
Davenport, Simeon, son of S. and S. Davenport, died September 14, 1843; age, 16 years, 2 months, 14 days
Sidney, son of S. and S. Davenport, died Jan. 29, 1852; age, 12 years, 6 months, 10 days
Donovan, L. H., born September 24, 1817, died June 8, 1886

Donovan, Marion, born January 1, 1832, died September 20, 1902
Douglass, Elizabeth, wife of W. T. Douglass (mother), born 1821, died 1910
Downey, B. T., died January 17, 1907; age, 76 years, 2 months, 25 days
    "Resting in the hope of the first Resurrection"
  Elizabeth D., wife of B. T. Downey (mother), died April 12, 1905; age, 7- years, 11 months, 19 days
Duncan, Margaret, wife of J. W. Duncan, born September 28, 1849, died March 12, 1893
Duncan, Thomas, died January 22, 1899; age, 78 years, 29 days
  Martha, wife of Thomas Duncan, died April 22, 1895; age, 64 years, 11 days

> "Dear mother thou art gone to rest,
> Thy toils and cares are o'er,
> And sorrow, pain and suffering now
> Shall ne'er distress thee more."

Eib, Jacob, died March 2, 1906; age, 72 years, 5 months, 1 day
Eib, Elizabeth, died November 15, ——; age, 45 years, 1 month, 13 days
Estes (mother), Martha Ann, born February 26, 1835, died April 18, 1895
Estes (father), Richard J., born 1829, died January 3, 1882; age, 52 years, 6 months, 27 days
Estes, Mary J., born 1866, died 1881
Estes, Edward, born 1860, died 1881
Estes, Quintilla R., born 1858, died 1885
Finnell, B. W., born December 23, 1815, died June 28, 1905
  J. S., born November 30, 1842, died April 28, 1898
Food, William, born 1843, died 1913
  Emma Jane, wife of William Food, born 1843, died 1922
Foree, Alice G., born August 9, 1848, died February 3, 1917
Foree, Lewis W., born November 18, 1830, died January 27, 1917
Foree, Joel, died March 2, 1882; age, 60 years, 11 months, 16 days
Foree, Mary J., born 1856, died 1923
Gilham, Captain J. Newton, member of Co. "D" 101 Ill. Vol. Inf., born in Scott County, Illinois, October 4, 1838, died in Jackson County, Missouri, August 24, 1883
Gore, Lewis, born September 24, 1813, died May 15, 1860
  Sophia, born November 22, 1827, died September 6, 1917
  Natives of Lexington, Ky. Erected by J. T. Gore and Mary E. Wells of Sacramento, Cal.
Grogger, Susan, wife of Bernhardt, born March 4, 1834, died February 4, 1899
Hampton, Enoch, died March 19, 1894; age, 64 years, 4 months, 27 days
  Mary, wife of E. Hampton, died March 20, 1890; age, 64 years, 7 months, 19 days
Havron, J. M., born December 18, 1823, died July 29, 1896
Hudson (father), Rufus M., died September 17, 1888; age, 60 years
James, Jacob Wolf, born November 8, 1823, died October 8, 1903
  Elizabeth E. Noble, wife of J. W. James, born February 9, 1826, died November 19, 1895
Johnson, G. W., died November 23, 1912; age, 87 years
Johnson, Jesse S., born April 13, 1835, died March 6, 1912
  Sarah, wife of J. S. Johnson, born August 11, 1836, died October 10, 1919
King, J. R., kin
King, A. J.
King, R. B.
Knouse, Caroline, born August 14, 1836, died February 18, 1909
Maddox, Alfred B., died February 23, 1895; age, 71 years, 8 months, 27 days
Marquette, P. H., died October 18, 1884; age, 35 years, 8 months, 28 days
McKay, Robert, born February 3, 1823, died January 6, 1908
  Rachel E., wife of Robert McKay, born May 8, 1840, died June 25, 1907
Miller, Charles, born February 25, 1809, died June 28, 1896
Miller, Elizabeth, wife of Charles Miller, died Jan. 31, 1891; age, 75 years, 4 months, 4 days
Miller, Simpson, born January 24, 1843, died February 21, 1899
Muir, John S., born November 29, 1828, died October 28, 1914

Muir, Fannie C., born October 10, 1848, died April 1, 1882
Odell, Matilda A., wife of Edward Odell, born May 20, 1834, died February 25, 1907; age, 72 years, 9 months, 6 days
Oliver, John, died May 17, 1894; age, 80 years, 4 months, 12 days
  "A chair is vacant in our home"
    Elizabeth, wife of John Oliver, died October 28, 1884; age, 69 years, 2 months, 24 days
Palmer, Jacob T., born 1833, died 1912
    Catherine M., born 1840, died 1904
Rollins, Perlona J., wife of J. T. Rollins, died 1883; age, 46 years, 5 months, 9 days
Rucker, John T., born 1843, died 1923
Rutherford, Hamilton, born July 6, 1831, died March 29, 1893
Searcy, Charles W., born 1845, died 1908
Searle, John, born in England, 1824, died January 22, 1882
Sechrest (mother), Martha, born 1835, died 1916
Sechrest (father), John R., died September 14, 1901; age, 67 years, 4 months, 6 days
Smith, Cornelia, wife of J. A. Smith, died June 28, 1881; age, 42 years, 8 months, 12 days
Stout, Elder G. W., died September 29, 1891; age, 62 years, 1 month, 20 days. Joined the Regular Baptist Church August, 1848. Ordained to the work of the ministry A. D. 1857.
    Martha, born August 10, 1835, died November 7, 1920
Stubbs, Peter Harris, born March, 1820, died August 27, 1904
    Lou Cinda, wife of P. H. Stubbs, born December, 1834, died August 16, 1907
Talley, Beverly, died February 2, 1893; age, 57 years, 2 days
Talley, Eliza J., born September 27, 1837, died October 25, 1903
Talley, Joseph, died December 7, 1892; age, 60 years, 8 months, 9 days
Talley, Sarah, wife of Joseph Talley, died March 27, 1895; age, 68 years, 2 months, 25 days
Young, John, born March 10, 1818, died October 3, 1883; age, 64 years, 10 months, 14 days

    Copied June 17, 1933, by Mrs. May T. Crosby and Miss Jessie M. Crosby

THOMPSON BURYING GROUND
Section 14, Township 47, Range 33
Located at the east side of the Blue Ridge Cemetery

This plot is twenty feet square, enclosed by a fence.

Thompson, Matilda V., wife of O. P. Thompson, born August 12, 1816, died August 17, 1858
    Outside of the fence are buried the following:
Caldwell, William, born April 21, 1813, died October 4, 1866
Caldwell, Ann Caroline, wife of Wm. Caldwell (sister of Matilda V. Thompson), born December 21, 1823, died April 30, 1889
Caldwell, Martha, daughter of W. and A. C. Caldwell, born September 15, 1860, died April 25, 1861

    Copied May 6, 1933, by Miss Jessie M. Crosby

WADE FAMILY BURYING GROUND
Near New Santa Fe, Missouri
Township 47, Range 33 W

Mrs. Alice Keeney McPherson (Mrs. Edward), of Belton, Missouri, gives the information that on the farm near New Santa Fe, Jackson County, owned by her grandfather, Sam Wade, were buried several members of the family whose bodies were later removed to Union Cemetery, Kansas City, Missouri.

Besides Sam Wade and his wife, who were buried on the farm, there were:
Lou Ann Wade, a daughter of Sam and Polly Wade, born July 20, 1836, died August 1, 1855; married, December 8, 1853, Thomas Keeney
Anna Eliza Wade, the first wife of William S. Gregory, Mayor of Kansas City in 1853

WATTS BURYING GROUND
Township 48, Range 33 W

The Watts Burying Ground south of Kansas City, near Dallas, about a mile and a half north of Watts' Mill, one of the landmarks of Jackson County, Missouri, was for many years the burial ground for that community. A number of the early pioneers were interred there, as were soldiers of the Union Army and of the Confederate Army who fell near that section during the Civil War. Those stones and all traces of the old historic burying ground which we are told Mr. Watts "deeded to the dead," have disappeared. Records were not kept so the number of pioneers interred there cannot be known. The names of but a few are recorded, among which are members of the Watts family, and of James Bridger and his sons, F. A. and William.

Mr. Stubbins Watts, realizing that the district south of Kansas City was in the path of this fast-growing community, and having seen other cemeteries completely erased, requested of his family that at his death all of the family who had been interred in this burying ground be removed to the Pleasant Valley Cemetery at Stanley, Kansas, where he himself wished to be laid to rest. This request was heeded. In 1922, upon the death of Mr. Stubbins Watts, the ashes of his father, A. B. Watts, which had lain in Jackson County, Missouri, for sixty-one years, were moved with those of other members of the family, to Stanley, Kansas.

The first buhrstone used by Mr. Watts in the early days in grinding corn at the mill on Indian Creek in Jackson County, which bears his name, has been most appropriately used as a monument on the Watts' lot in the Pleasant Valley Cemetery in Kansas. Small buhrs, which were also used by Mr. Watts, are used for headstones at the graves of Mr. Stubbins Watts and his wife.

The age which is given for Mr. A. B. Watts on his headstone is said by members of the family to be incorrect, as he ran away from home at the age of fifteen years and joined the Lewis and Clark Expedition up the Missouri River to the mouth of the Yellowstone.

This family burying ground was in use in 1890, for a little grandson of Stubbins Watts died and was interred there in that year. The inscription on the stone is as follows: George V., son of T. J. and S. L. Douglas, died June 23, 1890; age, 2 months, 21 days.

It is appropriate that in collecting and compiling facts concerning a large number of the early pioneers of Jackson County, Missouri, that the inscriptions on the stones found in a Kansas Cemetery, belonging to this family, appear in this book.

Cummings, Hiram, died January 6, 1879; age, 60 years, 5 months, 27 days
Cummings, Sarah, wife of Hiram Cummings, born September 18, 1826, died March 26, 1896
Watts, A. B., died January 6, 1861; age, 62 years, 11 months, 5 days
Watts, Sally, wife of A. B. Watts, died January 18, 1861; age, 51 years, 7 months, 2 days
Watts, Turner S., son of S. and N. C. Watts, died September 29, 1883; age, 1 year, 6 months, 3 days
Watts, Stubbins, born May 15, 1838, died March 17, 1922
Watts, Nancy C., born October 13, 1851, died September 30, 1926

Watts, Lafayette, son of A. B. Watts and wife Sally Watts, removed to cemetery at Stillwell, Kansas
Watts, Harriett Douglas, wife of Lafayette Watts, removed to the cemetery at Stillwell, Kansas

> The above information was obtained from Mrs. Lizzie Watts Cummins, daughter of the late Stubbins Watts, for many years owner and operator of the historic Watts Mill at Dallas, Missouri.

JAMES BRIDGER
Born March 17, 1804
Died July 17, 1881

The above inscription is on one side of the monument which for twenty-three years marked the grave of James Bridger in the Watts Burying Ground just south of Kansas City, near which James Bridger lived.

On the opposite side of the monument is the following:

> We miss thee in the circle
>   Around the fireside;
> We miss thee in devotion,
>   At peaceful eventide:
> The memory of thy nature
>   So full of truth and love
> Shall lead our thoughts to
>   Seek thee, among the blest above.

December 5, 1904, the body of this frontiersman was moved to Mt. Washington Cemetery. A granite monument by his grave has the following inscription carved upon it:

JAMES BRIDGER
1804 - 1881

CELEBRATED AS A HUNTER, TRAPPER, FUR TRADER AND GUIDE. DISCOVERED GREAT SALT LAKE 1824. THE SOUTH PASS 1827. VISITED YELLOWSTONE LAKE AND GEYSER 1830. FOUNDED FT. BRIDGER 1843. OPENED OVERLAND ROUTE BY BRIDGER'S PASS TO GREAT SALT LAKE. WAS GUIDE FOR U. S. EXPLORING EXPEDITIONS, ALBERT SIDNEY JOHNSON'S ARMY 1857, AND G. M. DODGE IN U. P. SURVEYS AND INDIAN CAMPAIGNS 1856-66. THIS MONUMENT IS ERECTED AS A TRIBUTE TO HIS PIONEER WORK BY MAJ. GEN. G. M. DODGE

The following inscriptions were copied from the stones which marked the graves of two of the sons of James Bridger in the Watts Burying Ground. The bodies of the sons were never removed from their first burial place.

F. E. BRIDGER
Died July 19, 1876
Age, 34 years

> "Dearest brother thou
>   hast left us
> Here thy loss we
>   deeply feel,
> But 'tis God that
>   hath bereft us,
> He can all our
>   sorrows heal."

WILLAM BRIDGER
Born October 10, 1857
Died July 12, 1887
Age, 29 years, 9 months
Requiescat in Pace

WELLS FAMILY BURYING GROUND
Section 18, Township 47, Range 33 W

John M. Wells came with his parents when he was quite small, to Lafayette County, Missouri, from Madison County, Kentucky. In about the year 1853 he came to Jackson County and purchased a farm near New Santa Fe, Missouri, in 1854.

The Wells, Lipscomb and Gill families were neighbors in the "Little Santa Fe" neighborhood and members of these three families have remained close friends during these many years.

On each of these neighboring farms were Family Burying Grounds. The one on the Wells' Farm was small, only members of the family were laid to rest there; later the bodies were removed to the cemetery at Belton, Cass County, Missouri. The following names and dates of this Jackson County family were copied from the stones found on the lot in the Cemetery at Belton:

Rippeto, O. H. P., born February 2, 1826, died September 7, 1896
Wells, John Mercer, born July 12, 1826, died December 9, 1893
Wells, Catharine J., daughter of T. B. and Ann Rippeto, born April 24, 1830; married to John M. Wells March 30, 1854; died June 28, 1887
Wells, Henrietta, died April 4, 1873; age, 15 years, 3 months, 8 days
Wells, "Our Babes," son and daughter of J. M. and C. J. Wells, born and died March 26, 1865
On an adjoining lot is the monument for Dr. James W. Spruill, born January 12, 1846, died March 15, 1895, who married Anna Eliza Wells, daughter of John M. Wells and wife
Close by is found a stone with the following inscription: "John McKeney, born 1803; age, 80 years"
Wells, Perry, son of John Mercer and Catherine Wells, died and buried in the "Klondike" about 1895

WHITSETT CEMETERY
Section 36, Township 48, Range 33 W

Muir, Leonidas M., son of J. S. and A. A. Muir, born June 17, 1854, died October 9, 1857
Muir, infant son of J. S. and A. A. Muir, died November 18, 1860
Whitsett, Martha M., wife of J. S. Whitsett, born August 21, 1844, died July 1, 1878
Whitsett, Mary Leslie, daughter of J. S. and Mattie Whitsett, born February 21, 1871, died September 22, 1872
Whitsett, John R., died June 1, 1892; age, 87 years, 3 days
Whitsett, Eliza L., wife of John R. Whitsett, born October 8, 1808, died April 25, 1883
Whitsett, John N., born November 10, 1842, died September 8, 1857
Whitsett, infant son of J. R. and E. L. Whitsett, born July 19, 1847

Copied July 3, 1933, by Miss Jessie M. Crosby

VAN BUREN TOWNSHIP
Organized May 3, 1837

The data on all the cemeteries in Van Buren Township, with the exception of Koger and Adams, was compiled and copied by Mrs. Hale Houts, assisted by her son, Oliver Lee Houts.

ADAMS CEMETERY
Section 10, Township 47, Range 30 W
1 Mile East and 2 Miles North of Cockrell, Missouri

Adams, Wm., died September 29, 1859; age, 50 years, 7 months, 24 days
Adams, Mary, wife of Wm., died January 19, 1862; age, 54 years, 1 month, 15 days
Adams, Jacob M., died April 5, 1876; age, 48 years, 3 months, 3 days
Adams, Nancy Jane, daughter of Jacob M. and M. J., born and died September 2, 1874
Adams, Margaret Jane, born January 22, 1838, died December 7, 1916
Adams, Noah F., born September 2, 1865
Adams, Louisa J., wife of Noah F., born August 12, 1867, died January 9, 1928
Alley, Henry C., born April 25, 1835, died February 29, 1880
Alley, Melinda E., wife of Henry C., born October 9, 1840, died December 18, 1916
Alley, infant twins of H. C. and M. E., died December 11, 1873
Alley, Francis N., son of H. C. and M. E., died June 23, 1876; age, 9 months, 24 days
Bradley, Mary E., wife of T. J., born November 14, 1836, died September 19, 1903
Bradley, Marvin, son of T. J. and M. E., born September 25, 1871, died November 19, 1873
Bradley, Jimmy, son of T. J. and M. E., born August 19, 1869, died April 2, 1894
Browning, Tabitha A., wife of O. N., died August 5, 1862; age, 29 years, 10 months, 4 days
Burhrle, John, born November 25, 1837
Burhrle, Mary Ann, wife of John, born October 6, 1842, died January 21, 1910
Burhrle, Edith, born December 29, 1885, died March 6, 1890
Burhrle, Leonard, born February 24, 1871, died April 17, 1887
Cash, Wm., born March 16, 1814, died June 13, 1891; age, 77 years, 1 month, 27 days
Cash, Elizabeth, born Oct. 3, 1824, died Dec. 12, 1891; age, 67 years, 2 months, 9 days
Crawford, Dudley J., died July 27, 1878; age, 28 years
Crawford, infant son of D. J. and S. C., born and died March 27, 1877
Daily, R. L. (mother), born November 20, 1820, died May 11, 1900
Daily, Berthena, daughter of J. W. and C. A., died August 10, 1872; age, 1 year, 4 months
Dealy, David, born February 14, 1793, died October 12, 1876
Dealy, Rebecca, wife, born June 4, 1796, died April 28, 1852
Dealy, Wm., died March 4, 1885; age, 67 years, 11 months, 17 days
Dealy, Florence G., died August 13, 1874; age, 1 year, 6 months, 28 days
Dealy, Alvis M., died September 16, 1879; age, 9 months
Dealy, Dolly, died December 25, 1875; age, 2 months
Dealy, Henry W., born December 27, 1865, died February 3, 1905
Dealy, Mary E., born August 12, 1843, died March 12, 1820
Dealy, Francis B., wife of Wm., born March 11, 1811, died March 29, 1858
Dealy, James D., son of Wm. and Frances, born September 11, 1840, died October 1, 1842
Dealy, Zerelda, born March 14, 1836, died April, 1852
Dealy, Benjamin, born June 4, 1837

Dealy, Thomas B., born July 10, 1836, died April, 1852
Dealy, Samuel, born March 23, 1869
Dealy, Anna, his wife, born January 14, 1877, died August 15, 1919
Duncan, E. A., born November 7, 1825, died January 5, 1910
Duncan, Mary F. Culp, wife of E. A., born April 25, 1825, died May 14, 1897; age, 71 years
Duncan, Tabitha E., born June 28, 1859, died January 19, 1922
Duncan, Thornton, husband of Polly Duncan, died 1871; age, 71 years, 7 months, 14 days
Duncan, Mary, wife of Thornton Duncan, died January 16, 1892; age, 89 years, 8 months, 15 days
Duncan, Hansford, son of Thornton and Mary, born June 8, 1837, died April 30, 1858
Duncan, George T., son of Mary and Thornton, born January 1, 1842, died June 7, 1858
Duncan, Nimrod, son of Thornton and Mary, born Dec. 1, 1835, died Dec. 25, 1857
Gadle, David, born January 10, 1795, died September 20, 1842
Gadle, Esther, born November 20, 1797, died September 13, 1875
Gary, J. N., died January 2, 1892; age, 52 years
Hammond, Charley, son of W. C. and Ina, born August 17, 1877, died November 6, 1899
Hammond, Ina, born 1855, died 1923
Hammond, W. C., born 1847
Hoffman, Jacob, born 1852, died 1917
Hoffman, Olive, his wife, born 1863, died 1903
Lindley, Mary A., wife of John H., born November 25, 1854, died October 31, 1871
Merritt, Richard S., Sr., born September 12, 1837, died September 2, 1866
Merritt, Susie E. (mother), died March 15, 1930; age, 79 years
Merritt, Richard S. (father), born 1856, died 19—
McCandless, James K., born February 14, 1837, died March 20, 1911
McCandless, Agnes T., born November 13, 1841, died January 7, 1916
Moore, J. H., born November 24, 1838, died 1928
Moore, Simara A., born August 20, 1840, died September 17, 1879
Moore, Angelind P., born May 5, 1838, died July 3, 1903
Moore, Mary E., wife of J. N., born 1841, died 1924
Moore, infant son of J. N. and S. A., died September 13, 1879
Moore, infant son of J. N. and S. A., died March 19, 1877
Moore, infant son of J. N. and S. A., died August 27, 1876
Moore, Henry W., died May 13, 1920; age, 52 years, 10 months, 9 days
Pancake, Burton P., born July 30, 1849, died February 20, 1921
Rust, Catherine, wife of W. M., died July 12, 1887; age, 62 years, 4 months, 7 days
Rust, W. M., born January 31, 1821, died July 30, 1891
Rust, James S. W., died February 2, 1843; age, 1 month, 14 days
Rust, Louisa M., died November 7, 1871; age, 10 years, 6 months, 1 day
Rust, Andrew, died November 3, 1871; age, 16 years, 8 months, 6 days
S——, Rev. T. J. (last name not visible), born August 7, 1844, died November 7, 1871
Sheppard, Louisa E., wife of A. S., and daughter of James Dealy DCD, died January 29, 1873; age, 26 years, 26 days
Sheppard, Albert S., son of A. S. and L. E., born December 11, 1870, died March 21, 1871
Sheppard, Sarah Ellen, wife of A. S., died November 29, 1890; age, 41 years
Sheppard, Elma G., born February 20, 1873, died November 18, 1873; daughter of A. S. and Sarah E.
Sheppard, Chester A., son of A. S. and Sarah E., born December 1, 1882, died March 1, 1883
Smallwood, M., born July 30, 1839, died April, 1852
Smallwood, Geo. W., born July 17, 1841, died April 25, 1852
Stokes, Sarah A., wife of L. P. Stokes, born October 26, 1818, died March 23, 1904
Stokes, L. P., born October 18, 1812, died August 3, 1901
Workman, Hugh, died June 19, 1900; age, 71 years, 4 months, 2 days
Workman, Mary E., died June 27, 1912; age, 87 years, 1 day

Copied April 19, 1933, by Mrs. C. M. Uhlig

ALLEY CEMETERY
NE Quarter Section 34, Township 48, Range 30 W

Alley, F. M. (father), born April 8, 1838, died October 4, 1921
Alley, Mary F. (mother), born February 12, 1844, died July 27, 1916
Alley, Major H., died January 14, 1884; age, 66 years, 11 months, 27 days
Alley, Elizabeth, wife of M. H. Alley
Alley, Sarah D., daughter of M. H. and E. Alley, died October 2, 1855; age, 1 year, 2 months, 6 days
Alley, George W. (father), born 1845, died 1928
Alley, Sarah E., born 1866, died 1929 (mother)
Alley, Marion E., son of F. M. and M. E. Alley, died January 12, 1885; age, 2 years, 3 months, 2 days
Brizzendine, Samanthia A., wife of J. J. Brizzendine, died September 17, 1877; age, 18 years, 6 months, 4 days
Brizzendine, James W., son of J. J. and S. A. Brizzendine, died September 20, 1877; age, 3 days

ABANDONED CEMETERY ON FARM OWNED BY MR. J. H. PHILLIPS, LONE JACK, MISSOURI
Section 32, Township 47, Range 29 W

The following information is supplied by Mr. Phillips regarding the cemetery on his farm; there being no markers and the descendants seemingly not interested in its care and preservation, it has been converted into a corn field.

The following burials are known by Mr. Phillips to have taken place:

Mrs. Hopper, died 1855 (remaining members of her family moved to California)
Mr. James, first school teacher of Mr. J. H. Phillips' father (Mr. J. H. Phillips was born in 1855)
Mr. Jesse Riding's mother, maiden name Bradley

Mr. R. W. Pilcher supplied the following pertaining to members of the Pilcher family who were also buried in this cemetery:

Daniel Pilcher, buried on Phillips' farm in 1848; age, 40 or 50 years
Isaac Pilcher and James Pilcher, buried in 1847 or 1848; ages, 10 or 12 years

CONFEDERATE CEMETERY
On the farm of Mr. J. H. Phillips
Section 32, Township 47, Range 29 W

John D. Hunter, born September 28, 1831, died September 6, 1863
Andrew W. Owsley, died September 6, 1863; age, 17 years
Benjamin Potter, born May 17, 1788, died September 6, 1863
John G. Cave, born September 18, 1809, died September 6, 1863
William J. Hunter, died September 6, 1863; age, 48 years
William C. Tate, born January 23, 1831, died September 6, 1863

CUMMINGS CEMETERY
On farm entered from Government by Fleming Harris
NW Quarter Section 27, Township 48, Range 30 W

Martha Ann, wife of G. W. Alley, born July 28, 1849, died December 21, 1872 (daughter of Fleming Harris)
One Confederate soldier (name unknown) who was harboured in the home of Mr. Fleming Harris and died there

THE GOSNEY CEMETERY
Section 35, Township 48, Range 30 W

Gosney, W. W., husband of S. A. Gosney, born January 7, 1812
Gosney, S. A., wife of W. W. Gosney, born February 14, 1814, died August 14, 1883
Gosney, J. T., born 1856, died 1917
Benard, William R., died April 28, 1930; age, 66 years, 3 months, 24 days

HARE CEMETERY
NW Quarter Section 33, Township 47, Range 30 W

This is reputed to have been a cemetery of fair size, but no burials have been made here since the Civil War. A recently constructed road runs through the cemetery. The only markers at graves were those of the Hare family. These were removed to Pleasant Hill Cemetery in Cass County, Missouri.

HOLINESS CEMETERY
SE Quarter Section 29, Township 48, Range 29 W

Cline, Harry, born April 14, 1842
Cline, Margaret Z., wife of Harry Cline, born October 24, 1837, died May 12, 1903
Davis, Christopher Columbus, born 1847, died 1895
Davis, S. F., born 1845, died 1914
Davis, Henry C., born May 21, 1854
Davis, Margaret, wife of Henry C. Davis, born June 14, 1852, died January 27, 1917
Frankenberry, Sarah E., died April 1, 1932; age, 84 years, 8 months, 29 days
Frankenberry, James, died February 2, ——; age, 76 years, 6 months
Gilchrist, John H., born 1842, died 1914
Gilchrist, Phiniah, wife of John H. Gilchrist, born 1847, died 1917
Hayden, J. P., born February 20, 1840
Hayden, Martha S., wife of J. P. Hayden, born November 3, 1848, died May 29, 1914
Hutchens, Benjamin F., born August 3, 1836, died April 24, 1909
Hutchens, Martha E., born February 2, 1839, died May 3, 1910
Hutchens, Joe N., born 1839, died 1916, husband of Lucy A.
Keller, Janie, wife of Isaac Keller, died January 27, 1899; age, 56 years, 11 months
Keller, George T., born 1849
Keller, Louise E., wife of George T. Keller, born 1854, died 1932
Keller, J. H., born January 25, 1853, died March 25, 1920
Landon, Arthur S., born 1846, died 1929
Paddock, Jeremiah, born August 24, 1847, died August 16, 1915
Paddock, Martha J., born July 29, 1850, died September 28, 1927 (wife of Jeremiah Paddock)
Phillips, William Clark, died March 2, 1930; age, 92 years
Shore, Elizabeth L., born 1831, died 1914
Zimmerman, John, born August 28, 1848, died June 1, 1918 (Flag on grave)

CEMETERY ON THE HUTT FARM
Formerly known as the Alexander Farm
Section 35, Township 47, Range 29 W

Families by the names of Alexander, Crisp and Graham were buried here. The tombstones have been removed from the original site and only two are in such condition that the inscriptions can be read:

Crisp, Ruth, wife of Reddin Crisp, died December 7, 1852; age, 69 years
Graham, Daniel, died September 13, 1858; age, 64 years
   Other burials:
   (The following data was supplied by Mrs. Luther Rowland, Cockrell, Mo., a granddaughter of Daniel Graham.)
Graham, Celey, wife of Daniel Graham
Crisp, Reddin
Edmonston, Mary and Martha (twins)
   N. B. The Edmonstons were related to the Grahams, Celey Graham was thought to be a sister of Reddin Crisp.

KOGER CEMETERY
SE Quarter Section 23, Township 47, Range 30 W
Copied July 28, 1933, by Mrs. Hale Houts, Miss Julia Kinney and Miss Ethel Merwin

Basham, Elizabeth, wife of Benjamin Basham, died September 11, 1880; age, 56 years
Basham, Lydia A., wife of G. E. Basham, born October 4, 1838, died November 2, 1902
Bault, Thomas, died December 12, 1884; age, 44 years, 10 months, 11 days
Barnard, Charity J., wife of G. Barnard, died April 17, 1895; age, 63 years, 27 days
Barnard, Greenbury, died November 25, 1876; age, 50 years, 11 months
Deemer, Elizabeth, wife of George Deemer, born 1833, died March 18, 1902
Dyer, Mary A., wife of G. W. Dyer, died January 25, 1890; age, 74 years, 4 months, 10 days
Dyer, Mary C., wife of D. P. Dyer, died January 30, 1888; age, 47 years, 7 months, 2 days
Dyer, Lee, son of D. P. and M. C. Dyer, born 1875, died 1892
Gregg, Nancy, wife of Jacob Gregg, born July 2, 1806, died December 29, 1885
Glauder,—(given name nor dates)
Harris, F. S., died November 19, 1885; age, 63 years, 8 months, 27 days
Harris, Mary, wife of F. S. Harris, died February 21, 1894; age, 66 years, 7 months, 29 days
Huffman, Matilda A., born May 30, 1850, died September 2, 1918
Johnson, E. R., born March 16, 1840, died April 24, 1905
Koger, Jacob, born February 22, 1788, died December 12, 1851 (?) (stone broken)
Koger, Sinai, wife of J. Koger, died July 14, 1878; age, 74 years, 4 months, 27 days
Koger, J. P., born October 28, 18—, stone broken, died November 27, 1847
Koger, Martha E., born November 12, 1829, died December 28, 1848
Koger, Henry E., born April 14, 1832, died January 13, 1857
Lynch, Elijah, born July 24, 1829, died January 13, 1857
Lynch, Miranda A., wife of Elijah, born November 18, 1836, died October 22, 1923
Marble, Ephram K., son of F. M. and E. J. Marble, died September 9, 1869; age, 11 months, 2 days
Marble, Lydia A. L., daughter of F. M. and E. J. Marble, died September 6, 1875
Russell, Elijah, born 1836, died 1868
Russell, Samuel, born 1859
Russell, Ruey, wife of Samuel Russell, born 1858, died 1917
Russell, Mary, wife of James Russell, born December 4, 1858, died August 3, 1909
Russell, James, born April 5, 1855, died January 1-, 1916
Russell, Tipton, died March 14, 1886; age, 53 years, 1 month, 3 days
Russell, Roda, wife of Tipton Russell, died July 25, 1877; age, 35 years, 5 days
Russell, J. C., died May 10, 1879; age, 70 years
Russell, Charlotte, wife of J. C. Russell, born March 31, 1812, died February, 1893
Russell, Enoch O., born February 15, 1833, died September 23, 1876
Ryan, Mary, born September 24, 1835, died October 22, 1896; age, 61 years, 21 days
Rine, —— W., born June 6, 1836, died November 9, 1882

Raines, Nancy Jane, wife of David Raines, born November 1, 1862, died April 8, 1883
Selvey, Sarah J., wife of M. N. Selvey, born July 26, 1839, died April 6, 1879
Schoonover, George W., died January 3, 1878
Schoonover, Alice, wife of George W. Schoonover, born Jan. 17, 1836, died March 16, 1916
Thurman, Martha S., wife of R. Thurman, born February 4, 1819, died June 9, 1859
Thurman, Richard, born December 25, 1810, died September 20, 1868
Thurman, James H., born March 18, 1801, died December 5, 1875
Warren, Benjamin, died August 11, 1888; age, 85 years
Warren, Lucinda, wife of Benjamin, died July 7, 1877; age, 69 years
Warren, Zachariah, born March 2, 1829, died May 8, 1900
Warren, Nancy T., wife of Zachariah Warren, born October 11, 1829, died July 2, 1907
Wood, Sarah M. E., wife of R. D. Wood, died Sept. 1, 1869; age, 31 years, 4 months, 4 days

LONE JACK CEMETERY

SE Quarter Section ———, Township 47, Range 29

Extracts from a newspaper clipping, written in 1903 by Elizabeth Jackson giving the history and containing an appeal to the public for the care and maintenance of this cemetery. Clipping supplied by Mrs. Frank Cave, Lone Jack, Missouri.

"A short distance east of our town there is a city whose inhabitants number nearly three thousand. But despite this large population, in this city no anvils clang, no engines throb, no hammers ring. There is no strife nor envy, nor sweat, nor worry, for here no anger is carried, no sorrow grieves and there is no need of wealth. There are no courts or juries here for its citizens are beyond the reach of earthly law. No church bells ring—for these have solved the secrets which to us are mysteries. All here are in peace for there is neither nationality, rank nor creed.

This city has a history. While the state was yet young and Van Buren Township almost a wilderness there was an immigration from the eastern states, mostly North Carolina and Tennessee. Among these settlers was one James Snow, whose descendants still live among us. Into this family the grim reaper of death appeared and took from them their little daughter, Bettie Snow, aged four years. A place of burial was selected on the prairie near the summit of the divide between the waters of the Osage and the Sni on land belonging to the little girl's uncle, John Snow, father of Stephen I. Snow, and the writer's great grandfather. In this beautiful spot overlooking many a settler's cabin and a new plantation was builded the first house of the Silent City. (Bettie Snow died June 20, 1837.)

Soon after this death, Sophia, the seven-year-old daughter of John Wright was burned to death by her clothes catching fire from the fire place in the home of her sister, Mrs. Martha Faulkenberry, mother of John, Thomas, James and Frank Faulkenberry, and of Mrs. C. B. Snow, all of whom live near this place. And thus a second grave was made on the ridge of the great divide. Other settlers came from the east, loved ones died and were laid to rest on this sun kissed spot. And so the Silent City grew and is still growing even to this day."

The following names and dates copied from tombstones:
Adams, Mary A., wife of W. H. Adams, born August 21, 1840, died September 10, 1896
Arnold Andrew J., born 1837, died 1913
Arnold, Elizabeth, wife of Andrew J. Arnold, born 1841, died 1914

CEMETERIES--VAN BUREN TOWNSHIP

Ball, Nicholas, born March 6, 1855, died September, 1870
Ball, William, died February 6, 1852, in the 36th year of his age
Ball, Joseph, born January 10, 1843, died September 10, 1917
Ball, Mrs. Ellen, died April 18, 1932; age, 93 years, 8 months
Ball, William, born 1849, died 1924
Baity, Isaac W., son of T. and M. A. Baity, died April 11, 1853; age, 5 years, 1 month, 2 days
Baity, Thomas, died June 11, 1857; age, 43 years, 8 months, 11 days
Bailey, Moses E. (father), born December 25, 1814, died May 1, 1897
Bailey, Mahala, wife of Moses Bailey, born May 6, 1818, died January 19, 1868
Bailey, Oscar, born February 20, 1845, died November 11, 1890
Bays, John H., son of Joshua and Mary T. Bays, died March 30, 1848; age, 1 year, 4 months, 22 days
Benton, Mary, wife of C. L. Benton, born in Madison County, Kentucky, November 11, 1818, died December 22, 1869
Benton, Unity K., wife of Thomas B. Benton, born February 4, 1833, died July 27, 1870; age, 37 years, 5 months, 23 days
Bennett, Jacob, born 1833, died 1912
Bennett, Ella, wife of Jacob Bennett, born 1856
Bennett, Elizabeth, wife of J. Bennett, died November 16, 1874; age, 44 years, 16 days
Bennet, Mary F., daughter of John and Sarah Ann Bennett, born December 18, 1853, died October 20, 1855
Bays, Sarah E., daughter of Joshua and Mary T. Bays, died April 11, 1848; age, 3 years, 10 months, 21 days
Bissell, Margaretta, wife of Jas. E. Bissell, died June 24, 1874; age, 29 years, 3 months, 29 days
Bunton, Frank, son of Dr. T. L. and M. E. Bunton, died July 27, 1861; age, 1 year
Bunton, Bettie, daughter of Dr. T. B. and M. E. Bunton, died July 7, 1860; age, 3 months, 8 days
Burns, John W., born February 28, 1844, died September 4, 1914
Burns, Elizabeth Worline, wife of John W. Burns, born May 30, 1855, died July 16, 1916
Burns, Delia E., wife of Thomas Burns, born November 3, 1820, died March 16, 1891
Burns, Thomas, born July 24, 1816, died February 19, 1872; age, 56 years
Bynum, Galen G., died March 19, 1875; age, 25 years, 6 months, 11 days
Bynum, ―― 1846; age, 58 years (stone broken)
Bynum, John B., born July 17, 1822, died June 20, 1892
Bynum, Robert A., born March 24, 1846, died March 18, 1893

Cantrell, C. C., born March 10, 1818, died March 5, 1897
Cantrell, Narsises, wife of C. Cantrell, died August 19, 1881; age, 69 years, 3 months, 13 days
Carmean, Cordie M., daughter of J. W. and E. J. Carmean, died October 21, 1883; age, 2 years, 3 days
Carr, Martha C., wife of A. Karr, born April 29, 1829, died November 13, 1904
Cave, Nancy, wife of J. K. Cave, born June 6, 1819, died December 15, 1905
Cave, Lucinda, born 1832, died September 23, 1862; age, about 30 years
Cave, Phenellar H., born September 29, 1859, died 1863; age, 3 years, 6 months
Cave, Malinda B., daughter of B. B. and Lucinda Cave, born August 1, 1885, died March 26, 1858
Cave, Susanah, died April 17, 1892; age, 87 years, 17 days
Cave, Galen, died June 23, 1851; age, 50 years, 8 months, 8 days
Cave, William, died November 21, 1861; age, 31 years, 7 months, 25 days
Cave, Nancy E. (mother), born 1834, died 1919; wife of William Cave
Chamberlin, James H., son of A. and L. Chamberlin, died August 16, 1850; age, 2 years
Chism, Nancy, wife of J. G. Chism, born December 7, 1828, died October 26, 1907
Cline, Edgar, son of H. and M. Z. Cline, died September 11, 1872; age, 19 days
Cobbs, William E., son of R. B. and G. J. Cobbs, born April 13, 1852, died September 7, 1876
Cobbs, Albert L., son of R. B. and G. J. Cobbs, died December 11, 1849, died August 23, 1876

Cox, James H., died June 15, 1831, died October 19, 1861
Cox, Martha A., daughter of J. H. and E. Cox, died August 15, 1870; age, 15 years, 5 months, 23 days
Colbert, George, born October 11, 1820, died July 7, 1878
Colbert, Mary Katherine, born May 5, 1849, died September 14, 1859
Colbert, Eunice, wife of George Colbert, born December 1, 1825, died July 26, 1905
Cottier, Mary, wife of James Cottier, born January 16, 1844, died September 15, 1870
Cox, Jeremiah W., born 1832, died 1867
Cox, Mary F., wife of Jeremiah Cox, born 1839, died 1925
Cox, Corlena A., born 1860, died 1862
Cox, Lula B., born 1863, died 1863
Cravens, Robert F., born March 13, 1841, died April 27, 1898
Crocker, John H., born October 2, 1832, died June 4, 1905
Crocker, Nancy, wife of John H. Crocker, born 1837, died 1925

Daniel, Rachel (mother), born July 18, 1824, died August 27, 1890; age, 65 years, 1 month, 9 days
Davis, William (father), born May 16, 1819, died June 16, 1900
Davis, Nancy Winfrey (mother), born April 11, 1818, died April 28, 1892
Davis, John S., born June 28, 1844, died September 15, 1925
Davis, Sarah, first wife of John S. Davis, born October 9, 1852, died April 11, 1925
Dedman, William, born September 18, 1824, died April 12, 1881
Dimmitt, Miles (father), born September 17, 1815, died July 18, 1890
Dimmitt, Matilda West, wife of Miles Dimmitt, born in Bracken County, Kentucky, December 19, 1819, died in Lafayette County, Missouri, September 27, 1876
Dimmitt, Calvin M. (father), born 1841, died 1917; Co. "H" 7th Tenn. MTP. Inf.
Dimmitt, Nancy L. (mother), born 1840, died 1930
Doak, William G., son of John N. and Emily Boak, died March 23, 1842; age, 3 months, 11 days
Doub, Elizabeth, wife of John W. Doub, died May 27, 1871; age, 44 years, 4 months, 19 days

Easley, Warham, died November 16, 1874; age, 78 years, 3 months, 19 days
Easley, Sarah, wife of Warham Easley, born December 7, 1803, died December 23, 1887
Easley, Charles, son of Warham and Sarah Easley, died December 6, 1855; age, 22 years, 9 months, 2 days
Easley, John Rowland, son of Warham and Sarah Easley, died June 22, 1849; age, 1 year, 10 months
Easley, Susannah F., daughter of Warham and Sarah Easley, died January 26, 1848; age, 4 years, 11 days
Easley, Milton F., son of R. C. and Susanah Easley, died January 15, 1849; age, 2 years, 10 months, 28 days
Easley, James, son of Warham and Elizabeth Easley, died October 19, 1848; age, 3 months, 11 days
Easley, J. W., born October 18, 1834, died May 5, 1905
Easley, wife of J. W. (no name), born September 23, 1834, died February 21, 1888
Easley, James G., born December 1, 1829, died April 26, 1881
Easley, Laura B., born January 20, 1886, died December 28, 1897
Easley, Miller W., born October 22, 1800, died April 17, 1868
Easley, America, born April 16, 1818, died December 30, 1878
Easley, James O., son of Miller and America Easley, died November 24, 1847; age, 9 months, 16 days
Easley, Sarah, Consort of William Easley, died September 6, 1848; age, 85 years, 5 months, 25 days
Easley, Charles S., born October 30, 1807, died September 30, 1879
Easley, Lucinda, wife of C. S. Easley, born September 19, 1815, died August 9, 1893

CEMETERIES—VAN BUREN TOWNSHIP

Faulkenberry, Mary, wife of W. Faulkenberry (stone very old and dates indistinct)
Faulkenberry, Nancy E., daughter of J. D. and M. J. Faulkenberry, died February 12, 1863; age, 10 months, 9 days
Faulkenberry, William D., son of J. D. and M. J. Faulkenberry, died August 16, 1877; age, 13 years, 19 days
Faulkenberry, J. C., born July 11, 1835, died July 23, 1911
Faulkenberry, Margaret, born May 24, 1841, died March 6, 1914
Faulkenberry, Thomas A. J., born December 20, 1844, died June 7, 1912
Faulkenberry, Mary J., wife of Thomas A. J. Faulkenberry, born June 2, 1840, died May 13, 1896
Faulkenberry, Martha S., wife of Thomas P. Faulkenberry, born June 30, 1817, died August 14, 1895
Faulkenberry, J. D., born December 7, 1837, died January 1, 1899
Faulkenberry, M. J., wife of J. D. Faulkenberry, born Nov. 22, 1844, died March 17, 1920
Fish, Elnra A., wife of J. H. Fish, born November 14, 1838, died January 7, 1878
Franklin, Ann, wife of John Franklin, died March 30, 1873; age, 69 years, 9 months, 25 days
Franklin, Maggie E., died July 21, 1898; age, 62 years, 7 months, 4 days
Franklin, Henry H., died March 17, 1874; age, 28 years, 9 months, 4 days
Franklin, Mary Cleveland, born August 10, 1830, died August 16, 1914
Franklin, Susan Elizabeth, born December 29, 1835, died February 3, 1924
Franklin, James W., born May 14, 1839, died February 15, 1899
Franklin, Letitia V., wife of James W. Franklin, born Dec. 17, 1839, died Nov. 25, 1913
Frost, L. B. A., daughter of J. E. and N. Frost, died September 17, 1869; age, 1 year, 4 months, 17 days
Frizzell, Lucetta S., wife of J. P. Frizzell, born April 27, 1836, died July 14, 1919
Frizzell, J. P., born March 6, 1829, died August 13, 1891

Gibson, Washington P., born August 10, 1825, died March 25, 1899
Gibson, Susan E., daughter of W. P. and Elizabeth Gibson, born July 11, 1857, died October 19, 1902
Golding, Eliza J., wife of William Golding, died April 27, 1876
Golding, Thomas, son of J. and M. Golding, born October 15, 1836, died 1885

Haden, Jacob, born in Fayette County, Penn., May 18, 1785, died October 24, 1874
Haddix, William R., born 1830, died 1915
Haddix, Matilda, wife of William Haddix, born 1840, died 1910
Harman, Julia A., wife of William Harman, born December 7, 1851, died December 4, 1888
Hayden, Stephen W., son of J. and R. Hayden, born August 25, 1829, died December 31, 1875
Hayden, Virginia G., born December 4, 1844, died June 4, 1908
Hayden, W. T., born October 12, 1835 (death dates not legible)
Hayden, Hellen E., daughter of A. M. and L. E. Hayden, born August, 1871, died 1873
Helmig, Charles, born 1837, died 1925
Helmig, Lizzie, wife of Charles Helmig, born 1850
Hininger, John, born February 6, 1841, died November 11, 1911
Hininger, Elizabeth, wife of John Hininger, born February 4, 1843, died August 7, 1914
Horn, T. M., died July 10, 1884; age, 26 years, 10 months, 19 days
How, Edward, son of S. S. and T. A. How, born June, 1860, died July, 1860
Hopper, J. P. M., died November 26, 1876; age, 26 years, 6 months, 3 days
Humphreys, William, son of Ashery and Elizabeth Humphreys, died October 7, 1857; age, 7 months, 17 days
Hunt, Nathan G., born May 17, 1802, died October 22, 1872
Hunt, Mary, wife of Nathan Hunt, born October 4, 1799, died September 3, 1872
Hunt, Enoch F., born October 9, 1852, died May 10, 1884
Hunt, Noah (father), born February 20, 1831, died November 22, 1906
Hunt, Nancy E., wife of Noah Hunt, born April, 1838, died March 7, 1879
Hunt, Mary Elizabeth, wife of Noah Hunt, born May 25, 1834, died November 29, 1921
Hunt, Benjamin T., born 1838, died 1912

Hunt, Noah A., son of F. M. and S. Hunt, died May 11, 1877; age, 6 years
Hunt, infant son of F. M. and S. Hunt, died October 29, 1867
Hunt, Frances W., died July 19, 1871; age, 29 years
Hunt, John Buford, born April 29, 1859, died February 26, 1917
Hunt, Virginia Lee, daughter of Noah and Nancy E. Hunt, died November 13, 1850; age, 19 months, 6 days
Hunt, Sarah J., wife of F. M. Hunt, died May 22, 1905; age, 72 years, 3 days
Hunt, Charles T., son of N. and M. J. Hunt, died September 2, 1891; age, 18 years, 11 months, 1 day
Hunt, Bertie S., daughter of N. and M. J. Hunt, died September 1, 1892; age, 17 years, 7 months, 18 days
Hunt, Martha J., wife of N. Hunt, died December 14, 1891; age, 46 years, 7 months, 19 days
Hunt, Nathan, died April 4, 1908; age, 75 years, 8 months, 11 days
Hunt, J. M., died October 24, 1857; age, 23 years, 11 months, 2 days
Hunt, G. C., son of Noah and N. E. Hunt, died November 3, 1857; age, 3 years, 17 days
Hunt, Melvina E., wife of B. F. Hunt, born November 14, 1842, died August 22, 1865
How, Samuel S., born February 2, 1819, died November 3, 1880
Hunter, John, born March 16, 1789, died September 5, 1886
Hunter, Elizabeth, wife of John Hunter, born May 14, 1892, died October 25, 1878
Huninger, Franklin, son of J. and C. E. Huninger, died April 21, 1879; age, 10 years, 18 days
Hutchens, Nicholas, born April 22, 1812, died February 7, 1901
Hutchens, Margaret, wife of N. H. Hutchens, born March 18, 1812, died June 1, 1881; age, 69 years, 13 days
Hutchens, William D., born 1838, died 1918
Hutchens, Rebecca M., born 1849, died 1930
Hutchens, Charles T., born 1848, died 1914
Hutchens, Charity J., wife of Charles T. Hutchens, born 1848, died 1930
Hutchens, Elizabeth, wife of O. James Hutchens, died July, 1850; age, 24 years, 7 months

Jackson, Mary J., born 1846, died 1886
Johnson, Annie M., wife of T. T. Johnson, born December 28, 1844, died February 12, 1908
Jones, Lucy M., daughter of L. L. and S. F. Jones, born May 29, 1869, died August 1, 1869

Kinman, Nathan, born January 29, 1819, died May 25, 1898

Lester, Nannie E., wife of M. J. Lester, born August 8, 1855, died December 25, 1880; age, 25 years, 4 months, 17 days
Lester, Joseph U., born August 7, 1838, died April 27, 1902
Lester, J. S., died September 29, 1893; age, 47 years, 7 months, 9 days
Lester, Jimmie H., son of J. S. and S. F. Lester, died September 19, 1880; age, 12 years, 2 months, 8 days
Long, Henry, son of J. M. and E. J. Long, died October 2, 1871 (stone so sunken that remaining inscription cannot be read)
Long, Fred (father), born September 18, 1836, died July 30, 1905
Long, Lafayette, son of F. and E. Long, born September 28, 1858, died November 11, 1888
Long, Elizabeth, wife of E. Long, born June 3, 1832, died November 2, 1886
Long, Sarah, born October 5, 1823, died April 28, 1886
Long, Henry, died September 4, 1889; age, 86 years, 4 months, 26 days
Long, Mary, wife of Anderson Long, born 1840, died 1916
Long, Anderson (father), born August 20, 1825, died May 14, 1912
Long, Delia A., wife of Anderson Long, born September 24, 1838, died July 18, 1875
Lightfoot, Elkin D., born February 5, 1836, died November 28, 1893
Lightfoot, Sarah M., wife of Elkin D. Lightfoot, born July 13, 1842, died March 13, 1911

Martin, Sallie James, daughter of J. O. and S. Martin, died September 7, 1861
Martin, James C. (father), born May 24, 1815, died April 18, 1857
Martin, Sarah T., wife of J. C. Martin, born March 22, 1828, died March 7, 1908
Maxwell, John, died October 31, 1874; age, 22 years, 6 months

Maxwell, Oliver J., born November 22, 1818, died February 8, 1862
Mertins, Charles H., born in Germany, January 27, 1832, died June 6, 1895
Mullins, Moses, born September 14, 1814, died November 26, 1868
Mullins, Julia A., born October 21, 1821, died May 24, 1907
Martin, Benjamin E., son of J. O. and S., died December 25, 1864; age, 7 months
Maxwell, Margaret E., died December 6, 1874; age, 49 years, 5 months, 27 days
Myers, William H., born July 4, 1853, died October 12, 1858

McKnight, Lucinda, wife of R. B. McKnight, died July 17, 1847; age, 33 years, 9 months, 3 days
McKnight, Elizabeth, daughter of R. B. and Jane McKnight, died July 24, 1857

Nicholas, Frank, son of Dr. J. F. and J. M. Nicholas, died February 20, 1877; age, 6 months, 18 days
Nichols, Matilda, born September 17, 1805, died August 18, 1875; age, 69 years

Oldham, J. S., died October 8, 1876; age, 54 years, 2 months

Payne, Robert R., son of A. M. and M. E. Payne, born August 13, 1870, died January 6, 1873
Payne, George L., died May 9, 1873; age, 81 years, 3 months, 27 days
Payne, Letticia F., daughter of H. H. and S. Payne, died December 22, 1865; age, 20 years, 10 months, 13 days
Payne, Henry H., died September 4, 1873; age, 86 years, 2 months, 17 days
Perrow, Daniel B., born September 21, 1829, died September 9, 1880 (Masonic Emblem)
Potter, John, born March 12, 1840, died April 10, 1889 (Flag at grave)
Potter, Robert P., died August 30, 1876; age, 27 years, 10 months, 24 days
Potter, Catherine J., wife of R. P. Potter, born August 5, 1857, died December 4, 1900
Powell, Alvis, born October 6, 1824, died August 30, 1912
Powell, Sarah Frances Hunt, born March 13, 1835, died December 16, 1872
Powell, Lily Bell, born September 20, 1855, died January 11, 1875
Powell, Charles Absalom, born January 7, 1867, died March 17, 1869

Ragsdale, Thomas, born March 25, 1832, died May 2, 1911
Ragsdale, Parthenia Ann, born January 11, 1842, died April 13, 1920
Ragsdale, William, born September 3, 1823, died October 21, 1905
Ragsdale, Mary Ann, wife of William Ragsdale, born March 1, 1835, died April 6, 1921
Ragsdale, Edward, born July 30, 1836, died July 23, 1915
Ragsdale, Virginia W., born 1844, died 1917
Ragsdale, Daniel, born November 15, 1833, died May 6, 1895
Ragsdale, Maggie A., daughter of D. and M. Ragsdale, died 1876
Ragsdale, Elizabeth E., born 1841, died 1875
Ravenscraft, Patsy, born January 30, 1803, died November 15, 1898; age, 87 years, 9 months, 15 days
Renard, died September 23, 1851; age, 75 years, 8 months
Ridings, Laura E. (mother), born May 30, 1848, died June 27, 1931
Rhodes, William, born October 5, 1797, died August 3, 1851
Rhodes, B. M., dates gone
Rhodes, Lewis F., born November 2, 1838, died March 26, 1918
Rhodes, Julia A., wife of L. F. Rhodes, born February 23, 1848, died October 27, 1901
Rhodes, John U., born May 12, 1832, died April 18, 1881
Rhodes, Elenor, born April 10, 1810, died April 21, 1895
Rhodes, A. M., died March 7, 1862 (stone broken)
Rowland, Bluford M., born November 4, 1824, died December 10, 1907
Rowland, Nancy, wife of Bluford M. Rowland, born May 31, 1831, died January 18, 1920
Rich, Eliza M., wife of —— Rich, died November 26, 1870; age, 23 years
Rumbaugh, John M., born 1849, died 1929
Rumbaugh, Estella, wife of John M. Rumbaugh, born 1870, died 1930
Russel, Mary Ellen, daughter of J. E. and M. A. Russel, died 1859 (stone so worn that other dates impossible to read)

Shawhan, William, born December, 1832, died August 21, 1905
Shawhan, Eliza A., wife of William Shawhan, born August 31, 1844, died December 14, 1904
Shawhan, John T., husband of J. P. Shawhan, born Sept. 25, 1847, died Feb. 26, 1891
Shawhan, Minerva (mother), born May 15, 1807, died August 21, 1890; age, 88 years, 3 months, 6 days
Simpson, Abbegill, daughter of Alfred and Rebecca Simpson, born November 6, 1866, died September 13, 1867
Smith, Thomas G., born December 1, 1828, died October 22, 1899
Smith, Francis, born December 4, 1832, died January 3, 1908
Smith, Noah H., born February 2, 1860, died March 27, 1888
Smith, Nancy, died August 21, 1878; age, 60 years (stone broken and part of inscription gone)
Smith, Charles, died October 16, 1879 (stone very worn)
Smith, Thomas, born June 1, 1918, died October 22, 1902
Smith, Frances T., wife of Thomas Smith, born August 20, 1824 (no date of death)
Spainhouer, Elizah, died April 16, 1869; age, 64 years, 7 months, 4 days
Spainhouer, Rebecca C., wife of E. Spainhouer, died October 13, 1862; age, 60 years, 2 days
Spainhouer, William H., born March 22, 1836, died April 10, 1918
Spainhouer, Elizabeth, wife of William H. Spainhouer, born January 8, 1832, died March 26, 1918
Smyth, Andre W., died October 20, 1846; age, 62 years, 2 months, 22 days (stone very old)
Snow, Frances, born December 14, 1793, died September 22, 1859
Snow, John, died June 23, 1851; age, 61 years, 3 months, 11 days
Snow, Elizabeth S., born 1825, died 1880
Snow, A. Lee, born 1822, died 1883
Snow, daughter of A. L. and Elizabeth Snow, died July 15, 1848
Snow, Charles E., son of John and Frances Snow, died December 5, 1858; age, 21 years
Staenaker, Thomas J., son of A. and M. C., died February 14, 1864; age, 9 months, 19 days
Staenaker, Nancy C., wife of Asher Staenaker, died December 7, 1874; age, 47 years, 3 months, 11 days
Staenaker, Asher, died September 21, 1879; age, 68 years, 2 months, 10 days
Steagall, Hattie N., wife of G. W. Steagall, died March 20, 1877; age, 23 years
Steagall, Luny, son of G. W. and H. N. Steagall, died September 3, 1873; age, 1 year, 1 month
Swinford, Samuel, born November, 1810, died June 23, 1854

Talbot, Frances, consort of Peter H. Talbot, and daughter of S. and P. Easley, died October 23, 1849; age, 19 years, 11 months, 3 days
Thomas, David, born May 4, 1816, died April 29, 1872
Thomas, Lewis H., born (no date), died March 22, 1883
Thomas, Isabell J., wife of D. T. Thomas, born April 2, 1829, died July 8, 1888
Thomas, Catherine E., born August 2, 1810, died February 14, 1898
Thomas, Thomas P., died July 29, 1873
Thomas, Benjamin, born January 20, 1805, died April 29, 1862
Thompson, William, born June 21, 1831, died September 1, 1919
Thompson, Elizabeth A., born July 5, 1840, died June 1, 1921
Tucker, Thomas B., born December 10, 1824, died January 8, 1908
Tucker, Martha A., born May 16, 1835, died July 17, 1926
Trundle, Nicholas A., died January 10, 1896; age, 77 years, 11 months
Trundle, Sarah A., died August 10, 1903; age, 67 years, 10 months

Weathebson, T. G., died September 22, 1876, in 34th year of his age
Williams, Thomas D., born October 2, 1824, died December 16, 1892
Williams, Robert M., born 1831, died 1916
Wilhite, Martha Elizabeth, died August 12, 1876; age, 30 years
Wilson, James H., born 1838, died 1905
Wilson, Malissa M., born 1854, died 1926
Williams, Lewis, husband of Nancy Williams, born December 9, 1809, died June 30, 1869

Williams, Nancy, wife of Lewis Williams, born March 21, 1813, died November 18, 1898
Winfrey, Isaac, died October 6, 1857; age, 28 years, 10 months, 16 days
Weaver, Lillet, daughter of Rev. A. and S. B. Weaver; age, 2 years, 3 months
Witherspoon, Lulie, born 1862, died 1890
Wright, John W., died June, 1849; age, 56 years, 6 months
Yankee, Sarah S., born January 5, 1827, died April 5, 1908

THE MARTIN CORN CEMETERY
SE Quarter Section 30, Township 48, Range 29 W

Corn, Martin, died August 5, 1894; age, 81 years, 2 months, 6 days
Corn, Martha, died October 14, 1909; age, 86 years, 7 months, 14 days
Corn, Martin L., son of S. H. and L. Corn, died May 28, 1837; age, 1 year, 3 months, 1 day
Corn, Joseph M., son of J. S. and R. Corn, died June 2, 1881; age, 10 days
Corn, G. E., son of G. W. and B. Corn, born February 5, 1892, died March 4, 1892
Corn, George M., son of S. W. and E. Corn, died December 4, 1891; age, 2 months, 12 days
Bradley, Mattie T., wife of Murphy Bradley, died April 1, 1895; age, 19 years
Branam, Martha A., wife of W. M. Branam, born November 6, 1854, died September 13, 1880

PERDUE CEMETERY
NW Quarter Section 35, Township 48, Range 30 W

Perdue, W. C., born September 7, 1847, died September 4, 1914
Perdue, Mark, born June 12, 1823, died April 19, 1900
Perdue, Dorcas, wife of Mark Perdue, died March 28, 1880; age, 57 years, 4 months, 29 days
Perdue, Luke, son of Mark and Dorcas Perdue, born July 12, 1842, died September, 1856
Perdue, Odly, daughter of W. T. and S. Smith, born Nov. 17, 1876, died Sept. 1, 1877

PLEASANT GARDEN CEMETERY
Also known as
THE RHEEMS CEMETERY, Lone Jack, Missouri
Section 25, Township 47, Range 29 W

Brewer, William, born March 3, 1820, died September 14, 1878
Butler, Mary E. Rice, wife of W. L. Butler, born May 6, 1841, died June 17, 1909
Butler, William L., Co. "C" Mo. Cav. (Gov. marker)

Carter, Edward, born May 18, 1797, died September 18, 1844
Carter, Sarah, born September 22, 1800, died February 5, 1850
Carter, Elizabeth, born October 21, 1825, died January 11, 1847
Carter, Isaac D., born April 17, 1823, died April 22, 1842

Daniel, Sarah, wife of J. K. Daniel, died 1849; age, 82 years
Daniel, J. K., died 1851; age, 86 years (parents of John Daniel)
Davis, Silas C., died May 31, 1849; age, 39 years
Davis, John, born September 5, 1815

Elmore, William, died April 30, 1877; age, 81 years

Gibbons, Roann, wife of W. H., died September, 1865; age, 29 years, 10 months, 5 days
Gibbons, Mary E., daughter of W. H. and R. Gibbons, died March 3, 1862; age, 1 year
Gibbons, John D., son of W. H. and R. Gibbons, died September 22, 1857; age, 11 months
Graham, Sarah J., wife of Emblers Graham, born July 17, 1839, died February 17, 1892
Griffin, John, died October 4, 1859; age, 78 years
Griffin, Mary A., wife of John Griffin, died September 14, 1875

Griffith, Walter O., died September 10, 1878; age, 57 years, 9 months
Griffith, George W., born January 29, 1827, died January 3, 1901
Hinshaw, Benjamin, died in 1849; age, 55 years
Hinshaw, Thomas, died February 6, 1847; age, 26 years
Keirsey, John, born July 23, 1829, died July 10, 1915
Keirsey, Elizabeth, wife of Drury Keirsey, died August 30, 1879; age, 75 years, 11 months
Keirsey, Drury, born 1784, died 1855
Kincaid, Samuel, died January 18, 1867; age, 76 years
Kincaid, Francis M., died June 29, 1868; age, 23 years
Kreeger, M. B. Aminta, wife of G. W. Kreeger, died July 4, 1875; age, 45 years, 2 days
Kreeger, Sallie, daughter of above, died December 16, 1875; age, 5 years, 3 months, 1 day

Lawrence, Elizabeth, wife of James Lawrence, died May, 1844
Lawrence, Josiah W., 2nd son of Elizabeth and James Lawrence, died September 6, 1845; age, 15 years, 10 months, 14 days
Lawrence, Thomas J., born October 16, 1840 (stone sunken in ground)

Miller, John, died January 16, 1849; age, 56 years, 5 months
Miller, James, died August 13, 1855; age, 36 years, 7 months, 14 days
Moutrey, J. D., born May 11, 1833, died July 28, 1908

Nixon, Emma M., died July 17, 1894; age, 28 years, 4 months, 1 day
Nixon, William, born November 8, 1817, died March 26, 1888
Nixon, Mary J., daughter of W. M. and Eveline E. Nixon, born January 26, 1852, died July 30, 1893
Noel, James, born November 3, 1808, died March 28, 1877
Noel, Louisa A., born October 28, 1835, died May, 1854
Noel, Alvis T., born June 12, 1837, died December 28, 1862
Noel, John P., born July 23, 1831, died January 16, 1852
Noel, Rachel (wife), born April 6, 1812, died August 17, 1893
Noel, Absalom M., born February 1, 1843, died June 25, 1851
Noel, Emmaline, born September 23, 1844, died June 7, 1849
Noel, Martha A., born June 25, 1849, died October 27, 1850

Perdue, Daniel G., born July 30, 1830, died October 9, 1915
Perdue, Icy G., wife of Daniel G. Perdue, born August 19, 1838, died September 20, 1905
Poindexter, Martha Ann, daughter of T. M. and M. A. Poindexter, died September 18, 1846; age, 5 years
Poindexter, son of T. M. and M. A. Poindexter, died September 7, 1846; age, 3 years
Powell, Oliver, born February, 1840, died October 4, 1862
Powell, Elizabeth, born 1800, died 1856
Powell, Absalom, born March 27, 1803, died April 28, 1851

Rheem, Daniel, born 1806, died March 19, 1878
Rheem, Sarah, born 1811, died March 14, 1876
Rice, Enoch, died July 25, 1851; age, 60 years
Rice, Mary, wife of Enoch Rice, born March 16, 1792, died March 11, 1881
    (Mary, wife of Enoch Rice and mother of Marten Rice, the poet)
Rice, James A., died November 13, 1851; age, 25 years
Rice, Marten, died December 5, 1903; age, 89 years
Rice, Mary, wife of Marten Rice, died December 11, 1855; age, 35 years
Rice, Fendel T., son of Charles and Sally Rice, died February 25, 1848; age, 18 years
Rice, Sally, wife of Charles Rice, died January 15, 1848; age, 43 years

Tate, Martha J., wife of William C. Tate, born February 11, 1838, died January 4, 1870
Tucker, James H., born 1786, died July 9, 1843; age, 57 years

Vestal, Rebekah, died August 18, 1845; age, 18 years, 10 months

Watts, Nancy J., born September 15, 1833, died March 21, 1897

CEMETERIES—VAN BUREN TOWNSHIP

SCOTT CEMETERY
SE Quarter Section 31, Township 48, Range 29 W
On the old Scott Farm, now owned by a Mr. Salzberger

About fifty years ago this was a family cemetery, numbering more than a dozen graves. Now only one tombstone remains.

Children of C. A. and S. A. Scott:
Winfield, born June 10, 1856, died March 13, 1862
Infant, born June 1, 1857, died July, 1857

The following information is supplied by Mrs. Frank Cave, who, as a child, was present at the burials:
Mrs. James Allen (a wife and mother), buried in the early 70's
Lizzie Powers, age, 7 or 8 years (widowed mother, lived near Sni Mills)

SOLDIERS' CEMETERY
Section 9, Township 47, Range 29 W
LONE JACK, JACKSON COUNTY, MISSOURI

Old settlers supplied the information that 87 Union soldiers and 53 Confederate soldiers are here buried. The names are not given.

One large monument, bearing the following:
"In memory of The Confederates who fell in Lone Jack Battle, August 16, 1862."

Also the following:
Allen, Eastham, born March 11, 1825, died January 2, 1904
Allen, Margaret, wife of Eastham Allen, born January 1, 1827, died May 7, 1902
Jackson, James A., died September 3, 1882; age, 72 years, 9 months, 3 days
Owen, John, husband of G. E. Owen, born May 29, 1832, died August 25, 1862
Riggs, George A., born 1846, died 1928
Riggs, Jennie, wife of George A. Riggs, born 1852, died 1922

UNDERWOOD CEMETERY
Section 21, Township 47, Range 29 W

Bradley, Griselda, wife of Tompkins Bradley, died February 22, 1833; age, 40 years

Easley, Nancy, daughter of S. and R. Easley, died February 17, 1843; age, 10 years

Lawrence, Mary E., daughter of E. M. and R. A. Lawrence, born January 24, 1859, died May 13, 1859

Sanders, James, born January 11, 1809, died September 1, 1904

Sanders, Mary A. Yankee, wife of James Sanders, born July 11, 1821, died August 13, 1877

Sanders, S. Y., died July 28, 1930; age, 80 years

Sanders, Thomas A., born April 10, 1825, died October 23, 1872

Sanders, Charles H., son of J. and M. S. Sanders, born April 11, 1810, died February 1, 1842

Sanders, Georgie, died July 26, 1878; age, 2 years, 9 months, 26 days; daughter of S. Y. and R. Sanders

Sease, Martha M., wife of J. H. Sease, died April 4, 1861; age, 30 years

Spainhower, Alpha N., born 1830, died 1915

Spainhower, Julia A., born 1842, died 1913

Underwood, Amanda, wife of J. K. Underwood, born Sept. 4, 1814, died Oct. 22, 1859

Underwood, William G., son of J. K. and Amanda Underwood, born August 12, 1836, died September 6, 1854

Underwood, Susan M., daughter of J. K. and Amanda Underwood, born March 14, 1843, died August 15, 1854

Underwood, Martha, wife of Wesley Underwood, born March 11, 1821, died Dec. 1, 1850

Underwood, Eliza D., born — 30, 1822, died November 14, 1853 (stone broken)

Underwood, Joel, born March 12, 1796, died September 19, 1841

Underwood, Susannah, wife of Joel Underwood, born January 28, 1782, died May 25, 1839

Underwood, Henry H., son of J. H. and A. Underwood, born March 9, 1849, died December 18, 1866

Underwood, James F., born September 17, 1816, died February 13, 1871

Underwood, Malinda, born October 22, 1822, died May 19, 1896

Underwood, Susan R., daughter of Joel and Susannah, born February 28, 1820, died December 30, 1839

Yankee, Sallie Underwood, born July 9, 1818, died July 17, 1854

Yankee, Wesley, born April 22, 1823, died January 24, 1910

Yankee, Sarah, wife of Wesley Yankee, died July 17, 1854; age, 36 years, 9 days

Yankee, Samuel, born January 15, 1846, died September 18, 1918

Yanke, Adelia, born February 12, 1856

Yankee, James A., born July 12, 1844, died July 26, 1908

Yankee, Loutitia J., born 1859, died 1926

Yankee, Joel K., son of Wesley and Sarah Yankee, died September 18, 1872; age, 23 years, 11 months, 23 days

YANKEE CEMETERY

Section 20, Township 47, Range 29 W

Hays, Matilda, born May 30, 1831, died March 30, 1897

Hays, William, born March 7, 1801, died February 7, 1892

Hays, Ann, wife of William Hays, born May 26, 1798, died December 20, 1869

Harris, Reece, infant son of Dr. J. B. and S. Harris, died September 14, 1852

Violett, Henry G., born July 14, 1843, died July 28, 1889

Windsor, Mary Jane, died July 21, 1930; age, 84 years

Yankee, David, born January 28, 1829, died March 27, 1873

Yankee, Orlena, wife of David Yankee, born May 14, 1831, died May 10, 1929

Yankee, Nancy R., wife of Jacob Yankee, died May 1, 1876; age, 49 years, 8 months

Yankee, Samuel, born December 9, 1797, died January 16, 1879; age, 81 years, 1 month, 7 days

Yankee, Permelia, wife of Samuel Yankee, born March 3, 1802, died March 3, 1882; age, 80 years

Yankee, Zachariah, son of Samuel and Permelia Yankee, died March 3, 1849; age, 23 years

Yankee, George W., son of D. and O. Yankee, born August 30, 1859, died June 27, 1860

PRAIRIE TOWNSHIP
Organized June 4, 1860

CHRISMAN CEMETERY
Section 15, Township 47, Range 32

Belcher, Elizabeth, wife of J. M. Belcher, died January 30, 1872; age, 44 years, 5 months, 24 days

Chrisman, James M., born February 25, 1834, died March 6, 1900

Chrisman, Permelia, daughter of James M. Chrisman, born September 26, 1860, died July 12, 1886

———, David, son of Permelia

Information secured from ——— of the following also buried this cemetery:

Chrisman, Gabriel

Chrisman, Cynthia, wife of Gabriel

Chrisman, Monroe

Nave, Amelia Chrisman

Copied September 23, 1933, by Mrs. Hale Houts

COWHERD CEMETERY
SE Quarter Section 14, Township 49, Range 31 W

Cowherd, America E., wife of Chris. J. Cowherd, died May 18, 1848; age, 18 years, 8 months, 18 days

Freeman, William L., born December 3, 1810, died January 19, 1869

Freeman, Elizabeth, wife of T. E. Freeman, died August 11, 1849; age, 27 years, 18 days

Freeman, Sarah H., daughter of T. E. and E. H. Freeman, died January 5, 1848; age, 2 years, 4 months, 10 days

Bush, infant son of L. N. and M. W. Bush, born and died August 24, 1857

Others known to have been buried in the Cowherd Cemetery, but markers now gone:

Cowherd, Francis K., died 1863

Cowherd, Sarah A., wife of Francis Cowherd, born 1799, died July, 1853 or 1854

Freeman, Elizabeth Cowherd

Cowherd, Henry and wife

Young, Virginia

Freeman, Lude

Freeman, Mrs. Ed.

Freeman, wife of Richard Freeman

Freeman, W. M. H., son of T. E. and E. H. Freeman, died January 11, 1848; age, 9 months, 10 days (stone broken)

Bush, Sarah, said to have been first burial and the oldest person buried in this cemetery

Mr. and Mrs. Charles Cowherd, buried here, but later removed to the Lee's Summit Cemetery.

Copied August 14, 1933, by Mrs. Hale Houts

GREENWOOD CEMETERY
GREENWOOD, MISSOURI
Copied by Mrs. C. M. Uhlig

Allen, Harriette M., wife of Dr. J. M. Allen, died March 20, 1894; age, 63 years, 7 months, 24 days
Autle, L. D., born 1818, died 1898
Autle, M. A., born 1821, died 1898
Autle, H. C., born 1860, died 1888

Barker, Charles H., born 1808, died 1893
Bowman, Wm. G., died October 2, 1881; age, 61 years, 8 months, 18 days
Bowman, Lea J., died May 21, 1902; age, 69 years, 11 days
Bowman, Sarah E., died February 8, 1877; age, 12 years, 4 months
Bowman, Lelia E., died February 28, 1877; age, 4 years, 9 months, 11 days
Bowman, W. N., born March 3, 1848
Bowman, Melissa, his wife, born September 18, 1855, died December 29, 1909
Bowman, S. G., mother of W. N., born January 1, 1813, died February 22, 1903
Boone, Mary, wife of Wm., born 1827, died 1875
Branham, N., died December 22, 1872; age, 72 years
Branham, Eliza, wife of N., died November 16, 1871; age, 63 years, 11 months, 18 days
Branham, Ann E., daughter of James and Eliza, born June 2, 1870, died July 28, 1871
Branham, John A., son of T. L. and M., born March 25, 1866, died August 20, 1890
Bricker, David C., born October 30, 1846, died February 13, 1905 (Soldier)
Bricker, Amanda, his wife, born July 2, 1851, died June 9, 1927
Brooks, Jane, born 1812, died 1884
Brown, Squire F., born September 12, 1835, died December 7, 1872
Brown, Julia Fannie, daughter of S. F. and E. H. Brown, born September 16, 1868, died September 30, 1868
Brown, J. P., born January 23, 1841, died April 24, 1928; age, 87 years, 3 months, 1 day
Brown, Melissa, born May 7, 1846, died January 17, 1914
Brown, Mahlon J., son of J. P. and C. M., born November 30, 1868, died September 26, 1887
Brown, Mattie E., daughter of J. P. and C. M., born November 27, 1877, died November 27, 1879
Brown, James R., born 1806, died 1885
Brown, Georgia A., son of Robert and Jennie, died 1869
Brown, Ross, born 1852, died 1876

Caruthers, Rev. J. S., born 1839, died 1914
Carwood, Betsey E., wife of Wm. M., died 1873; age, 66 years
Cramer, Clara Belle, wife of G. C., born 1858, died 1883
Craig, Perry (father), born November 25, 1839, died November 22, 1914
Craig, Esther, his wife, born September 4, 1835, died August 25, 1897
Collins, S. Burrell, born October 27, 1820, died March 24, 1891
Crockett, Rev. D. R., born July 20, 1843, died November 3, 1892
Cline, Daniel D. (father), born 1840, died 1914
Cline, Sarah A. (mother), born 1841, died 1911
Custer, Joel M., born 1826, died 1911
Custer, Mary, his wife, born 1836, died 1919
Custer, Sophia M., born 1872, died 1877

Davenport, Susan J., wife of Ira F., born 1845, died 1883
Davenport, Charles F., born 1867, died 1867
Davenport, Edgar, born 1869, died 1870
Drake, Zerelda Gratten, died December 31, 1928; age, 72 years, 5 months, 15 days

Gambrel, Melstead, born June 15, 1835, died August 11, 1907
Gambrel, Emma R., born June 8, 1847, died September 13, 1930

CEMETERIES—PRAIRIE TOWNSHIP

Gambrel, Olive, wife of George L., born August 20, 1873, died May 30, 1899
Geryn, Robert Newton, born 1839, died 1915
Geryn, Elizabeth A., his wife, born 1845, died 1922
Garrison, Mary C., wife of D. M., born 1847, died 1895
Goff, A. J., born March 27, 1829, died May 18, 1875
Gibson, Benjamin, died April 12, 1932; age, 76 years, 5 months, 21 days
Gibson, Hattie, died March 24, 1933; age, 74 years, 3 months, 21 days
Graham, David, born March 1, 1832, died January 10, 1912
Graham, Sally, his wife, born November 16, 1846, died May 22, 1927
Ghormley, John B., born April 14, 1827, died March 15, 1895

Hamilton, Emily F., born 1846, died 1920
Hamilton, James Polk, born 1844, died 1929
Henderson, Ella J., wife of R. G., died March 8, 1871; age, 26 years
Hicklin, Sally, wife, born September 20, 1842, died January 18, 1910
Hicklin, Ingram, born September 27, 1836, died September 27, 1911
Hamilton, Fannie A., born 1839, died 1909
Haney, Wm., born September 10, 1845, died August 11, 1909
Haney, Melissa M., wife, born October 12, 1857
Harris, S. B., born 1830, died 1923
Hartnett, Rebecca, born 1794, died 1869
Holtzclaw, Peter L. (father), born February 5, 1842, died December 27, 1918
Holtzclaw, Mary E. (mother), born October 12, 1840, died February 20, 1907
Holtzclaw, Thomas A., born October 28, 1867, died September 13, 1916
Holtzclaw, Taylor B., born October 12, 1870, died June 23, 1929
Hoover, David M., born 1833, died 1908
Hoover, F. E., wife of David M., born 1833, died 1894
Hoover, David E., son of D. M. and F. E., born 1871, died 1871
Huggins, Henry J., born 1823, died 1897
Huggins, Esther Jane, born 1823, died 1911
Huggins, Josephine, died July 3, 1920; age, 60 years, 10 months, 20 days
Hurt, Richard T., born August 15, 1836, died August 10, 1915
Hurt, Minerva O., his wife, born February 1, 1839, died November 2, 1919
Hurt, Wayne B. (Baby)
Huston, P. B., died August 15, 1875; age, 55 years, 6 months

Jenkins, Mary J., born 1852, died 1924
Jennings, —, born February 17, 1843, died February 9, 1922
Jennings, Arthur L., born August 22, 1881, died November 12, 1925
Jennings, J. H. (father), born 1873, died 1926
Jennings, Bessie Bare, his wife, born 1876, died 1915
Johnson, C. A., born 1809, died 1866
Johnson, John W., born April 1, 1839, died March 2, 1914
Johnson, Margaret, wife, born February 16, 1841, died July 13, 1912
Johnstone, J. B., born September 22, 1805, died July 20, 1892
Johnstone, Polly, born December 25, 1789, died August 5, 1876
Johnstone, M. M., born 1837, died 1925 (father)
Johnstone, Annie E., wife of M. M., born October 16, 1837, died January 18, 1891
Johnstone, Sally, daughter of M. M. and A. E., born 1875, died May 29, 1875
Johnstone, Minnie, daughter of M. M. and A. E., born 1873, died 1874
Johnstone, Ollie L., daughter of M. M. and A. E., born November 16, 1877, died January 24, 1891

Kennedy, Alexander, born 1828, died 1895
Kennedy, Sarah A., born 1838, died 1919
Kerr, E. H., wife of Wm. Kerr, born 1825, died 1891
Kissell, Nancy, born July 21, 1860, died February 25, 1931

Kissell, Robert, born September 22, 1848, died October 1, 1930
Kissell, Vollie, their son, born February 14, 1884, died July 21, 1907
Kissell, Minnie, born 1882, died 1898
Kissell, Charles, born 1875, died 1915
Kissell, Robert A., born 1874, died 1898

Lasley, J. J., born 1825, died 1889
Lasley, Margaret, wife of J. J., born 1833, died 1922
Leviston, James W., born July 5, 1835, died November 7, 1909
Leviston, Thomas J., born November 3, 1832, died January 7, 1896
Leviston, Ann, born April 27, 1822, died October 8, 1895
Leviston, Mary Alice, born June 2, 1849, died January 2, 1899
Leviston, Walla, born May 7, 1856, died March 14, 1927
Long, John L., born July 2, 1849, died December 9, 1924
Long, Martha S., wife of John, born December 1, 1861, died February 14, 1914
Long, Erwin, died March 20, 1933; age, 60 years, 1 month, 3 days

McBride, Harrison, born October, 1812, died Oct. 21, 1875; age, 63 years
McBride, Phoebe, born September 25, 1818
McCullough, Francis T., born June 23, 1885, died December 20, 1903
McCullough, Nancy Jane, his wife, born April 21, 1826, died July 9, 1910
McCullough, John T., born January 18, 1862, died October 31, 1903
McGillivray, Katy, born 1854, died 1874
McGillivray, D. A., born 1858, died 1890
McGillivray, Rebecca B. (mother), born 1825, died 1905
McFarland, Wm. M., died 1883; age, 42 years, 8 days
McKinney, Wm., born 1829, died 1875
McKinney, Mary Ann, born 1833, died 1904
McKitrick, Mary, wife of A. H., born 1786, died 1880
McNeil, Charles W., born 1841, died 1874
McRoberts, Lydia, born 1800, died 1880

Mardock, Edwin W., born October, 1819, died August 31, 1908
Mardock, Mary J., born April 25, 1839, died May 18, 1929 (?)
Marsh, Wm. H., died 1848
Micholson, Jane, wife of Robert S., born 1827, died 1891
Miller, Mathew B., born 1823, died 1892
Miller, Agnes F., born 1834, died 1890
Miller, George (father), born April 14, 1796, died January 20, 1875
Miller, Isabelle (mother), born July 3, 1822, died July 18, 1875
Miller, John, son of Geo. and Isabelle (dates not visible)
Miller, Mathew White, born 1859, died 1913
Mogard, Ann, wife of Henry, died 1872
Mogard, Ed, son of J. T. and R. H. Mogarth, died 1877; age, 1 year, 6 months
Morland, Lou Woods, born 1834, died 1915
Morland, Delmar Brooks, born 1830, died 1916
Morland, Kate Woods, born 1866, died 1886
Morlan, Wm., died October 3, 1897; age, 61 years, 15 days

Nicholson, John R. (father), born April 25, 1837, died November 22, 1906
Nicholson, Marion C., wife of H. J., born February 20, 1856, died December 9, 1892
Nicholson, Geo. W., son of C. J. and S. J., died December 2, 1873; age, 4 years, 11 months 20 days
Nicholson, John R., son of J. R. and M. L., died November 10, 1871; age, 26 days
Nicholson, Phila V., daughter of J. R. and M. L., died August 20, 1870; age, 14 days
Newall, Eliza Jane, wife of James, died 1871; age, 56 years

Page, Fannie H., wife of Rev. D. G. Page, born 1841, died 1870
Paswater, John P., born January 28, 1850, died October 17, 1913
Paswater, Mary E., his wife, born January 28, 1850, died September 2, 1918
Phillips, Milton, born 1826, died 1903
Phillips, Maggie S., born 1858, died 1878
Phillips, Mattie L. Miller, died 1855
Post, William, born January 27, 1802, died September 12, 1888
Post, Phoebe, wife of Wm., born October 23, 1804, died September 30, 1853

Rafferty, A. C., born 1834, died 1916
Rafferty, Ethel M., born 1890, died 1891
Rafferty, Elizabeth A., born 1836, died 1906
Roberts, Margaret, wife of John W., born 1846, died 1918

Sample, David, born 1843, died 1918
Sample, Mary J., born 1851, died 1924
Sample, William A., born 1822, died 1908
Skiles, Isaac M., born March 25, 1845, died August 18, 1909
Skiles, Mary E. McKirahan, his wife, born November 30, 1861
Skiles, son of I. M. and M. E., born 1898, died 1899
Skiles, Henry, died May 11, 1893; age, 75 years, 2 months, 7 days
Skiles, Jane A., wife of Henry, died July 7, 1891; age, 74 years, 2 months, 22 days
Skilling, Samuel R., born April 10, 1824, died May 18, 1907
Skilling, Emeline, born April 30, 1832, died February 5, 1907
Skilling, Charles E., born April 12, 1859, died March 8, 1923
Skilling, Edgar B., born January 8, 1867, died February 13, 1889
Smith, Elizabeth, wife of W. M., born 1811, died 1894
Smith, J. A., born 1828, died 1895
Smith, Sealah B., wife, born 1833, died 1885
Smith, Mary J., wife of T. J., born 1839, died 1873
Smith, Sarah P., wife of Rev. Ezra C., born 1813, died 1871
Spainhower, H. W., died March 19, 1874
Spainhower, Sarilla (dates not visible)
Speer, Wm. W., died May 24, 1877; age, 46 years, 5 months, 24 days
Speer, Nancy, his wife, died January 5, 1886; age, 52 years, 28 days
Sweetland, Rebecca, born April 26, 1846, died March 16, 1886

Taborn, Anna, born 1811, died 1888
Totten, Wm., born 1826, died 1898
Totten, Prudence, born 1817, died 1899
Totten, Elizabeth S., born 1849, died 1928
Totten, Margaret A., born 1850

Whitehurst, T. J., born 1820, died 1887
Whitehurst, Elizabeth, wife of T. J., born 1843, died 1891
Whitehurst, James A., son of A. D. and P. Kennedy, born 1864, died 18—
White, Francis M., born 1834, died 1911
Wilkin, Robert J., born June 15, 1837, died October 10, 1911
Wilkin, Mary E., wife of R. J., born March 20, 1839, died August 11, 1899
Wilkin, John, born July 30, 1813, died January 29, 1893
Wilkin, Elizabeth, wife of John, born September 28, 1871, died May 29, 1917
Wise, Julia C., wife of J. H., born 1847, died 1871
Woods, T. D., born 1850, died 1926
Woods, Rev. J. V. A., born 1804, died 1891
Woods, Lucinda, wife of J. V. A., born 1816, died 1899

Young, Elizabeth, wife of Wm., born August, 1841, died October 27, 1896

THE HARDUP CEMETERY

Situated upon farm now owned by Mr. Goodman,
formerly owned by Mr. Thomas B. Hagen
Section 30, Township 48, Range 31

This cemetery was situated at Hardup Church, which existed before the War between the States. There were between 30 and 40 graves. No marker of any kind.

Harry Younger, the brother of Cole Younger's father, was first buried here, but removed to Harrisonville after the War

John Hagen and two daughters, buried July or August, 1864

James Speperd, buried 1860

Carlton, John, born 1852, died September, 1859; son of Ezekiel and Mary Carlton

Contributed by Mr. Thomas Hagen, born April 11, 1852

HINK CEMETERY

Section 23, Township 48, Range 31

Samuel Hink, Captain in the War of 1812, died 1865
Charity Busley, wife of Samuel Hink, died 1874
Edward Hink, son of above, died 1861-64

Contributed by Mr. H. J. Davis, of Lee's Summit, a grandson of Samuel Hink

LEE'S SUMMIT CEMETERY

LEE'S SUMMIT, MISSOURI

Copied by Mrs. Hale Houts, Mrs. M. A. Christopher, Mrs. John N. Kinyoun

A

Acock, James, died April 27, 1929; age, 87 years
Adams, John T., born February 24, 1848, died June 15, 1919
Adams, Isaac W., died March 4, 1880; age, 51 years
Adams, Mary A. B., wife of Isaac W. Adams, born July 7, 1833, died October 1, 1915
Adams, John D., died December 11, 1902; age, 63 years, 1 month, 20 days
Adams, Barbery E., wife of John D. Adams, died December 18, 1898; age, 48 years, 10 months, 20 days
Agre, Nathan, born August 29, 1854, died June 19, 1918
Akers, Henry H., died July 13, 1920; age, 82 years
Alexander, James, born 1830, died 1914
Alexander, Amanda A., wife of James Alexander, born 1836, died 1918
Alexander, Peter S., born 1839, died 1927
Alexander, Sarah Ann, wife of Peter S. Alexander, born 1844, died 1932
Alexander, Ida W., wife of W. T. Alexander, and daughter of Isaac W. and Mary A. B. Adams, born 1853, died 1876
Allen, Adison H., died July 10, 1932; age, 77 years, 19 days
Allen, Mary E., wife of Adison H. Allen, born 1861, died 1918
Anderson, W. P., born January 24, 1848, died November 23, 1892
Anderson, Mary A., born 1848, died 1924
Anderson, John C., born 1840, died 1932
Anderson, Eliza F., born 1848, died 1924
Anderson, James C., born 1854, died 1915
Armstrong, Charlotte, wife of Joseph Armstrong, born July 17, 1812, died June 29, 1893

Armstrong, Thomas J., born 1843, died 1925
Armstrong, Elizabeth Andrees, born 1847, died 1924
Armstrong, Nancy T., wife of Jas. S. Armstrong, born November 30, 1853, died June 14, 1887
Armstrong, Belle, daughter of W. T. and M. A. Kennedy, wife of J. S. Armstrong, born November 30, 1853, died June 14, 1887
Arnold, William P., born 1845, died 1921
Arnold, Malinda J., wife of Wm. P. Arnold, born 1851, died 1921
Arnett, David Solomon, born October 20, 1850, died April 29, 1928
Arnett, Thomas J., born 1849, died 1923
Arnett, Martha L.
Ash, William W., born July 20, 1829, died February 12, 1910
Ash, America A., wife of Wm. W. Ash, born April 9, 1833, died June 4, 1911
Ashcroft, Benjamin G., Co. "F" 52nd Inf. (Gov. marker)
Ashcroft, Alexander, born 1853, died 1925
Ashcroft, Mary E., wife of Alexander Ashcroft, born 1847, died 1922
Asher, Emeline (mother), born 1849, died 1928
Asher, Charles (father), born 1845, died 1888; Co. "D" 54th Ill. Inf. (Gov. marker)

B

Bagby, William F., born 1849, died 1923
Bailey, Jesse W., Sr., born October 5, 1827, died July 30, 1905
Bailey, John Mark (father), born 1860, died 1929
Bailey, Mary F. (mother), born May 31, 1929, died November 18, 1914
Bailey, Alice, daughter of J. W. and Mary J. Bailey, died August 31, 1877; age, 18 years, 11 months, 3 days
Baird, Margaret E. (wife), born 1843, died 1912
Baird, Amzi E., born 1835, died 1917
Baxter, Robert, born 1844, died 1916
Baxter, Abigail, born 1845
Bayles, James A., born 1834, died 1916
Bayles, Louise G. Allen (wife), born 1833, died December 24, 1874
Bayles, Esther G. (wife), born 1827, died 1906
Beal, Permelia W. (mother), born 1830, died 1910
Beach, N., born 1847, died 1926
Belser, Charles F., born 1844, died 19— (Flag upon grave)
Bennet, George W. (father), born 1827, died 1923
Bennet, Dorcas E. (mother), born 1836, died 1888
Berry, Marander V., wife of J. A. Berry, born November 16, 1844, died March 11, 1887
Berry, J. A., born June 18, 1837, died October 13, 1899
Best, William B., son of T. H. and M. E. Best, born June 10, 1855, died June 15, 1856
Bishop, Sergt. William M., Co. "G" 48th Ohio Inf. (Gov. marker)
Bishop, Wayne S., born December 29, 1810, in Nelson County, Kentucky, died May 21, 1902
Blair, Mrs., born 1843, died 1910
Black, Barbara B., wife of Thomas Black, born September 18, 1820, died December 13, 1911
Black, Emma E., born 1841, died 1899
Blackwell, John Randolph, born January 20, 1824, died June 20, 1904
Blackwell, Matilda Chenauet (wife), born June 12, 1835, died February 24, 1884
Blackwell, Sallie M., born March 31, 1839, died August 30, 1920
Blackwell, J. W., born 1844, died 1922
Blackwell, Margaret Q. (wife), born 1849, died 1917
Boggs, H. J., died July 14, 1931; age, 89 years, 25 days
Boggs, Mrs. Mary L., wife of H. J., died September 24, 1929; age, 88 years, 5 months, 21 days
Boggs, John O., born October 30, 1818, died September 16, 1900
Boggs, Peace, wife of John Boggs, died March 27, 1876; age, 58 years, 6 months, 23 days
Bollinger, Joseph, born March 15, 1812, died June 8, 1880
Boten, Thomas J., born August 13, 1841

Boten, Emily G., wife of Thomas J. Boten, born March 26, 1844, died February 25, 1913
Bowers, Hattie E. Trewett, wife of William G. Bowers, born Aug. 10, 1868, died May 18, 1906
Bowers, Lydia, died October 10, 1929; age, 75 years, 2 months, 3 days
Bowers, John H., died September 18, 1904; age, 55 years, 10 months, 10 days
Bowin, George A., born August 10, 1814
Bowin, Sallie A., born August 20, 1824, died October 23, 1911
Bowin, Joseph, born March 4, 1850, died November 9, 1901
Bowin, S. B., born 1854, died 1923
Bowin, Frank, died November 6, 1930; age, 71 years, 8 months, 12 days
Browning, Anna Harvey, wife of O. N. Browning, born Nov. 24, 1844, died Sept. 24, 1904
Browning, O. N., born 1826, died 1917
Boyer, W. E., born 1842, died 1924
Boyer, Josephine, born 1843, died 1921
Boys, Anna W., born October 24, 1839, died September 16, 1904
Boys, Leonard Andre, born October 13, 1837, died September 30, 1912
Brewer, Daniel K., died March 14, 1881; age, 58 years
Brewer, Hannah J., born July 26, 1823, died May 9, 1898
Brewer, James E., son of A. E. and M. A., died October 2, 1873; age, 5 years
Broughton, C. P., born February 23, 1844, died May 4, 1924
Broughton, Etta B., born December 28, 1849, died December 24, 1903
Brownfield, William, born May 1, 1827, died January 13, 1892
Brownfield, Sarah A., born December 11, 1827, died November 19, 1893
Brown, C. Rachel, born December 20, 1830, died July 27, 1906
Browning, Abbie, wife of C. A. Browning, born 1855, died 1914

C

Calfee, John V., died October 26, 1878
Calfee, Christine, died April 20, 1907
Callaghan, Michael, born 1850, died 1923 (flag at grave)
Camp, Calvin, born January 21, 1817, died October 20, 1893
Campbell, Robert F., died December 8, 1885; age, 58 years, 3 months, 3 days
Campbell, J. T., born January 1, 1859, died December 19, 1911
Campbell, James B., Corporal, Co. "G" 8th Ill. Inf. (Gov. marker); born 1838, died 1890
Campbell, Mrs. M. A., born 1844, died 1925
Cantrell, Pleasant J., born 1857, died 1884
Cantrell, Mary C., born 1865, died 1908
Cantrell, Sarah C., born 1863, died 1883
Cantrell, Benjamin A., born 1826, died 1912
Cantrell, Mary, born 1833, died 1930
Casey, James H., born October 17, 1845, died March 3, 1914
Casey, Dradenna J., wife of James H. Casey, born December 4, 1840
Carlton, Mary A., born August 13, 1828, died October 9, 1906
Carlton, Ambrose J., born December 15, 1861, died July 4, 1911
Carter, Jane, born January 17, 1818, died June 5, 1887
Carter, Joseph H., born September 17, 1839, died June 24, 1907; Co. "H" 89th Ohio Vol. Inf. (Gov. marker)
Carter, Virginia Morrow, wife of Joseph H. Carter, born Feb. 2, 1840, died May 17, 1920
Carr, J. E., born 1837, died 1916
Carr, Annie V., born 1848, died 1917
Cattlett, William O., born March 30, 1839, died November 14, 1906
Chambers, O. H., born November 2, 1838, died March 10, 1904
Chambers, Amanda G., wife of O. H. Chambers, born November 30, 1843, died March 5, 1913
Childs, Andrew J., died December 9, 1901; age, 79 years
Childs, Emily E., died October 5, 1898; age, 81 years
Clayton, Tabitha A., born 1842, died 1921
Clayton, Warren, born January 11, 1824, died March 18, 1895

Clayton, Charles B., son of W. and L. Clayton, died October 29, 1885; age, 31 years, 7 months, 21 days
Clarke, Leroy, son of C. H. and J. P., born August 2, 1850, died September 22, 1875
Cline, William A., born October 30, 1846, died May 20, 1923
Clifford, Sarah Ann, wife of J. B. Clifford, born May 10, 1834, died February 19, 1914
Chrismas, W. T., died February 11, 1874; age, 53 years, 6 months
Chrisman, Edward P., born August 22, 1835, died September 7, 1919
Chrisman, Abraham, born 1837, died 1918
Chrisman, J. M., born January 6, 1827, died January 1, 1893
Chrisman, Joseph M., born October 3, 1820, died May 1, 1881
Chism, William, died January 27, 1879; age, 89 years
Chism, Gabrm, died January 17, 1879; age, 37 years
Colburn, W. H., born March 22, 1829, died July 23, 1892
Colburn, Jerusha, wife of W. H. Colburn, died May 12, 1880; age, 47 years, 3 months, 11 days
Collins, Josiah, born October 4, 1819, died July 29, 1902
Collins, Sallie A., born October 11, 1826, died January 5, 1904
Cooper, William H., born January 1, 1822, died May 6, 1881
Cooper, Blewford, born August 29, 1807, died January 8, 1889
Coley, G. W., born September 3, 1832, died January 18, 1906
Coley, Mary J., wife of G. W. Coley, born June 27, 1849, died July 13, 1916
Collins, Rev. W. K. (father), born 1848, died 1928; Co. "I" Reg. 132nd Ind.
Collins, Harriet E. (mother), born 1851, died 1916
Colebank, Mrs. Elizabeth, died January 19, 1926; age, 82 years, 10 months, 11 days
Consolver, R. E. (mother), born September 6, 1844, died June 20, 1926
Consolver, J. L. (father), born March 21, 1843, died February 6, 1885
Cooper, Robert, son of Jos. M. Cooper, born September 29, 1869, died March 5, 1870
Cooper, Blewford, son of J. M. and P. Cooper, died June 17, 1873; age, 2 years, 3 months, 6 days
Colwell, Anna, died July 9, 1919; age, 78 years
Cowherd, Charles J., born March 3, 1830, died April 11, 1914
Cowherd, Charles J., born May 11, 1827, died April 29, 1893
Cowherd, Edmund, born July 21, 1816, died May 20, 1889
Cowherd, Martha H., born April 25, 1827, died November 15, 1904
Conradfehr, Hs., Geborne in Maach, Slnieizerland, September 26, 1826, Gestobben in Lee's Summit September 27, 1878
Cramer, Mary J., wife of B. Cramer, died Dec. 27, 1900; age, 62 years, 3 months, 14 days
Cramer, Benedict, born March 2, 1838, died January 29, 1915
Crane, Samuel, born 1828, died 1894
Crane, Malinda, his wife, born 1833, died 1897
Croh, Henry, born January 18, 1847, died April 23, 1832 (flag at grave)
Croh, Sarah M., born November 10, 1851, died May 20, 1909
Crozier, John P., born May 21, 1836, died October 3, 1890
Cooper, Zachariah G., born 1815, died 1908
Cooper, Olivia D., born 1820, died 1910
Corlew, Nancy A., born 1839, died 1917

D

Davis, Maria, wife of Francis Davis, died September 28, 1875; age, 52 years, 11 months
Davis, W. M., husband of Rebecca Davis, died June 30, 1895; age, 58 years
Davis, Rebecca, born 1848, died 1925
Davis, Louvia A., wife of T. O. Davis, died November 7, 1880; age, 45 years
Davis, Lemuel, born 1845, died 1920
Davis, L. W., born March 1, 1860, died October 10, 1909
Davenport, Tillman T., born 1834, died 1897
Davenport, Lucinda, wife of Tillman T. Davenport, born 1835, died 1915

Dark, Edwin, born February 2, 1820, died September 6, 1876
Dark, Caroline, wife of Edwin Dark, born September 6, 1822, died February 9, 1900
Dark, John, born 1848, died 1924
Dark, Henry, born 1846, died 1922
Dark, Nellie, daughter of H. and F. E. Dark, died January 28, 1875; age, 8 months
Daily, James A., born 1854, died 1917
Dawson, Rosella, born 1817, died 1886
Dawson, Mary E. (mother), born 1857, died 1903
Dennis, sons of W. and M. Dennis
Dennis, William H., born November 3, 1840, died July 13, 1862
Dennis, Fletcher S., born March 9, 1844, died February 17, 1866
Dennis, John Reese, son of Milton and Irene Dennis, born September 20, 1876, died September 22, 1879
Dennis, William, born May 12, 1809, died June 3, 1872
Dieffenderfer, Ida M., wife of Theo. Dieffenderfer, born October 10, 1868, died July 24, 1904
Dickhout, Peter S., born February 12, 1841, died December 29, 1903
Dickhout, Eliza J., born October 24, 1847, died March 6, 1909
Donington, Jennie E., born 1847, died 1925
Donovan, William G., born 1848, died 1905
Doudna, Lucinda (mother), born 1830, died 1923
Doudna, Joseph B. (father), born 1830, died 1912
Driskell, ——, born 1844, died 1917
Dryden, Mary Atherton, mother of T. C. and W. H. C. Dryden, died July 9, 1883; age, 91 years, 9 months, 7 days
Dryden, W. H. C., born 1824, died 1878
Dryden, Mary E., wife of W. H. C. Dryden, born 1846, died 1917
Dryden, Samuel, born April 17, 1840, died April 12, 1918
Dryden, Sarah E., born September 26, 1848, died March 10, 1888
Dryden, Lula M., born 1874, died 1877
Dunn, James W., born in Virginia, July 17, 1811, died October 14, 1891
Dunn, Maria Jane, wife of James W. Dunn, born June 12, 1818, died March 26, 1900
Duffield, Thos., born April 18, 1880; age, 58 years
Duncan, Willis, born 1846, died 1923
Durrett, John D., born 1848, died 1931

E

Easley, Stephen H., born 1853, died 1930
Egton, Susan B., wife of J. W. Egton, born 1829, died 1886
Ellis, Mary E., born 1846, died 1926
Emanuel, Casper, born March 11, 1828, died July 19, 1908
Evans, Samuel P., born February 29, 1856, died May 20, 1918
Evans, Joseph, died June 13, 1873; age, 19 years, 15 days
Ervin, Mary Ann, wife of J. M. Ervin, born June 22, 1835, died September 28, 1868
Ervin, John H., born December 13, 1832, died May 20, 1905
Ervin, Isabelle, wife of John H. Ervin, born 1845, died 1923
Earles, A. T., died June 26, 1874; age, 37 years, 11 months, 23 days
Earles, Claire

F

Fearman, R. J., born 1834, died 1898
Fields, R. M., born 1838, died 1925
Fields, Susan A., wife of R. M. Fields, born May 7, 1823, died January 16, 1898
Fields, Lucy A. (mother), born 1843, died 1900
Fields, John, died May 17, 1884; age, 71 years
Fields, Margaret, wife of John, died April 28, 1898; age, 82 years
Fields, Joseph, born March 3, 1843, died April 2, 1906
Flinn, Isham, born March 10, 1823, died January 3, 1906
Foster, Jeremiah, born December 14, 1835, died April 19, 1899

Foster, Isabelle Brookouer, wife of Jeremiah, born January 27, 1850, died December 26, 1886
Foster, Sarah, born November 13, 1832, wife of H. U. Foster
Foust, David M., Co. "G" 187th Ohio Inf. (Gov. marker)
Fristoe, John L., died June 18, 1876; age, 63 years
Fristoe, Busheba A., born March 9, 1885; age, 45 years
Fowler, Jane, wife of Robert, born August 25, 1789, died December 5, 1858
Fowler, Robert Y., born June 8, 1788, died August 27, 1847
Fuqua, George R., born May 30, 1844, died July 28, 1892
Fulk, Elvira, wife of Samuel Fulk, died April 27, 1896; age, 65 years
Fulk, Samuel, died June 26, 1892; age, 51 years

G

Gammon, Martha P., wife of Thos. Gammon, died September 4, 1871; age, 20 years, 1 month, 4 days; also infant son
Garvin, William, born June 13, 1835, died March 22, 1904
Garvin, Susan A., born June 12, 1839, died October 16, 1932
Garrison, Solomon F., born 1844, died 1915
George, Richard B., born September 12, 1833, died June 11, 1896
George, Martha T., born November 7, 1840, died October 1, 1912
Gray, Mollie, died May 11, 1932; age, 74 years, 7 months, 13 days
Greene, Mary (mother), born 1843, died 1923
Ground, Harrison, born 1830, died 1874
Ground, Mary A., wife of Harrison Ground, born 1835, died 1926
Grubb, Mahala E., died January 4, 1871; age, 1 year, 7 months, 29 days
Grubb, Myra S., died September 29, 1873; age, 2 years, 2 months, 22 days
   Children of A. W. and M. A. Grubb
Gibbons, John E., born December 9, 1830, died December 27, 1809
Gibbons, Nancy G., wife of John E. Gibbons, born March 8, 1846, died November 6, 1931; age, 86 years
Gibbons, William, born December 9, 1830, died January 21, 1917
Gibbons, Margaret J., wife of Wm. Gibbons, born August 10, 1848, died November 20, 1922
Gibson, Robert W., born September 29, 1822, died January 17, 1864
Gibson, Constantia, wife of Robt. W. Gibson, born Nov. 16, 1822, died Nov. 13, 1895
Giffin, John, born 1815, died 1870
Giffin, John W., born 1845, died 1871
Giffin, Eddie C., born 1861, died 1870
Gillen, Sarah, born 1863, died 1919
Gillet, Orsamus, born October 13, 1803, died February 26, 1883
Glare, Robert, born January 27, 1814, died December 8, 1905
Glouser, Anna Ramsey, born 1849, died 1914
Gorlew, James A., born 1828, died 1902
Gorlew, Mary A., wife of James A. Gorlew, born 1828, died 1914
Green, Henry A., born June 23, 1843, died March 12, 1890
Greenlee, Nicodemus, husband of M. J. Greenlee (Masonic Emblem), born November 13, 1842, died February 24, 1895
Greenlee, Malinda J., born July 30, 1847, died July 16, 1921
Grimsley, Frances G., wife of A. P. Grimsley, died 1869; age, 19 years
Grinter, Perry N., born 1820, died 1913
Grinter, Sally D., wife of Perry N. Grinter, born 1832, died 1924
Grinter, John F., died March 5, 1877; age, 22 years, 26 days
Guinn, Mary Lou, died February 16, 1933; age, 79 years
Guinn, David W., died January 26, 1925; age, 82 years, 6 months, 4 days

H

Hagen, William (father), born May 15, 1829, died December 13, 1916
Hagen, Sedelia (mother), born May 18, 1832, died March 27, 1912

Hale, J. F., died March 11, 1904; age, 56 years
Hale, Sarah A., wife of J. F. Hale, died November 1, 1914; age, 67 years
Hall, Richard A., son of R. S. and F. L. Hall, died August 28, 1873; age, 16 years, 3 months, 8 days
Haller, John
Hanlon, Edward M., born 1844, died 1918
Hann, Andrew S., son of William and Ellen Hann, died March 10, 1884; age, 27 years, 11 months, 27 days
Hann, Ellen V., wife of William Hann, died 1883; age, 50 years, 2 months, 12 days
Hann, William, born May 1, 1832
Harrington, Thomas, son of A. and M. A. Harrington, died November 14, 1874; age, 1 year, 1 month, 5 days
Harris, James F., died December 23, 1930; age, 74 years, 5 months, 18 days
Harris, John H., born July 20, 1832, died September 23, 1918
Harrison, Clementina, born 1823, died 1906
Harrison, Mathew T., born 1846, died 1927
Harbaugh, Frank, born April 12, 1831, died September 14, 1908
Harbaugh, Mary E., wife of Frank Harbaugh, born April 20, 1838, died November 22, 1913
Harsel, Joseph, born 1843, died 1905
Haynes, Joseph, born October 11, 1816, died March 1, 1892
Haynes, Lamira, wife of Joseph Haynes, born August 15, 1819, died March 8, 1897
Hedges, James P., born 1844, died 1916
Hedges, Sarah R., born 1835, died 1913
Hedges, Isaac, born March 15, 1811, died December 23, 1881
Hedges, Artemesie, wife of Isaac Hedges, born January 24, 1822, died September 10, 1881
Hensler, Joseph, died October 24, 1885; age, 40 years
Hendrickson, Mary E., wife of A. W. Hendrickson, born July 18, 1849, died June 29, 1902
Hertzog, Mary E., born 1849, died 1917
Hertzog, Daniel G., born 1840, died 1915
Herron, James, born 1847, died 1902
Hess, William H., born December 25, 1831, died January 29, 1906
Hess, Mary F., wife of William Hess, born June 9, 1839, died July 7, 1910
Hess, Catherine, born March 8, 1828, died May 8, 1911
Hess, Abraham J., born October 16, 1827, died March 9, 1899
Heubach, Eleonora, born April 29, 1830, died January 3, 1892
Heubach, George, born July 19, 1829, died March 14, 1889
Hiatt, Clara Elizabeth, died May 18, 1933; age, 75 years, 4 months, 14 days
Hibson, Samuel A., died May 21, 1931; age, 69 years
Hickman, J. T., born 1826, died 1904
Hickman, Elizabeth C., wife of J. T. Hickman, born 1832, died 1879
Hickman, Anna B., their daughter, born 1855, died 1879
Hickman, infant daughter, died April 8, 1873
Hicks, Davidson B., born March 30, 1826, died January 4, 1904
Hilligoss, Sarah F., wife of Isaac W., born June 29, 1824, died October 8, 1907
Hilligoss, Isaac W., born October, 1818, died January 26, 1892
Hinton, Lettie, daughter of E. H. and Elizabeth Hinton, born August 3, 1849, died November 2, 1868
Holmes, William N. (father), born 1831, died 1919
Hoke, William, born August 2, 1841, died October 20, 1903—his wife
Hoke, Harriet, born May 12, 1842, died February 5, 1919
Hollyday, Anna Maria (mother), born January 1, 1832, at Readbourne, Maryland, died August 23, 1908
Hollyday, Clarence (father), born June 19, 1843, died June 21, 1916
Hollyday, Elizabeth G. (mother), born October 16, 1856, died April 24, 1927
Hood, John W., born January 19, 1842, died December 30, 1915
Houchin, John M. Chester, Mo. Mil. (Gov. marker)

House, Almeda, born 1854, died 1914
Hostetler, Noah, died September, 1897, in his 65th year, 4th month, and 27th day
Hostetler, Noah, his wife, born 1832, died 1910
Hopper, Anna, wife of Edward Hopper, died February 27, 1874; age, 70 years
Howard, Harriet, died August 19, 1869; age, 75 years
Howard, John C., died November 18, 1885; age, 70 years, 9 months, 25 days
Howard, Mary C., born 1845, died 1908
Howard, Mary Etta, daughter of J. C. and Mary A., died May 25, 1869; age, 15 years, 1 day
Howard, infant son of L. H. and E. A. Howard
Hughes, William P., died March 3, 1885; age, 59 years, 5 months, 1 day
Hulse, William, born 1841, died 1890
Hulse, Thormas Ann Cooper, wife of William Hulse, born 1850, died 1890
Hutchings, John T., born 1840
Hutchings, Savilla A., born 1855, died 1913

I

Ince, Robert Lee, born 1870, died 1880

J

Jackson, Rev. James B., born February 22, 1820, died July 18, 1901
Jackson, Helen Knight, wife of Rev. James B. Jackson, born April 20, 1830, died November 21, 1902
Jones, W., born 1850, died 1924
Jones, William S., born October 3, 1820, died May 23, 1908
Jones, Jemima, born February 20, 1823, died April 22, 1897
Jones, infant daughter of T. and E. Jones, died August 29, 1871; age, 7 days
Jones, Thomas, born October 20, 1838, in Llandsyenan, Anglesea, North Wales, died January 4, 1926; age, 87 years, 2 months, 10 days
Jones, Ellen, wife of Thomas Jones, born March 15, 1835, in Gaeriven, Anglesea, North Wales, died September 7, 1888; age, 53 years, 5 months, 23 days
Jones, Ann, wife of J. J. Jones, died June 17, 1871; age, 41 years, 1 month, 13 days
Jones, J. J., born 1823, died 1901
Jones, Lucinda M., born 1844, died 1914
Jones, Edgar A., born 1859, died 1900

K

Keller, Michael M., born 1842, died July 3, 1929; 27th Ind. Inf.
Keller, Martha Jane, born 1845, died 1922
Keirsey, Jonathan, born August 29, 1831, died June 14, 1902
Keirsey, Alice Madora, born March 11, 1855, died September 23, 1912
Kendall, Adam B., born 1829, died 1911
Kendall, Elmira L., born 1847, died 1923
Kennedy, William T., born July 1, 1816, died May 24, 1898
Kennedy, Mary A., born December 3, 1826, died July 23, 1891
Kerr, James F. (father), born 1812, died 1884
Kerr, Nancy C. (mother), born 1831, died 1909
King, Angelina (wife of Jesse), died March 20, 1899; age, 80 years, 10 months
King, Jesse, died December 31, 1879; age, 66 years, 7 months
King, Sarah E., born 1835, died 1916
King, George W., died November 1, 1899; age, 61 years
King, M. P., born 1840, died 1914
King, Martha L., born 1850, died 1931
King, Mary E., wife of Thomas King, born 1846, died 1925
Kinne, Melville A., born 1849, died 1912
Kinne, Mary A., wife of Melville A., born 1851, died 1919
Knepp (mother), born April, 1847, died January, 1927
Knepp, (father), born March, 1847, died December, 1923

Knox, Mrs. Margaret, died January 2, 1931; age, 74 years, 9 months, 21 days
Koons, Dr. R. P., born 1847, died 1921
Koons, Ella, wife of R. P. Koons, born 1859, died 1923
Kreeger, Jacob, born December 14, 1818, died May 29, 1885
Kreeger, Martha J., born September 2, 1827, died July 22, 1921
Kreeger, William H., born August 5, 1847, died April 25, 1930
Kreeger, Catherine (mother), born 1828, died 1919
Kreeger, John (father), born 1822, died 1880
Kreeger, John W. (father), born 1858, died 1930
Kreeger, Lydia J. (mother), born 1863, died 1930
Kreeger, Ada May
Kurzweil, Katherine Z., born November 18, 1841
Kurzweil, Joseph, born 1836, died 1931

L

Lamkin, Lewis, born March 7, 1832, died May 24, 1907
Lamkin, Helen K., wife of Lewis, born September 2, 1847, died December 14, 1916
Langsford, Nicholas B., born February 6, 1839, died September 22, 1898
Langsford, Fannie M., wife of Nicholas B., born June 21, 1849, died September 9, 1898
Landis, John, died January 6, 1899; age, 65 years, 3 months, 4 days
Lain, Ephram A., born December 17, 1830, died May 22, 1898
Latham, Joseph V., born December 10, 1819, died May 17, 1897
Latham, Martha, wife of Joseph, born September 11, 1823, died March 17, 1907
Latham, Harrison A., born 1845, died 1926
Latham, Elutheria J., wife of Harrison A., born 1855, died 1924
Lawrence, George W. (father), born 1841, died 1925
Lawrence, Lydia B. (mother), born 1849, died 1926
Lawrence, John, born 1812, died 1886
Lesher, Henry C., born 1838, died 1923
Lesher, Ella, wife of Henry C., born 1845, died 1929
Lea, Dr. P. J. G., born 1807, died 1862
Lea, Lucinda F., wife of Dr. P. J. G., born 1821, died 1867
Lea, Stephen A., born October 14, 1839, died February 23, 1898
Lacey, J. W., born 1812, died 1846
Lacey, Sarah, born 1816, died 1876
Lacey, Sarah A., born 1839, died 1913
Lacey, John T., born 1838, died 1908
Lewis, William F., born April 27, 1830, died August 18, 1888
Lewis, Janet T. Compton, wife of William Lewis, born Feb. 11, 1841, died March 19, 1926
Lewis, Zachary T., born April 26, 1846, died October 30, 1919
Lewis, David, born 1847
Lewis, Mary C., born 1852
Lewis, Oliver H., born 1847, died 1916
Lewis, Louisa E., born 1842
Longfellow, Rev. Perry W., born 1854, died 1915
Longfellow, Rev. N. M., born April, 1830, died December 24, 1893
Longfellow, Mary C., wife of Rev. N. M. O., born December 14, 1829, died January 19, 1914
Lucas, D. B., born 1848, died 1912
Lucas, Deborah, wife of D. B., born 1848, died 1908
Lytle, Mary A., born 1820, died 1878

M

Maxwell, William H., born 1850, died 1917
Maxwell, Eliza D., born 1853, died 1921
Martin, Joseph, born 1845, died 1914
Martin, Mrs. Emma, died September 10, 1931; age, 76 years, 8 months, 3 days

Mason, John D., born May 4, 1858, died March 27, 1872
Mason, Peter, born February 4, 1838, died January 6, 1898
Mason, Mary, born 1840, died 1910
Mason, Samuel A., born 1852, died 1919
Mason, Samuel C., born 1810, died July 20, 1887
Mason, Anne E., born March 22, 1817, died December 3, 1874
Maxwell, Arthur F., born April 13, 1850, died February 17, 1907
Maxwell, Mary B., wife of Arthur F. Maxwell, born Sept. 1, 1857, died Jan. 19, 1918
Maxwell, Thomas, died April 19, 1887; age, 48 years, 5 months, 22 days
Moore, William, born July 8, 1825, died December 25, 1893; age, 68 years, 5 months, 17 days
Moore, Eliza, wife of William Moore, born November 10, 1826, died February 8, 1911
Merton, Andrew
Mozier, R.
Mozier, Rebecca, died 1894; age, 84 years
Munns, Sanford T. (stone broken)
Munn, Mary M., wife of S. T. Munn, died September 23, 1870; age, 32 years
Markham, Byron A., born October 26, 1839, died June 29, 1907; Co. "G" 14th Wis. Inf. (Gov. marker)
Mercer, Mrs. Jennie, died February 8, 1821; age, 71 years, 3 months
Mercer, Clinton, died 1931; age, 88 years, 6 months, 26 days
Mitchell, Sarah, wife of Alvin Mitchell, died January 9, 1878; age, 42 years
Moss, S.
Murphy, James, died September 17, 1873; age, 76 years, 5 months, 20 days
Mulligan, Mrs. Sarena, died March 12, 1933; age, 88 years, 7 days
Moore, Luzetta, wife of James N. Moore, born March 13, 1849, died July 19, 1908
Moore, Thomas K., died September 18, 1890; age, 63 years
Muse, John M., born 1833, died 1917
Muse, Annie E., wife of John M. Muse, born 1854, died 1922
Myers, Frances, born 1845, died 1903
Myers, Jacob, born 1841, died 1921
Mackay, George, born 1850, died 1898
Martin, Mary J., born February 5, 1832
Martin, W. G., born March 22, 1832, died July 13, 1895
Mapel, Mark G., born June 24, 1846, died June 10, 1903
Miller, Sarah E., born 1830, died 1877
Mansell, J. E., wife of R. H. Mansell, born September 6, 1841, died March 16, 1902

Mc

McBride, G. W., —— emblem
McCarter, O. P. (father), born 1842, died 1925
McCarter, M. E. (mother), born 1848, died 1927
McClanahan, Adam Irvine, Sr., died 1870
McClanahan, Ezekiel, died 1869
McClanahan, Irvine, Jr., died 1871
McClanahan, Maria E., died 1895
McCloud, Walter, born 1850, died 1921
McCloud, Mattie H., wife of Walter McCloud, born 1862, died 1928
McGraw, Losia J., wife of G. W. McGraw, born 1839, died 1917
McKisson, Margaret, born December, 1827, died March 3, 1905
McNutt, Henry D., born December 16, 1835, died January 26, 1925

N

Newby, Jerimah, born April 29, 1842, died October 10, 1910
Newby, Martha, born April 8, 1842, died August 24, 1925
Nichols, James, born October 13, 1820, died February 19, 1908
Nichols, Mary, wife of James Nichols, born October 29, 1818, died August 30, 1890

Nichols, John, born 1845, died 1923

Niederauer, Roxanna D., wife of M. Niederauer, born November 17, 1839, died 1880 (stone broken)

Noel, James W., born 1841, died 1919

Noel, William A., born February 13, 1846, died September 29, 1901

Noland, Ann R., wife of James, born in Richmond, Kentucky, January 21, 1821, died August 11, 1894

Norvell, J. W., 22nd Ind. L. A. (Gov. marker)

Norvell, Lucinda E., daughter of J. W. and M. A. Norvell, died January 22, 1868; age, 1 year, 9 months

Norvell, Lucinda, wife of J. C. Norvell, born June 12, 1820, died September 21, 1882; age, 62 years, 3 months, 12 days (stone also bears the name "father," no dates)

Norvell, M. A., son of J. C. and Lucinda, born August 18, 1833, died September 22, 1869

O

Ocker, M. B., born 1845, died 1921

Ocker, Eliza Jane, wife of M. B. Ocker, born 1849, died 1919

Ohaus, Anna, wife of Henry Ohaus, born 1838, died 1923

Ohaus, Henry, born 1859, died 1920

Owen, Mary E. (mother), born 1842, died 1931

Owen, Lerick, Co. "E" 94th Ill. Inf. (Gov. marker)

Owen, Robert W., born October 24, 1840, died February 22, 1893

Owen, Mary E., born August 18, 1840, died May 4, 1927

Owens, Elizabeth D., born 1832, died 1885

Orrick, Minerva, died January 16, 1896; age, 60 years

P

Parker, Zachariah, born May 20, 1810, died June 29, 1896

Parker, Mary, wife of Zachariah Parker, born September 1, 1814, died May 10, 1900

Parks, Sarah L., born 1810, died 1887

Parry, Thomas, born in Baerwen, Angelsea, North Wales, July 11, 1838, died Nov. 26, 1922

Parry, Jeannette, wife of Thomas Parry, born in Barhead, Scotland, February, 1838, died October 18, 1914

Parry, Robert O., son of T. and J. Parry, died September 2, 1870; age, 2 months, 22 days

Parry, infant son of T. and J. Parry, born and died January 18, 1873

Pate, Jeremiah, died November 25, 1874; age, 53 years, 7 months, 3 days

Payton, Presley M., born 1837, died 1823; 3rd Ind. Cavalry (Gov. marker)

Payton, Rhoda E., wife of Presley M. Payton, born 1845, died 1888. "100% Christian, 100% American"

Patton, Rebecca, born 1843, died 1929

Patton, W. J., died March 8, 1878; age, 45 years

Peacock, John E. (father), born April 11, 1811, died February 5, 1884

Peacock, Annah V. (mother), born October 28, 1829, died October 30, 1902

Perdue, Daniel, born November 13, 1850, died September 27, 1910

Perdue, Amanda F., born November 6, 1854, died January 17, 1921

Peters, Clara A., died June 13, 1875; age, 12 years

Pettenger, William H., born November 17, 1836, died June 5, 1898

Pettenger, Maria L., born February 28, 1845, died March 27, 1928

Phillips, K. C., born March 4, 1845, died July 30, 1919

Phillips, Matilda J., died September 5, 1925; age, 74 years, 4 months, 16 days

Prather, Frances W., born 1815, died 1901

Price, Fannie M., born 1830, died 1917

Price, Captain Jesse L., born 1824, died 1886

Primley, Ruth, wife of E. Primley, died May 24, 1878; age, 45 years, 9 months, 26 days

Porter, Elvira R. Hutchings (mother), born 1841, died 1916

Porter, Samuel C. (father), born 1843, died 1869

Proudfit, John, born 1836, died 1920
Proudfit, Harriet L., born 1836, died 1920
Proudfit, infant son of J. and H. L. Proudfit, died February 5, 1871
Powell, John B., born February 14, 1834, died November 3, 1914
Powell, Mary J., wife of J. B. Powell, died November 11, 1891; age, 53 years
Powell, William, died October 29, 1879; age, 70 years, 2 months, 24 days
Powell, Rebecca, wife of William Powell, died December 20, 1882; age, 68 years, 4 months, 9 days
Children of William and R. Powell
Powell, Thomas, born August 29, 1848, died August 10, 1870
Powell, Elizabeth, born June 22, 1833, died February 25, 1897
Powell, Archibald McC., born April 2, 1840, died April 1, 1906
Powell, William A., born September 18, 1841, died December 10, 1897
Powell, Laura B., wife of William A. Powell, born 1847, died 1932
Powell, Sarah E., born September 3, 1844, died February 18, 1825
Rawles, William N., born August 12, 1839, died July 26, 1908; Co. "E" 21st Ohio Vol. Inf. (Gov. marker)

Q

Quog, J. E., born December 1, 1832, died August 23, 1914
Quog, Mary E., born December 18, 1844, died February 5, 1905

R

Reeder, Daniel, born May 2, 1828, died March 26, 1894
Reeder, Mary, wife of Daniel Reeder, born March 15, 1832, died July 28, 1907
Rhea, William M., born August 7, 1840, died February 20, 1893
Rheem, Clark, born 1848, died 1901
Rheem, Ida A., born 1852, died 1902
Rhodes, Mary D., daughter of A. J. and K. Rhodes, died August 20, 1875; age, 1 year, 7 days
Rider, Dora A. (wife), born April 28, 1839, died July 29, 1881
Rider, J. W. (son), born April 10, 1839; age, 10 months
Ritter, Henry T., died February 24, 1903; age, 79 years
Ritter, Mary M., wife of Henry T. Ritter, died June 15, 1901; age, 69 years
Ritter, Lockey J., daughter of H. T. and M. M. Ritter, died November 14, 1873; age, 5 years
Ritter, Elvis G., son of H. T. and M. M. Ritter, died September 13, 1873; age, 2 years
Ritter, J. L., born December 27, 1850, died May 7, 1905
Ritter, Rebecca, wife of J. L. Ritter, born January 1, 1850, died August 1, 1913
Rogers, William, born 1845, died 1913

S

Sampson, Sue (Christopher), born 1838, died 1881
Sampson, H. T., born 1811, died 1892
Sampson, Ellen G., born 1835, died 1923
Sampson, J. B., born 1844, died 1921
Sampson, T., born 1852, died 1875
Sanders, Mrs. Elizabeth Jane, died 1931; age, 97 years
Sanders, Elza, Co. "B" 6th Kansas Cav. (Gov. marker)
Saunders, Lewis W., born September 28, 1835, died November 11, 1926
Saunders, Julia A., wife of Lewis W. Saunders, born August 22, 1838, died July 15, 1884
Scheer, Nicholas, born 1839, died 1916
Scheer, Mary E., born June 27, 1847, died February 11, 1888
Scheer, Henry J. (father), born 1849, died 1923
Schrole, Lewis, born March 28, 1841, died May 18, 1907 (Flag at grave)
Schrole, Matilda, wife of Henry J. Schrole, born September 3, 1847, died July 7, 1911
Scott, Martin H., born 1844, died 1928
Scott, Sophis F., wife of Martin H. Scott, born 1849, died 1928

Scruggs, Henrietta, daughter of J. Alex. and Amanda Scruggs, born April 11, 1870, died April 20, 1870
Sears, Thomas L., born March 13, 1848, died August 11, 1919 (Masonic Emblem)
Sechler, Michael, born February 28, 1837, died March 27, 1912; Co. "L" 3rd Penn. H. A. (Gov. marker)
Sechler, Susan, wife of Michael Sechler, born January 17, 1839, died January 25, 1914
Shaw, Louis, born 1842, died 1912
Shaw, Sallie D., born 1843, died 1923
Shaw, Pearl, daughter of J. A. and E. E. Shaw, died July 16, 1880; age, 25 days
Shaw, Captain Jas. A., Co. "B" 10th Ill. Inf. (Gov. marker)
Shaw, Rebecca Jane, wife of Jas. A. Shaw, died February 1, 1873; age, 28 years, 5 months, 11 days
Shaw, Cora Irene, daughter of J. A. and R. J. Shaw, died August 24, 1872; age, 7 months
Shaw, Ellae, died August 23, 1888; age, 49 years, 5 months, 8 days
Shawhan, George R., born 1843, died 1912
Shepard, Oliver B., born November 25, 1842, died March 4, 1868 (first burial in Lee's Summit Cemetery)
Short, Martha J., wife of E. W. Short, born July 29, 1845, died June 7, 1901
Short, E. W. (father), born 1843, died 1917
Short, J. M., born January 20, 1841, died March 3, 1912; Co. "F" 5th Prov. En. Mo. Mil. (Gov. marker)
Short, Jasper, born 1839, died 1911
Short, Josephine, born 1850, died 1911
Shrout, Elizabeth, wife of J. M. Shrout, born September 25, 1845, died October 19, 1872
Shrout, James M., born August 8, 1843, died April 5, 1924
Shy, Jacob (father), died November 22, 1869; age, 80 years, 20 days
Shy, Sarah, wife of Jacob Shy, died March 3, 1872; age, 64 years, 5 months, 7 days
Smelser, Sarah, wife of John Smelser, born 1815, died 1887
Smith, Frank P., born October 13, 1849, died September 28, 1916
Smith, Napoleon B., born 1836, died 1922
Smith, Fannie A. (mother), born 1853, died 1926
Smith, Ketteman
Smith, Henry, born 1848, died 1927
Smith, Lydia A., born July 16, 1856, died December 3, 1926
Smith, William W., born March 24, 1840, died February 11, 1919
Smith, Mary E., wife of William W. Smith, born December 28, 1840, died March 24, 1905
Smith, Augustus S., born May 29, 1834, died January 22, 1895
Smith, Pattie, wife of A. S. Smith, born February 9, 1844, died September 29, 1885
Snediker, Isaiah F., born August 10, 1842, died December 29, 1918
Snider, Emily J., wife of U. M. W. Snider, born March 28, 1833, died September 11, 1922
Snider, U. M. W., born August 5, 1827, died December 14, 1897
Spencer, James R., born 1850, died 1932
Sprout, Clara M., daughter of J. M. and E. Sprout, born January 30, 1871, died Oct. 19, 1872
Spoonamore, George G., died December 14, 1894; age, 75 years, 4 months
Seiler, Frank, born 1851, died 1910
Seiler, Amelia, wife of Frank Seiler, born 1858, died 1923
Simmons, John F., born June 10, 1840, died January 24, 1903
Simmons, Marjeline, wife of John F. Simmons, born October 15, 1839, died March 26, 1896
Soper, Archie A., wife of B. F. Soper, born July 7, 1844, died May 7, 1918
Stevenson, Albert F., born 1854, died 1912
Stralley, William, born September 9, 1847, died March 28, 1893
Stralley, Camillia Ann, wife of William Stralley, born July 4, 1849, died November 19, 1881
Stone, Sergt. Caleb, Co. "F" 5th Prov. En. Mo. Mil. (Gov. marker)
Strother, Dr. William D., born March 10, 1827, died April 21, 1907
Strother, Julia S., wife of Dr. Wm. D. Strother, born August 29, 1836, died July 9, 1885
Stottlemyer, Howard (brother), born February 9, 1850, died February 2, 1922

CEMETERIES—PRAIRIE TOWNSHIP

St. Raley, Pearley Don, daughter of W. and S. St. Raley, died 1874
Stauffer, Mary C., daughter of B. F. and A. A. Stauffer, died April 22, 1867; age, 1 year, 4 months, 22 days
Stoner, George B., born May 12, 1849, died December 21, 1913
Stoner, Jennie M., wife of George B. Stoner, died December 23, 1921
Sutton, Robert, born 1846, died 1922

T

Taggart, Martin V., born April 6, 1844
Taggart, Mary E., wife of Martin V. Taggart, born May 2, 1847, died February 20, 1901
Taylor, Sarah, wife of Theodore W. Taylor, born December 6, 1838, died March 23, 1908
Taylor, Theodore W., born January 11, 1837, died December 22, 1917
Thalheim, Albert, born March 19, 1848, died June 11, 1910
Talheim, Minna, born June 22, 1854, died May 14, 1925
Thrail, W. B., born March 20, 1811, died April 5, 1888
Thomas, Harriet P., wife of Adam Thomas, died April 16, 1874; age, 61 years, 1 month, 3 days
Thornton, Sarah H., born July 8, 1829, died January 7, 1874
Townsend, Icyphene, born May 22, 1813, died January 2, 1877
Tyer, Columbus F., born May 5, 1848, died September 20, 1925 (American flag at grave)
Tyer, Martha A., wife of Columbus F. Tyer, born April 15, 1852, died May 17, 1907
Tyler, John W., born January 16, 1839, died October 25, 1919
Tyson, O. V., born 1838, died 1920
Tyson, Luvenia, wife of O. V. Tyson, born 1848, died 1930
Tyson, Hannah, wife of Thomas S. Tyson, born February 21, 1828, died August 15, 1914
Tyson, Thomas S., born February 26, 1830, died June 13, 1911
Tweedler, Chris, born 1850, died 1927
Thompson, William, died April 22, 1885; age, 66 years
Thompson, Hester, wife of William Thompson, born July 27, 1820, died November 24, 1906

V

Vanhook, George C., born 1846
Vanhook, Margaret L., wife of George C. Vanhook, born 1852, died 1918

W

Walker, J. A., born 1845, died 1929
Warden, Mary A., wife of J. G., born August 30, 1834, died March 21, 1911
Warden, John G., died December 6, 1901; age, 74 years
Warden, Thaddeus W., born November 28, 1831, died September 4, 1901
Warren, Thomas V., born 1841, died 1898
Warren, Almeda House, born 1854, died 1914
Warren, G. W., born April 30, 1847, died May 23, 1893
Warren, Rev. George J., born 1847, died 1922
Warren, Sarah E., wife of Rev. Geo. J. Warren, born 1845, died 1921
Weeks, Tully, Co. "E" 53rd Ind. Inf. (Gov. marker)
Whiting, A. B., born 1833, died 1914
Whiting, Lucy E., wife of A. B. Whiting, born 1840, died 1911
Whiting, Daniel, born January 22, 1825, died August 5, 1900
Whiting, Elizabeth (wife), born January, 1837, died November 25, 1910
Whitton, John, died January 1, 1925; age, 81 years, 10 months, 9 days
Whitworth, Barthena, died November 6, 1869
Wigginton, Mary C., born February 2, 1842, died February 17, 1899
Wigginton, Mary Ann, died June 8, 1882; age, 73 years
Wigginton, G. W., born 1843, died 1918
Wilson, Willie A., son of J. W. and Bettie Wilson, died Aug. 31, 1873; age, 9 months, 26 days
Wilson, G. H., born August 10, 1810; age, 60 years, 3 months, 3 days

Wilson, John W., born 1845, died 1915
Wilson, Louisa G., born 1831, died 1905
Wilson, Robert G., born 1820, died 1911
Williams, William, born 1856, died 1923
Williams, Jane Thomas Williams, born 1860, died 1925
Williams, Younger R., son of A. G. and G. J. Williams, died November 29, 1874; age, 7 years. 1 month, 16 days
Williamson, H. G., born 1838, died 1914; Co. "H" 62nd Ill. Inf.
Williamson, Emily E. (wife), born 1841, died 1930
Winburn, Thomas, born April 29, 1827, died August 31, 1897
Winburn, Martha, wife of Thomas Winburn, born July 2, 1848, died August 22, 1895
Winship, Willie F., born December 22, 1873, died May 2, 1877
Winship, Mary Ann, born 1836, died 1920
Winship, Thomas, born 1829, died 1906
Wood, J. L., born 1834, died 1915
Wood, Eliza A., wife of J. A. Wood, born June 19, 1842, died December 7, 1907
Woods, W. H., born 1839, died 1911
Wood, Nancy, died 1890; age, 63 years
Wood, J. P., died 1892; age, 71 years
Worthington, Eli Jefferson (father), born 1841, died 1916
Worthington, Mary Josephine, born 1852, died 1880 (mother)
Worthington, James, born July 28, 1815, died July 30, 1897
Worthington, Holland, born August, 1810, died February 28, 1889
Worthington, Martha E., born 1847, died 1915
Wright, Thomas J., born September 22, 1829, died March 7, 1900; Co. "E" G. Ky. Cavalry
Wright, Lucretia, wife of Thomas J. Wright, born June 5, 1821, died June 13, 1914
Wright, Robert H., born 1845, died January 5, 1921
Wright, Susan F., wife of Robert H. Wright, born 1848, died January 12, 1932
Wright, Fannie B., daughter of William T. and A. Wright, born September 15, 1858, died July 9, 1870
Wright, Sarah F., daughter of Wm. T. and A. Wright, born October 22, 1849, died November 22, 1886
Wright, William T., born October 12, 1822, died September 27, 1897; age, 75 years

Y

Yankee, Jacob, born January 6, 1827, died March 17, 1895
Yankee, Fannie S., wife of Jacob Yankee, born March 20, 1849, died June 12, 1921
Younger, Cole, born 1844, died 1916

MASON CEMETERY
SE Quarter Section 19, Township 48, Range 30 W

Mason, Elizabeth, daughter of Samuel G. and Anna E. Mason, died December 9, 1847; age, 5 years
Mason, Margaret S., daughter of Samuel G. and Anna E. Mason, died December, 1844; age, 8 years
Mason, Marchia P., daughter of Samuel and Anna E. Mason, born June 9, 1844, died January 11, 1846
N. B. Other unmarked graves in the cemetery.

CEMETERIES—PRAIRIE TOWNSHIP

MOORE CEMETERY
Land entered by John Moore; now a part of Unity Farm
Section 25, Township 48, Range 32

Tombstones and all trace of cemetery now gone.
Information by Mr. James Dark, Lee's Summit, Missouri, and
Mrs. Carlton, Lee's Summit, Missouri, R. R. No. 2

Moore, John, died 1888; age, 90 years (Mason)
Moore, Katie, wife of John Moore
Moore, Charlie, son of Mr. Leck Moore, and grandson of John and Katie Moore
Yocum, Angeline, daughter of John and Katie Moore
Porter, Mary, daughter of John and Katie Moore
Oldham, Enoch

Secured by Mrs. Hale Houts October 24, 1933

STRODE CEMETERY
Section 20, Township 47, Range 32 W

Data by Mrs. Jennie Stone, daughter of James E. and Susan Chrisman Strode

Dews, Elizabeth Strode, was the first one to be buried on the Strode farm
Irvin, Bead
Rule, Martha
Rule, Nancy Strode
Strode, John, born January 13, 1795, died June 19, 1866
Strode, Nancy Evans, born June 15, 1817, died March 29, 1874
Strode, James E., born May 15, 1823, died 1882
Strode, Susan Chrisman, born January 29, 1830, died 1916
Strode, Rebecca Chrisman
Strode, Elizabeth Ann, born May 28, 1849, died 1887
Strode, Samuel M., born November 4, 1851, died July 25, 1852
Strode, John P., born March 18, 1854
Strode, Susan L., born February 18, 1857
Strode, Nancy Jane, born June 11, 1859
Strode, Mattie B., born March 14, 1865
Strode, James W., born March 7, 1862, died December 23, 1929
Talley, Mary Rule
Whiteman, Jesse I.
Whiteman, Tommy (small boy)
   There are 22 graves
John Strode married Nancy Evans March 3, 1816, near Nashville, Tennessee
James E. Strode married Susan Chrisman October 17, 1848, in Jackson County, Missouri

STRODE GRAVES
Section 17, Township 47, Range 32 W

Strode, William
Strode, son of William Strode
Strode slaves

Copied by Miss Jessie M. Crosby

TALLEY CEMETERY

Section 24, Township 48, Range 32 W

There are twenty-one graves in this cemetery, only the following are marked:

David C. Talley, born August 5, 1811, died May 19, 1869
Mary A., wife of D. C. Talley, born September 10, 1820, died December 23, 1884
Talley, Albert H., son of S. L. and Susie Talley, died March 8, 1901; age, 4 days

Buried in the Talley Cemetery, but not marked, are the following:

Benjamin Talley, died 1902; age, 70 years
Robert Talley, died 1866; was an old man at time of death
Five Talley children

Copied August 14, 1933, by Mrs. Hale Houts

WELLS CEMETERY

Old Myers Farm, now owned by Unity School of Christianity
Section 26, Township 48, Range 32
Information by Mrs. Carlton, R. R. No. 2, Lee's Summit, Mo.

Wells, Wash, a son of Samuel Wells, known to have been buried on this farm

Secured by Mrs. Hale Houts October 24, 1933

WESTPORT TOWNSHIP

Organized May 17, 1869

Westport Township taken into Kansas City (Kaw Township) 1909

BOONE HAYS CEMETERY

Sixty-third Street and Brooklyn Avenue, Kansas City, Missouri
Data contributed by Col. James H. Rout and Mrs. Lem Stevenson,
descendants of the Boone family

This land was a part of the farm of Daniel Morgan Boone. In 1836 he sold it to Boone Hays. The first person buried there was a Mr. McCorkle, who worked for Daniel Morgan Boone.

The following members of the Boone family were buried there:

Col. Daniel Morgan Boone, born December 23, 1769, died July 13, 1839.*
    Sarah Griffin Lewis, wife of Daniel Morgan Boone, born Jan. 29, 1786, died June 19, 1850
Edward Boone, born July 30, 1813, died 1860
Elizabeth Levica Boone, wife of Jesse White, born April 22, 1815, died 1850
James Boone, born 1819, died 1852
Lorinda, wife of James Boone, died 1865
William, son of James Boone
Cassandra Boone Cosby, born November 3, 1821, died May 20, 1845
Morgan Boone, born August 3, 1824, died 1852
Disa Stewart, wife of Morgan Boone, died before 1851
Daniel Boone, born March 27, 1809, died 1880 (removed to Forest Hill Cemetery)
Samuel Hays, son of Boone Hays, born December 12, 1824, died December 6, 1872
Rebecca Berry, wife of Samuel Hays, died June, 1873
Mrs. Mariam Hays McMurtry, born March 12, 1826
Mr. and Mrs. Linville Hays (removed to Belton, Missouri)
Upton Hays, died 1867; age, 6 years
Mrs. Cepriande Philabert (removed to Forest Hill Cemetery)
Mr. and Mrs. Charles Thompson
Lucinda Thomas Davis (removed to Independence, Missouri)
William Benham Carmichael, born March 9, 1828, died April 21, 1890
Jerusha Mattison Cornett, wife of Wm. B. Carmichael, born Jan. 5, 1840, died Oct. 7, 1900
Martha Hefford, wife of J. R. Reynolds, died July, 1880; age, 60 years
Henry Clay Rout, born April 6, 1838, died August 24, 1863 (removed to Forest Hill Cemetery)
Eliza M. Hays, wife of H. C. Rout, born 1844 (removed to Forest Hill Cemetery)
Frank Thomas (removed to Forest Hill Cemetery)
Leon Thomas (removed to Forest Hill Cemetery)
Three Rout children (removed to Forest Hill Cemetery)

    *In collecting the early records of the county, the committee found a difference of opinion as to where Daniel Morgan Boone was buried. Some say he was buried in Westport Cemetery; others say he was buried in the Boone Hays Cemetery.

The following inscriptions were copied from stones in the Boone Hayes Cemetery June 22, 1933:

Flacy, George A., son of Samuel and Louise Flacy, born Nov. 29, 1893, died July 29, 1903
Frey, Ida Bell, wife of John J. Frey, born September 4, 1865, died February 26, 1890; age, 24 years, 5 months, 22 days
Fuqua, William, born March 8, 1800, died January 3, 1855
Grummett, Albert, born January 31, 1882, died December 5, 1897
Hays, Linville Upton, born February 6, 1864, died July 15, 1893
Sharon, John W., born December 3, 1846, died July 18, 1886
Thompson, Elizabeth R., died February 14, 1892; age, 86 years, 26 days
Thompson, George V., died January 3, 1888; age, 53 years, 8 months, 27 days
Thompson, Martha A., died June 26, 1893; age, 42 years, 10 months, 2 days

Compiled and copied by Miss Jessie M. Crosby

BROOMFIELD CEMETERY

Seventy-fifth Street and Indiana Avenue, Kansas City, Missouri

Mr. Samuel Broomfield set aside one acre of his farm as a neighborhood burying ground. This cemetery was destroyed when Seventy-fifth Street was opened. Mr. F. X. Self is the authority for recording the following as having been buried there:

The wife and only child of Samuel Broomfield
Warren Self, died in 1866
Two children of S. L. Woolf
Two wives of Griffith Dodson
Mrs. Price

The following record of removals from Broomfield Cemetery to the Palestine Cemetery was furnished by Mr. Greenberry Ragan, acting sexton of the Palestine Cemetery.

Date of Removal April 11, 1916

Nash, Riley; age, 52 years
Nash, Raymond, a baby
Nash, two babies
Cooper, a baby

Cared for by Mrs. Cooper

Burch, baby; age, 2 days
Burch, Charles T.; age, 14 years
Burch, David; age, 61 years
Burch, David, Jr., infant
Burch, John; age, 2 years
Burch, Mary; age, 74 years
Nash, Garrett; age, 45 years
Nash, Baby J. H., infant
Nash, Tabitha; age, 14 years
Williams, Baby, infant
Williams, George; age, 4 years
Williams, John; age, 7 years
Williams, Martha; age, 95 years

Copied by Miss Jessie M. Crosby

CEMETERIES—WESTPORT TOWNSHIP

THE CONFEDERATE SOLDIERS' CEMETERY
Sometimes called the Self Cemetery
SE Corner Seventy-first Street and Troost Avenue
Data gathered from interviews with Mr. Kemp Mockbee, Mr. G. M. Toliver,
Mr. Greenberry Ragan and Mrs. Lem. Stevenson.

The Federal Government cared for the dead Union soldiers in the Civil War but it was left to the family and friends to care for the Confederate dead. During the war the dead were generally buried near where they fell. Several years after the war it was decided to gather together as many as possible of the Confederate soldiers buried in and near Kansas City, and place them in an acre of ground at 71st Street and Troost Avenue. Captain Napoleon Davis was one of the leaders in this undertaking. Many friends and relatives attended the services held at the time these soldiers were reburied. The soldiers rested there until 1892 or 1893 when they were removed to Forest Hill Cemetery across the street.

In 1902 the Kansas City Missouri Chapter 149, United Daughters of the Confederacy, erected a monument "To the Brave Southern Soldiers Who Fell in the Battle of Westport, October 23, 1864."

The monument stands almost upon the exact spot where General Jo Shelby and his soldiers slept the night before the battle of Westport. Jo Shelby's grave is close to the base of the monument. Eighty unknown soldiers, who were killed in the battle of Westport, were buried together upon the field. The monument was dedicated May 30, 1902.

It is known that the following were buried at 71st and Troost Avenue:
Upton Hays
Richard Yeager
William McGuire
Officer Jones from Arkansas

In the quit claim deed recorded in connection with the sale of the burying ground at 71st Street and Troost Avenue the name mentioned is the Byram Ford Cemetery Association.

CONFEDERATE SOLDIERS BURIED ON MOCKBEE FARM

On the Mockbee Farm, which would now be located at 76th and Holmes Streets, were buried Confederate soldiers who were killed in that neighborhood during the Civil War. The bodies were moved to the Byram Ford Confederate Cemetery of Jackson County, which was located at what would now be the southeast corner of Seventy-first and Troost Avenue, and still later they were moved into Forest Hill Cemetery.

CORINTH CEMETERY
On SW Corner Westport Township
See Corinth Cumberland Presbyterian Church Records

Ballard, Charles, born 1846, died 1919
Barrow, Casandria, died November 2, 1873; age, 76 years, 5 months, 19 days
Cogswell, M. H., born 1829, died 1918
Cogswell, Julia Bailey, wife of M. H. Cogswell, born August 16, 1829, died August 18, 1876
Cook, Ruth H., wife of Wilson Cook, died 1860; age, 22 years, 14 days
Cross, James W., born January 6, 1837, died August 30, 1907
Cross, Perry C., born April 3, 1841, died August 6, 1918
Cross, Hettie M., wife of Perry C. Cross, born February 5, 1845, died April 13, 1909
Cross, Benjamin, born 1846, died 1922
Cross, Sarah M., born January 8, 1849, died November 22, 1896

Dodson, Lucinda B., wife of D. Dodson, died September 24, 1852; age, 35 years, 6 months, 22 days
Dugan, Victoria (mother), born 1848, died 1872
Dyche, John, born December 4, 1825, died November 17, 1898
Dyche, Louanna, wife of John Dyche, died June 12, 1889; age, 60 years, 9 months
Flanner, William (father), born August 8, 1824, died November 27, 1889
Flanner, E. R. (mother), born August 6, 1829, died March 15, 1909
Flanner, W. T., born April 2, 1856, died February 5, 1879
Finch, David E., died May 6, 1918; age, 73 years
Finch, Robert S., born December 4, 1813, died January 5, 1884
Finch, H. W. G., died January 1, 1884; age, 74 years
Finch, Harriet, wife of H. W. G. Finch, died July 27, 1869; age, 36 years
Fitzwater, Melinda, born January 1, 1813, died March 12, 1888
Hoge, Rachel Penning, born March 10, 1814, died January 29, 1894
Hoge, Elmer James, born August 20, 1830, died November 24, 1906; age, 76 years
Hoge, Sarah Amanda, born March 30, 1839, died January 19, 1925
Hall, Susan D., daughter of E. E. and B. S. Hall, wife of H. B. Tower, died October 30, 1880; age, 41 years, 9 months, 2 days
Hall, Betsy S., wife of Elisha E. Hall, died April 15, 1880; age, 67 years, 10 months, 23 days
Hoyt, Mary Dell, daughter of A. F. and M. E. Hoyt, died July 12, 1873; age, 8 months, 15 days
James, Thomas, born January 16, 1825, died April 29, 1902
James, Barbara, wife of Thomas James, born May 19, 1828, died November 25, 1905
James, Charles W., son of Thomas and B. A. James, died June 30, 1884; age, 36 years, 2 months, 9 days
James, J. P., born 1841, died 1922
James, Hettie, wife of J. P. James, born 1839, died 1918
Lewis, Thompson A., born 1824, died 1915
Lewis, Bettie J., born 1829, died 1893
Lockard, Sarah, wife of James S. Lockard, born in Bedford County, Virginia, February 5, ———, died 1901; age, 7- years
Major, Ella M., infant daughter
   (daughter of Wm. & E. R. Flanner), died August 4, 1884; age, 31 years, 6 months, 24 days
Moore, Allen, born April 4, 1847, died September 4, 1918
McFall, Corporal William, Co. "B" 2nd Kentucky Inf.
McMinn, Benjamin, born 1844, died 1901
McMinn, Angemima, wife of Benjamin McMinn, born 1852, died 1929
McPherrin, born May 25, 1835, died September 13, 1902
Park, David, born 1835, died 1873
Park, Mary, wife of David Park, born 1848, died 1917
Park, Archibald (father), born 1851, died 1899
Patrick, William, born in Scotland, June 20, 1825, died April 14, 1891
Pitt, George L., born September 9, 1837, died December 3, 1901
Prosser, Henry, died July 3, 1923; age, 82 years, 9 months, 8 days
Schisler, Reuben, born 1837, died 1872
Schwartz, Christina, born 1827, died 1907
Shufeldt, George H., son of H. G. and M. A. Shufeldt, died September 23, 1874; age, 1 year, 12 days
Self, John M., born 1848, died 1924
Self, Annie, wife of John M. Self, born 1855, died 1878
Self, Nancy A., wife of W. M. Self, born November 26, 1850, died April 29, 1889
Self, Elizabeth, wife of Jobe Self, died July 23, 1882; age, 56 years, 9 months, 18 days
Staver, Tobias S., born May 12, 1838, died April 20, 1904
Staver, Emeline, wife of Tobias S. Staver, born April 4, 1847, died December 25, 1923
Steele, Philo Potter, born April 7, 1840, died June 18, 1922
Tomlinson, Mary J. (Mrs. G. U.), born February 12, 1832, died June 17, 1906

Tomlinson, G. U., born January 13, 1838, died March 6, 1918
La Tourrette, T. V., born 1850, died 1927
Tower, Susan D., daughter of E. E. and B. S. Hall, wife of H. B. Tower, died October 30, 1880; age, 41 years, 9 months, 2 days
Voigts, Herman W., born April 23, 1841, died May 3, 1913
Voigts, Emelie Gehring, born September 15, 1844, died March 17, 1880
Voigts, Wilhelm, born 1843, died 1918
Voigts, Dorris Meyer, wife of Wilhelm Voigts, born 1856, died 1920
Younger, J. W., born October 9, 1824, died December 28, 1894

Copied March 10, 1933, by Mrs. Hale Houts

McCOY CEMETERY
Fifty-fifth Street and State Line

Epitaphs from all tombstones in the old McCoy Cemetery were copied by William W. Harris, grandson of John Calvin McCoy, the founder of Old Westport. The J. C. Nichols Company removed the remains to Union Cemetery in 1916. The McCoy family had moved the bodies of members of their family to Union Cemetery many years before.

Adams, John Q., of Acton, C. W., died May 6, 1849; age, 21 years, 10 months, 15 days
"That life is long which answers life's great end"
"My Baby W. H. B. born October 28, 1879"
Farmer, William F., born August 26, 1809, died October 16, 1855
Horn, James H., died February 10, 1874; age, 24 years, 8 months, 28 days
Hornung, Charles, born May 3, 1848, died July 3, 1849
Mize, John, born March 8, 1799, died July 9, 1864
Mize, Mary, born June 29, 1807, died February 9, 1871
Noland, Rellie A., daughter of R. and S. L. Noland, died August 11, 1879; age, 10 months, 12 days
Polke, Robert, born June 7, 1797, died May 26, 1843
Polke, Elizabeth, wife of Robert Polke, died May 9, 1854; age, 55 years, 2 months, 5 days
Polke, Elizabeth, daughter of Thomas W. and Eliza Polke, died July 1, 1849; age, 8 years, 4 months, 6 days
Polke, Helen, another daughter, died June 30, 1849; age, 4 years, 7 months, 29 days
Polke, Henry L., son of Thomas W. and Eliza Polke, died October 28, 1839; age, 14 months
Polke, Walter, a son, died June 30, 1849; age, 2 years, 4 months, 15 days
"All died of Cholera"
Russell, Sallie G., daughter of C. J. Russell, died August 13, 1878; age, 2 years, 5 months
Swaghbach, Henry, born October 15, 1824, died September 15, 1856
Tate, George W., born January 5, 1790, died November 12, 1868
Tate, Nancy P., wife of Maj. George W. Tate, died September 7, 1839; age, 46 years, 5 months
Toliver, Lizzie B., daughter of G. and J. A. Toliver, died July 31, 1879; age, 2 years, 9 months, 18 days. "Asleep in Christ"
Thomas, N. B., born January 28, 1823, died February 7, 1872
Thomas, Julia A., wife of N. B. Thomas, died August 4, 1878; age, 52 years
"Farewell children. I could no longer stay.
I am gone but all is well; will meet in endless day."
Thomas, George W., died March 19, 1869; age, 23 years, 22 days
Thompson, Joseph, born April 20, 1805, died February 1, 1870
Thompson, Margaret
McCoy, Virginia C., wife of J. C. McCoy, died May 28, 1849; age, 28 years, 5 months, 6 days; her body was removed to Union Cemetery at a much earlier date

PARRISH CEMETERY
Thirty-fifth Street and Bales Avenue
Data contributed by Mrs. M. A. Pitcher

This plot of ground, 118 x 114 feet, was set aside as a burying ground by William Parrish in 1849. The first burial in the cemetery was in 1851 when Miss Missouri Parrish, a daughter of the founder, was interred. Mr. Parrish came to Kansas City in 1827.

In 1926 the bodies of those buried in this cemetery were exhumed and moved to Forest Hill Cemetery, Kansas City, Missouri.

Others buried there:
- William Parrish
- Robert L. Hall, a son-in-law, died 1876
- Andrew Johnson, a son-in-law, died 1882
- Eliza Jane Johnson, a daughter, died 1882
- Mary R. Montgall, a daughter, died 1869
- Henry C. Parrish, a son, died 1860
- Angeline Parrish, a daughter, died 1889
- Mary R. Montgall, a granddaughter, died 1881
- William Parrish, a son, died 1873
- Eliza Parrish, wife, died 1871
- Joseph Braden, a brother-in-law, died 1880
- Missouri Parrish, a granddaughter, died 1881
- William A. Priest, a grandson, died 1859
- William Montgall, a son-in-law, died 1871
- Three infant sons of Wm. Montgall, died in 1859, 1861, 1863
- Margaret Bradley, a daughter, died 1886
- Ralph Bradley, a grandson, died 1879
- Margaret Bradley, a granddaughter, died 1882
- Maletus Bradley, a grandson, died 1863
- James W. Bradley, a grandson, died 1859
- Thomas E. Bradley, a grandson, died 1851
- Edith Bradley, a granddaughter, died 1880
- Levi W. Bradley, a son-in-law, died 1882

Copied by Miss Jessie M. Crosby

WESTPORT CEMETERY
Westport Avenue near Penn Street, Kansas City, Missouri

The land for this cemetery was given by Mr. Ed Price. It was established about 1835 and was about two hundred feet square. The land is now occupied by the Badger Lumber Company.

The families of Wornall, Yoakum, Richters and Gov. Boggs had lots there. It is only possible to record a very few of the names of those buried there.

Judith A. Wornall, wife of Richard Wornall, and mother of John Bristow Wornall, died 1849

G. Thomas Wornall, died 1849

John B. Wornall's first wife (she was a Miss Polk)

Several members of the Boone family, descendants of Daniel Boone, were buried there.

The only mention of the plague (cholera) was on the stone at the head of Elizabeth Richter's grave. One of the oldest dates was on the headstone of Luke Lea, an Indian agent at Westport. He was born in 1783 and died June 17, 1851.

Rosie Mae Yochum, died 1846

Henry Sager's wife

Lieut. Jos. Boggs, died January 22, 1843, served in the Pa. Mil. Rev. War

In 1915 the Elizabeth Benton Chapter of the Daughters of the American Revolution placed a marker to his memory in the wall of the Badger Lumber Company's building.

Compiled by Miss Jessie M. Crosby

PARTIAL LIST OF SMALL BURYING GROUNDS NOW EXTINCT

Located within what is now Kansas City, Missouri
Compiled by Miss Jessie M. Crosby

ADAIR BURYING GROUND
Fifty-ninth Street and Swope Parkway, on the Thomas Farm

Mary Ann Adair, wife of Abner J. Adair
Infant son and daughter

N. B. These bodies were removed to the cemetery in Independence, Mo., when Swope Parkway was graded.

BURYING GROUND
NW Corner Fifty-second Street and Troost Avenue

In the early days there was a cemetery at Fifty-second Street and Troost Avenue. When Troost Avenue was graded a part of the cemetery was destroyed. Oda Cantrell entered this land from the Government in 1834. The Duke family was the next owner, buying it in 1847.

It is called by some the John Moore Cemetery. There are no traces of it at this time, but it is well remembered by the old settlers of the neighborhood and few, if any, of the remains were ever removed.

HARPER CEMETERY
Sixty-third Street near Brooklyn Avenue

This cemetery was south of the Boone Hays Cemetery.
Harper, George
Harper, Dudley, son of George Harper
Gregg, daughter of Darius Gregg
Noland, Malinda, daughter of Russel and Zeralda (Harper) Noland

N. B. These bodies were removed to the Woodlawn Cemetery, Independence, Missouri.

Contributed by Mr. Russell Noland, whose mother was a Harper

HORNBUCKLE BURYING GROUND
Fifty-third and Main Streets

Mrs. Nancy Hornbuckle died November, 1877
Henry Hornbuckle
Sarah Hornbuckle Patton
Mr. Alfred Hornbuckle was buried near Hale, in Carroll County, Missouri

LAWS CEMETERY
Thirty-sixth Street Terrace and Drury, Kansas City, Missouri

Allen, Laws
Allen, Willis
Grandchildren of Alfred Laws, owner of the Laws Farm

Contributed by Mrs. Samuel H. Laws

MOUNTFORTT BURYING GROUND
Thirty-ninth Street and Cleveland Avenue

Mountfortt, Gustavus Augustine, born April —, 18-0, died July 1, 1868

Mountfortt, Adelade, daughter of G. A. Mountfortt, born Aug. 3, 1865, died Jan. 6, 1868

These bodies were removed from the Mountfortt yard to Forest Hill Cemetery.

Mr. Mountfortt was the first passenger and freight agent of the Missouri Pacific Railroad, the first railroad to enter Kansas City.

Data contributed by Mrs. E. Mont Reily

RAGAN CEMETERY
Near Thirty-sixth and Cherry Streets

Jacob Ragan, born in Lexington, Ky., December 7, 1792; removed to Jackson County, Mo., October 31, 1837; died November 7, 1878. Was a Color Bearer in the War of 1812.

Joseph H. Ragan, born December 29, 1834, died September 7, 1857

Ragan, Rane, son of G. L. and Jane P. Ragan, born April 6, 1851, died March 30, 1868

Javens, Everline T., born August 16, 1825, died January 29, 1852

Johnson, Jacob S., born January 1, 1847, died May 7, 1849

Johnson, James H., born August, 1822, died August 10, 1851. Was the first Undertaker in what is now Kansas City, Mo.

N. B. In 1886 these remains were removed to Union Cemetery, Kansas City, Mo.

RUGGS GRAVE
Near 36th Street and Van Brunt
Data contributed April 2, 1933, by John M. Johnston of Taylor, Missouri

"I have in mind a lone grave, which I came upon in 1903 or 1904, while strolling through the woods as a boy. It was located about three or four blocks east of Elmwood Avenue and south of 36th Street, on a slight hillside south of a large pond. The grave had been surrounded by an iron fence which was toppled over; tombstone was marked 'Dr. H. H. Ruggs, Kansas City, died 1855.' At that time it was completely surrounded by the woods known as 'Vineyards.'"

SECKINGER GRAVE
In the block east of Montgall between Forty-third and Forty-fourth Streets
Data contributed by J. J. Seckinger

Martha or Nancy Hendricks, wife of John Seckinger, died 1865 or 1866. She was buried on the Seckinger farm and her body has never been removed. Her husband was buried in Forest Hill Cemetery.

John Seckinger was the first dairyman to sell milk in Kansas City.

STEWART CEMETERY
SW Corner Thirty-sixth Street and Lydia Avenue

There were about 25 graves in the family burying ground on the William Stewart farm.

THOMAS BURYING GROUND
Forty-first Street and Benton Boulevard
Data contributed by Mr. W. O. Thomas

Thomas, Jesse, and his first wife

Davenport, James and his wife, Polly; James Davenport was a brother of Jesse Thomas' first wife

Bishop, Thomas F., born June 25, 1849, died August 15, 1866

The Bishops were related to the Davenports.

Davis, Jesse, and wife, Lucy

Davis, Elizabeth, daughter of Jesse Thomas

BROOKING TOWNSHIP

Organized March 13, 1872

BROOKING CEMETERY

Section 33, Township 49, Range 32 W

Compiled and copied by Miss Jessie M. Crosby and Mrs. May T. Crosby

Abstract records show that the land on which Brooking Cemetery is located, was entered by James Kimsey from the Government, December 10, 1831. James Kimsey and his wife, Hannah Kimsey, deeded it to Alvin Brooking, April 13, 1839, "eight hundred acres, more or less," for a consideration of $5,000.00.

The first burial was that of Mrs. John Herndon, a relative of Judge Brooking, in 1844. Mrs. Marcus Pendleton recalls that an old neighbor related the incident of one morning meeting Alvin Brooking with an ax over his shoulder. He said there had been a death in the family and he was going out to locate a burying ground. The Brooking slaves built a stone wall around the plot. The wall is still standing, and marks the original burying grounds.

Alvin Brooking had three children,—a son, Henry C. Brooking; two daughters, Serena Brooking, who married William C. Debord, and after his death married Logan Pendleton; and Mary Brooking, who married John T. Campbell.

Alvin Brooking died November 30, 1857, and his son, Henry C. Brooking, in accordance with his father's request, completed the wall and cared for the cemetery. There are twenty members of the family and two slaves buried within the inclosed plot. In later years a few friends were buried outside the family burying ground.

Henry C. Brooking inherited this land, and in order to protect the graves, formed the Brooking Cemetery Association, and deeded five acres to the Association. A Charter was granted the Association by the State, May 8, 1894. The By-laws for the Association were adopted by the Trustees at their first annual meeting, June 5, 1894. "The Trustees of the Brooking Cemetery Association met in first regular meeting at Raytown, Jackson County, Missouri, this, the first Saturday in November, 1894, and proceeded to elect officers for said association for the ensuing year. The Ballot being taken resulted in the election of Henry C. Brooking as President, John T. Campbell as Secretary, Robert Pendleton as Treasurer." (This record was copied from the Association minute book.)

After platting the land, Henry C. Brooking gave a lot to each of his nephews and nieces, and also to some of his friends. After his death, his widow deeded the adjoining thirty-five acres to the Cemetery Association.

After the organization of the Cemetery Association, the Brooking Cemetery was open to the public, and bodies from several of the old pioneer family burying grounds were removed to this cemetery.

Adams, Mary, wife of Isaac Adams, died December 5, 1877; age, 86 years
Alcock, Mary, wife of A. G. Dennis, born March 17, 1835, died May 2, 1900
Allen, W. M., born August 10, 1837, died September 30, 1897
Anderson, Rev. J. O., born 1835, died 1888 (father)

Anderson, Louisa D., born 1837, died 1918 (mother)
Anthony, Rua Catherine, born 1840, died 1923
Anthony, David L., born 1842, died 1915
Argo, Moses B., born September 28, 1822, died December 28, 1898

Ballenger, James B., born 1831, died 1917
Ballenger, Camileet (wife), born 1832, died 1916
Barrett, Robert W., died June 10, 1880; age, 47 years, 5 months, 20 days; he was removed from the Lane Burying Ground August 19, 1932
Betts, William, born 1835, died 1908
Betts, Elizabeth, born 1838, died 1920
Bishop, Thomas F., born June 25, 1849, died August 15, 1866; he was first buried in Thomas Cemetery
Blume, Christina E., born August 13, 1845, died April 4, 1932
Brauninger, Gottlog John, born 1844, died 1928
    Clara Eugenie, born 1847, died 1928
Braun, Gustav A., born 1844, died 1918
Braun, Mary H., born 1846, died 1922
Brody, T. J., born 1847, died 1924
Brooking, Alvan, born March 7, 1796, died Nov. 30, 1857; age, 61 years, 8 months, 23 days
    "In Civil Life an Upright Judge,
        And an —— State Senator"
Brooking, Frances C., wife of A. Brooking, died April 27, 1892; age, 91 years, 7 months, 9 days
Brooking, Jula A., born December 9, 1829, died August 1, 1847
Brooking, Robert W., died January 8, 1854; age, 27 years, 3 months, 21 days
Brooking, Martha J., wife of Robert W. Brooking, died November 7, 1848; age, 20 years
Brooking, John S., died March 3, 1841; age, 22 years, 8 months, 19 days
Brooking, Wallace U., died November 18, 1840; age, 18 years, 14 days
Brooking, Henry Clay, born in Scott Co., Ky., April 23, 1832, died May 18, 1901
    Elyira F., wife of H. C. Brooking, born August 19, 1849, died October 8, 1922

Campbell, Benjamin A., Co. "E" 45th Mo. Inf., born January 22, 1847, died May 30, 1914
Campbell, John W., died March 19, 1855; age, 45 years, 4 months, 4 days
Campbell, Mary L., wife of John W. Campbell, died August 7, 1858; age, 38 years, 4 months, 23 days
Cassell, George W., born May 24, 1838, died June 25, 1909
Coleman, W. W., born May 25, 1842, died August 1, 1905
Cook, Enoch B., born February 23, 1823, died August 10, 1899
    Nancy Ann, wife of Enoch Cook, born August 1, 1826, died April 26, 1899
Crouse, Jacob, born March 4, 1844, died August 7, 1914
    Mary D., his wife, born December 30, 1850, died January 22, 1922

Debord, William C., died January 5, 1860; age, 37 years, 1 month, 15 days
Debord, Susan A., daughter of W. C. and S. Debord; age, 1 year, 2 months, 15 days
Dehoney, Leander M., born December 28, 1825, died August 20, 1910
Dehoney, Sarah, wife of L. M. Dehoney, born February 25, 1835, died July 9, 1906
Duncan, Emory, born November 28, 1833, died July 9, 1903
Duvall, Adelaide, wife of Silas L. Duvall, born March 27, 1836, died November 16, 1907

Faulconer, Nelson, born August 21, 1819, died January 29, 1897
Fellers, Alonzo, born October 7, 1845, died December 18, 1905
Finch, M. A., born 1841, died 1913
Frost, James M., born 1835, died 1917
Frost, Charlotte J., born 1846, died 1918

Gault, James A., born February 26, 1842, died January 28, 1929
Gault, Rebecca Jane, wife of James A. Gault, born December 16, 1842, died May 7, 1907

Goodwin, William, born 1841
Green, Gilbert L., born 1847, died 1928
Guleman, Martha E., born May 8, 1848, died May 14, 1921

Harrill, Napoleon S., died July 25, 1903; age, 57 years, 6 months
    Sarah E. Wood, born June 17, 1850, died November 14, 1923
Herndon, Catherine, wife of John Herndon, died September 18, 1844, in the 77th year of her age
Holder, Joseph N., died November 23, 1893; age, 63 years, 1 month, 13 days
    Arretta J., wife of J. N. Holder, died February 2, 1869; age, 35 years, 9 months, 22 days
House, J. T., born 1838, died 1924
    Alice, his wife, born 1869, died 1900
Hudgens, Mollie, born 1848, died 1917
Hunter, S. R., born May 22, 1815, died February 9, 1901
    Julia A., his wife, born January 10, 1825, died August 23, 1921
Hutchinson, Thomas H., born 1843, died 1916
Hussey, Daniel, born November 4, 1830, died March 7, 1902
    Mary C., wife of Daniel Hussey, born June 10, 1840, died April 8, 1904
Hyde, M. A., born January 24, 1842, died November 27, 1906

Jackson, James, born 1848, died 1929

Knight, William A., born 1843, died 1911
    Mary A., born 1848, died 1931
Kritser, Henry Clay, died June 12, 1932; age, 88 years
    Elizabeth, wife of H. C. Kritser, born July 28, 1845, died October 2, 1915

La Cross, Maurice, born April 15, 1835, died July 27, 1906
Lane, Frances, born 1845, died 1923
Larison, Rosana, born 1825, died 1915
Leach, Father, born 1843, died 1925
Leach, Mother, born 1848, died 1899
Lewis, William F., born 1845, died 1924
Lewis, Louisa E., born 1851, died 1931

McCormick, O. A., born March 29, 1838, died November 15, 1909
    E. F., wife of O. A. McCormick, born February 19, 1842, died June 23, 1923
McCormick, Elizabeth, wife of J. F. McCormick, born February 10, 1831, died July 31, 1901
McCraw, George, died September 7, 1893; age, 84 years. He is buried beside his mother who died many years before. Their graves are unmarked.
McCraw, Sarah Hendrix, mother of George McCraw, and wife of Major William McCraw, of Halifax County, Virginia
McInteer, E. T., born December 18, 1822, died March 14, 1899
McInteer, D. V., born December 14, 1834, died August 8, 1913
McKeever, J. B., born 1838, died 1917
McKeever, Sarah, wife of J. B. McKeever, born 1841, died 1923

Miller, Joseph, born December 10, 1846, died April 28, 1913
Morris, C. M., born March 10, 1835, died May 24, 1903
Moses, Argo, born September 28, 1822, died December 28, 1898

Nixon, Isaiah W., born 1848, died 1929
Noland, Date, born 1847, died 1925
Noland, Sarah C., wife of G. M. Noland, died November 5, 1874; age, 26 years, 11 months, 22 days

Ochsner, Michael, born November 17, 1837, died January 9, 1921
    Louisa Ellen, born October 20, 1842, died December 4, 1924
Overstreet, James R., died April 22, 1899; age, 73 years, 10 months, 14 days

Pendleton, Alfred, born December 23, 1838, died December 8, 1898
    Permelia, wife of Alfred Pendleton, born August 15, 1842, died April 28, 1910
Pendleton, William, born January 26, 1841, died January 27, 1914
    Levina B., wife of William Pendleton, born November 27, 1843, died February 28, 1921
Pendleton, Logan, born December 30, 1830, died March 30, 1903
Pendleton, Serena M., born February 1, 1834, died May 26, 1904

Read, Margaret, wife of J. L. Reed, died September 15, 1893; age, 75 years, 3 months, 15 days
Redford, John H., born February 14, 1848, died November 23, 1914
Renick, George, born 1816, died 1880
Renick, Parthenia, born 1839, died 1925
Rhoades, Susan A., born August 12, 1838, died September 20, 1916
Rice, Ella, born August 20, 1855, died August 31, 1895
Rice, James W., born March 10, 1849, died May 23, 1930
Rice, William B., born October 6, 1831, died August 22, 1911
Rice, Experience Hewitt, born November 16, 1832, died August 6, 1891

Sechrest, Newton J., born November 18, 1850, died December 7, 1920
Sellers, Elijah M., born 1835, died 1916
Sellers, Martha J., born 1843, died 1924
Sewell, Dr. Franklin L., born January 24, 1827, died July 5, 1905
Shepherd, Walter F., died December 22, 1905; age, 65 years
    Ann, born 1840, died 1922
Slater, Cyras A., died 1859
Slater, Emily R.
Slater, William
Smith, Dr. Minor T., born March 25, 1827, died December 28, 1914
Smith, Laura B., born February 24, 1851, died February 16, 1929
Stilley, John R., born 1840, died 1900
Stilley, Mary E., born 1842, died 1925
Storms, Henry W., born April 3, 1830, died December 14, 1916
Storms, Louisa, born September 6, 1848, died November 8, 1924

Whitehouse, William, died September 3, 1898; age, 76 years, 7 months, 15 days
    Maranda W., wife of Wm. Whitehouse, died January 23, 1897; age, 70 years, 1 month, 15 days
Wilson, James M., born 1845, died 1907
Wolfe, William K., born December 20, 1840
Wolfe, Susan A., born April 16, 1844, died January 5, 1908
Wright, B. M., born May 18, 1812
    Susan, wife of Bryan Wright, born June 27, 1829, died June 24, 1893

Young, David, born 1830, died 1901
Young, Elizabeth J., born 1838, died 1891

COLE CEMETERY
Section 25, Township 49, Range 33W
Contributed by Mrs. L. R. Lane

Brown, Benjamin, died September 11, 1883; age, 65 years, 22 days
Brown, Sidney Blevins, wife of Benj. Brown, died September 27, 1897; age, 76 years
Brown, Abraham, son of B. and S. Brown, born December 17, 1853, died March 11, 1857
Brown, Andrew J., son of B. and S. Brown, born March 26, 1858, died April 14, 1858

CEMETERIES—BROOKING TOWNSHIP

Brown, Martha E., daughter of B. and S. Brown, born February 22, 1856, died Oct. 20, 1861
Brown, James, son of B. and S. Brown, born May 2, 1851, died September 12, 1873
Buckles, Ruben, son of T. M. and M. J. Buckles, born November 9, 1855, died June 21, 1858

Calhoun, D. V., died January 3, 1870; age, 41 years, 2 months, 23 days
Calhoun, Samuel, son of D. V. Calhoun, died Oct. 22, 1906; age, 54 years, 3 months, 12 days
Calhoun, Louisa Brown, wife of Samuel Calhoun, died September 1, 1923; age, 80 years
Cates, Joshua, died October 14, 1898; age, 63 years, 4 months, 15 days
Cates, Mary Brown, wife of Joshua Cates, born January 21, 1846, died July 10, 1879
Cates, Louisa, born February 24, 1869, died March 3, 1905
Cole, Alfred, born March 9, 1814, died February 9, 1854
Cole, Harriet Blevins, wife of Alfred Cole, born June 1, 1814, died July 10, 1876
Cole, Andrew Jackson, born February 24, 1836, died March 15, 1860
Cole, William, born September 1, 1838, died January 26, 1854
Cole, James, born June 4, 1837, died October 6, 184-
Cole, Jesse, born March 5, 1840, died December 29, 1915
Cole, Harriet Brown, wife of H. H. Cole, died March 24, 1884; age, 34 years, 6 months, 10 days
Collings, Jennie A., daughter of Wm. H. and C. P. Collings, died March 8, 1878; age, 5 years, 7 months, 24 days

Dodson, Frank, born December 25, 1892, died November 4, 1900
Dodson, Nancy, born April 2, 1891, died October 22, 1896

Gamer, Lilie Cates Gamer, born May 5, 1879, died February 18, 1904

Higgins, Dan, born June 11, 1810, died November 3, 1890
Higgins, L. J. (Grandma Higgins), born December 12, 1810, died December 17, 1899

Lewis, F., born October 19, 1868, died March 8, 1869

Prater, F. L., born November 15, 1865, died June 13, 1884

Rice, James, died 1850; age, between 60 and 65 years
Rice, second wife of James Rice. His first wife was buried in Caswell County, N. C. James Rice came to Jackson County, Mo., from Rockingham County, N. C.
Rice, George, son of James Rice
Rice, Littleton, son of James Rice

West, Annie L., daughter of H. M. and H. West, born July 2, 1873, died October 24, 1873
West, Etta A., daughter of H. M. and H. West, born May 18, 1871, died August 20, 1872
West, James, son of H. M. and H. West, born August 21, 1869, died May 13, 1876
West, twins of H. M. and H. West, born June 6, 1870, died June 9, 1870

Compiled by Miss Jessie M. Crosby

HOUSE CEMETERY
East Part Section 32, Township 48, Range 32 W
On farm owned by Mr. John House

William F. McMonigle, died April 18, 187-; age, 31 years, 6 months, 3 days
Winnie McMonigle, daughter of E. E. and J. House, died January 31, 1869; age, 27 years, 11 months, 19 days
Ephram E. House, died November 23, 1861; age, 57 years, 2 months, 6 days
Irene House, wife of E. E. House, died August 17, 1872; age, 49 years, 9 months, 28 days

Copied August 11, 1933, by Mrs. Hale Houts

HOWELL CEMETERY
Section 17, Township 48, Range 32 W

Howell, Butler, born October 15, 1780, died December 19, 1864; age, 84 years, 2 months, 4 days
Howell, Elizabeth, wife of Butler Howell, died October 18, 1856, in the 69th year of her age
Howell, Daniel M., died February 11, 1849; age, 25 years, 4 months, 29 days
Howell, George W., died May 5, 1855; age, 44 years, 4 months, 25 days
Howell, Lucretia, born June 27, 1812, died July 10, 1901
Howell, Rebecca, born July 21, 1809, died November 8, 1902
Howell, Elizabeth, daughter of W. B. and W. M. Howell, died June 13, 1852; age, 19 days
Howell, Elizabeth C., daughter of G. W. and L. Howell, died December 22, 1857; age, 10 years, 2 months, 15 days
Howell, Laura Cyrena, daughter of W. B. and W. M. Howell, died June 22, 1854; age, 1 year, 1 day
Howell, Sarah Ann, daughter of Wm. B. and Winny Ford M. Howell, died August 26, 1849; age, 2 years, 5 months, 4 days
Parsons, Malinda E., wife of John C. Parsons, born January 2, 1830, died March 22, 1857
Steele, Winna A., wife of Harden Steele, born May 20, 1805, died December 15, 1848
Tevebough, Lucinda, wife of J. Tevebough, died December 29, 1852; age, 45 years, 6 days
Whitlock, Sarah, wife of Robert Whitlock, died September 6, 1856; age, 40 years, 1 month, 8 days

Copied June 12, 1933, by Miss Jessie M. Crosby and Mrs. May T. Crosby

HYLTON CEMETERY
Section 6, Township 48, Range 31

Holland, infant son of J. N. and A. J. Holland, born February 18, 1871
Holland, Jennie, wife of J. N. Holland, died Jan. 29, 1889; age, 44 years, 1 month, 29 days
Hylton, Jeremiah W., died September 1, 1847; age, 39 years, 5 months, 18 days
Hylton, Jane E., wife of J. W. Hylton, born March 10, 1812, died July 4, 1882
Hylton, John, died January 29, 1857; age, 22 years, 6 months, 2 days
Morgan, John J., born in Sussex County, Delaware, October 16, 1813, died Nov. 7, 1871
Spoonamore, Sallie B., daughter of C. C. and E. Spoonamore, born 1867, died 1873
Tatum, Mary E., daughter of T. B. and S. A. Tatum, born December 2, 1866, died March 2, 1868
11 other graves marked only with native stone, without inscriptions

Copied September 21, 1933, by Mrs. R. E. Shryock and Mrs. Hale Houts

LANE CEMETERY
Section 31, Township 49, Range 32 W

Basye, James D., died September 22, 1856; age, 36 years, 7 months
Basye, Mary Ann, wife of James D. Basye, died January 22, 1890; age, 64 years, 2 months, 27 days
Basye, Armilda, daughter of J. D. and M. A. Basye, died July 20, 1854; age, 1 month, 16 days
Basye, Lovelace, son of J. D. and M. A. Basye, died September 23, 1853; age, 1 year, 15 days
Basye, infant daughter of J. D. and Grace Basye, born and died October 3, 1891
Bush, Sarah, wife of L. N. Bush, died September 3, 1853; age, 32 years, 8 months, 11 days
Bush, Nancy W., daughter of L. N. and S. Bush, died August 4, 1859
Lane, Luciehr, son of F. H. and E. Lane, died January 29, 1854; age, 19 days
Lane, James, died May 1, 1886; age, 42 years, 5 months, 24 days

Lane, Silas, son of F. H. and E. L. Lane, died May 28, 1859; age, 22 years, 1 month, 16 days
Parr, William P., died January 14, 1857; age, 25 years, 8 months, 22 days
Sampson, C. H., born February 17, 1840, died December 12, 1881
Thomas, John B., son of J. and S. S. Thomas, died October 25, 1880; age, 10 years, 10 months, 29 days

Mr. L. R. Lane, a member of this family, furnished the following names of members of the family buried there in unmarked graves:

Lane, Fielding H.
Lane, Elizabeth, wife of Fielding H. Lane
Payne, George, died 1913; age, 70 years

Compiled and copied April 23, 1933, by Miss Jessie M. Crosby

McPHERSON CEMETERY
Section 6, Township 48, Range 31
Located on the Ess Farm

Elizabeth Ann Fitzhugh McPherson, born in Virginia, August 4, 1799, died 1856
Wife of Murdock Mordecai McPherson, born in Edinburgh, Scotland, December, 1781

Mr. McPherson was drowned while trying to cross the Ohio River, upon his return from a business trip East where he had gone to settle an estate. His will is recorded in Independence, Mo.

Solomon McPherson, brother of Murdock Mordecai McPherson
Elizabeth Ann McPherson, daughter of Murdock Mordecai and Elizabeth Ann McPherson

Information supplied by Mrs. E. L. Harris, 320 S. White Ave., Kansas City, Mo.
Compiled by Mrs. Hale Houts September 28, 1933

RICHARDS CEMETERY
Section 25, Township 49, Range 33 W
Forty-seventh Street and Eastern Avenue
Data contributed by L. A. Renick

Richards, Richard
Richards, Jennie McCraw, wife of Richard Richards
Richards, Lue
Richards, Samuel
Richards, Martha Lovelace, wife of Thomas Richards
Richards, George, son of Thomas and Martha Richards
Richards, Richard, son of Thomas and Martha Richards
Noland, Sue Richards, wife of J. D. Noland
Noland, Sarah Catherine Richards, wife of George M. Noland
Noland, Sue

N. B. These bodies were removed to the Brooking Cemetery. No markers except for Sarah Catherine Noland.

Copied by Miss Jessie M. Crosby

Sechrest, Charles, died June 25, 1864; age, 60 years
Sechrest, Catharine, born October 7, 1813, died September 27, 1894 (mother)
Sechrest, Jacob, husband of Alice, born November 12, 1831, died September 15, 1870
Sechrest, C. W., died September 28, 1863; age, 29 years, 9 months, 28 days
Sechrest, Thomas D., son of C. and C. Sechrest, died February 11, 1863; age, 18 years, 9 months, 11 days
Sechrest, Louisa, wife of J. R. Sechrest, born January 27, 1847, died February 7, 1876
Sechrest, Lee, son of J. R. and L. Sechrest, died December 30, 1869; age, 6 years
Sechrest, Catharine, daughter of J. R. and L. Sechrest, died October 8, 1867; age, 6 years, 2 months
Sechrest, Baby, son of J. R. and L. Sechrest, February 10, 1875
Sechrest, Elearia J., died October 29, 1856; age, 10 months, 5 days
Sechrest, Edward D., son of S. and M. P. Sechrest, died March 17, 1866; age, 2 years, 1 month
Sechrest, Mattie, daughter of S. and M. P. Sechrest, died August 10, 1870; age, 4 months, 11 days
Simmons, Jane, died July 29, 1872; age, 23 years, 7 months
Vang, Sarah, wife of Ebenezer Vang, died August 8, 1869; age, 64 years, 2 months, 11 days
Young, Robert E., son of S. and L. Young, died Aug. 26, 1867; age, 2 years, 6 months, 7 days

Copied June 12, 1933, by Miss Jessie M. Crosby and Mrs. May T. Crosby

WOODS CHAPEL CEMETERY
Cumberland Presbyterian
Section 8, Township 48, Range 31

Adams, Rachel, died September 19, 1870; age, 53 years, 4 months, 10 days
Baxter, Elizabeth J., wife of Robert Baxter, died April 3, 1877; age, 35 years
Baxter, son of Elizabeth and Robert Baxter, died July 3, 1873; age, 15 months
Baxter, Robert D., son of E. and R. Baxter, died July 3, 1875; age, 4 months
Beal, M. S., died August 29, 1888; age, 61 years, 10 months, 25 days
Bowlin, Lesley M., son of J. G. and M. A. Bowlin, died August 14, 1884; age, 11 months, 21 days
Bowlin, Jacob C., died December 17, 1890; age, 53 years, 6 months, 22 days
Brown, Mary Ann Bemuth, wife of John Brown, died September 10, 1876; age, 69 years, 1 month, 6 days
Brown, John, died September 10, 1876; age, 69 years, 4 months, 15 days
Cabness, William R., born March 20, 1827, died March 15, 1911
Cabness, Agnes T., wife of William R. Cabness, born September 22, 1829, died Jan. 12, 1888
Cairns, John M., born September 25, 1836, died May 1, 1916
Etzenhouser, Lucy A., wife of H. Etzenhouser, born March 24, 1845, died October 23, 1894
Ferguson, Ebenezer F., died December 19, 1930; age, 74 years, 11 months, 15 days
Ferguson, Margaret, born August 13, 1854, died August 11, 1890
Frans, Sophia A., died February 16, 1874; age, 39 years, 5 months, 15 days
Green, Mary, died September 23, 1886; age, 83 years, 8 months, 3 days
Harrold, Charles E., died January 20, 1890; age, 24 years, 11 months, 20 days
Harrold, Emma, wife of Charles Harrold, born January 23, 1867, died February 14, 1909
Hulse, Freeman, died February 26, 1875; age, 61 years, 5 months, 24 days
Hulse, Judith, died March 12, 1898; age, 87 years, 10 months
Hulse, James (father), born January 1, 1849, died April 16, 1926
Hulse, Armatha (mother), wife of James Hulse, born March 26, 1848, died Dec. 26, 1911
Johnson, Mary A., died January 31, 1892; age, 66 years, 5 days
Jones, Elizabeth D., wife of M. O. Jones, born March 4, 1832, died May 5, 1898
Jones, Martin O., died January 6, 1888; age, 66 years, 5 months, 22 days

CEMETERIES—BROOKING TOWNSHIP

Jones, William H., died February 16, 1873; age, 16 years, 16 days
Kerr, Jemima, died April 1, 1883; age, 89 years, 8 months, 19 days
Kerr, James W., son of J. R. and N. J. Kerr, died February 22, 1881; age, 23 years, 11 months, 27 days
Kerr, Nancy J., wife of J. R. Kerr, born October 16, 1837, died September 10, 1901
Kerr, John R., born July 12, 1833, died December 16, 1929
Kinney, Annie, died December 4, 1874; age, 86 years
Kinney, Sarah F., born December 24, 1861, died November 3, 1889
Lea, Mrs. A. F., wife of T. C. Lea, died September 13, 1881; age, 29 years
Lea, John R., son of T. C. and A. F. Lea, died March 5, 1875; age, 4 years
Lewis, Mrs. Serena, died February 18, 1933; age, 72 years, 8 months, 27 days
Mitchell, George, died June 8, 1897; age, 68 years, 6 months, 22 days; member of Co. "G" 13th Ill. Cavalry
Myers, George T., son of A. and S. Myers, died March 18, 1873; age, 1 month, 28 days
Newton, infant daughter of J. S. and E. Newton
Reynolds, Sanford M., son of E. E. Reynolds, died October 9, 1872; age, 1 year, 13 months, 22 days
Ritter, John Franklin, died February 22, 1933; age, 76 years, 10 months, 16 days
Rucker, Malinda R., died May 9, 1887; age, 74 years, 6 months, 17 days
Sandridge, Mary E. Bowlen, wife of G. E. Sandridge, born April 29, 1840, died Jan. 21, 1912
Schmidt, Caroline, wife of Robert Schmidt, died July 30, 1883; age, 42 years
Stone, Lambert Mu—p, son of J. W. and A. A. Stone, died 1870 (infant)
Stone, Mrs. Agnes Ann, died May 16, 1929; age, 66 years, 11 months, 25 days
Stone, James W., died December 15, 1831; age, 75 years, 2 months, 14 days
Strohm, Mary M., died January 31, 1930; age, 60 years, 4 months, 22 days
Strohm, Samuel J., died September 14, 1893; age, 73 years, 7 months, 16 days
Strohm, Charles A., died June 18, 1929; age, 67 years, 6 months
Smith, Sarah, wife of J. M. Smith, died December 24, 1885; age, 32 years, 9 months, 8 days
Smith, Josiah, born February 19, 1858, died November 7, 1892
Smith, Noah, born December 2, 1860, died November 7, 1901
Spotts, David, son of L. and H. Spotts, born July 7, 1872, died September, 1873
Trogge, Nancy E., wife of Theadore Trogge, died January 5, 1885; age, 31 years, 9 months, 3 days
Trogge, Arminda, wife of A. R. Trogge, died January 23, 1877; age, 46 years
Trogge, A. B., died January 17, 1877; age, 46 years

Copied April 23, 1933, by Miss Julia Kinney and Mrs. Hale Houts

SMALL CEMETERIES

Data on these small cemeteries in Brooking Township was compiled by
Miss Jessie M. Crosby

BARNES GRAVES
Section 18, Township 48, Range 32 W
Data contributed by O. V. Slaughter and Carl Davenport

Jesse Barnes and his wife were early settlers of Brooking Township. He owned the NW quarter of Section 17, Township 48, Range 32. They were buried on the NE quarter of Section 18, Township 48, Range 32 W. The markers at their graves have disappeared but Morris Hartman remembers the dates on Mr. Barnes' tombstone as being, born 1776, died October 15 or November 15, 1849.

William Gore, who was murdered near this burying place, was buried here, but was later removed to the Palestine Cemetery.

COLLINGS CEMETERY
Section 31, Township 49, Range 32 W
Data contributed by Mr. Ed Collings

Collings, Ann Yates, born February 24, 1822, died March 11, 1905
Collings, Frank, died 1860; age, 23 years
Collings, William Hellier, born May 11, 1821, died April 25, 1904
Collings, Caroline, wife of Wm. H. Collings, Jr.
Compton, Amanda, born February 16, 1817, died December 13, 1904
Compton, Joel, born September 7, 1816, died September 21, 1892

COX CEMETERY
Section 5, Township 48, Range 32 W

Cox, William, died before 1854. He came to Jackson County in 1831 from Scott County, Virginia (Lynch River)
Cox, Nancy Ervin, wife of Wm. Cox, died before 1854
Cox, John, died May 28, 1898; age, 77 years, 1 month, 2 days
Cox, Charlotte Price, wife of John Cox, born January 18, 1832, died 1915
Cox, Mary, wife of Henry Cox, died April 13, 1854; age, 24 years, 2 months, 23 days
Cox, James M., son of J. and C. T. Cox, died November 20, 1863; age, 1 year, 6 months, 10 days
Cox, Miriah, daughter of J. and C. T. Cox, died January 13, 1867; age, 3 years
Cox, Birdie, daughter of J. and C. T. Cox
Cox, Mary, wife of G. L. Cox
Price, Martin, died December, 1890
Price, wife of Jack Price
Rice, Eviline, daughter of James Rice; married first, —— Hilton; second, Henderson Graves (no marker)

MELTON BURYING GROUND
Section 1, Township 48, Range 33 W

There were several members of John Melton's family buried on this farm.

BEN RICE CEMETERY
Section 36, Township 49, Range 33 W

Rice, B. L., born April 6, 1822, died January 17, 1918
Rice, Jane, wife of B. L. Rice, born September 22, 1827, died February 1, 1901
Benjamin L. Rice went to the Mexican War with Col. Doniphan.

COFFEE RICE CEMETERY
Section 5, Township 48, Range 32 W
Data contributed by Mrs. Mary Kritzer Dunn

Rice, Archibald, born December 18, 1782, died October 14, 1849
He came to Jackson County, Missouri, in 1832 from North Carolina
Rice, Sallie, wife of Archibald Rice, born February 29, 1794, died August 5, 1852
Rice, Mary, born July 20, 1820, died November 8, 1826
Rice, Martha B., born August 15, 1822, died November 24, 1838
Rice, Mary Ann, born March 29, 1827
Rice, Mamervia R., born April 9, 1829
Rice, Louisana, born March 10, 1835, died February 2, 1848
Rice, Quintiller, born October 1, 1831, died July 31, 1848
Stone, Sarah R. Rice, died May 25, 1866

CEMETERIES—BROOKING TOWNSHIP

RHOADES CEMETERY
Section 32, Township 49, Range 32 W
Contributed by Mr. Walter Cassell, Raytown, Mo., heir of Rhoades' estate

Rhoades, George T.
Rhoades, George W.
Rhoades, Mary A.
Stovall, Harry, son of John Stovall
Thompson, three children of M. T. Thompson
Woodson, three children of A. M. Woodson
   These bodies have been removed to the Brooking Cemetery.

SEARCY CEMETERY
Section 6, Township 48, Range 32 W
Contributed by Mrs. Omer Davenport (nee Searcy)

Brusaw, Leonard, son of Joseph Brusaw
Cox, Delie, daughter of Carter Cox
Cox, Julia, wife of Carter Cox
Cox, Magg, wife of Carter Cox
Cox, W. W.
Mockbee, Reuben, died 1878
Morris, Cora May, born May 15, 1868, died March 15, 1870
Morris, John Henry, born June 27, 1866, died June 29, 1866
Morris, William, died 1873
Searcy, Christopher Reed, died 1897; age, 40 years
Searcy, Sarah Jane Cox, wife of Christopher Reed Searcy, died October, 1915; age, 67 years
   These bodies have been removed to the Brooking Cemetery. Graves not marked.

WEST CEMETERY
Section 5, Township 48, Range 32 W

Davenport, George, born 1842
   Susan, born 1848, died 1914
Goins, B. E., born 1847, died 1919
   Mariah C., wife of B. E. Goins, born December 25, 1835, died October 20, 1913
Rice, Nathaniel, died January 10, 1892; age, 63 years, 9 months, 6 days
   Harriet L., wife of N. Rice, died September 9, 1872; age, 37 years, 10 months, 29 days
   Serelda J., wife of N. Rice, died August 28, 1873; age, 44 years, 11 days
Rice, infant daughter of Nathaniel and Harriet L. Rice, born February, 1863
West, James N., died August 2, 1871; age, 69 years, 8 months, 18 days
West, Dicea, wife of James N. West, died June 8, 1883; age, 74 years, 4 months, 15 days
West, Mary E., daughter of James N. and Dicea West, died November 14, 1862; age, 20 years, 6 months, 5 days
West, Henry M., son of J. N. and D. West, died November 24, 1873; age, 35 years, 6 months, 7 days
West, Mary A., wife of J. H. West, died September 6, 1856; age, 19 years, 6 months, 2 days
West, Mary A., daughter of J. H. and M. A. West, died November 18, 1862; age, 7 years, 2 months, 28 days
              Copied April 8, 1933, by Miss Jessie M. Crosby

WEST FORK CHURCH CEMETERY
NW Quarter Section 3, Township 48, Range 32 W

   There were a number of graves near the old West Fork Baptist Church.
   The only record obtainable is that of:
Thomas Dehoney, born 1784, died March 31, 1853
Martilia, daughter of Thomas Dehoney, born September 8, 1824, died June 20, 1851
   Thomas Dehoney married Harriet Gatewood February 12, 1819.

www.ingramcontent.com/pod-product-compliance
Lightning Source LLC
Chambersburg PA
CBHW081455040426
42446CB00016B/3257